Rethinking Social Policy

turned

Rethinking Social Policy
This Reader provides some of the set readings for a 16-week module (D860 *Rethinking Social Policy*) which is offered by The Open University Masters Programme in the Social Sciences.

The Open University Masters Programme in the Social Sciences
The MA/MSc Programme enables students to select from a range of modules to create a programme to suit their own professional or personal development. Students can choose from a range of social science modules to obtain an MA in the Social Sciences, or may choose to specialize in a particular subject area by studying modules in one of the offered study lines. D860 *Rethinking Social Policy* is the core module for both the MA in Social Policy and the MA in Social Policy and Criminology.

OU Supported Learning
The Open University's unique, supported ('distance') learning Masters Programme in the Social Sciences is designed to facilitate engagement at an advanced level with the concepts, approaches, theories and techniques associated with a number of academic areas of study. The Social Sciences Masters Programme provides great flexibility. Students study in their own environments, in their own time, anywhere in the European Union. They receive specially prepared course materials, benefit from structured tutorial support throughout all the coursework and assessment assignments, and have the chance to work with other students.

How to apply
If you would like to register for this programme, or simply find out more information, please write for the Masters Programme in the Social Sciences Prospectus to The Open University, Course Reservations Centre, PO Box 625, Milton Keynes, MK7 6ZW, UK (Telephone +44 (0)1908 858585) (E-mail: ces-gen@open.ac.uk)

Rethinking Social Policy

edited by
Gail Lewis, Sharon Gewirtz and John Clarke

The Open
University

in association with

SAGE Publications
London • Thousand Oaks • New Delhi

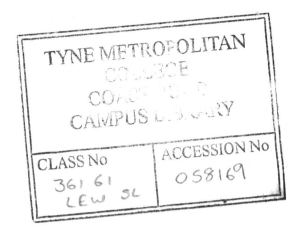
First published 2000

 SAGE Publications Ltd
6 Bonhill Street
London EC2A 4PU

SAGE Publications Inc
2455 Teller Road
Thousand Oaks, California 91320

SAGE Publications India Pvt Ltd
32, M-Block Market
Greater Kailash – I
New Delhi 110 048

British Library Cataloguing in Publication data

A catalogue record for this book is available
from the British Library

ISBN 0 7619 6754 0
ISBN 0 7619 6755 9 (pbk)

Library of Congress catalog record available

Typeset by Mayhew Typesetting, Rhayader, Powys
Printed in Great Britain by The Cromwell Press,
Trowbridge, Wiltshire

Contents

Notes on Contributors

Jean Carabine is Lecturer in Social Policy at Loughborough University where she is Programme Director of the BSc. Social Policy Degree. She is also an editor of the journal, *Critical Social Policy*. She has written extensively on the intersection between discourses of sexuality and social policy.

John Clarke is Professor of Social Policy at The Open University. His recent research has explored the role of managerialism in the restructuring of the welfare state. More generally, he is fascinated by the possible intersections of cultural analysis and social policy.

Celia Davies was founding Professor of Women's Studies at the University of Ulster in the late 1980s and is now Professor of Health Care at The Open University. Her publications on professions and organizations in the health field include *Gender and the Professional Predicament in Nursing* (Open University Press, 1995). *Interpreting Professional Self-Regulation*, written jointly with Abigail Beach (Routledge, 2000), extends the themes developed in her chapter in this collection.

Sharon Gewirtz is Lecturer in Social Policy at The Open University. Her recent research has focused on the rise and operation of managerialism in education and its consequences for social justice. She is co-author of *Specialisation and Choice in Urban Education* (Routledge, 1993) and *Markets, Choice and Equity in Education* (Open University Press, 1995), and is currently writing a book on the *Managerial School* for Routledge.

Paul Hoggett is Director of the Centre for Economic and Social Research and Professor of Politics at the University of the West of England, Bristol. He is the author of *Partisans in an Uncertain World* (Free Association Books, 1992) and *Emotional Life and the Politics of Welfare* (Macmillan, 2000).

Bob Jessop is Professor of Sociology at Lancaster University. He is best known for his contributions to state theory, the regulation approach, and the analysis of post-war British political economy. He has recently begun to study the restructuring of welfare regimes.

Gail Lewis is Lecturer in Social Policy at The Open University. Her research interests centre on the intersection of social policy and the construction of gender and racial formations. Her forthcoming book *Race, Gender, Social Welfare: Encounters in a Post-colonial Society* will be published by Polity Press in 2000.

Jane Lewis is Barnett Professor of Social Policy at the University of Oxford. She is the author of numerous books and articles on gender and social policy, including (with K. Kiernan and H. Land) *Lone Motherhood in Twentieth-century Britain* (Oxford, U.P., 1998) and (ed.) *Gender, Social Care and Welfare State Restructuring in Europe* (Ashgate Publishing Ltd, 1999).

Ruth Lister is Professor of Social Policy at Loughborough University. She is a former Director of the Child Poverty Action Group and served on the Commission on Social Justice and the Opsahl Commission into the Future of Northern Ireland. She has published widely on poverty, income maintenance and women's citizenship. Her latest book is *Citizenship: Feminist Perspectives* (Macmillan/New York University Press, 1997).

Maureen Mackintosh is Professor of Economics at The Open University. Her chapter draws on a recent ESRC-supported research project on 'Economic Culture and Local Governance'. She is currently working on issues of health care management and regulation, including a collaborative project on health care regulation in Tanzania. Her most recent book is *Economic Decentralization and Public Management Reform*, edited with Rathin Roy (Edward Elgar, 1999).

Gerry Mooney is Staff Tutor in Social Policy at The Open University. He has published widely on issues relating to developments in social policy and in the field of urban studies. He has recently edited a collection of essays on the theme of *Class Struggle and Social Welfare* with Michael Lavalette, to be published in 2000 by Routledge.

John Muncie is Senior Lecturer in Criminology and Social Policy at The Open University. His most recent publications include *The Problem of Crime* (Sage/O.U., 1996), *Controlling Crime* (Sage/O.U., 1996), *Criminological Perspectives* (Sage/O.U., 1996) and *Youth and Crime: A Critical Introduction* (Sage, 1999).

Ann Phoenix works in the Psychology discipline at The Open University. Her research interests include social identities; motherhood; gender and racialization. Her current ESRC-funded research (with Stephen Frosh and Rob Pattman) is on masculinities in 11–14-year-old boys.

Jane Pillinger is an independent policy adviser and researcher on European social, employment and regional policy, acting as a consultant to a number of EU institutions and European trade union organizations. She is also a specialist adviser to the House of Commons Select Committee on Employment. Jane was formerly the Associate Director for the Northern Institute for Continuing Education, and Senior Lecturer in Social Policy, based at Northern College. She is the author of *Feminising the Market: Women's Pay in the European Community* (Macmillan, 1992).

Sharon Pinkney is currently engaged in research on how the concept of 'participation' constructs, produces and reproduces children as 'new subjects' within social care. She is also involved in teaching and writing on a variety of social policy and social work courses with The Open University.

Lynne Poole is Lecturer in Social Policy at the University of Paisley. Her current research interests are social policy in Central and Eastern Europe, comparative social policy, health and community care and the contemporary restructuring of welfare.

Tom Shakespeare worked at the Disability Research Unit, University of Leeds, for four years, researching disabled sexuality and disabled childhood. He now works on the social implications of genetics at the Policy, Ethics and Life Sciences Research Institute, Newcastle. His latest book, *Help* (Venture Press, 2000), develops ideas discussed in his chapter for this volume.

Elizabeth Stanko, Professor of Criminology, Royal Holloway College, University of London, is the Director of the Economic and Social Research Council's Programme on Violence. Her research has explored the meanings of violence and its intersections with gender. She has published extensively in the areas of violence against women, fear of crime and feminist criminology.

Kevin Stenson is Professor of Social Policy and Criminology at Buckinghamshire Chilterns University College. He has applied and developed Foucault's theories in examining the growth of pluralistic forms of liberal governance, through studies of social work practice, the social control and self-organization of young people on the streets, community policing, social deprivation and the development of anti-deprivation strategies. Publications include (co-edited with David Cowell) *The Politics of Crime Control* (Sage, 1991).

Julia Twigg is Reader in Social Policy at the University of Kent. She has published extensively on the topics of community care and informal care. She has recently completed a study of the provision of help with bathing for frail older and disabled people, and is currently working on a book on the body and social policy.

Sophie Watson is Professor of Urban Studies at the University of East London and a former Professor at the School for Policy Studies at the University of Bristol. She has published many books including (edited with L. Doyal) *Engendering Social Policy* (Sage, 1999) and *Surface City: Sydney at the Millennium* (Sage, 1997).

Fiona Williams is Professor of Social Policy at the University of Leeds and Director of the ESRC Research Group for the Study of Care, Values and the Future of Welfare. She has written widely on gender, 'race', class and welfare, and on learning disabilities, community care and social theory and social policy. She is currently writing a book on *New Principles for Welfare* for Polity Press.

Introduction: Expanding the Social Policy Imaginary

Gail Lewis

The chapters in this volume are the outcome of a seminar series held at The Open University between October 1998 and March 1999.[1] Always envisaged as leading to a published volume, the seminar had four main aims – aims that centred on understanding the shifts in the contours and orientation of social policy. There have, of course, been many volumes, from varying political perspectives, published in the last decade or so that seek to describe, prescribe and analyse the impact of the shifts in social welfare (for example, Burrows and Loader, 1994; O'Brien and Penna, 1998; Jordan, 1998; Green, 1993). Although this book forms part of this growing literature, our concerns have a distinctive flavour in that we have focused on the reconfiguration of 'the social'. Our four aims, then, were envisaged as speaking to different dimensions of 'the social' in social policy.

First, we wanted to outline and explore some of the challenges to and reconceptualizations of social policy that had occurred over the previous thirty years. Second, we were concerned to identify the ways in which social policy was both constitutive of and constituted by a series of intersecting and unequal social relations. Third, we wanted to map the dimensions and directions of change that were contained in the visions for a reworked and expanded social policy that had been expressed by various constituencies of new welfare subjects. Finally, we wanted to plot out briefly some of the new agendas for welfare in the twenty-first century that emerged from these processes of rethinking. In sum we could say that we wanted to cast a glance backwards – over the forms, practices and effects of the 'old' social policy – and forward, toward the new claims, issues and relations that emerge from contemporary struggles over the terms of inclusion in the social relations of welfare.

These are issues that have implications for the academic field of social policy. What counts as 'social' as a focus of social policy in a specific society at a particular historical moment matters deeply for members of that society. Whether unemployment is a focus of social policy; whether children are private property, subjects of social concern and without agency; how gender or ethnic divisions are conceptualized and how they are seen to link to the aims and practices of welfare agencies – such issues have significant social consequences. They also have academic implications: they raise questions about how social policy is to be defined and analysed. Indeed, one critical dimension of the process of rethinking social policy derives from challenges to conventional assumptions about what is – and what is not – social.

Individually and collectively the chapters that follow show that any project of rethinking social policy raises a multiplicity of highly complex issues. They also show that this complexity is compounded by the points of theoretical and political tension that result from the intersection of two issues that potentially pull in opposite directions. Thus, on the one hand, rethinking social policy involves trying to think through an agenda that will ensure greater equality across numerous social divisions. On the other hand, this requires recognition of the specificity of particular relations of inequality without privileging any one of these relations as primary.

Such concerns require us to think about how to discern the parameters and targets of social policy, and whose values should underwrite and shape these boundaries of legitimacy. This in its turn raises issues as to which categories of analysis are most appropriate for a project aimed at a refashioned, emancipatory social policy. One such issue concerns the conceptual categories capable of directing analysis and research, whilst capturing the multiple social divisions that welfare regimes reflect, produce and address: for example, how best to hold on to the 'old' analytic category of class in a way that neither privileges this form of social division as the primary one, nor sidelines it as a central arena of difference and inequality. Or, to take a second example, how to introduce and work with 'age' as an analytic category in ways that enable a grasp of the subordinating effects that social policy has on the elderly and children.

The question of which conceptual categories are the most appropriate for developing a new analytical framework points to another concern. This is how to create a social policy capable of being fluid and dynamic whilst simultaneously being able to define the points of, at least, temporary, closure around the scope of the discipline, or the criteria of entitlement to welfare services and benefits. How do we decide whose interests to privilege at what moments in, for example, the social relations of care in familial or public settings? How do we characterize and analyse the state and define the legitimate boundaries of its role in social welfare? Some of these issues have been endemic to social policy for at least this century; others are more the product of the theoretical and political perspectives that have emerged in the last thirty years or so. Among these new issues are questions of the body, the emotions and the psychic dimensions of welfare; time and temporalities; experience, identity and social agency.

In this sense, then, *Rethinking Social Policy* is concerned with the dislocation of social policy that has occurred over the last two to three decades in the context of wider social, political, economic and cultural changes. Its silent starting-point is the crisis of the liberal and Fabian influenced welfare state that emerged in the UK in the wake of the Second World War. At the core of the issues addressed in this volume are those questions, challenges and visions associated with a diverse range of political and theoretical perspectives and 'new' constituencies of welfare subjects. The challenges, visions and projects articulated by these constituencies in part expressed, in part converged with fundamental shifts and realignments in the economic and spatial organization of production within and across the boundaries of nation-states. Together these forces combined to profoundly destabilize the welfare 'settlements' (Clarke and Newman, 1997; Hughes and Lewis, 1998) that had characterized the Beveridge insurance revolution. It was not just the form, content and distributive criteria of social welfare that were subjected to challenge but the very categories and boundaries through which welfare was conceptualized, produced and distributed. Thus, the destabilization was profound because in its very breadth and depth it struck at the social organization of state-regulated (though not necessarily produced and/or distributed) welfare and the social relations that were constituted by, and constitutive of, this social organization. Moreover, the challenges came from opposing political directions. On the one hand, there were the forces and voices of that amalgam of social authoritarians and neo-liberals that became known as the 'New Right' and captured the heart, mind and governments of the Conservative Party for two decades or more.[2] On the other hand, there were the critiques, emanating from radical Marxists and 'new social movements', of the social and material inequalities that persisted despite the existence of 'the welfare state'. The clash of these two sets of opposing forces was to disrupt the old assumptions about the aims, methods and effects of social welfare (Lewis, 1998a). At the core of this disruption was a struggle over the connections between state, 'people' and social welfare and the relative distribution of rights and responsibilities between state and citizen. Moreover, these critiques were occurring in a context where the scalar units that formed the boundaries of the nation-state, and so represented the geo-political parameters within which welfare agencies practised, were themselves being subjected to a reconfiguration brought on by the combined and uneven processes of regionalism and globalization.

These critiques and challenges have resulted in a wide-ranging debate about a number of issues central to the field of social policy. These include definitions of the parameters and content of social policy, including the definition of the term itself; concerns about the scope and purpose of the state's role in social policy, and the related but distinct issue of the links between social policy and constructions of national belonging; questions as to the most appropriate criteria to use in facilitating access to social welfare; questions relating to how to conceive agency and who can be, or are, defined as subjects with agency. Moreover questions of difference and identity have had the effect of introducing 'new' issues and methods in social policy research, issues such as recognizing the importance of the emotions for social policy, or the relation between social policy and the temporalities that govern and flow through familial, employment and leisure relations. These 'new' issues sit alongside the 'old' ones such as social disadvantage, inequality and access to welfare services and practices. Some of these are addressed in chapters in this volume and in the rest of this Introduction I want to provide some context for the arguments they present by considering five themes. These are: defining social policy; rethinking the social; state, nation, people; social divisions, social differences and democratization; new dimensions – time, bodies, emotions.

Defining social policy

The term 'social policy' always contains a certain ambiguity. The phrase can be – and is – used to refer to two different objects. It can refer to a cluster of government policies designed to promote social ends or objectives. In this meaning it is usually understood as policies intended to improve social well-being or the welfare of citizens and is often treated as though it is equivalent to talking about 'welfare states'. This definition of social policy has a fairly long history, as the following quotation from Titmuss, one of the key figures in the Fabian tradition of social policy, indicates:

> Social administration may broadly be defined as the study of the social services whose object . . . is the improvement of the conditions of life of the individual in the setting of family and group relations. It is concerned with the historical development of these services, both statutory and voluntary, with the moral values implicit in social action, with the roles and functions of the services, with their economic aspects, and with the part they play in meeting certain needs in the social process. On the one hand, then, we are interested in the machinery of administration, which organizes and dispenses various forms of social assistance; on the other, in the lives, the needs, and the mutual relations of those members of the community for whom the services are provided by reason of their belonging to that community. (Titmuss, 1958a, pp.14–15)

In this definition, Titmuss, using the term 'social administration' that was common at the time he was writing, extends the scope of social policy beyond the issue of collective provision for individual well-being by touching on the connections between welfare and other aspects of social life. Thus, he includes issues of historical develop-ment, ethics, economic questions and the patterns of what we would now call the mixed economy of welfare. Moreover, he embeds these issues in the social relations of family and community. Social policy is, then, about the interface between forms of integration and belong-ing and the administrative or organizational mechanisms devised for the delivery of welfare services and benefits. These issues continue to be central to the domain of social policy. Thus, the breakdown of the Beveridge welfare settlements, and the restructuring that both reflected and effected this process of breakdown, have had a range of effects. Among them are shifts in the balance between statutory and voluntary provision; struggles over welfare moralities; and attempts to redefine the criteria of welfare (and wider societal) belonging and legitimacy (for example, Clarke and Newman, 1997; Hughes and Lewis, 1998; Hay, 1996).

In this context, one central issue at stake in rethinking social policy is the causes and consequences of the break-up – or unsettling – of the welfare state that developed in the post Second World War period. Such analysis requires more than an investigation of changes in the administrative arrangements, the lines of connection between welfare organizations, or the criteria of access to welfare services. As the critiques and challenges articulated by numerous constituencies of welfare subjects have shown, it also involves examining how, and on what basis, any given social organization of welfare excludes, subordinates or disempowers groups of welfare users. The explora-tions of the exclusions and subordinations that result from the social organization of welfare also point to questions about the boundaries and aims of social policy. This inevitably impacts upon social policy as an academic field of study concerned with examining welfare policies and their conditions, causes and consequences – in other words, their links to wider social processes and relations. Again, Titmuss provides us with a useful definition of the elements that need to be addressed in the *study* of social policy:

> It is clear that the study of social policy cannot be isolated from the study of society as a whole in all its varied social, economic and political aspects. An essential background for the study of social policy is a knowledge of population changes, past and present and predicted for the future; the family as an institution and the position of women; social stratification and the concepts of class, caste, status and mobility; social change and the effects of industrialisation, urbanisation and social conditions; the political structure; the work ethic and the sociology of industrial relations; minority groups and racial prejudice; social control, conformity, deviance and the uses of sociology to maintain the status quo.

> Policy, any policy, to be effective must choose an objective and must face dilemmas of choice. But to understand policy, to distinguish between ends (what we want or think we want) and means (how to get there), we have to see it in the context of a particular set of circumstances, a given society and culture, and a more or less specified period of historical time. In other words, social policy cannot be discussed or even conceptualised in a social vacuum . . . (Titmuss, 1974, pp.15–16)

So it is difficult to entirely separate 'social policy' as referring to policies, procedures, practices and values related to social welfare and 'social policy' as a field and practice of study. Even when we are caught up in arguments about the appropriate scope, content, methods and perspectives for the study of social policy, social policies are at least an implicit presence. There are, however, problems about defining and delimiting social policy in both meanings.

Take, for example, the term 'policy'. Immediately this raises an issue about which policies – from which institutions – we should concentrate on. Should we only be looking at *government* policies? Why not the policies of other social institutions: markets, corporations, voluntary bodies? Why not the policies of non-governmental or supra-national institutions: the United Nations, the International Monetary Fund, the European Union? As Titmuss made clear, the study of social policy has to engage with questions about the different institutions and agencies that might shape or affect social welfare. In part this is because in some cases governments have chosen to pursue social objectives through other agencies or in 'partnership' with them. Indeed, the legitimate scale and scope of government action has always been a subject of huge debate and disagreement in Britain (see Lewis, 1998b) and, as such, has varied within societies historically, as well as between societies. Moreover, if we focus attention on government policies, or even those related to the domain of the public more generally, we occlude the pivotal role that familial relations and practices have in the organization and distribution of care and welfare. The same can be said of the role that the voluntary and private sector play in care and welfare. This issue reflects the way in which social policies always intersect with complex economic, social and political arrangements that have social welfare consequences or effects of their own.

Alternatively, we could limit our focus to those policies *designed* to promote social ends. This, however, only begs the question about other policies that might have social effects or consequences: forms of economic organization, building technologies, transport policies, environmental policies and so on. These differences show that which policies and agencies are included in the remit of the study of social policy is itself subject to debate and contestation. For example, Ginsburg would argue for a broad definition of social policy:

I would define the welfare state very broadly indeed to include all public action and inaction to meet fundamental human needs to mitigate social inequalities including direct public provision of benefits and services, subsidisation and regulation of occupational and other private provisions, and the impact of taxation. The welfare state is also an ideology, a potent symbol within contemporary political currency in Britain at least, which is much greater than the sum of its policy parts – the idea of social welfare support from cradle to the grave is extremely attractive, engendering a sense of social belonging, social solidarity and meaningful citizenship. (Ginsburg, 1996, p. 1)

In contrast to this, the ideological dimension of the reforms instituted by successive governments in the last two decades has attempted to define welfare narrowly, as the provision of income maintenance benefits and services to individuals and families. This has been related to attempts to shift the bases of welfare responsibilities and their links to the formation of social solidarities and connections between state and citizen.

If, however, we want to define social policy in broad terms – and particularly if we want to make a multiplicity of social inequalities and the struggles against them central to our concerns – then three sets of questions emerge. First, there is the question of how other policies – and other parts of the state not commonly identified with social welfare, such as the criminal justice system – play important roles in the definition and management of social problems. As McLaughlin (1998) has noted, the criminal justice system and the personnel who staff its agencies have operated in a discursive environment that casts this system as at once different from other public sector agencies (such as education or health) whilst dealing with 'fundamental *symbolic* issues of principle – rights, duties, order, equity, justice, punishment – that lie at the heart of a social order that is governed by the rule of law' (ibid., p.163). In other words, the criminal justice system is a constitutive 'other' of social welfare – one that establishes or defines the discursive and political limits of social welfare.

This is the issue addressed in the chapters in this volume by Muncie, Stenson and Stanko, each of which focuses on conceptualizations of crime and the criminal justice system. In different ways, each insists on the necessity to rethink the relation between welfare policies and practices and those of the criminal justice system. Each argues that failure to do so maintains and reproduces an artificial divide between crime, policing and social control, on the one hand, and need, welfare and social policy on the other. In contrast 'crime' and criminal justice ought to be understood as one facet of social policy, with discourses of crime, criminality and policing representing a constitutive outside of social policy. Indeed it is through analysis of the discourses and practices at work in this 'outside' that attempts by the state to redefine the objectives, scope and practices of welfare agencies can be understood. Again, in their different ways, the chapters by Muncie and Stanko point to the social harms, and those who are hurt, that dominant discourses of crime and criminality exclude. Moreover, the arguments of both these authors give a central position to multiple social inequalities as they move the debate away from a simple binary divide between victim and perpetrator of crime. In this way, they attempt to lay the ground for an expanded notion of social policy.

The question of that which is different from, but constitutive of, the legitimate horizons of social welfare raises a second set of questions. The study of social policy has always had to deal with a tension between assessing whether policies are delivering their claimed effects and assessing what other intentions or interests might be the forces behind policies. The tension was classically posed in the work of the American scholars Frances Fox Piven and Richard Cloward in their study of poverty programmes in the United States (1971). Conventionally understood as programmes to 'relieve poverty' (to reduce the economic and social toll on poor people), such policies, Piven and Cloward argued, were primarily designed to contain, manage or 'regulate' poor people. In so doing, Piven and Cloward, like the authors concerned to explore the links between constructions of crime and those of social welfare, were pointing to the difficulty of separating the 'care' aspects of social policies from their 'control' aspects. This raises the difficult and politically loaded issue of the extent to which social welfare is designed to ameliorate the excessive effects of capitalist social relations (as T.H. Marshall, 1950/1996 believed) or is linked to a more broadly defined project of social justice and radical democracy. It also raises the thorny and persistent issue of the character and role of the state in relation to social welfare. This is an issue to which we return briefly in a later section.

Finally there is the issue, already touched on, of the 'private' dimensions of welfare. There are at least two interrelated aspects to this area of concern. On the one hand, defining social policy as being concerned only with the domain of 'the public' occludes the mutually constitutive relation of definitions of 'the public and the private'. Feminists have long pointed to the gendered character of the designation of these domains – and their implication for gendered inequalities (see, for example, Davidoff and Hall, 1987; Riley, 1988). They have also stressed the profound implications for the social organization of welfare that the discursive divide between public and private realms has had (see Land, 1976, and Wilson, 1977, for early examples of this analysis).

Indeed, it is precisely these points that are addressed in the chapters by Lister, Jane Lewis and Shakespeare which open the present volume. These chapters have issues of gender and care as common concerns and as such they introduce themes that recur throughout the book. Nevertheless these three (and subsequent chapters) approach the issues in different ways and with different priorities. In so doing, they point to two matters of importance for the rethinking of social policy. First (individually and together) they indicate the ways in which the social relations of gender and care have been central to a rethinking of social policy. This focus has extended the parameters of what is included in social policy and widened understanding of the effects of welfare policy and practices on diverse constituents of welfare subjects. Second, they are indicative of the debates *among* those concerned to rethink social policy. They show a diversity of opinion about, and approach to, common concerns. The divergence of their points of engagement with relations of gender and care also illustrate the rich analytical insights that it has been possible to develop as a result of the stretching of the boundaries and imaginary of social policy.

Rethinking the social

Each of these issues indicates the fundamental question of what we mean by *social* in social policy. What conditions, what categories of people, what patterns of life are seen as 'social'? And what are not 'social' but natural, or biological, or private, or economic, or environmental? In these terms, 'social' exists in relation to a complicated set of other categorizations of the world. Again we return to Titmuss, who offers an implicit definition of the 'social' of social policy when he writes,

> The grant, or the gift or unilateral transfer – whether it takes the form of cash, time, energy, satisfaction, blood or even life itself – is the distinguishing mark of the social (in policy and administration) just as exchange or bilateral transfer is the mark of the economic. (Titmuss, 1968, p.22)

Identifying the character and limits of 'the social' is, then, particularly significant for rethinking social policy. These are not just 'academic' questions, although they have implications for the academic field of social policy. Indeed, one way of characterizing the challenges to the policies, practices and values that underpinned the Fabian welfare state is as a set of struggles over what counted – and counts – as social. For Titmuss the domain of the social is constituted through the chains of connection that are formed by the altruistic behaviour of social actors. In this context, social policy – understood as comprising three areas of policy and practice: social services, fiscal welfare and occupational welfare (Titmuss, 1958a and b) – has a central role to play in promoting both greater equality and a more

cohesive society, with a strong sense of community. 'The social' of
social policy in this view, then, is about the recognition and development of reciprocal obligations through which organic connections
among individuals and groups might be expressed and fostered. For
some writers, Titmuss' approach to 'the social', and the role of social
policy in sustaining this domain, meant that 'questions of power,
inequality and the division of labour' stood at the centre of discussions on welfare (Mann, 1992, p.24, quoted in Wilding, 1995). This
is an important observation and indicates the enduring quality of
these issues in debates about social welfare. However, how 'power,
inequality and the division of labour' are conceptualized, and what
specific social relations they are understood as referencing, have been
subjected to change in the light of the political and theoretical challenges of the last thirty years.

Some of this movement is reflected in the shift to definitions of the
social that mark it as a domain formed by the struggles of individual
and social actors to establish their own normative orientations and
interpretations of need as the bases for the distribution of resources
(Baynes, 1993). These are struggles over the ability to fix meanings as
much as they are struggles over material resources. However, in
contrast to the approach by Titmuss, who placed altruistic transfer at
the heart of the social, this more contemporary definition of the social
places 'struggle' or 'contestation' at the core.

This latter approach is in many ways indebted to Foucault, who in
his shifting theoretical stance (and especially in his work after the
events of May 1968)[3] came to understand the social as the product of
the flow of conflictual strategic action. This gives a central place to
power in the definition of the social, but an understanding of power
not as the possession of a specific social actor or agency but as
capillary-like, flowing through the multiple fibres of the social body:

> Power comes from below: that is, there is no binary and all-encompassing
> opposition between rulers and ruled at the root of power relations, and
> serving as a general matrix – no such duality extending from the top down
> and reacting on more and more limited groups to the very depths of the
> social body. One must suppose rather that the manifold relationships of
> force that take shape and come into play in the machinery of production,
> in families, limited groups, and institutions, are the basis for wide-ranging
> effects of cleavage that run through the social body as a whole. (Foucault,
> 1978, p.94)

It operates as follows:

> Between every part of a social body, between a man and a woman,
> between members of a family, between a master and his pupil, between
> every one who knows and every one who does not, there exist relations of

power which are not purely and simply a projection of the sovereign's great power over the individual; they are rather the concrete, changing soil in which the sovereign's power is grounded, the conditions which make it possible for it to function. (Foucault, 1980, p.156)

Foucault's work is not alone in marking shifting configurations and conceptualizations of the social, but of the structuralist/post-structuralist French theorists he has perhaps been the most influential in the discipline of social policy. Moreover, it is in relation to shifts in conceptions of the social and the insistence on the importance of meaning and discourse for establishing the known, knower and knowable, that we can most clearly see the impact of the political and theoretical challenges to the policies, practices and effects of Fabian social policy. There are two effects highlighted here. First, there is the redefinition of the object of analysis that accompanies the linguistic or cultural turn. In this case the effect is to focus the analytic gaze of the discipline of social policy on the relations of meaning that are internal to the discourses embedded in policies themselves rather than to seek an objective truth 'out there' which the policy documents then describe. The second is to insist that the study of social policy involves an identification and analysis of the forms of agency adopted by diverse welfare subjects.

The chapters by Watson, Carabine and Pinkney illustrate this shift in the object of analysis. Watson's chapter works in a way similar to that of Lister in that it introduces the key dimensions of a parti-cular approach to social policy. Whereas Lister looked at the new analytic gaze that the lens of gender facilitated, Watson outlines the elements of a Foucauldian approach. Carabine deploys a Foucauldian approach to explore the connections between discourses of poverty and discourses of sexuality in nineteenth-century Britain. In different ways, the question of what is known and who can be constructed as a knowing subject with the power of agency is addressed in the chapters by Pinkney and Phoenix. Phoenix, for example, goes straight to the issue of who can be a 'knowing' subject in social policy. She does this by developing an argument for recognizing children as active agents who negotiate their gendered and racialized positions in the social relations of schools on the basis of the discourses avail-able to them. Pinkney shows that despite the existence within welfare agencies of competing discourses on children, they all tend to con-struct children as without agency. By drawing on research conducted in a social constructionist framework Phoenix demonstrates that this view is contestable. She points to children as 'knowing' subjects embedded in the social relations of welfare. Indeed the dynamic tension between discursive positioning in the social relations of wel-fare and expression of agency by diverse constituencies of welfare subjects is a theme running throughout this volume.

State, nation, people

Each of the concerns considered so far implies that social policy may be a distinctive academic field because of the particularity of its focus on the relation between shifting social and political action and forms of social welfare. If what counts as 'social' in social policy is not a fixed or eternal category, then part and parcel of the study of social policy is the historical analysis of its changing configuration. More than just what policies are produced is involved. The complexity of the study of social policy lies in its focus on relationships between different aspects and institutions of society. Social policy marks the intersection of patterns of economic inequalities and insecurities; forms of household organization and family networks; shifting alignments of political membership, political action and social movements; forms of social division and challenges to them. It also marks the intersection of this cluster of social institutions and relations and the discursive formations that legitimize and organize the inequalities that filter through and across these social domains.

Because of the intersection of social welfare with the state and the way the state articulates social differences, the study of social policy is also engaged by issues about nation and nationality: the boundaries (geographical, social and political) of 'membership' and citizenship. Indeed, social policies may be viewed as attempts to 'settle' these tensions, problems and conflicts – to resolve or accommodate them in particular ways (see Clarke and Newman, 1997; Hughes and Lewis, 1998; Williams, 1989), not only by establishing the terms of access to welfare services and benefits but also by expressing the distribution of rights and responsibilities between state and citizen. In many ways, then, the shape of the 'settlements' characterizing British social welfare at any particular time contain within them views about the state, the respective moral obligations of state and citizen and boundaries of who does and does not (fully) belong to the nation.

These are, of course, issues that have plagued the development of competing ideologies of welfare and which have been, and continue to be, central to the process of rethinking social policy. In broad terms it is possible to characterize debates about the role of the state in social welfare as comprising a three-cornered dispute between liberal democratic, collectivist (including Fabian) and Marxist approaches. They therefore mark some of the points of departure for the rethinking of social policy going on at the end of the twentieth century.

In late twentieth-century Britain the question of the state – and specifically its relation to and responsibilities for social welfare – has been put on to the agenda by the convergence of a number of contradictory trends. On the one hand, there has been the decline of modernist meta-narratives, including those central to the ideologies of social democratic and working-class movements. This decline in the interpellative and interpretative power of traditional ideologies of progress sat alongside the articulation of a politics by new social movements wanting to address hitherto unrecognized inequalities. On the other hand, there were the political successes of the Conservative Party, with its radical right-wing agenda. The election of New Right governments in Britain (and other liberal democracies) had a number of effects. These included a growing gap between rich and poor, an increase in the numbers in poverty, such that in Britain in the late 1990s one in three children lived in poverty, and a realigned 'statecraft' alongside the liberalization of the economy. Moreover, the context of these growing material inequalities and realignments of state, economy and welfare has been a growing globalization, a process presented and accepted as 'inevitable' by the national and supranational institutions and governments it serves (Massey, 1999).

The ascendancy of right-wing political parties and ideologies represented a shift away from the statist and collectivist approaches that had found their most articulate expression in the welfare state. These approaches faced a concerted political and ideological onslaught from New Right politicians and 'think-tanks', who promoted and (at least partly) effected a shift towards a liberal democratic state. In this approach the state is defined by its place as the guarantor of the rights and liberties (including electoral rights) of the individual. Itself subject to the rule of law, this state must be both 'strong' – to enable it to defend the individual and the nation – and 'small' – i.e. restricting its field of intervention in civil society and the family to a minimum. The individual of liberal democracy is an equal, autonomous and rational actor. But this is 'a specifically instrumentalist type of rationality [with] a fundamental interest in the acquisition of more and more goods' (Smith, 1998, p.11). However, as Hall and Schwarz (1985) have noted, this state has always intervened to ensure that the conditions for the working of the free market and capital accumulation are secured. Thus, the notion of the minimal state characteristic of the liberal democratic approach does not mean the 'absence of controls, but a specific means by which market forces are politically regulated' (p.19).

Jessop's chapter addresses the changing form of the state and its relation to social welfare in the context of shifting regional, national and supra-national alignments. Embedded within a social regulationist approach his argument can be broadly located within a Marxist perspective. Rather than focusing on the balance of class forces, or the shape of a class compromise, as has been common in Marxist analyses of the welfare state, he outlines a shift in the general contours of the state in a post-Fordist era. This is summed up in a shift from a 'Keynesian welfare state' to a 'Schumpeterian workfare post-national regime' – a shift that in his view represents a greater subordination of social policy to economic imperatives. Jessop's argument points to the realigned but nevertheless continuing and contradictory relationship between capitalism and the welfare state. This shift also raises key issues about the changing spatialities of social welfare, an issue that Clarke takes up in his chapter. Cautioning against both too strong a focus on the agencies of the state at the expense of other social agencies, such as non-governmental organizations (NGOs), and an approach that explains all realignments in the state/social welfare nexus in terms of the logics of capital, Clarke points to the utility of cultural analysis of the discourses of globalization. Importantly, he draws attention to the continued significance of the nation-state as the legitimate geo-political entity in social welfare, even while recognizing the dislocations that have occurred in the nation-state/welfare state relation. In part this dislocation is linked to an increasing welfare pluralism and the emergence of new organizational linkages between welfare agencies. Thus, the multiple spatialities, scalar units and organizations involved in the production, mediation and delivery of welfare services 'pose significant analytical problems for the study of social policy' (Clarke, Chapter 13, p.211).

What these chapters do is raise the question of boundaries, boundaries of the geographical or scalar variety, particularly in their intersection with, and impact upon, the social policies of nation-states. There are also boundaries between forms of private, public, familial and community based welfare provision – a multiplicity that confounds any simple distinction between the state or the market. In their different ways each chapter explores the interaction of shifts in the organization of spatial boundaries, how these shifting boundaries are, or should be conceptualized, and the objectives, effects and possibilities of national welfare policies.

Social divisions, social differences and democratization

Earlier I noted some of the implications for the study of social policy that result from a remapping of the social in terms of power and struggle between diverse social groups. In large part this redefinition of the social is the product of the convergence of post-structuralism and the emergence of new social movements. Laclau and Mouffe (1985) have argued that the new forms of social conflict articulated by new social movements have resulted in both theoretical and political destabilization and crisis. They see the need for new forms of political understanding and organization that are capable of creating a new democratic imaginary.

In relation to social policy the effect of the convergence of new social movements and post-structuralist theory has been to place the

issues of difference, identity, particularity, and the subjective vari-
ability of historical experience on the agenda. This has resulted not
only from the disruptions of the old grand narratives and their certainties but also from the insistence by new claims-making constituencies (Drover and Kerans, 1993) that the categories, practices
and relations of welfare that were previously taken for granted be
explored for their emancipatory or subordinating effects. The refusal
to treat social differences as pre-social or as essential characteristics of
particular groups or individuals draws attention to them as the
outcomes of processes of *subject formation*. Fabian social policy was
concerned with the social divisions of class albeit in a gradualist,
ameliorative or statist fashion. Pushed by the political challenges of
new social movements, those involved in rethinking social policy are
seeking to understand the relationships between the 'knowledges'
and practices of social welfare and the production of forms of social
difference. Centrally, exploration of this link involves conceptualizing
difference as a set of social practices.

However, it is not just from the effects of domination and inequality that social differences emerge. Social differences also emerge from
the challenges to domination and inequality and the struggle for
self-defined identities, as the chapters by Phoenix and Shakespeare
illustrate. Thus, social differences are formed in the dynamic interplay
of domination and the struggle against it; between the attempt to
establish the boundaries of the 'normal' and attempts to dislodge
and/or expand those boundaries; between the attempts to limit the
criteria of access to resources and the struggle to breach or replace
those criteria.

In practical terms new issues emerge for social policy agencies
and professionals. Among them are the following. How can welfare
agencies and professionals identify and respect cultural diversity
whilst simultaneously resisting racializing or racist practice? How
can diverse sexualities and sexual practices be respected without
placing one form as 'normal' and normative? How can welfare
benefits and services be provided in ways that do not reproduce
traditional gender relations, yet enable care of home and dependants
to be practised by men as much as women? How can those in
poverty have their material needs met without being positioned as
abnormally or deviantly dependent? What kinds of services and
benefits need to be produced to enable people to develop forms of
relationship that meet their mental and emotional needs alongside
their physical needs? What would it mean to accept children as equal
citizens and agents as adults?

What all of these questions speak to is the issue of how to create
the conditions for a democratization of social policy, and the great
majority of the chapters in this volume address one or other of
the dimensions that are central to issues of equality, justice and

democratization. Gail Lewis, for example, picks up the theme of racialization first raised in the chapter by Phoenix, by considering the racializing effects of current government policy on school exclusions and truancies. She explores the ways in which social policy can be implicated in the constitution of social difference and inequality. Gewirtz also explores the links between social policy, welfare practices and the construction of social inequalities in schools. Her concern, however, is to show that when used to analyse policy documents, frameworks that take the question of social justice as their guide can provide a keen analytic way to discuss processes that produce social inequality. Like other authors in the volume, both Lewis and Gewirtz consider in general terms the issue of differentiated subject positions and their links to inequality.

Mooney agrees that social divisions, inequality and the issue of democracy are central to a rethinking of social policy but cautions against what he identifies as dangerous trends in current approaches to these issues. Noting not only the continued existence of poverty, the widening gap between rich and poor *and* the deepening levels of poverty in contemporary Britain, Mooney argues for a return to an older agenda in debates about social policy. For him, this will involve the re-centring of poverty as an issue as well as the re-emergence of the social divisions of class and the use of 'class' as an analytic category. Rooted in forms of Marxism, Mooney's chapter sits along-side that of Jessop. It is also illustrative of radical Marxist critiques of Fabian, New Right, New Labour and post-structuralist approaches to social policy.

The chapter by Poole provides a partial link between some of the concerns about the form and role of the state that Jessop and Clarke consider and the production of social differences. Poole explores the implications of new approaches to the analysis of social policy for the study of social welfare in Central and Eastern Europe. She high-lights the importance of identifying which social divisions are seen as the concern of policy-makers and why, exploring how social differ-ences are represented, how they are connected to social problems and how these understandings impact on policy development. Analysis of these factors is crucial, she argues, if we are to begin to untangle the confusing picture of welfare transformation in the wake of the demise of actually existing socialism and explore the impact of these changes on a range of social differences and inequalities.

New dimensions – emotions, bodies, time

The discussion so far has indicated two effects of the claims and perspectives articulated by constituencies of new welfare subjects. One is the demand for new, more democratic and dialogic ways of interpreting and meeting need. The other is the promotion of more holistic approaches towards both the user of welfare services and benefits and those who are employed by the agencies that produce and deliver these services. Both of these suggest that the redefinition of 'the social' around conceptions of struggle should not be interpreted as an evacuation of the moral aspects of the social that was integral to Titmuss' definition. Indeed, it is precisely the articulation of demands for more emancipatory and inclusive value systems in social welfare that distinguishes the claims of the new social movements from the New Right attacks on social democratic welfare.

The push for more holistic and liberatory value systems suggests that the boundaries of social policy should be expanded to include debates about how the individuals who people welfare practice (as both recipients and providers) are conceptualized. Indeed this is the implication of the introduction to the study of social policy of new concerns. The chapters by Hoggett, Twigg and Pillinger explore some of these new dimensions of social policy, adding to the process of rethinking social policy in two ways. On the one hand, they are examples of criticisms of certain post-structuralist perspectives (a concern they share with Mooney), especially those associated with the work of Foucault, and in the case of Hoggett that of the psychoanalyst Jacques Lacan. They are, then, further examples of debates among those concerned to rethink social policy.

On the other hand, by arguing that the psychic or emotional, the bodily and the temporal are central to welfare policy and practice they expand the intellectual horizons of the study of social policy in ways that make it more attuned to the multifaceted character of welfare. Thus, they argue not only for a rethinking of social policy because of the potentially exclusionary or subordinating effects of existing welfare practices, but also for an expanded conceptualization of the very elements of human life that social policy is concerned with and has effects upon. Each of these chapters points to the complex negotiations that have to be entered into by individuals and groups if supportive and respectful relationships are to occur. Here, then, 'the social' is not just demarcated by 'struggle' – with all the suggestions of conquest and defeat that this term conveys – but also by negotiation, integration and the pursuit of justice or equality. By drawing on Kleinian psychoanalysis to develop his argument, Hoggett points to the connections between the integration of ambivalent desires and emotions that individuals must achieve if they are to be able to develop fruitful and fulfilling *social* relationships. Such an approach holds much for social policy in that it implies that individuals require more than material goods to achieve a state of well-being (see also Rustin, 1991, especially Ch.2). Moreover, by highlighting (what in the Kleinian view are) universal human mechanisms for resolving ambivalence and creating relationship, this psychoanalytic approach offers social policy the tools with which to pursue more successfully its stated aims of promoting social cohesion. It also offers the potential for resolution of the tensions and contradictions between service users and those employed to deliver these services.

Twigg explores the ambiguities and ambivalences within social policy itself in terms of the body. She uses the body and its place in social care to critique the Foucauldian conception of power and in this moves away from depictions of care in mechanical or technicist terms – with all the disembodied, emotionless implications these depictions carry. Instead she points to the complexity both of social policy's engagement with the body and of the face-to-face inter-actions between carer and cared-for as they negotiate the multiple boundaries of body and emotions in the practice of welfare.

Spaces of the body and the emotions are, then, central elements in existing social relations of welfare and must be central to any rethinking of social policy. But so, too, are time and temporalities. In reminding us of the connections feminists made between gendered inequalities, divisions of labour and social policy, the chapter by Lister already indicated something of the way in which the social relations of welfare are also social relations of time. The Fordist family as a modality connecting circuits of production and consumption was also marked by the temporalities of bourgeois time. How-ever, the simultaneous interconnection and relative autonomy of the social relations of family, gender and production means that changes in one have implications for the temporal relations among them all. As Nowotny notes,

> With the intensification of working life and increasing pressure of time, but above all with the emergence of women from the private time of the family and their participation in the public time of working life, there grew the desire for a new category of disposal: disposal of one's own time, rights to which are declared, as if it were a question of acquiring possession of it. (Nowotny, 1994, p.13)

'Time' can provide a useful analytical tool for understanding the interrelated processes of the reorganization of production and welfare across countries of the European Union. For Pillinger this is a key issue as she explores experiments to realign the balance of working time, domestic time and leisure time and the implications this may have for gendered inequalities. She not only considers the links between the social organization of gender relations and social policy but also shows how the dimension of 'time' is both constituted by and constitutive of the social relations of paid work, care and gender.

The introduction of new arenas, dimensions and conceptual categories into the horizon of 'the social' offers social policy the opportunity to develop richer, more textured analyses of the social relations of welfare. This is evident in relation to the recipients of welfare services and benefits, but the chapters by Davies and Mackintosh suggest that our understanding of 'the social' should extend inside welfare agencies to those who are paid to produce and deliver welfare services and benefits. Davies' chapter illustrates the connections between the shape of institutions regulating and monitoring welfare practices and the social and discursive patterns that are dominant at any one time. She shows that differentiated and hierarchically ordered subject positions affect not only the dynamics of personal and group interaction but also the very mode of organizing the institutional boundaries and rules demarcating professional groups. In this way she historicizes institutional form and therefore contextualizes the uncertainties and contradictions of contemporary attempts to change the form of regulation in health and social care professions. Mackintosh is concerned to explore the effects of organizational change on the dynamics and relations within welfare agencies in shifting the modes and points of identification within and across professional occupations in these sectors. She uses primary data in the form of interview material to analyse how personnel in social care agencies negotiate shifts in the structures of their work organization by adopting positions within the new managerialist discourses that now govern these agencies' practices. Her chapter also notes an important and interesting reminder of the distinction Titmuss made between the social and the economic when he said that unilateral transfer was the key characteristic of the former, bilateral transfer characteristic of the latter. Mackintosh indicates both the blurring of this boundary that has resulted from managerialist restructuring of welfare and the importance of treating 'the economic' as no more nor less socially constructed than other spheres of life.

The chapter by Williams brings together many of the themes raised earlier in the volume. She summarizes some of the main political sources that have led to a rethinking of social policy and begins to elucidate the principles that might help shape a more democratic and emancipatory social policy of the future. Importantly she highlights the centrality of values in social policy, indicating that if struggle is a defining characteristic of the social, a more emancipatory and democratic social policy will depend on the formation of a value system capable of engaging diverse constituencies in dialogic connection.

'Rethinking' social policy thus involves a series of overlapping issues. Those about the boundaries or limits of the subject, some of which hinge on the shifting contextual definitions of social policy with the implication that these cannot be fixed abstractly. There are also issues about how to analyse social policy, as well as what the focus of analysis should be. Thus there are potentials for arguments between different sorts of theoretical and political perspectives. In some senses, these issues have become central to the task of studying social policy during the last twenty years. The process of 'rethinking', of course, implies a challenge to existing ways of thinking. The idea of rethinking provides us with a convenient way of registering a set of arguments, conflicts and challenges around the study of social policy. These arguments, conflicts and challenges are part of a continuing process of rethinking. This does not reflect a finished state of affairs in which social policy has been rethought. Rather, we are placed within these processes – reflecting on the conditions, directions and implications of an unfinished process.

Notes

1. The editors thank the Social Policy Discipline at The Open University for hosting the seminar series from which this volume has been produced.
2. Margaret Thatcher became leader of the Conservative Party in 1975.
3. Such as *The History of Sexuality, Vol. 1* (1978).

References

Baynes, K. (1993) 'Translator's preface', in Honneth, A., *The Critique of Power: Reflective Stages in a Critical Social Theory*, Cambridge and London, The MIT Press.
Burrows, R. and Loader, B. (eds) (1994) *Towards a Post-Fordist Welfare State?* London, Routledge.
Clarke, J. and Newman, J. (1997) *The Managerial State: Power, Politics and Ideology in the Remaking of Social Welfare*, London, Sage.
Davidoff, L. and Hall, C. (1987) *Family Fortunes: Men and Women of the English Middle Class 1780–1850*, London, Hutchinson.
Drover, G. and Kerans, P. (eds) (1993) *New Approaches to Welfare Theory*, Aldershot, Edward Elgar.
Foucault, M. (1978) *The History of Sexuality, Volume 1: An Introduction*, New York, Random House.
Foucault, M. (1980) 'Interview with L. Finas', in Gordon, C. (ed.) *Power/Knowledge*, New York, Pantheon Books.
Ginsburg, N. (1996) 'The future of the welfare state'. Professorial inaugural lecture, University of North London.
Green, D. (1993) *Reinventing Civil Society: The Rediscovery of Welfare without Politics*, London, IEA.
Hall, S. and Schwarz, B. (1985) 'State and society 1880–1924', in Langan and Schwarz (1985).
Hay, C. (1996) *Re-Stating Social and Political Change*, Milton Keynes, Open University Press.
Hughes, G. and Lewis, G. (eds) (1998) *Unsettling Welfare: The Reconstruction of Social Policy*, London, Routledge/The Open University.
Jordan, B. (1998) *The New Politics of Welfare*, London, Sage.
Laclau, E. and Mouffe, C. (1985) *Hegemony and Socialist Strategy*, London, Verso.

Land, H. (1976) 'Women: supporters or supported', in Barker, D.L. and Allen, S. (eds) *Sexual Divisions in Society: Process and Change*, London, Routledge & Kegan Paul.

Langan, M. and Schwarz, B. (eds) (1985) *Crises in the British State 1880–1930*, London, Hutchinson.

Lewis, G. (1998a) 'Coming apart at the seams: the crises of the welfare state', in Hughes and Lewis (1998).

Lewis, G. (ed.) (1998b) *Forming Nation, Framing Welfare*, London, Routledge/The Open University.

McLaughlin, E. (1998) 'Social work or social control: remaking probation work', in Hughes and Lewis (1998).

Mann, K. (1992) 'The making of an English underclass', quoted in Wilding (1995).

Marshall, T.H. (1950/1996) 'Citizenship and social class', in Marshall, T.H. and Bottomore, T. (eds) *Citizenship and Social Class*, London, Pluto.

Massey, D. (1999) 'Imagining globalization: power-geometries of time-space', in Brah, A., Hickman, M. and Mac an Ghaill, M. (eds) *Future Worlds: Migration, Environment and Globalization*, London, Macmillan.

Nowotny, H. (1994) *Time: The Modern and Postmodern Experience*, Cambridge, Polity Press.

O'Brien, M. and Penna, S. (1998) *Theorising Welfare: Enlightenment and Modern Society*, London, Sage.

Piven, F. Fox and Cloward, R. (1971) *Regulating the Poor: The Functions of Public Welfare*, New York, Pantheon Books.

Riley, D. (1988) *Am I That Name? Feminism and the Category of 'Women' in History*, Basingstoke, Macmillan.

Rustin, M. (1991) *The Good Society and the Inner World*, London, Verso.

Smith, A.M. (1998) *Laclau and Mouffe: The Radical Democratic Imaginary*, London, Routledge.

Titmuss, R.M. (1958a) 'Social administration in a changing society', in *Essays on the Welfare State*, London, Unwin University Books. (First published 1951.)

Titmuss, R.M. (1958b) 'The social division of welfare', in *Essays on the Welfare State*, London, Unwin University Books. (First published 1955.)

Titmuss, R.M. (1974) 'The international perspective', in Abel-Smith, B. and Titmuss, K. (eds) *Social Policy: An Introduction*, London, George Allen and Unwin.

Titmuss, R.M. (1976) 'The subject of social welfare', in *Commitment to Welfare* (2nd edn), London, George Allen and Unwin. (First published 1968.)

Wilding, P. (1995) 'Titmuss', in George, V. and Page. R. (eds) *Modern Thinkers on Welfare*, London, Prentice-Hall/Harvester Wheatsheaf.

Williams, F. (1989) *Social Policy: a Critical Introduction*. Cambridge: Polity Press.

Wilson, E. (1977) *Women and the Welfare State*, London, Tavistock.

1

Gender and the Analysis of Social Policy

Ruth Lister

Contents

1 Introduction

The traditional world of social policy (or administration) was peopled by ungendered subjects and objects of analysis; women and their concerns were marginalized. Today, while not all social policy analysis is gendered and women are still frequently marginalized within it, social policy has probably gone as far as, if not further than, any of the other social sciences in taking on board some, at least, of the insights of feminist analysis. As acknowledged by George and Wilding in a key textbook, these insights have 'enormously enriched the study of social policy' (George and Wilding, 1994, pp.157–8). This chapter is, thus, outlining perspectives which are now taken for granted by many in the field of social policy, but which are so only because of the work done by feminists in the 1970s and 1980s.

The gendering of social policy can be understood in two ways. First, as foregrounded in this chapter, it provides a lens through which to describe and analyse the institutions, relations and dis-courses which constitute social policy. Second, it represents a norma-tive, and often political, attempt to reconstruct or to 're-gender' those institutions, relations and discourses in ways which better reflect the perspectives and needs of women in their diversity.

Of course, gendering is not just about women, and a recent development has been the beginnings of the discovery of men in social policy, not, as hitherto, as a hidden norm, but now problematized in their relations to welfare (Popay et al., 1998). Nevertheless, women are the main focus of this chapter for, as Elizabeth Wilson stated in one of the pioneering texts in contemporary feminist social policy analysis, 'only an analysis of the Welfare State that bases itself on a correct understanding of the position of women in modern society can reveal the full meaning of modern welfarism' (Wilson, 1977, p.59).

After a brief description of the sources of the feminist challenge to traditional practices and analysis of social policy, the chapter outlines a key set of related moves and questions involved in analysing social policy through a gendered lens.

2   The sources of the feminist challenge

A number of the insights of contemporary feminist social policy analysis can be found implicitly, or sometimes explicitly, in the writings and actions of early and mid-twentieth-century feminist campaigners. The needs of women (and their children), together with the implications for women's citizenship, were highlighted by them in debates about the emergent welfare services and benefits. A classical piece of gendered analysis can be found in Eleanor Rathbone's *The Disinherited Family* (1924; republished 1986). Deploring women's economic dependence upon their male partners, she suggested that 'there is perhaps no relation in life as it is lived in a modern industrialized community where the temptations to selfishness are greater and the checks on it fewer than the relationship between a wage-earning husband and a wholly dependent wife' (1986, p.205).

The issue of economic dependence was a key one for feminist campaigners in the 1970s who were attempting to 're-gender' social policy. In 1974 'financial and legal independence' was adopted as one of the demands of the British women's liberation movement. It aimed to challenge 'the way the state upholds the family in its present form and, thereby, forces women into a position of dependence on men' (WLCLFI, 1975, p.1). The Women's Liberation Campaign for Legal and Financial Independence campaigned against a range of social policies, particularly in the income maintenance area, which reinforced women's economic dependence. Similar issues began to be raised by feminist academics such as Hilary Land and Elizabeth Wilson. Their work was consolidated and extended during the following two decades as a growing number of feminist academics established themselves and helped to shape the direction of the 'discipline' of social policy – increasingly from the centre rather than the margins.

There is, of course, no 'one' feminist analysis and it is customary to categorize the different approaches (see, for instance, Williams, 1989, 1997; George and Wilding, 1994). In practice, though, contemporary feminist social policy analysis tends to draw fairly eclectically on these different strands, for the boxes into which they were allocated were arguably 'always much too neat and tidy' (Lewis, 1998, p.86). This chapter therefore takes a broad brush approach to feminist analysis, while acknowledging the roots of this analysis in different strands of feminism.

3   The key moves in gendering social policy

The gendering of social policy from a feminist perspective or perspectives has involved a set of key, interrelated moves concerning locale, people, resources and concepts.

3.1   Locales I: family, labour market and state

Social policy analysis is located in a number of institutional bases. The state and, to a much lesser extent, the labour market were the traditional loci of social policy analysis, augmented more recently by the voluntary and private sectors with the development of 'the mixed economy of welfare'. The lens of gender opened up a further key institutional base – the family – and it illuminated the ways in which the family interacts with these other institutional bases and also their gendered nature. How you experience the family, the labour market and different forms of welfare provision depends crucially on gender (mediated by and through other sources of social division such as class, 'race' and disability).

The family

Feminist analysis has helped to puncture the myth that in the modern welfare state, the state has taken over the welfare functions of the family. It reveals the myriad ways in which the family continues to operate as a site not just of welfare consumption but also of production. Families still represent the main source of care of children and of older people. Much of this care is provided by women. Likewise, the consumption of welfare involves a certain amount of work liaising with welfare providers, again mainly undertaken by women.

The family has been shown to operate not only as an institutional basis of welfare but also at the level of ideology or discourse. In an influential text, Michèle Barrett and Mary McIntosh (1982) articulated a critique of 'the ideology of the family' which privileges the institution of the 'the family' to the detriment of those living outside it. Familialist (and heterosexist) discourses serve to devalue alternative forms of living arrangements and sexualities and to promote a particular, traditional, model of 'the family', namely that of two married parents (preferably a male breadwinner and a female carer) with children. Families headed by a lone mother have been the most public target of familialism; feminist analysis underlines how their position has to be understood in gendered terms. The use of the more neutral term 'families' represents for many a deliberate move to dissociate the family as an institutional base of welfare from 'the family' as an ideological and discursive model.

Both as a material site of welfare consumption and production and as an ideology or discourse, the family has been identified by many feminists as a key site of women's oppression rather than 'the haven from a heartless world' it has traditionally represented for men (Lasch, 1977), a 'cosy' picture to which, Richard Titmuss, one of social policy's great names, subscribed (Pascall, 1997). However, this formulation by feminists has, itself, been challenged as ethnocentric, representing as universal the experiences of particular groups of women. For many black women their families have been seen as a site of resistance to racist oppression; the family was thus the locus of a major critique of white feminism by black feminists in the 1980s (Amos et al., 1984; Carby, 1982; and see Mirza, 1997, which brings together many of these early critiques). Likewise, for many Central and Eastern European women their families were a source of solidarity against an oppressive state under the former totalitarian regimes (Einhorn, 1993). More recently, feminist analysis has also tended to become more sensitive to the perspectives of children and of older people within families.

These caveats notwithstanding, the family plays an important role in shaping both women's and men's relationship to the labour market and the state. Like the family, these are highly gendered institutions.

The state

Initially, feminist analysis challenged both the liberal conceptualization of the state as a neutral benign instrument to which women could appeal and the Marxist and socialist conceptualizations which dismissed the state as serving only the class interests of capitalism. The state was cast by feminists as a patriarchal state, reinforcing and regulating unequal gender relations in the interests of men. Engagement with the state was therefore, for many, suspect. Subsequently, though, a growing number of feminists have engaged with the state from both within and without, often in a context of welfare retrenchment. The analysis of the gendered nature of the welfare state has, accordingly, become more nuanced, in acknowledgement of the ways in which it can simultaneously be supportive and oppressive of (different groups of) women, who do not necessarily share an identical set of interests (Misra and Akins, 1998). Thus the welfare state might be promoting traditional gender relations through some of its programmes, while at the same time generating 'political resources' for women as both welfare state workers and users (Fox-Piven, 1990).

This more nuanced analysis also reflects a recognition that the state has to be understood not as a monolithic unity but as a site of struggle and of the expression of a variety of social interests (Pringle and Watson, 1992). Welfare states change over time and they operate differently in different countries (see Chapter 2 this volume). Thus the notion of the 'woman-friendly' state has been coined alongside that of the patriarchal state. What remains is the understanding of the state as a gendered institution and as such it interacts with the family to help shape gender relations (Fox Harding, 1996). Through family law and policies, income maintenance provisions, care policies, immigration laws and laws around sexuality the state impacts on the family and reacts to changing family patterns, always with gendered consequences. The state also regulates, to varying degrees, the relationship between the family and the labour market.

The labour market

Despite the 'feminization' of the labour market, as increasing numbers of women participate in paid employment, and despite the widespread endorsement of equal opportunities policies, the culture and organization of paid work are still imbued with its earlier masculinist ethos. Sexual harassment has been named as the unacceptable face of this ethos. It can be interpreted as a message to women that they do not belong in the public sphere of the workplace; by sexualizing them, men transgress the public–private divide (see below) in a way which undermines women's position in the public sphere.

Occupational segregation persists in most labour markets so that, by and large, women and men do different kinds of work, with implications for the grading and evaluation of their jobs and for the rewards which flow from that (Crompton, 1997). The wage itself is a gendered phenomenon. The ideology of the family wage earned by a male breadwinner still runs deep, so that even when women's earnings make a substantial contribution to household income, there is a tendency to devalue them and to treat them as marginal. To the extent that the labour market is organized on the assumption that women's wages are secondary to a male-breadwinning wage, all women stand to be affected, regardless of whether they live with a male breadwinner or not.

In explaining women's labour market position, feminists differ in the relative importance they attach to the gendered structuring and operation of the labour market itself and to women's position in the family. A major dispute has also emerged between those who emphasize the constraints faced by women and those who regard women's choices and 'preferences' as key (see, for instance, Crompton and Harris, 1998, and Hakim, 1998). Few, though, would dispute that women's labour market position has to be understood with some reference to their position in the family. As Arber and Gilbert (1992, p.1) conclude from an overview of women's working lives, 'the nature and extent of women's participation in waged work is intimately connected with their unpaid domestic labour as mothers and housewives' – and also, we could add, as carers. This unpaid domestic labour and the responsibilities it involves can limit the time which women are able to commit to paid work and the responsibilities they are able to take on. The very work they do in the labour market tends to reflect that which they do in the home and for some the home itself (either their own or other people's homes) is the location of their paid work.

At the same time, the position of women and men in the labour market feeds back into their position in the family. The economic logic generated by unequal labour market rewards encourages a traditional domestic division of labour. Differential economic rewards for labour market participation can translate into differential power within the family itself.

3.2   Locales II: connecting the public and private

The analysis of the interactions between family and labour market and family and state reflects feminism's challenge to what was previously treated as an impermeable divide between public and private spheres. Whereas traditionally social policy's interest in the relationship between public and private was framed in terms of the state and the market (i.e. the private *sector*, which is itself a gendered site: see Chapter 2 this volume and also May and Brunsdon, 1996), a gendered analysis opens up the private, domestic *sphere*. It is a sphere which political theory has traditionally associated with women, thereby serving to exclude them from the public sphere, the sphere of citizenship, associated with men. It overlaps with the sphere of civil society, the locale for informal, voluntary forms of welfare which are again highly gendered.

The feminist reconceptualization of the relationship between public and private has had three main implications for social policy:

- It has translated a number of issues previously deemed 'private' into legitimate concerns of public policy. Prime examples of this process of 're-gendering' include domestic violence and marital rape.
- It has turned the spotlight on the impact of public policies and practices on relations within the family.
- It has demonstrated the ways in which gender relations in the private sphere differentially shape the access of men and women to the public sphere, with implications for their economic and political power.

Resources: opening up the closed box of the family

The impact of gender relations in the private sphere on access to the public sphere is most notable with respect to the gendered division of domestic labour. Women's continued responsibility for the bulk of unpaid domestic labour simultaneously limits their access to the public sphere of the political system and the labour market (together with the rewards to be derived from paid work) and underpins the access of men. Time has to be understood as a resource in this equation (see Chapter 21 this volume). It is a resource which feminist analysis has revealed as having a qualitative as well as a quantitative dimension. Thus not only do women tend to have to devote more time than men to domestic responsibilities, but the time left over for other pursuits, including leisure, tends to be more fragmented. Both the use and experience of time are highly gendered, reflecting what women and men do in both public and private spheres and the interrelationship of the two (Glucksman, 1998).

The distribution of material resources within the family has been a critical issue in gendered social policy analysis. Social and economic policy has all too often treated the family as a closed box, into which resources can be channelled without any concern for what then happens to them. The assumption is that resources are shared equally among different family members. The reality, as Eleanor Rathbone warned back in the 1920s, is frequently otherwise. Both money and the resources which it can buy, such as food, clothes and access to leisure pursuits, are often unequally distributed within families (Millar and Glendinning, 1989). This maldistribution is a reflection of gendered power relations within the family which, again, reflect in part the economic resources which each partner is able to bring into the household.

One consequence is that women can experience hidden poverty which is obscured by measurements of poverty which take the family or household as the unit of measurement (Pahl, 1989; Jenkins, 1991; Glendinning and Millar, 1992). The implications for income maintenance policies of the distribution of resources within the family has also been underlined by feminists in an attempt to 're-gender' these policies (Lister, 1992; Goode et al., 1998).

People: gendered welfare subjects

As we have shown, men and women are, by and large, positioned differently within the family–state–labour-market triad, reflecting the interaction of private and public spheres. They thus represent gendered welfare subjects. As parents, children, workers, migrants, public, private and informal service users or benefit recipients, our relationship to welfare is gendered (and racialized). Following Helga Hernes (1987), it is common to identify three subject positions in relation to welfare states: clients, employees and citizens, which I have reformulated as users, providers and shapers (see also Hallett, 1996a). While women are over-represented as users and providers, they are under-represented as shapers in the formal policy process.

Because of their disadvantaged economic position, women as a group are more likely to be reliant on social security than men and are more likely to look to the state sector for housing. In each case, they are less likely to use private sources of welfare. Because of their caring responsibilities within the family, as observed above, women tend to act as mediators with welfare state services on behalf of other family members. Laura Balbo (1987) suggests the (gendered) image of 'patching and quilting' to capture the complex survival strategies that can be involved in negotiating the complexities of getting by in modern welfare systems.

It is in their role of welfare providers in the private sphere that women patch and quilt the resources together as they care for children and adults and service partners. They are also major providers in the public sphere of welfare services which has provided women with one of their main sources of employment in the statutory, voluntary and private sectors. It is, though, in the lower echelons of service provision that women, and especially minority ethnic women, tend to predominate. Women are also often the providers of alternative forms of welfare, such as alternative health projects, in the first, second and third worlds (Doyal, 1995). In Norway, Arnlaug Leira (1992) has described how, in the absence of adequate state provision, women developed their own informal childcare economy, thereby acting as 'change agents'. This is also an example of how, through their actions, for example decisions about when to return to work after having children, women can behave in ways which are not congruent with state social policies.

The Norwegian example reflects how women's role as welfare state shapers has tended to be played out in informal, more opposi-tional arenas, rather than through formal policy-making channels. Through provision of services outside the state sector and through campaigning, women have, both historically and today, had some *influence* on the shape of welfare (in ways which are neither necess-arily straightforward nor all pointing in one direction). But they have rarely had *power* as welfare state shapers. Today's welfare states are thus patterned primarily with male rather than female fingerprints.

As welfare subjects, women and men also have to negotiate their movements within the family–state–labour-market triad. How they do so will be influenced by their positions within both public and private spheres and the interaction of the two. Nevertheless, they are active agents in this negotiation and as gendered agents may approach the process in different ways. Social policy analysis has tended, implicitly or explicitly, to be premised on a construction of the welfare subject as 'rational economic man', attempting to maxi-mize their economic position. This paradigm has been challenged by Simon Duncan and Rosalind Edwards (1999), who argue that welfare subjects' behaviour has to be understood also in the context of culture and of moral beliefs which are grounded in specific geo-graphical and historical contexts. They have introduced the notion of 'gendered moral rationalities' to capture the gendered nature of this broader understanding of rational decision-making. They apply it to lone mothers, showing how their decisions about whether or not to undertake paid work are influenced not only by economic considerations but also by their beliefs about their children's needs and what constitutes good mothering (beliefs which are socially patterned according to factors such as class, 'ethnicity' and geo-graphical location).

Concepts: gendering the building blocks of social policy

Duncan and Edwards' formulation is an example of how basic concepts such as rationality can be transmogrified when examined through the lens of gender. Other examples include the following:

Work has tended to be equated with paid employment in social policy analysis and practice, reflecting the public–private divide discussed earlier. Yet, if work is understood as 'physical or mental effort directed towards making or achieving something' (*Chambers Dictionary*, 1993), feminism has illuminated how physical and mental effort are also expended in maintaining a home, raising children and caring for relatives. Nor is it accurate to equate unpaid work solely with the private sphere and paid with the public. Unpaid volunteering and community work operate across the public–private divide and paid work can be undertaken as homework or child-minding in one's own home or as caring and cleaning work in the homes of others.

Closely linked to this broader understanding of the meaning of work is feminism's deconstruction of the meaning of **care**. The first breakthrough in feminist social policy analysis was to reveal that care *is* work, often extremely hard work, involving long hours. A key distinction was that made by Clare Ungerson (1983) between the work involved in caring *for* someone and the emotions and feelings of affinity involved in caring *about* someone. The two are, nevertheless, often closely intertwined, especially, but not solely, in the context of unpaid caring, prompting Hilary Graham's formulation: 'a labour of love' (1983). This labour of love was shown to be undertaken mainly by women, underlining the gendered impact of community care policies, although more recently men's role as carers of their spouses has been acknowledged. Since the early 1980s, there have been a number of developments in the theorizing and empirical study of care. These include:

- a challenge to the dualist distinction between paid and unpaid forms of care, as new methods of paying for care evolve (Ungerson, 1997);
- the theorizing of care as a value which should inform social policy and citizenship (Knijn and Kremer, 1997), inspired by feminist philosophizing around 'an ethic of care'; and
- a greater emphasis on care as a relationship in which the perspectives of both those providing and those receiving care need to be taken into account. This is partly in response to the critique by disabled feminists, such as Jenny Morris (1991), of feminism's preoccupation with carers at the expense of disabled and older people, many of whom are also women (see also Chapters 3 and 22 this volume).

Julia O'Connor points out that care-giving (and also receiving) is 'inextricably related' to **dependence**, as the care relationship involves 'a layering of dependency relations' (1996, p.13), in part linked to and promoted by a 'male breadwinner model' of income maintenance (see Chapter 2 this volume). Contemporary feminists have taken the analysis further, unpicking the ideological as well as material force of the male-breadwinner–female-economic-dependant model and revealing the unequal relationship of interdependence of which it is a part. Economic dependence is the price many women have had to pay for the hidden dependence of their families and partners upon them for care and servicing (Graham, 1983).

Feminist critiques of dependence in the private sphere have acted as a corrective to public discourses about dependence on the state. These public discourses have grown increasingly vocal in recent years, particularly in the US and the UK, and often focus on lone mothers. One feminist response has been to emphasize human inter-dependence, distinguishing between 'socially necessary' and illegitimate forms of dependence (Fraser and Gordon, 1994; see Chapter 22 this volume).

The failure to recognize the significance of private economic dependence for **citizenship**, a concept traditionally premised on independence, has been the focus of feminist social policy critiques of T.H. Marshall and many subsequent citizenship theorists (Pascall, 1997). Although the Marshallian tradition has promoted citizenship as an inclusive, universal, ostensibly gender-neutral concept, critics today point to the ways in which it has been predicated historically on the exclusion of women. Citizenship has been associated with the (male) public sphere, so that women's relegation to the private sphere has meant that they have been deemed unsuitable for and incapable of citizenship. The continued power of the public–private dichotomy means that women's formal admission to citizenship has been on terms different to those enjoyed by men. The challenge facing feminism today is to reconceptualize and re-gender citizenship in ways which meet the concerns of women as well as men and which acknowledge the contribution made to citizenship by unpaid care work, alongside paid work. This project is thus closely tied in with the revaluation of the concepts of work, care and independence. It also involves taking on board the interests and perspectives of a range of 'minority' groups and of nation-state 'outsiders' in an attempt to construct a more inclusive and differentiated conceptualization of citizenship (Lister, 1997).

Citizenship has traditionally been located within a national community. Both **nation** and **community** are also gendered and racialized concepts. Women and men's relationship to nation has been constructed differently according to their gendered and racialized citizenship rights and responsibilities (Yuval-Davis, 1997). Nowhere was this portrayed more clearly than in the Beveridge Report which formulated married women's duties as 'vital unpaid service' which would ensure 'the adequate continuance of the British race and of British ideals in the world' (Beveridge, 1942, paras 108, 117; see also Williams, 1989).

The concept of community has been used more frequently at local level in social policy analysis. Fiona Williams (1993) has illuminated how 'community' can be seen both as the *space* within which women organize, often traversing the public–private divide, and the *place* to which they are confined. A key finding of Andrew McCulloch's study of community activism is 'the very significant difference between the genders on almost every dimension of community life' (1997, p.66). Nevertheless, politicians still tend to appeal to 'community' as some kind of homogeneous, unified entity, despite the evidence from critical academics and activists of the ways in which actual communities can be riven by gender and other intersecting social divisions (Hoggett, 1997).

Finally, gender analysis itself has had to take greater account of these intersecting social divisions, to the extent that the very category **'woman'** (and to a lesser extent 'man') has come to be challenged, partly reflecting post-modernist critiques (see Chapter 4 this volume). Whatever the area of social policy, an undifferentiated gender analysis obscures the concerns of different groups of women in the same way that an undifferentiated class analysis has ignored gender and other social divisions (which is not to deny the continued importance of social class). Thus, for example, so long as a gendered analysis of community care focused simply on women as carers, it elided the sometimes different perspectives of disabled and older women. Likewise, a heterosexist norm serves to write lesbians out of the welfare picture. The most concerted challenge, though, has come from black feminism, which has exposed the failure of much feminist analysis to represent or address the needs of black women (Bryan et al., 1985; Nasir, 1996). The searching spotlight which these challenges have thrown on the differential experience of women represents the most important development in feminist thinking since the 1970s.

For the most part the concepts of 'woman' and 'gender' have, nevertheless, survived these critiques in the belief that 'gender functions as a "difference that makes a difference", even as it can no longer claim the legitimizing mantle of *the* difference' (Hallett, 1996a, p.11). Stripped of this mantle, a gendered social policy analysis has to be transformed from a uni- or even bifocal into a multifocal lens when looking both at women's and men's relationships to welfare. It is probably fair to say that much feminist analysis still has a long way to go in applying such a lens systematically.

4 Conclusion

The insights which derive from a gendered analysis prompt a series of questions when 'doing social policy', such as:

- Who stands to gain and lose from any particular set of welfare relations and practices – the 'who' being a gendered subject, but also a differentiated gendered subject?
- What are the effects on gender relations in both public and private spheres of particular configurations of the family–state–labour-market triad and of particular social policies? And what

manner of gender relations do they underpin, promote or challenge at both a material and a discursive level?
- Who are the actors in the development and execution of particular welfare policies, at the level of shapers, providers and
users?
- How does the relationship between public and private spheres
affect women's and men's positions as shapers, providers and
users of welfare and how does it frame their varying needs and
demands?
- How is any resource, material or otherwise, distributed between
different groups of women and men in both public and private
spheres?
- What are the gendered meanings of the key concepts used in
social policy analysis?

The application of such questions to social policy analysis by
feminists has led to its transformation. It has also laid the ground-
work for the 're-gendering' of social policy as both a subject and a
practice. Over the three decades of contemporary feminist theory and
politics, what has become clearer is that both the gendering and re-
gendering of social policy is a complex process, involving intersecting social divisions and throwing up a range of contradictions
and strategic possibilities.

References

Amos, V., Lewis, G., Mama, A. and Parmar, P. (eds) (1984) 'Many voices: one chant:
   black feminist perspectives' (special issue), Feminist Review, 17.
Arber, S. and Gilbert, N. (eds) (1992) Women and Working Lives, Basingstoke, Macmillan.
Balbo, L. (1987) 'Crazy quilts', in Sassoon, A.S. (ed.) Women and the State, London,
   Hutchinson.
Barrett, M. and McIntosh, M. (1982) The Anti-Social Family, London, Verso.
Beveridge, W. (1942) Social Insurance and Allied Services (The Beveridge Report), Cmd.
   6404, London, HMSO.
Bryan, B., Dadzie, S. and Seale, S. (1985) The Heart of the Race, London, Virago.
Carby, H. (1982) 'White woman listen: feminism and the limits of sisterhood', in Centre
   for Contemporary Cultural Studies, The Empire Strikes Back, London, Hutchinson.
Crompton, R. (1997) Women and Work in Modern Britain, Oxford, Oxford University
   Press.
Crompton, R. and Harris, F. (1998) 'Explaining women's employment patterns:
   "orientations to work" revisited', and 'A reply to Hakim', British Journal of Sociology,
   49 (1), pp.118–36, 144–9.
Doyal, L. (1995) What Makes Women Sick, Basingstoke, Macmillan.
Duncan, S. and Edwards, R. (1999) Lone Mothers, Paid Work and Gendered Moral
   Rationalities, Basingstoke, Macmillan.
Einhorn, B. (1993) Cinderella Goes to Market, London, Verso.
Fox Harding, L. (1996) Family, State and Social Policy, Basingstoke, Macmillan.
Fox-Piven, F. (1990) 'Ideology and the state: women, power and the welfare state', in

Gordon, L. (ed.) *Women, the State and Welfare*, Madison, WI, University of Wisconsin Press.

Fraser, N. and Gordon, L. (1994) '"Dependency" demystified: inscriptions of power in a keyword of the welfare state', *Social Politics*, 1 (1), pp.4–31.

George, V. and Wilding, P. (1994) *Welfare and Ideology*, Hemel Hempstead, Harvester Wheatsheaf.

Glendinning, C. and Millar, J. (ed.) (1992) *Women and Poverty in Britain in the 1990s*, Hemel Hempstead, Harvester Wheatsheaf.

Glucksman, M.A. (1998) '"What a difference a day makes": a theoretical and historical exploration of temporality and gender', *Sociology*, 32 (2), pp.239–58.

Goode, J., Callender, C. and Lister, R. (1998) *Purse or Wallet? Gender Inequalities and Income Distribution within Families on Benefits*, London, Policy Studies Institute.

Graham, H. (1983) 'Caring: a labour of love', in Finch, J. and Groves, D. (eds) *A Labour of Love: Women, Work and Caring*, London, Routledge & Kegan Paul.

Hakim, C. (1998) 'Developing a sociology for the twenty-first century: preference theory', *British Journal of Sociology*, 49 (1), pp.137–43.

Hallett, C. (1996a) 'Social policy: continuities and change', in Hallett (1996b).

Hallett, C. (ed.) (1996b) *Women and Social Policy: An Introduction*, Hemel Hempstead, Harvester Wheatsheaf.

Hernes, H. (1987) *Welfare State and Woman Power*, Oslo, Norwegian University Press.

Hoggett, P. (ed.) (1997) *Contested Communities*, Bristol, The Policy Press.

Jenkins, S. (1991) 'Poverty measurement and the within household distribution', *Journal of Social Policy*, 20 (4), pp.457–83.

Knijn, T. and Kremer, M. (1997) 'Gender and the caring dimension of welfare states: towards inclusive citizenship', *Social Politics*, 4 (3), pp.328–61.

Lasch, C. (1977) *Haven in a Heartless World: The Family Besieged*, New York, Basic Books.

Leira, A. (1992) *Welfare States and Working Mothers*, Cambridge, Cambridge University Press.

Lewis, J. (1998) 'Feminist perspectives', in Alcock, P., Erskine, A. and May, M. (eds) *The Student's Companion to Social Policy*, Oxford, Blackwell/Social Policy Association.

Lister, R. (1992) *Women's Economic Dependency and Social Security*, Manchester, Equal Opportunities Commission.

Lister, R. (1997) *Citizenship: Feminist Perspectives*, Basingstoke, Macmillan.

McCulloch, A. (1997) 'You've fucked up the estate and now you're carrying a briefcase!' in Hoggett (1997).

May, M. and Brunsdon, E. (1996) 'Women and private welfare', in Hallett (1996b).

Millar, J. and Glendinning, C. (1989) 'Gender and poverty', *Journal of Social Policy*, 18 (3), pp.363–81.

Mirza, H.S. (ed.) (1997) *Black British Feminism: A Reader*, London and New York, Routledge.

Misra, J. and Akins, F. (1998) 'The welfare state and women: structure, agency and diversity', *Social Politics*, 5 (3), pp.259–85.

Morris, J. (1991) *Pride against Prejudice*, London, The Women's Press.

Nasir, S. (1996) '"Race", gender and social policy', in Hallett (1996b).

O'Connor, J. (1996) 'From women in the welfare state to gendering welfare state regimes', *Current Sociology* (Trend Report), 44 (2), pp.1–130.

Pahl, J. (1989) *Money and Marriage*, Basingstoke, Macmillan.

Pascall, G. (1997) *Social Policy. A New Feminist Analysis*, London and New York, Routledge.

Popay, J., Hearn, J. and Edwards, J. (1998) *Men, Gender Divisions and Welfare*, London, Routledge.

Pringle, R. and Watson, S. (1992) '"Women's interests" and the post-structuralist state', in Barrett, M. and Phillips, A. (eds) *Destabilizing Theory*, Cambridge, Polity.

Rathbone, E. (1986) *The Disinherited Family*, Bristol, Falling Wall Press. (First published 1924.)

Ungerson, C. (1983) 'Why do women care?' in Finch, J. and Groves, D. (eds) *A Labour of Love: Women, Work and Caring*, London, Routledge & Kegan Paul.
Ungerson, C. (1997) 'Social politics and the commodification of care', *Social Politics*, 4 (3), pp.362–81.
Williams, F. (1989) *Social Policy: A Critical Introduction*, Cambridge, Polity Press.
Williams, F. (1993) 'Women and community', in Bornat, J., Pereira, C., Pilgrim, D. and Williams, F. (eds) *Community Care: A Reader*, Basingstoke, Macmillan/The Open University.
Williams, F. (1997) 'Feminism and social policy', in Robinson, V. and Richardson, D. (eds) *Introducing Women's Studies*, Basingstoke, Macmillan.
Wilson, E. (1977) *Women and the Welfare State*, London, Tavistock.
WLCLFI (1975) *The Demand for Independence*, London, Women's Liberation Campaign for Legal and Financial Independence.
Yuval-Davis, N. (1997) *Gender and Nation*, London, Sage.

2

Gender and Welfare Regimes

Jane Lewis

1   Gender and social provision

Beginning in the 1990s, comparative work on modern welfare states has emphasized the importance of the relationship between state and economy, and in particular between work and welfare. Esping-Andersen (1990) defined 'welfare regime' in terms of this relationship. In so doing, he defined work as paid work and welfare as policies that permit, encourage or discourage the decommodification of labour. His empirical work, like that of many other comparativists, focused on the development of social insurance programmes, which are by definition tied to labour market participation. While this work represents a substantial advance on the older literature which focused only on the comparative development of policies of social amelioration (for example, Wilensky and Lebaux, 1965), it has missed two of the central issues in the structuring of welfare regimes that are relevant to the development of women's social citizenship.

The first issue is the problem of valuing the unpaid work that is done primarily by women in providing welfare, mainly within the family, and securing social entitlements for those providers. In other words, the crucial relationship is not just between paid work and welfare, but between paid work, unpaid work and welfare (Taylor-Gooby, 1991), and this is particularly important for understanding women's position as clients in welfare systems. Second, the recent literature on modern welfare regimes has tended to pay insufficient attention to the significance of the mixed economy of welfare provision. Such provision means that the state, the voluntary sector, the family and the market all play a part, and although the balance among them has shifted over time, the amount of informal provision through the family has remained remarkably constant. The nature of the mixed economy of welfare has proved important historically for understanding how women's contribution as providers of welfare has been elicited.

The relationship between paid work, unpaid work and welfare is gendered in that while it is possible to argue that the divisions in paid work have substantially diminished to the extent that greater numbers of women have entered the labour market, their pay, status and hours remain less than those of men.

Inge Persson and Christina Jonung (1993) in Sweden and Catherine Hakim (1996) in Britain have shown that there has been very little change in the number of women working full-time in those countries. Indeed, in Britain, notwithstanding the huge increase in women's labour market participation rate since the war, the percentage of full-time women workers was less in 1991 than it was in 1951. In respect of unpaid work, the evidence suggests that gender divisions remain substantially the same (Morris, 1990; Anderson et al., 1994). Thus concepts such as 'decommodification' or 'dependency' have a gendered meaning that is rarely acknowledged. While Esping-Andersen wrote of decommodification as a necessary prerequisite for workers' political mobilization, the worker he had in mind was male and his mobilization may depend as much on unpaid female household labour as on state policies. Commodification has proved difficult for many women seeking a degree of autonomy via wage-earning (Hobson, 1994), while decommodification via social security systems is likely to result in women carrying out unpaid caring work. In other words, 'welfare dependency' on the part of adult women is likely to result in the greater independence of another person, young or old. The unequal division of unpaid work thus blurs the dichotomous divisions between 'dependent' and 'independent', 'commodified' and 'decommodified'.

As Kohlberg (1991) noted, the interface between the private in the sense of the informal provision of welfare, the market and the state has not been subjected to close analysis. Just as informal, unpaid, family-based care was absent from Titmuss' (1963) division of welfare, so it is also absent from more recent categorizations of welfare regimes (Langan and Ostner, 1991). In the work of Esping-Andersen, or of Leibfried (1991), women disappear from the analysis when they disappear from labour markets. Yet consideration of the private in the sense of domestic is crucial to any understanding of women's position, because historically women have typically gained social citizenship entitlements by virtue of their dependent status within the family as *wives*, the justification being a division of labour perceived to follow 'naturally' from their capacity for motherhood. Women have thus tended to make contributions and draw benefits via their husbands in accordance with assumptions regarding the existence of a male-breadwinner family model (Land, 1980; Lewis, 1992, 1997). Further-more, in welfare regimes such as that of the United States and in early and mid-twentieth-century Britain, where the social security systems developed a dual insurance/assistance model, this in and of itself was gendered, with first-class (insurance) benefits going mainly to men and second-class (assistance) benefits to women (Gordon, 1990). Thus the first unemployment insurance legislation in Britain in 1911 covered those trades in which mainly skilled, male workers were employed.

Modern welfare regimes have all subscribed to some degree to the idea of a male-breadwinner model and have therefore treated women as dependants of men, although the persistence of this assumption in the late twentieth century has varied considerably between countries. In France, because of the very different occupational structure and in particular because of the importance of independent agricultural producers, women have tended to gain entitlements both as wives and mothers on the one hand, and as paid workers on the other. Patriarchal control seems to have remained more private than public, existing within private family law in respect of the rights of husbands more than in the public law governing social provision as has been the case in the English-speaking countries. While virtually all western welfare states began by assuming the existence of a male-bread-winner model, different countries have moved away from the model to different degrees (Lewis, 1992, 1997). The Scandinavian countries moved furthest away, pulling women into paid employment from the 1970s by the introduction of separate taxation and parental leaves, and by increasing childcare provision, to the point where the dual-breadwinner family has become the norm.

In regard to women as providers of welfare, their position has been affected greatly by the nature of the mixed economy of welfare. Informal, unpaid provision in the family, usually by women, has remained remarkably constant. As the state came to play a much larger part in social provision in the twentieth century, so it has often been charged that government has usurped the role of the family, providing institutional care for elderly people and day care and education for children (Parsons and Bales, 1955; West, 1965). Many writers have pointed out that there is little evidence of the family doing less: for example the percentage of elderly people in institutions in Britain has been remarkably stable throughout the twentieth century (Anderson, 1983), and while schools and clinics have taken on many responsibilities for children, the family has found new tasks, especially in fostering the emotional development of children and in playing a complementary role to the school in securing their intellectual development, supervising homework and the like (Smith, 1988).

While the level of the family's contribution has not changed markedly, the balance between the voluntary and the statutory sector has, with significant effects for women as providers, clients and agents in modern welfare states. In Britain, the size of the voluntary sector at the turn of the century is hard to measure, but if the medical charities are included as well as those relieving poverty, then the amount of money distributed by this sector was probably greater than that distributed by the state poor law (Humphreys, 1991; Prochaska, 1988). At that time, women played a large role as providers of welfare in the voluntary sector in many European countries, which, together with their involvement in the work of the local authorities that financed and administered the Poor Law and education, was perceived as a legitimate extension of their role in the family (Koven and Michel, 1990; Lewis, 1994). In contrast, employment in the service of the central state was not seen as legitimate and as social provision became a matter of 'high politics' in the early twentieth century, with central government financing and administering the key programmes of pensions and social insurance, so women failed to make the transition from the local level and the decision-making positions in the 'welfare state' were filled by men. As Skocpol (1992) has also pointed out, the central programme of modern European welfare states – social insurance – was, perhaps not surprisingly, aimed primarily at the male worker.

By limiting the subject of its study to social insurance, the recent comparative study of the nature of modern welfare regimes has missed the major gendered dimensions of social provision which relate to the provision of cash benefits in the form of social assistance, which is more likely to be drawn upon by those marginal to the labour market; the issue of unpaid work and the provision of care; and the issue of the provision of welfare, in the form of cash and care, above and beyond the state, particularly by the family and the voluntary sector. The next section of this chapter explores these issues further by focusing on the issue of the provision of care. This has not been the centre of any major comparative analysis to date, yet it demonstrates the complicated interrelationships of public, market and family provision, and of cash and services.

2 Care-centred analysis of welfare regimes

The dichotomous thinking of governments in terms of 'dependent' and 'independent', 'citizen mother' and 'citizen worker' ignores the complicated shifting and interrelated material and emotional dependencies of the late twentieth century. Women who give care to the young or to the old (who are also likely to be disproportionately female) on an unpaid basis may require state support in their turn. Historically, they have been unlikely to receive very much because of the attachment of governments to social insurance schemes which operate through the labour market and because care is widely believed to be the province of the private sphere. An academic commentator, Alan Wolfe (1989), has argued that while it is appropriate for governments to redistribute cash, care-giving should remain the work of families and communities, but he does not spell out the implications of this view for the gendered division of labour.

No modern welfare regime has found a way of valuing the caring work performed by women in the family, which in some measure accounts for why the gendered division of labour in respect of unpaid work remains so unequal (that it is not a sufficient explanation is shown by the low take-up of parental leave by men in Sweden, where up to 90 per cent replacement income has been provided). It has been possible for governments to give cash benefits to those who cannot, for demonstrable reason, enter the labour market, or to those who are prepared to demonstrate their willingness to re-enter the labour market, without violating the principle that (above all) male individuals should provide for themselves and their families. But historically it has been more difficult for governments to square the collective provision of care with family responsibility. The fear has been that state provision necessarily usurps care by family members, something that was being articulated clearly and loudly in the USA by the end of the 1980s (for example, Glazer, 1988).

It should not therefore be surprising that the development of the collective provision of care has been secondary to the elaboration of cash benefits, although in the case of the elderly, 'Poor Law' type systems had long provided both the means of subsistence and a semblance of care in institutions. As Anttonen and Sipilä (1996) have pointed out, the amount of social care provided by the state in the post-war period has varied enormously between countries, from very little in Ireland, to an expectation of social care as a right in some of the Scandinavian countries. In addition, provision for children and for elderly people may vary considerably within countries. Thus, The Netherlands, Norway and Britain have good state coverage for elderly people, but little for children, while France, Belgium and Italy have large-scale provision for children and little for the elderly. From a gender perspective, what is interesting is the way in which different countries have justified state intervention. In 1992 the European Council of Ministers adopted a Recommendation on Child Care, which explicitly encouraged 'the more equal sharing of parental responsibilities between men and women' (Article 6). However, the development of publicly provided social care has owed little to the aim of promoting gender equality in respect of sharing unpaid work in any country (even in Scandinavia), although enabling women to share more equally in paid work has been on the political agenda in many, but not all, countries.

If we look more closely at the factors driving the state provision of child care, we immediately hit a basic divide between the English-speaking countries, which maintain a strict division between public and private, and the continental European states (Hantrais and Letablier, 1996). Most notably, France sees a legitimate role for government in helping parents to 'reconcile' employment and family responsibilities, whereas British governments have tended to take the view that adult men and women have the right to enter the labour market, but that if they are parents then it is up to them to make their own arrangements regarding child care. Public childcare provision in Britain and Ireland has been primarily for children deemed to be 'at risk'. This is also in keeping with the broader orientation of their welfare provision towards poverty, rather than, as in the more social-insurance-centred regimes of continental Europe, towards the main-tenance of labour-market-related differentials. It is noteworthy that the debate about child care in countries such as Britain and Germany is about provision for children aged over three years. In France, provision for these children is virtually complete and the debate centres on the under-threes.

2.1   Child care

Countries where state childcare provision has been more generous have, on the whole, tended towards a more child-centred approach. In France, for example, the social security system has sought to redis-tribute in favour of families with children, rather than, as in Britain, between the social classes. Therefore it should come as no surprise that the contributions of various kinds of child care to children's development should have been such a strong driving force in the development of provision, or that provision should be so nuanced and dense. The political consensus in favour of state provision for pre-school children is striking in France and many of the Scandinavian countries. In Britain, not only has such consensus been absent, but there has also been division between the government departments with responsibility for health and for education as to what should be provided.

Finally, there is the question of the part played by women them-selves in lobbying for child care. Randall (1996) has commented on the absence of such a lobby among British women compared to other European countries. As she notes, this may well have been a rational response to the political realities. However, Hakim (1996) has argued that the British female labour market is divided into a large number of women who want to work part-time and spend a significant amount of time caring for their children, and a much smaller number of career-oriented women. Hakim's argument is controversial because she argues that women choose this pattern of work. In this interpretation, women do not want large-scale, formal day-care provision. Hakim does not give much place to the reverse pattern of causation, whereby the lack of child care may operate as a constraint on women's labour market participation. One of the implications of her argument (which would also fit the Dutch and German cases) is that there are not many women who would want to lobby for extensive childcare provision in these countries, which accords with Randall's empirical observations.[1]

2.2   Care of the elderly

If we look more closely at the factors driving the public provision of care for elderly people we see that the issues have been somewhat different and the development of different forms of care has varied considerably. In Britain, there is evidence to show that the proportion of elderly people in institutional care did not change much from the late nineteenth century to the late 1970s (Thomson, 1983). Other countries, such as Ireland and the Netherlands, have experienced a large growth in institutional care. Domiciliary care has on the whole, developed very slowly compared to other forms of service provision (Jamieson, 1991).

This is undoubtedly related to the expectation that women will care for elderly relatives. Evidence for such an expectation takes many forms. In Germany, it is underpinned by a legal obligation to maintain that extends to the care of one's parents as well as one's children (something that was abandoned in Britain in 1948). In Britain, which alongside Ireland offers a cash allowance to carers, married women were initially deemed ineligible for the invalid care allowance because it was assumed that they would be available to care. Just as increased levels of employment among married women and changing family structure has pushed child care on to the political agenda, so it has done so for elder care. (It is noteworthy that the reverse approach, looking at the impact of services for elderly people on women's employment rates, has not been the subject of analysis.) As early as 1976 Moroney warned that the pool of potential female carers was shrinking. In the meantime, the proportions of frail elderly people increased dramatically in virtually all Western European countries except Ireland. In addition, the proportions of elderly people living in separate households also increased significantly across Europe.

Assumptions regarding the availability of women as informal carers (see, for example, Beveridge, 1942), while not susceptible to quantifiable measurement, are likely to have been important in accounting for policy developments in respect of formal services for elderly people.

As adults, elderly people have always been able to claim the 'right' to care in the way that children have not. However, only in the Scandinavian countries have entitlements to social (as compared to health) care services been recognized. Female carers have been less active as a lobby group, although in Britain campaigning groups representing informal carers have had a degree of success in getting the government to acknowledge the monetary value of their contribution and in claiming their own right to assessment, the hope being that more assistance will then be given, for example in the form of respite care, that will enable them to continue caring.

The nature of this claim highlights the complicated issues surrounding care from a gender perspective. The early work on informal care stressed the extent to which it was both 'labour and love', 'affection and duty' (Finch and Groves, 1983). There is considerable evidence to suggest that women want to care for elderly relatives as well as for children (e.g. Lewis and Meredith, 1988). But at what cost? Is the work of informal, unpaid care freely chosen, or is it more a question of 'compulsory altruism' (Land and Rose, 1985)? The balance between informal and formal provision is a delicate one. In large measure the fear that collective provision will necessarily substitute for informal, family-based care is historically unfounded (Horden and Smith, 1998). The informal carer who receives a measure of formal respite care may indeed be enabled to continue caring. Furthermore, this may be what she wants. However, the work of caring – paid and unpaid – is very unequally shared between men and women. It is also woefully undervalued. This is why from a gender perspective it is, as Clare Ungerson (1997) has argued, impossible to separate the consideration of informal from formal care.

2.3   Formal or informal, cash or kind

In regard to formal care, social provision has been subjected to substantial restructuring in many European countries in the 1990s. First has been the desire to effect a shift in the mixed economy of welfare, such that the state provides fewer services and the voluntary, market and informal sectors provide more. Second, as part of this goal some countries have moved towards 'marketization' in the form of privatization and the contracting out of state services to the independent sector. Third, some countries have experienced another form of marketization, with the introduction of market principles, and hence, it is hoped, market disciplines, into the public sector. Even a country such as Norway, conspicuous within Europe for its lack of economic problems, has introduced many of the reforms associated with this third form of restructuring. In some countries, even though there has been substantial change in the way in which social care is provided, the reforms have been characterized more by continuity than by change. This helps to account for the very different views of the changes that have come from observers in different countries. Writing from Germany, Evers and Svetlik (1993) and Evans et al. (1994), for example, took a much more positive view of the more 'pluralist' provision of care, believing diversity of provision is inevitable in a pluralist society. In a country such as Britain, where the implementation of the social care reforms in 1993 sometimes appeared to public sector providers on the ground as a rather punitive zero-sum game, this seems to be an overly rosy view. But in the corporatist German or Dutch models, which have continued to operate in a spirit of consensus, it makes more sense.

A logical concomitant of more market-oriented services is the shift in some countries from service provision towards cash benefits. A cash benefit does make the service user the purchaser of the service and is arguably more effective in securing genuine choice. However, when this was tried in Britain in the 1980s (with the Independent Living Allowance) and in the 1990s in The Netherlands, it proved not only popular (especially with the young physically disabled, a particularly vocal lobby group) but expensive. In Germany the provision of care services has always been slight in comparison with the provision of cash benefits, but these have taken the form of an additional social insurance, which automatically places a limit on the payments received. Other governments implementing systems of cash payments for care rapidly learned the need to impose cash limits during the 1990s. A majority of Western European governments have experimented to some degree with 'payments for care', whether in the form of payments to care recipients, to carers, or to volunteers. (Ungerson, 1997 has offered the most elaborated and convincing typology of the form that such payments take.) However, the shift from services to cash has dominated recent changes in only one country, France. Here again, the driving force behind the trend towards cash payments to enable those requiring care, whether for children or elderly people, to buy services has not so much been the desire for whatever reason to limit the role of state bureaucracies as the wish to do something about the huge problem of unemployment by effectively re-creating domestic service, albeit with access to social entitlements. The exigencies of the French case demonstrate the importance of understanding the specific conjuncture from which changes emanate (and into which reforms are inserted). Evers et al. (1994, p.27) also welcomed the move towards cash payments, arguing that they are 'far from being exclusively linked with pure consumerism' and that, given that some diversity and fragmentation are inevitable in pluralistic societies, cash solutions 'may be looked at as the better way to guarantee equal rights under such conditions'. However, this last hope does rather depend on the amount of money that the service user is given to bring to the market.

All the trends discussed in this section have implications for the quality of care. If the state continues to finance, but sets new limits on the extent to which it will provide, there may well be an argument in favour of it increasing its role as a regulator. In the British case, market principles in the form of contracts have been regarded as the main method of regulation. At present, the evidence seems to suggest that the quality of services is an issue for recipients in many countries. Both the provision of relatively low cash benefits that enable users to hire their own care-givers, and the separation of purchasing and providing in the public sector, which means that provision may come from the market sector where pay and conditions are worse than in the public sector, may result in a poorer-quality service. At present, the evidence is largely confined to knowledge that the terms and conditions of many front-line, female care-providers have deteriorated (for instance in Britain and Norway but not, seemingly, in Finland); the implications for the care recipient are then inferred. In France employment policies have driven the new arrangements regarding cash payments and the idea is to take care work out of the underground economy and make sure that the workers qualify for social entitlements. However, it seems that the quality of child care has nevertheless declined because child development is no longer at the centre of policy.

The changes also all have implications for the informal, family-based care provided mainly by women. This under-studied aspect of the restructuring of formal provision is all the more remarkable given that one of the fears underlying many of the changes was the idea that state provision substituted for that by the family and, indeed, other elements of civil society. In Germany, where family-based social care was among the strongest in Europe, the introduction of care insurance could be interpreted as a shift towards more collective provision, contrary to the trend in most countries. However, given that most care insurance recipients have opted to take a cash payment for care, the insurance is probably working to reinforce family-based provision by women. In all countries where aspects of the new public management have been tried, or market principles have been introduced, the result has tended to be a more systematic targeting of those in need of services, which has in turn meant that some – whether elderly people with lower levels of dependency and risk, or children with unemployed parents – no longer qualify for assistance. In this case it is the family that must pick up the slack. This has been as true in 1990s Sweden as in Britain.

For feminists, there have always been two main questions concerning women's unpaid care work: (a) how to value it; and (b) how to share it more equally between men and women. No country has succeeded in valuing unpaid work and in no country has the gendered division of unpaid work shifted substantially. However, it would probably be a mistake to elevate social provision for caring and for carers into a measure of 'woman-friendliness'. The whole history of feminism shows that it is by no means unproblematic to advocate policies that seek to recognize female 'difference' in respect of the disproportionate amount of caring work women do as opposed to policies that seek to achieve equality with men, usually in respect of paid employment (Scott, 1988; Bacchi, 1990; Lister, 1995). Indeed it was possible for Sir William Beveridge, the architect of the British post-war welfare state, sincerely to argue that his proposals to insure women via their husbands constituted an appropriate recognition of their valuable caring work (Lewis, 1983). The problem is that, however well meaning, such policies also entrenched women's economic dependence on men. Nor is this debate dead, as contributions to the first issue of *Social Politics* showed, where Trudie Knijn (1994) argued for the right to claim income from caring, while Bettina Cass (1994) warned that this would enshrine care work as women's work.

As McLaughlin and Glendinning (1994) have pointed out, two ways of valuing caring have emerged in the last two decades: payment by the state for care, and individual rights under the social security system to caring benefits. Pay rates in the case of the former tend to be extremely low and employment conditions poor or non-existent (Evers et al., 1994; Glendinning and McLaughlin, 1993). The latter are potentially radical, involving, as they do, the recognition of claims based on caring. However, the basis of such benefits may not in fact be so clear-cut. For example, the British invalid care allowance was introduced in recognition of the impact of caring on paid work; it was therefore conceived of as a compensation for income forgone rather than as a wage for caring. The eligibility criteria for the benefit are also linked to the receipt or non-receipt of other benefits by the person being cared for, which, as Lister (1997) has pointed out, means that it is not an independent citizenship benefit. This, of course, is to be expected in a country in which the policy logic deriving from the assumption of the existence and desirability of a male-breadwinner model is still influential. One trend is clear in many European countries: the shift from paying benefits to carers to paying the people cared for, who may in turn choose to pay their informal carers. It must be noted, however, that the care relationship, which is usually a relationship between women, is not without tensions and such a trend substantially changes the power balance.

Care is thus at the intersection of a number of relationships that are crucial to a gendered understanding of social provision: of paid and unpaid work, of providers and clients, of cash and care, of public and informal provision. If a gender-centred analysis of the development of welfare regimes must take on board historical assumptions about the male-breadwinner model, so the analysis of late twentieth-century welfare must pay due attention to care.

3 Conclusion: women's agency and welfare regimes

The late nineteenth-century British government aimed to set up a framework of rules within which society would more or less run itself. In some ways the late twentieth-century state looks somewhat similar, as governments attempt to retreat from taking the responsibility for social provision. There are continuities especially in the concern to get the family to provide welfare in the form of both money/maintenance and care. But the conditions under which this contribution is being elicited are quite different. Governments of the 1990s were exerting a far more centralized control than their late nineteenth-century counterparts, while at the same time denying responsibility for provision. The introduction of 'quasi-markets' in health, community care services, education and housing was intended to make services more responsive to the needs of 'consumers', rather than 'citizens'. But market mechanisms, while holding out the promise of a better deal for people as consumers, offer nothing by way of participation to the citizen.

Women are left in a very vulnerable position. Because access to paid and unpaid work, income and resources is profoundly gendered, men and women do not start out equal when it comes to establishing their rights to social citizenship. Assuming men and women to be capable of exerting equal pull in the market will not do; women's caring responsibilities mean that they start out unequal. State benefits and services, particularly for children and the domiciliary services for elderly dependants, have played their part in permitting women to exist without being wholly dependent on male relatives; given the unequal division of unpaid work, a majority of women do not stand a good chance of being able to be 'dependent' on the labour market throughout their adult lives.

Many feminists in English-speaking states have remained at best ambivalent about their expectations as to what state policy can deliver. While recognizing that the outcomes of social policies have changed familial and other structures in society such that male power has been challenged, they have argued that the state has also served to perpetuate patriarchal structures. Undoubtedly the conditions under which women have been offered benefits and services have often reflected normative expectations regarding female behaviour. Thus, in Britain, lone mothers have been denied benefit if they cohabit with a man, the logic being that if there is a man present he will maintain the woman and children. On the other hand, Scandinavian feminists have insisted on the possibility of a 'woman-friendly' state (Hernes, 1987). Kohlberg (1991) has gone one step further and dismissed any idea that the Scandinavian welfare state might be patriarchal, insisting that it has increased women's independence, empowerment and emancipation. Certainly without state intervention it is likely that women will be forced back to dependence on men. State provision of social services is crucial if women are to have equality of access to the public sphere.

Women's social entitlements are therefore crucial to securing them equal access to resources in society. State social provision may also be decisive in securing their participation as citizens. Laura Balbo (1987) has argued that modern welfare states have called forth greater female public participation. In the Nordic parliaments, with the exception of Iceland, women's representation has reached a critical mass of between 30 and 40 per cent, and this has in part led to Scandinavian women's optimism about the role of the state. The states that have granted the most comprehensive citizen-based social entitlements have also secured the most extensive female political participation. It seems that women's social citizenship rights and entitlements are crucial to their broader participation in society.

Note

1 This is not of course to infer that Hakim believes the provision of child care in Britain to be optimal.

References

Anderson, M. (1983) 'What is new about the modern family? A historical perspective', in British Society for Population Studies, *The Family*, London, OPCS.

Anderson, M., Bechhofer, F. and Gershuny, J. (eds) (1994) *The Social and Political Economy of the Household*, Oxford, Oxford University Press.

Anttonen, A. and Sipilä, J. (1996) 'European social care services: is it possible to identify models?', *Journal of European Social Policy*, 5 (2), pp.87–100.

Bacchi, C. (1990) *Same Difference*, Sydney, Allen & Unwin.

Balbo, L. (1987) 'Family and the state: notes toward a typology of family roles and public intervention', in Maier, C.S. (ed.) *Changing Boundaries of the Political: Essays on the Evolving Balance between the State and Society, Public and Private in Europe*, Cambridge, Cambridge University Press.

Beveridge, W. (1942) *Social Insurance and Allied Services* (The Beveridge Report), Cmd. 6404, London, HMSO.

Cass, B. (1994) 'Citizenship, work and welfare: the dilemma for Australian women', *Social Politics*, 1 (1), pp.106–24.

Esping-Andersen, G. (1990) *The Three Worlds of Welfare Capitalism*, Cambridge, Polity Press.

Evers, A. and Svetlik, I. (eds) (1993) *Balancing Pluralism: New Welfare Mixes in Care for the Elderly*, Aldershot, Avebury.

Evers, A., Pijl, M. and Ungerson, C. (1994) *Payment for Care: A Comparative Overview*, Aldershot, Avebury.

Finch, J. and Groves, D. (1983) *Women, Work and Caring*, London, Routledge & Kegan Paul.

Glazer, N. (1988) *The Limits of Social Policy*, Cambridge, MA, Harvard University Press.

Glendinning, C. and McLaughlin, E. (1993) *Paying for Care: Lessons from Europe*, Research paper 5, Social Security Advisory Committee, London, HMSO.

Gordon, L. (1990) *Women, the State and Welfare*, Madison, WI, University of Wisconsin Press.

Hakim, C. (1996) *Key Issues in Women's Work: Women's Heterogeneity and the Polarization of Women's Employment*, London, Athlone Press.

Hantrais, L. and Letablier, M.-T. (1996) *Families and Family Policies in Europe*, London, Longman.

Hernes, H. (1987) *Welfare State and Women Power: Essays in State Feminism*, Oslo, Norwegian University Press.

Hobson, B. (1994) 'Solo mothers, social policy regimes and the logics of gender', in Sainsbury, D. (ed.) *Gendering Welfare States*, London, Sage, pp.170–87.

Horden, P. and Smith, R. (eds) (1998) *The Locus of Care: Families, Communities, Institutions and the Provision of Welfare since Antiquity*, London, Routledge.

Humphreys, R. (1991) 'A public management for all seasons', *Public Administration*, 69, pp.3–16.

Jamieson, A. (1991) *Home Care for Older People in Europe*, Oxford, Oxford University Press.

Knijn, T. (1994) 'Fish without bikes: revision of the Dutch welfare state and its consequences for the (in)dependence of single mothers', *Social Politics*, 1 (1), pp.83–106.

Kohlberg, J.E. (1991) 'The gender dimension of the welfare state', *International Journal of Sociology*, 21 (2), pp.119–48.

Koven, S. and Michel, S. (1990) 'Womanly duties: maternalist politics and the origins of welfare states in France, Germany, Great Britain and the United States, 1880–1920', *American Historical Review*, 95 (4), pp.76–108.

Land, H. (1980) 'The family wage', *Feminist Review*, 6, pp.55–78.

Land, H. and Rose, H. (1985) 'Compulsory altruism for some or an altruistic society for all?', in Bean, P., Ferris, J. and Whynes, D. (eds) *In Defence of Welfare*, London, Tavistock.

Langan, M. and Ostner, M. (1991) 'Gender and welfare', in Room, G. (ed.) *Towards a European Welfare State?*, Bristol, School of Advanced Urban Studies.

Leibfried, S. (1991) 'Towards a European welfare state? On the integration potentials of poverty regimes in the EC', Typescript, Bremen University.

Lewis, J. (ed.) (1983) *Women's Welfare, Women's Rights*, London, Croom Helm.

Lewis, J. (1992) 'Gender and the developments of welfare regimes', *Journal of European Social Policy*, 2 (3), pp.159–73.

Lewis, J. (1994) 'Gender, the family and women's agency in the building of "welfare states"': the British case', *Social History*, 19 (1), pp.37–55.

Lewis, J. (1997) 'Gender and welfare regimes: further thoughts', *Social Politics*, 4 (2), pp.160–77.

Lewis, J. and Meredith, B. (1988) *Daughters Caring for Mothers*, London, Routledge.

Lister, R. (1995) 'Dilemmas in engendering citizenship', *Economy and Society*, 24 (1), pp.1–40.

Lister, R. (1997) *Feminism and Citizenship*, London, Macmillan.

McLaughlin, E. and Glendinning, C. (1994) 'Paying for care in Europe: is there a feminist approach?' in Hantrais, L and Mangen, S. (eds) *Family Policy and the Welfare of Women*, University of Loughborough, Cross National Research Papers.

Moroney, R.M. (1976) *The Family and the State: Considerations for Social Policy*, London, Longman.

Morris, L. (1990) *The Workings of the Household: A US–UK Comparison*, Cambridge, Polity Press.

Parsons, T. and Bales, R.F. (1955) *Family Socialization and Interaction Process*, Glencoe, IL, Free Press.

Persson, I. and Jonung, C. (1993) 'Women's employment: current developments', *Work, Employment and Society*, 7 (2), pp.259–74.

Prochaska, F.K. (1988) *The Voluntary Impulse*, London, Faber & Faber.

Randall, V. (1996) 'Feminism and child daycare', *Journal of Social Policy*, 25 (4), pp.485–506.

Scott, J.W. (1988) 'Deconstructing equality versus difference: or, the uses of post-structuralist theory for feminism', *Feminist Studies*, 14 (1), pp.33–50.

Skocpol, T. (1992) *Protecting Soldiers and Mothers: The Political Origins of Social Policy in the US*, Cambridge, MA, Belknap Press of the Harvard University Press.

Smith, D. (1988) *The Everyday World as Problematic: A Feminist Sociology*, Buckingham, Open University Press.

Taylor-Gooby, P. (1991) 'Welfare state regimes and welfare citizenship', *Journal of European Social Policy*, 1 (2), pp.93–105.

Thomson, D. (1983) 'Workhouse to nursing home: residential care of elderly people in England since 1840', *Ageing and Society*, 3 (1), pp.43–70.

Titmuss, R.M. (1963) *Essays on the Welfare State*, London, Allen & Unwin.

Ungerson, C. (1997) 'Social politics and the commodification of care', *Social Politics*, 4 (3), pp.362–82.

West, E. (1965) *Education and the State*, London, Institute of Economic Affairs.

Wilensky, H.L. and Lebaux, C.N. (1965) *Industrial Society and Social Welfare*, New York, The Free Press.

Wolfe, A. (1989) *Whose Keeper? Social Science and Moral Obligation*, Berkeley, CA, University of California Press.

3

The Social Relations of Care

Tom Shakespeare

Contents

1 Introduction: disability rights and social policy

Many disability rights commentators have reached the conclusion that not only has the welfare state failed disabled people, but that the academic discipline of social policy has added insult to injury (Oliver, 1990; Morris, 1991; Oliver and Barnes, 1998). After all, the birth of the disability movement lay in the 1970s split between the social policy academics of the Disability Alliance, and the grassroots radicals of the Union of Physically Impaired Against Segregation. This chapter focuses on the provision and delivery of personal support services, in order to show that prevailing discourses of dependency have been unhelpful in understanding the experience of disabled people and other user groups, and have resulted in an inadequate response to the issue of disability.

The first half of the discussion develops a critique of existing approaches to care, drawing on disability rights perspectives. In the second half, two alternative approaches are explored in terms of their potential for challenging the existing social relations of care and promoting the interests of disabled people and others receiving services. It is argued that the independent living model developed by disabled people provides a major advance on the status quo, but that the best basis for reforming care would require this to be balanced by the new feminist ethic of care.

2 Challenging the discourse of care

The caring literature is broad, but has tended to concentrate on the location of care, in institutions or the community; whether care is paid or unpaid; and whether the delivery of care involves exploitation, either of women and/or children. My concerns touch all these issues, but focus on the absence of a consideration of the receiver of care from any of these debates. From a disability movement perspective, it is important to challenge the assumptions about dependency that underlie these approaches, and the way that debates start from a medical model of disability. However, the argument applies more widely than just to disabled people, narrowly conceived: there are areas of relevance to other care receivers, particularly to older people, children, and people with HIV/AIDS. These are all constituencies who are often 'othered' and subordinated within the social relations of welfare, and from social policy analysis.

It seems suggestive to characterize prevailing models of care as a colonial relationship (Memmi, 1990). Broader structural relations are reconceptualized in terms of the inadequacies of the victim. Prejudice against the victim is widespread, based on models of infantilization and incapacity. Rather than helping the victim, policies are paternalistic and undermining, and leave the victim in a state of dependency. In the field of care, the 'colonizing' process comprises the way in which recipients of services are described, the way in which their voices are often ignored, and the way that the issue is constructed as a social problem. These claims will be developed in the next three sections.

2.1 The burden of dependency

First, it is suggested that people who receive care are conceptualized as dependent. Within social policy, there is a dangerous tendency to objectify those people who receive welfare services. This critique builds on Warnes' (1993) argument about the treatment of older people. Making a comparison with Jonathan Swift's notorious *Modest Proposal*, Warnes counsels against the mindset of burden becoming or remaining a characteristic of social policy or political analysis, even for those with progressive intentions:

What happens is that the agents carrying the burdens are misidentified: the more graphic the portrayal of the wearisomeness of old age, poverty or sickness, the greater the sense of grievous load upon others. Sometimes the distortion is so great that, following Swift's modest proposal, it turns out that those who experience the burden are of so little concern that they become disposable. (Warnes, 1993, p.329)

In the case of older people, the experience of old age is essentialized and problematized, as if older people were invariably incapable and physically dependent (Phillipson et al., 1986). Emotive words about the 'demographic timebomb', and the 'growing burden' of elderly people serve to undermine the individuality and agency of older people. This ignores the reality, which is that the majority of older people live independent lives in their own homes and do not rely on support or care from others.

The discourse of burden also applies to disabled people who are placed in situations where their children have to take up a caring role. The literature on young carers tends to objectify disabled parents as 'dependants', and to characterize the situation as a 'plight' or 'curse'. A positive attempt to challenge the social exclusion of child carers slips all too easily into a tendency to pathologize people with impairments who choose to have children (Olsen, 1996; Olsen and Parker, 1997). By focusing on the single issue of young carers, this research can obscure other issues: for example, it may ignore the fact that disabled people can be carers. In problematizing families with a disabled parent, there is a danger of ignoring the ways in which all families involve interdependence: for example, older children looking after younger children, and other age-appropriate responsibilities for children (Keith and Morris, 1995, p.53). In general, the accounts of families with a disabled person as mother or father are guilty of essentializing and pathologizing disability, infantilizing disabled people and suggesting that they cannot make good parents, and that their children become the victims of this incompetence and selfishness, all on the basis of very scant research.

The literature on disabled children similarly has tended to rely on the assumption that having a child with impairment is to experience inevitable burden, for example in the titles of older books on the subject such as *A Constant Burden* (Voysey, 1975). Emotive and offensive terms like 'severely disabled' implicitly blame the victim for their situation. The literature tends to make a range of normative assumptions about the effects on the family dynamic of having a child with impairment; for example it suggests that having a disabled child means that relationships break down, or that siblings suffer. There tends to be a suggestion that, in the case of a child with impairment, the typical loving parental relationship is replaced by a relationship of caring and physical support based on the performance of certain tasks.

Services provided for families with disabled children reflect this assumption of burden: there is a considerable stress on the need for respite care, on the basis that the intolerable responsibilities of having a child with impairment typically necessitate a break, or a rest. Practice literature on fostering and adoption stresses the special qualities needed to look after disabled children, and the particular problems which carers of disabled children have to deal with, in ways which sometimes make disabled children sound like sacks of potatoes, or exotic zoo animals. The emphasis of many policies is on the needs and wishes of parents and siblings: it is rare that disabled children themselves are asked what they think about it.

Broader debates in the area of social policy also reflect the tendency to view disabled people as an inevitable burden on their families, and to biologize and individualize the problem of disablement. The carer movement has redefined care in a way which enshrines this: according to Jill Pitkeathley, a carer is 'someone whose life is in some way restricted by the need to be responsible for the care of someone who is mentally ill, mentally handicapped, physically disabled or whose health is impaired by sickness or old age' (Pitkeathley, 1989, p.11). Similarly, Morris (1991) has drawn attention to the work of feminists such as Finch, Groves and Dalley, whose critique of the ways in which women perform the majority of care in the community led to their demand for more residential care, a view which ignores the views and rights of disabled people and other recipients of care. Ironically, the focus on women as carers fails to notice that women can also be disabled people.

Finally, another important area of literature which constructs disabled people (especially children) as burdens is the discussion of pre-natal screening and termination of foetuses affected by congenital impairment (Shakespeare, 1999). This discourse rests on a number of assumptions: that being a disabled person involves a life of suffering; that disabled people are inevitably dependent on others; that the state will ultimately have to bear the cost of supporting disabled people. Public health writers such as Nicholas Wald make explicit the ways in which screening programmes are evaluated on the basis of cost-benefit analysis regarding the avoidance of the burden of disabled children (Wald et al., 1992).

The various discourses on disability and dependency which have been referred to share the common tendency to abnormalize the physical experience of impairment, or ageing. The fact that 'normal' life involves mutual aid and that everyone is in some measure dependent on others tends to be ignored. It is assumed that there is a polar dichotomy between families with disabled members, and other, 'normal' families. It is suggested that one set of relationships is normal and benign, and the other is problematic and pathological. It is argued that the problem inheres in the individual with impairment, not in the wider social context in which the whole family finds itself.

2.2   Silencing receivers of care

There is a tendency to ignore the voices of those people who are constructed as the problem: whether it is older people, disabled people, children or people with HIV/AIDS, it is not common for first-hand accounts to be available. We therefore rely for our information on the projections of policy-makers and academics, or professionals, or sometimes the testimonies of non-disabled relatives and carers.

It is very rare to hear directly from the disabled child in research on disabled childhood (Shakespeare and Watson, 1998). A review of the literature concludes: 'We lack children's accounts of pain, discomfort, dependence on others for feeding, bathing and toileting. We do not know how they feel about the way doctors, social workers, therapists and other children treat them' (Baldwin and Carlisle, 1994, p.35). As other analysts have shown, we seldom hear from the person who is cared for in the literature on caring, whether it is the feminist literature on community care, or the new literature on children as carers. Thus, Jenny Morris criticizes Gillian Dalley's models of collective residential care, for failing to let disabled people's voices be heard (1991, p.157). There has been criticism of researchers who use terms which respondents are unwilling to use themselves, for example where the young carers' researchers are accused of imposing their own definitions and perceptions on the subjects of their research (Keith and Morris, 1995, p.39).

In fact, the rise of carer literature displaces the voices of the cared-for even further (Keith and Morris, 1995, p.37), just as in the political and policy arena the development of a carers' movement challenges the gains of disabled people's organizations: one activist said to me, 'to my mind, the more you increase the rights of carers, the more you take them away from disabled people'. Warnes argues that the construction of the debate itself implies the submergence of the service recipient's voice: 'the focus on care-giver burden by definition gives a primary position to the provider of care' (Warnes, 1993, p.326). For example, Pitkeathley (1989) talks about the need to move away from a nuclear family model towards a collectivist approach to care. She also opposes direct payments to disabled people, suggesting that the money should go direct to carers, not to service users. Both these suggestions are directly contrary to disabled people's own demands for independent living and direct payments.

The failure to hear the voices of those who receive care means that the problematic aspects of the experience for them are neglected. For example, the family may be the site of oppression for disabled people (Morris, 1991, p.143). This may be to do with the paternalism or over-protectiveness of parents to children with impairments. Alternatively, it is clear that there is a high prevalence of abuse of disabled children, but also of older people, which is attributable to the uneven dependencies which can emerge from the role of care within the family, as well as to the behaviour of people outside the family.

It is not suggested that we should not listen to or research the experiences of carers. However, it is a priority to consider and research the voices of people placed in a situation of dependency, by the social relations of (dis)ability, rather than to use carers, parents or professionals as proxies. It is true that we must consider the civil rights of parents and carers, but this can only happen on the basis of the full and prior consideration of the civil rights of disabled people and older people.

2.3   Dependency individualized

The third critique grows out of the construction of care-receivers as burden, and the silencing which is connected with this. Approaches to care are based on a medical model, rather than on the view of disability and dependency as socially constructed. This results in an assumption that older people or disabled people or people with HIV/AIDS need care: their lives are often medicalized, and their problems are inextricably connected with particular problems of body or mind.

Disabled people's reliance on benefits is often an outcome of factors such as employment discrimination, and high levels of structural unemployment. The solution is not to limit entitlement to incapacity benefit, which is just blaming the victim in order to cut the social security budget. A government which really wanted to help disabled people would provide effective civil rights and real support in finding work, in the short term and in the long term, would investigate redistribution of work, a reduction in the working week, and other ways of bridging the divide between full-time working and total unemployment.

People are disabled by society, not by their bodies. It is the social and environmental barriers, prejudicial attitudes and other exclusionary processes which make living with an impairment so hard for disabled people and their families. This social model parallels the work within social gerontology on the structured dependency of old age (Townsend, 1981). Thus Estes argues:

> The needs of older persons are reconceptualized as deficiencies by the professionals charged with treating them, regardless of whether the origins

of these needs lie in social conditions over which the individual has little
or no control, in the failings of the individual, or in some policy-maker's
decision that a need exists. (Estes, 1979, p.235)

Equally, Keith and Morris (1995, p.45ff.) focus attention on the
factors which make a disabled parent reliant on the personal assistance of a young carer. These include poverty, disabling professional
attitude, disabling services, disabling environments and the broader
problems of disabling experiences and disabling communities. Disabled parents rely on their children as carers not because they wish
to, but because society has failed to provide them with adequate
social support. A social model of disability relocates the problem of
dependency from being a corollary of impairment, to being a product
of a disabling society. Rather than putting resources into support for
young carers, it would be appropriate to put resources into integrated living schemes and personal assistance, which would render
dependence on child carers unnecessary.

When Keith and Morris make the following comment about child
carers, it is equally relevant to the debate about disabled children:
'The choice both parent and child have in these circumstances is
often dependent on access to external support, accessible housing
and appropriate aids and equipment' (1995, p.54). Rather than seeing
the problems of disabled childhood as a result of the child's impairment, it is beneficial to look at the wider context of support and
services extended to different families. This point is made by parents
in Bryony Beresford's research on *Positively Parents* (1994): despite the
thrust of the research, there were many comments suggesting that it
was not the impairment itself which was the main problem. Many of
the experiences of families with disabled children did not differ
qualitatively from those of families with non-disabled children, many
of which are isolated and impoverished. As Beresford concludes, 'We
should not forget, therefore, that a parent caring for a disabled child
may also be facing other stresses which, to them, may be far more
problematic than those associated with the disabled child' (Beresford,
1994, p.111). Equally, the financial assistance provided by the Family
Fund is not usually used for particular specialist equipment, but for
the basics which make life better for all disadvantaged families:
washing-machines, holidays, transport costs.

Understanding dependency as a consequence of an ageing or
impaired body or mind ignores the broader social relations which
undermine and exclude disabled people. Often, it is the pressures
and stresses of trying to live in a hostile environment which exacerbate the physical and mental problems of the body. It is more
appropriate and more just to seek to remove disabling barriers and
structural disadvantage, than to provide services to deal with the
consequences of oppression.

3 Moving beyond care

Two alternative theoretical models for reforming care are currently available. One is based on the independent living principles which have been developed by the disabled people's movement. The second is the feminist ethic of care. Both share some criticisms of existing care, but offer significantly different strategies for developing new approaches. Disabled writers promote the civil rights of disabled people, and suggest that independence can be achieved via personal assistance schemes. Feminist writers favour replacing the discourse of rights with the discourse of care, and, like many from the disability movement, wish to deconstruct the notion of independence itself. Yet neither perspective has engaged with the other, despite the opportunities this might offer for a more holistic programme of reform. It is my argument that such a dialectic is the way forward.

The independent living model is based on several claims. First, that there is not a qualitative distinction between disabled and non-disabled people in terms of needs. Everyone has needs, and disabled people do not have special needs, but the same needs as everyone else: for housing, employment, health care, education and so forth. A discourse has been constructed in which independence is equated with 'normality' and dependence with 'disability'. Yet no one is independent. Everyone depends on others, whether to drive the bus or deliver milk, or perform any number of basic personal and systemic maintenance roles. As Aristotle says, the person who is independent is either a beast or a god.

Second, that 'dependency' has to be deconstructed. High levels of physical dependency do not have to translate into high levels of social dependency. For example, in the United Kindom, rich people depend on others to clean the toilet, do the ironing, and make the meals. Clearly, they are independent because they have control. This is exactly the distinction – i.e. the absence or presence of control – which the disability movement has insisted on.

Thus comes the third claim, as Richard Wood (1991) argues, that disabled people do not need or want care. They need personal assistance in order to achieve their goals. This means having the money to pay other people to perform personal services, be this driving the car, lifting in and out of bed or wheelchair, making meals or giving toileting and cleaning assistance. Finally, the advent of community care has led to a shift towards this vision of independent living, in which disabled people are given direct payments in order to pay personal assistants a proper wage for performing empowering roles in their lives (Morris, 1993).

No disabled person wants to be institutionalized, or to be dependent on family members or volunteers in order to survive. Disabled people want social independence, which is about autonomy and control over their lives. As Morris writes, 'Independent living is about both human and civil rights. If disabled people do not have control over the very basic activities of daily living then they cannot hope even to begin to participate in society on an equal basis' (Morris, 1993, p.162). The removal of social and environmental barriers, and the provision of direct payments and personal assistance schemes is the way to achieve this outcome, not the perpetuation of dependency through traditional care.

The feminist ethic of care originated partly in the work of Carol Gilligan, and particularly from her study *In a Different Voice* (1982), which criticized the traditional models of moral development advanced by psychologists such as Lawrence Kohlberg, and suggested that women were not morally underdeveloped, but had a different approach to morality. Jean Tronto (1993) summarizes three major distinctions between what has been called the 'ethic of rights' and the feminist 'ethic of care'. The ethic of care is based on relationships and responsibilities, while the ethic of rights is based on rights and rules. The former emerges from concrete circumstances, rather than formal and abstract situations. Finally, the ethic of care depends on activity, while the ethic of rights depends on principles. Drawing on these differences, feminist philosophers have argued that public discourse needs to draw on the neglected ethic of care, as a balance to the dominant ethic of rights, and they have elaborated the implications of this approach for welfare.

From a disability studies perspective, one could develop some critiques of this approach. For example, there is a tendency in some of this literature to idealize the caring role, and to develop an almost essentialist idea of women as carers (as in Noddings, 1984). Yet users of care services may well have reason to reject this for reasons outlined earlier: they may feel taken over, spoken for, undermined, disempowered or even neglected and abused by carers. Moreover, the literature on the feminist ethic of care perhaps fails to grasp a key problem, in the challenge to the ethic of rights, which is variously described as patriarchal in essence or in values (Larrabee, 1993), and which dominates within the public sphere. Abstract universals such as equality and justice are criticized, and a feminist ethic based on relationships and responsibilities is offered as an alternative. This may be a step forward in the public sphere, yet in the private sphere, where much caring takes place, the contribution of the feminist ethic of care would surely be resisted by those who come from a disability rights perspective. I (and possibly others connected to the disability rights movement) would argue that the fundamental need is for the application of the ethic of rights to the social relationship of care. So, for example, disabled people have promoted the slogan 'rights not charity', demanding personal assistance as of right, instead of dependency on care or kindness. As Anita Silvers argues, 'far from vanquishing patriarchal systems, substituting the ethics of caring for the ethics of equality threatens an even more oppressive paternalism' (Silvers, 1995, p.40).

However, more recent writers from the feminist ethic of care position move away from the opposition of care and rights, and also show more understanding of the problems of disempowerment. For example, amongst others, Sevenhuijsen has criticized what she calls 'the shadow side of virtue' (Sevenhuijsen 1998, p.12), meaning the conflict, aggression and ambivalence which is also sometimes present in caring:

> Even if care is to a certain extent generated by dependency and attentiveness, the concrete motives in social practices of care cannot always be derived from the urge to protect dependent people from vulnerability. Caring for others can also stem from less noble motives, such as the urge to meddle or to control others. (Sevenhuijsen, 1998, p.20)

Marilyn Friedman (1993) argues that justice and caring are compatible: that close relationships create special vulnerability to harm and abuse therefore it is important to introduce the notion of justice into debates about the social relations of care. In her work, and that of others (Tronto, 1993), there has been some progress towards dissolving the false dichotomy of care versus justice. Certainly, one would want to support the argument that care can bring benefits to democratic citizenship, as long as it was also accepted that justice and equality may bring benefits to caring relationships and the private sphere: this, after all, has been a central part of the feminist project.

Whereas disabled people campaign for independence, feminist ethic philosophers promote the notion of interdependence. They critique liberal ideals of autonomy and independence as being irredeemably bound up with a masculine view of people as separate subjects. For example, Sevenhuijsen criticizes autonomy and independence as a goal, and the whole idea of 'atomistic individualism':

> The ideal of abstract autonomy in fact overlooks what it is that makes care an element of the human condition, i.e. the recognition that all people are vulnerable, dependent and finite, and that we all have to find ways of dealing with this in our daily existence and in the values which guide our individual and collective behaviour. (Sevenhuijsen, 1998, p.28)

Because women have historically been the care providers, it is suggested that they are less likely to promote an unrealistic view of independence. They realize that a large proportion of people – babies and children, pregnant women, older people, and sick and disabled people – will rely on others in various ways and at various stages.

That is to say, over a life cycle, people will variously both receive and provide care: 'Dependence on care should not be seen as something which can suddenly overtake us; rather it should be seen as an integral part of human existence' (Sevenhuijsen, 1998, p.147). Here there is a revisioning of the idea of human nature to include dependence on others as a core concept.

Moreover, there is an argument in the feminist ethic literature that it is the denial of this basic interdependence which contributes to the devaluing of people who receive care. Joan Tronto highlights the social construction of dependency which undermines and objectifies 'helpless' people:

> Because neediness is conceived as a threat to autonomy, those who have more needs than us appear to be less autonomous, and hence less powerful and less capable. The result is that one way in which we socially construct those who need care is to think of them as pitiful because they require help. (Tronto, 1993, p.120)

Selma Sevenhuijsen argues along similar lines:

> In the ideal of the atomistic individual, the moral subject is primarily expected to pursue autonomy and independence. In this way, vulnerability and dependency easily become separated from the ideal self and localized in, or projected on to others: weak or 'needy' people. (Sevenhuijsen, 1998, p.57)

Attractive though these arguments are, the disability community may have a major problem with those who wish to displace independence as a goal. Here there is a parallel with those post-structuralists who seek to deconstruct the notion of identity. In response, feminists and others on the margins have argued that for people whose identity is not strong, or valued, or established, the need is to construct and defend a notion of identity, not to dissolve the concept of identity. In a similar way, disabled people might reply to the feminist ethic writers that while deconstructing independence sounds good in theory, in practice they would prefer schemes which offer them the choice and control which others already take for granted. With Silvers we need to argue that 'social policy that reconciles equality with difference can advance historically subordinated groups but that displacing equality in favour of positional ethics merely reprises the repression of those already marginalized' (Silvers, 1995, p.31).

Rather than challenging the goal of independence, disabled people want to be empowered to become independent. The crucial move here is not just to recognize that everyone has needs, but to break the link between physical and social dependency. While feminist ethic philosophers may see women's dependency as socially constructed, they retain an essentialist model when it comes to disability, seeing it as arising from particular physical limitations. They fail to deconstruct care. The independent living model argues that independence consists in being able to make choices and exert control over one's life. It does not mean being able to perform particular physical acts. Direct payments and independent living schemes are very direct ways of ensuring that people gain far greater independence and are not disempowered by inappropriate or demeaning care: by contrast, the stress that the ethic of care places on interdependence seems rather idealistic.

Yet the feminist ethic of care is also a valuable correlative to the independent living model. There can be too much stress on independence and autonomy within disability rights discourse. There is a contradiction between the collectivism of the disability movement, and the individualism of the proposed solution to care. Moreover, the direct payments model will never be appropriate for everyone. After all, many people want to be able to receive care from family and friends, or do not want the stress of employing their own workers, or may not be capable of the negotiation and responsibility which this involves. Finally, there is the danger of exploitation of the personal assistant, and an unreflexive reliance on a servant/employer solution.

Undoubtedly, the first step in any reform must be the removal of the gross obstacles to the inclusion and equality of disabled people: for example, with civil rights statutes, personal assistance schemes, and accessible housing and public environments. This might establish a 'level playing-field', in which there is more balance between disabled people and non-disabled people, and dependency is minimized. Yet, at this stage, the values of interdependence and the feminist ethic contribute an important dimension to social life.

4 Conclusion

Social policy cannot go on tinkering with prevailing arrangements, based on a discourse of care which is individualizing and excluding (see, for example, Brechin et al., 1998). If an independent living philosophy was applied widely, then many of the problems of disabled people and older people would change radically. At the current time, experimentation with personal assistants for children, and similar arrangements for older people, is challenging the idea that only young adults can benefit from these systems. Equally, people with learning difficulties or other cognitive needs could also benefit from having personal assistance in different forms. The common philosophy is to offer the person receiving help as much control as possible over the way in which that help is delivered. Unpaid carers and family members, often women, should no longer be exploited by the caring structures of the welfare state. But the key to this is recognizing the civil rights of service users and radically revising the way we understand need and independence. Centrally this requires a re-examination of the extent and configurations of interdependence and the social and moral dimensions of care in general and among specific constituencies.

Selma Sevenhuijsen promotes the idea of 'caring solidarity':

> The feminist ethic of care points to forms of solidarity in which there is room for difference, and in which we find out what people in particular situations need in order for them to live with dignity. People must be able to count on solidarity because vulnerability and dependency, as we know, are a part of human existence; we need each other's disinterested support at expected and unexpected moments. (Sevenhuijsen, 1998, p.147)

This notion of caring solidarity may perhaps offer some promise in the attempt to break down the dichotomy between disabled and non-disabled people, recognizing that everyone is variously dependent, that disabled people are themselves often carers, and that society is based on interdependence.

The independent living combination of direct payments and personal assistance cannot solve all the problems. Disabled people and others still often depend on good will and mutual aid, as all people do. The danger comes when disabled people have no choice and no alternative, and are reliant on unresponsive services or demeaning charity which renders them marginalized and dependent. Yet empowered disabled people will achieve a better quality of life in a community in which each recognizes their responsibility to the other, rather than a world made up of competing and selfish individuals seeking to maximize their own advantage.

Note

Many thanks to the participants in the Rethinking Social Policy seminar for their stimulating comments, and to John Clarke, Sharon Gewirtz, Gail Lewis and Fiona Williams for their help and support with this chapter.

References

Baldwin, S. and Carlisle, J. (1994) *Social Support for Disabled Children and their Families*, London, HMSO.
Beresford, B. (1994) *Positively Parents: Caring for a Severely Disabled Child*, London, HMSO.
Brechin, A., Walmsley, J., Katz, J. and Peace, S. (1998) *Care Matters: Concepts, Practice and Research in Health and Social Care*, London, Sage.

Dalley, G. (ed.) (1991) *Disability and Social Policy*, London, Policy Studies Institute.

Estes, C. (1979) *The Ageing Enterprise*, San Francisco, Jossey-Bass.

Friedman, M. (1993) 'Beyond caring: the democratization of gender', in Larrabee, M.J. (ed.) *An Ethic of Care: Feminist and Interdisciplinary Perspectives*, New York, Routledge.

Gilligan, C. (1982) *In a Different Voice*, Cambridge, MA, Harvard University Press.

Keith, L. and Morris, J. (1995) 'Easy targets: a disability rights perspective on the "children as carers" debate', *Critical Social Policy*, Issue 44/45, volume 15, nos 2/3, pp.36–57.

Larrabee, M.J. (ed.) (1993) *An Ethic of Care: Feminist and Interdisciplinary Perspectives*, New York, Routledge.

Memmi, A. (1990) *The Colonizer and the Colonized*, London, Earthscan.

Morris, J. (1991) *Pride against Prejudice*, London, The Women's Press.

Morris, J. (1993) *Independent Lives: Community Care and Disabled People*, Basingstoke, Macmillan.

Noddings, N. (1984) *Caring: A Feminine Approach to Ethics and Moral Education*, Berkeley, CA, University of California Press.

Oliver, M. (1990) *The Politics of Disablement*, Basingstoke, Macmillan.

Oliver, M. and Barnes, C. (1998) *Disabled People and Social Policy: From Exclusion to Inclusion*, Harlow, Longman.

Olsen (1996) 'Young carers: challenging the facts and politics of research into children and caring', *Disability and Society*, 11 (1), pp.41–54.

Olsen, R. and Parker, G. (1997) 'A response to Aldridge and Becker – "Disability rights and the denial of young carers: the dangers of zero-sum arguments"', *Critical Social Policy*, 17, pp.125–33.

Phillipson, C., Bernard, M. and Strang, P. (1986) *Dependency and Independency in Later Life*, London, Croom Helm.

Pitkeathley, J. (1989) *It's My Duty, Isn't It? The Plight of Carers in Our Society*, London, Souvenir Press.

Sevenhuijsen, S. (1998) *Citizenship and the Ethics of Care: Feminist Considerations on Justice, Morality and Politics*, London, Routledge.

Shakespeare, T. (1999) 'Losing the plot? Discourses of disability and genetics', in Gabe, J. and Conrad, P. (eds) *Social Perspectives on the New Genetics*, Oxford, Blackwell.

Shakespeare, T. and Watson, N. (1998) 'Theoretical principles in disabled childhood', in Stalker, K. and Robinson, C. (eds) *Growing Up with Disability*, London, Jessica Kingsley.

Silvers, A. (1995) 'Reconciling equality to difference: caring (f)or justice for people with disabilities', *Hypatia*, 10 (1), pp.30–55.

Townsend, P. (1981) 'The structured dependency of the elderly', *Ageing and Society*, 1 (21), pp.5–28.

Tronto, J.C. (1993) *Moral Boundaries: A Political Argument for an Ethic of Care*, London, Routledge.

Voysey, M. (1975) *A Constant Burden*, London, Routledge & Kegan Paul.

Wald, N.J., Kennard, A., Densem, J.W., Cuckle, H.S., Chard, T. and Butler, L. (1992) 'Antenatal maternal serum screening for Downs's syndrome: results of a demonstration project', *British Medical Journal*, 305, pp.391–94.

Warnes, A.M. (1993) 'Being old, old people and the burdens of burden', *Ageing and Society*, 13, pp.297–338.

Wood, R. (1991) 'Care of disabled people', in Dalley (1991).

4

Foucault and the Study of Social Policy

Sophie Watson

1   Introduction

During the 1970s and 1980s critical social policy analysis for the most part took place within a Marxist framework. Thus, the provision of welfare by the state was understood in terms of how it served the capitalist system by keeping society ticking comfortably along, by reproducing class relations and by shoring up the patriarchal family where women provided domestic labour for free. Though there were sophisticated debates as to who did, or did not, benefit from such a system, and on the role of the state and other complexities, the underlying social and economic structure was posited as capitalism, with class relations as the major social division. This approach was then developed to take account of other social divisions – gender and 'race' – which were also understood in terms of the big pictures – or grand narratives – of patriarchy, imperialism and so on.

In post-structuralist approaches, and in particular in the work of Michel Foucault, bodies of thought such as Marxism, which attempted to explain the social/political/economic world within one totalizing (to use a post-structuralist term) framework are called meta-narratives or are sometimes referred to as grand theory. Post-structuralists criticize the attempt to build grand theories, arguing instead that we can only understand the world in partial, specific and local ways. In relation to social policy what this means is that we can begin to see social policy as necessarily contradictory and complex. Some social policies in some contexts may reproduce capitalist relations. But other social policies will need to be understood and analysed in different ways using different frameworks of analysis. This means paying attention to the specificity of local contexts and times and the locally different effects of policies on different groups of people. The development of effective social policies will then require attention to specificity of time, place and constituency.

This approach acknowledges that the world is fluid, changing and inherently complex and fragmented. This chapter looks specifically at the work of Michel Foucault and considers what it offers for an analysis of social policy. In the first part we consider his notion of power and the power/knowledge nexus. We then discuss his notion of discourse and its relevance to understanding social policy. The third part of the chapter interrogates Foucault's view of the state and his notion of governmentality. In the last section a Foucauldian perspective is used to look at some aspects of social and housing policy in relation to women.

1.1 Power

In most radical traditions power is conceived as repressive and negative in its effects. Power is postulated as excluding and oppressive and as possessed by institutions or groups of people who use it for their own ends and to effect certain outcomes. One of Foucault's major contributions was to challenge this notion of power. In his work power is seen as exercised, not possessed, and as a strategy. It is a mechanism which has positive and useful effects. Power in this formulation is fluid and operates in a capillary-like fashion constituting all social relations, which must be conceived as a 'multiplicity of force relations immanent in the sphere in which they operate and which constitute their organization' (Foucault, 1977a, p.194). Power is thus not given but is exchanged, and is productive in that it constitutes the domain of the social. Power relations are present in all encounters, not just between labour and capital or citizen and the state: they are to be found in, for example, the relations between husband and wife, doctor and patient, and student and lecturer.

For Foucault, where there is power there is also resistance. Power is not about something done to people over which they have no control. People are not victims of power in the way that is sometimes suggested by Marxist and some feminist analyses. According to this view, subjects are both the targets of power and its articulation:

> When I think of the mechanics of power, I think of its capillary forms of
> existence, of the extent to which power seeps into the very grain of indi-
> viduals, reaches right into their bodies, permeates their gestures, their
> position, what they say, how they learn to live and work with other
> people. (Foucault, 1977b, p.10)

This 'micro-physics' of power implies, then, that there are
innumerable points of confrontation and instability and numerous
possibilities for tactics and strategies of resistance. Such a view stands
in clear opposition to the notion that the state or capital as a concentrated site of power needs to be overthrown or dismantled for
socialism or universal social justice to be achieved.

Another important element of Foucault's view of power for social
policy is his argument that power and knowledge are intimately
connected and intertwined – we cannot think of one without the
other. According to Foucault, all fields of knowledge are constituted
within power relations and all power relations constitute a field of
power. As he puts it, power 'produces reality, it produces a domain of
objects and rituals of truth' (1977a, p.194). This is particularly relevant
to analysing the social, medical and legal professions and the knowledge claims on which they are based. Foucault's work concentrates in
particular on two configurations of the power/knowledge nexus:
these are the notions of disciplinary power and bio-power which are
illustrated respectively in practices around discipline and sexuality. In
both of these the body is a key organizing concept which acts as the
site for the production, transmission and legitimation of knowledge.

Foucault's notion of disciplinary power is developed most extensively in his book *Discipline and Punish* (1977a). According to Foucault
the end of the eighteenth century marks a key point in the eclipse of
sovereign power – where the king represented the seat of power, the
source of government, and law and justice – by new forms of power.
In this later period, he suggests, it is no longer necessary to punish
crimes with overt forms of torture or control since a new range of
techniques, strategies, subtle forms of control and surveillance were
developed in their place. For Foucault the metaphor for this form of
disciplinary power was Bentham's panopticon. This was a model of a
prison where a central control tower was surrounded by cells which
could all be observed from one place. This meant that the potential
for constant surveillance of the prisoner's body – the all-pervasive
eye or gaze – regulated the behaviour of the inmates without force.
The surveillance cameras in shopping centres and on motorways
operate in just this way, since everyone must behave as if surveillance is total and perpetual even if no one is observing.

Foucault went further to examine a whole range of techniques that
were developed outside of the penal system – in the army, in schools
and in hospitals – to manipulate, control and produce 'A body is

docile [that] may be subjected, used, transformed and improved' (1977a, p.136). In schools, for example, children are subjected to intricate timetables to regulate their behaviour or to repetitive exercises which are standardized and individualized according to their rate of progress. With sufficient repetition, automatic responses to stimuli are created and reproduced without our awareness. The spatialization of this disciplinary power is also crucial – a place for everyone and everyone in her/his place. We can think of hospital wards here, or a child's place in a class, or a housing estate cut off from decent amenities or services.

Bio-power represents Foucault's other pole of power. The development of the social, medical and psychiatric professions of the nineteenth century brought new forms of control over the body and thus the population, through the collection of information on births, mortality, levels of health and life expectancy. Once again we see the power–knowledge nexus as inextricably connected. In *The History of Sexuality* (1979), Foucault analyses how discourses on sex and sexuality produced different forms of bodies, such as the homosexual body, in different cultures at different times. What interested him was not the discovery of different kinds of sexual practices as such, but the proliferation of discourses on sex and their social effects, and how and why sexuality became an object of knowledge at a particular time. Freud's friend, Dr Fleiss, for example, believed that many sexual problems in women were due to masturbation and could be cured by an operation on the nose.

Central to the power/knowledge nexus in Foucault's view was confession, which he argued had been taken from Christendom and incorporated into the wider domain of disciplinary power: 'It has spread its effects far and wide. It plays a part in justice, medicine, education, family relationships, and love relations, in the most ordinary affairs of everyday life' (Foucault, 1979, p.59). Confession in this sense plays a key part in social administration, social policy and social research. Surveys, questionnaires and interviews all investigate and intrude upon the most intimate aspects of personal and social life. In order to qualify for assistance or benefits the notion of privacy is stripped away. The homeless person, the criminal, the social security claimant are constantly monitored and surveyed and called upon to give information which may be prejudicial to them.

One consequence of the new forms of power, according to Foucault (1977a, 1977b, 1979), was an increasing appeal to decisions based on statistical measures of what is normal as opposed to decisions based on notions of right and wrong or justice. Classifying and ordering became standard techniques of normalization and the norm came to be as important as the law in determining social policies. This kind of normative ordering of the population in the nineteenth century continued apace throughout the twentieth century with a plethora of government surveys, reports, censuses and commissions establishing notions of average and expected forms of individual behaviour and social life. As Rabinow expresses it: 'The power of the state to produce an increasingly totalizing web of control is intertwined with, and dependent upon, its ability to produce an increasing specification of individuality' (1986a, p.22). Many feminists have developed Foucault's ideas to interrogate the reproduction of normative feminine practices in our culture. Bordo (1988) looks at eating disorders in these terms, while Cameron and Fraser (1987) suggest that the apparently motiveless killing of women by men in our society can best be understood in the context of a normative culture of misogyny and the objectification of women's bodies.

1.2   Discourse

Another significant contribution to thinking critically about social policy is Foucault's notion of discourse as a framework of meanings which are historically produced in a particular culture at a particular time. Discourses or discursive practices, for Foucault, have profound effects, and it is the effects of the discourses that matter, not whether they are scientific or not, or true or false. Rather than human subjects being the producers of truth as universal, sovereign and right, human subjects are themselves produced within discourses and the realm of the 'social'. This idea relates back to the power/knowledge nexus since what becomes crucial is which people and institutions have the power to define the terms of the debate or the way a problem is to be understood. In other words the place of the expert is key.

Mark Poster describes it in this way:

> Discourses, for Foucault, are already powers and do not need to [seek] their material force somewhere else, as in the mode of production. Most significantly for a critical theory of history, such a perspective shifts the focus of attention away from the sublime ideas of the intellectual elite and toward the mundane discourses of disciplinary institutions that more directly affect the everyday life of the masses. Ideology is no longer seen as the airy dialogue of great minds, but as the prosaic encounter of criminal and criminologist, neurotic and therapist, child and parent, unemployed worker and welfare agency. (Poster, 1984, p.87)

Thus, not only do material practices matter – for example, how homeless people are actually treated – but also how different discourses act to produce certain outcomes. From this perspective we may ask the question 'How does the Housing Act create particular notions of homeless people – marginalizing some groups, creating

others as victims, others as blameworthy and so on?' Also important
are discursive practices – how are particular discourses mobilized
and in what arenas and how can we intervene to change these?

2   Governmentality and the state

Foucault's ideas have played an important part in shifting contemporary understandings of the state. Within social policy, dominant
understandings of the state have derived from Marxist or liberal
traditions. Within Marxism the state is posited as having an independent and objective existence as a set of institutions or structures:
it is seen to play a key role in organizing relations of power and
assumed in the last instance to act in the interests of capital, even if
its role is sometimes contradictory (Gough, 1979). In liberal traditions
the state is posited as the neutral arbiter of competing interests, and
the welfare state is posited in similar terms. Given Foucault's views
about power, it is not surprising to find that he is wary about locating
power in the apparatuses of the state, and indeed there are very few
direct references to the state in his work. In its place he is more
concerned with the construction of the 'social' and in governmentality. Foucault distinguishes between two notions. First, there is a
notion of sovereignty, the aim of which is to maintain a territory
where the sovereign rule is preserved through the rule of the law and
the people's submission to it. Government, in contrast, is the exercise
of power which concerns the realm of the social, the object of which
is to manage or facilitate the best resolution of a population's needs,
resources and wealth. The catalyst for the development of the art of
government was the emergence of the problem of population which
was constituted by the deployment of bio-power.
     The new technology of government was constituted in the new
forms of knowledge available through the statistical monitoring of
the population. There was a shift from the model of government as a
higher order of the family to the adoption of the family itself as the
privileged site for the regulation and management of the population.
Donzelot (1979) refers to this displacement of the sovereignty of the
family as the shift from government by the family to government
through the family. Thus the family became the principal source of
information on the population and the target for population campaigns around health, mortality and marriage. Women, as mothers
and primary carers in the family, thus had a key part to play,
although Donzelot and Foucault in their work paid little attention to
these gendered dimensions. The aim of government became the
condition of the population (in the sense of both demographic
knowledge and the constitution of docile subjects) rather than the
power of the sovereign and new techniques and tactics of power

were developed as a result. It can be seen from this brief discussion that although Foucault did not focus on the state as such, he does address many of the issues which are central to an understanding of the development of the modern state.

Smart describes the shifts noted by Foucault in the realm of the social as follows:

> The emergence of the 'social' and the associated mechanisms directed towards such dimensions of population as fertility, age, health, economic activity, welfare and education, not only represent a major development or shift in the form of the exercise of power, but in addition it has produced significant changes in the nature of social relationships, and has since the mid-nineteenth century effected a particular form of cohesion or solidarity within society . . . it is at the political level that the various measures and technologies of power associated with the rise of the social have had their most critical impact. (Smart, 1983, p.121)

Other writers (such as Laclau and Mouffe, 1985; Pringle and Watson, 1992) have drawn on Foucault's ideas to criticize the dominant formulations of the state that are to be found in social policy analysis. In these analyses the state was postulated as having an objective existence as a set of institutions or structures which operated as a unity, albeit a contradictory and complex one. Hence, the notion of 'state' acting in the interests of capital, say, implies a body which acts with a coherent set of interests across the political, bureaucratic, judicial and other spheres. In their work, adopting a Foucauldian perspective, Pringle and Watson (1992) questioned the notion of a unified state on the one hand and, on the other, the notion of coherent interests of groups such as men, women and capitalists which are based on underlying economic or sexual relations that exist outside the state and are directly represented or embodied in it.

Instead, they argue that the state has to be seen as disconnected and erratic rather than contradictory, as a set of arenas or as a 'plurality of discursive forms'. This shifts the emphasis to analysing how particular discursive struggles define and construct the 'state' as a historical product and the ways in which various groupings are able to articulate their interests and hegemonize their claims. If we adopt this kind of formulation, there is no need to explain why the state acts contradictorily or to assume that it will act to maintain patriarchal or capitalist relations. The state can then be thought of as a diverse set of discursive arenas which play a crucial role in organizing relations of power. Particular interests – women's interests or the interests of specific ethnic or 'race' groups – can be seen as perpetually constructed in the process of interaction with specific institutions and sites, and within particular discourses which can be challenged and shifted strategically.

Laclau and Mouffe adopt a related set of arguments: for them, the state 'is not a homogeneous medium, separated from civil society by a ditch, but an uneven set of branches and functions, only relatively integrated by the hegemonic practices which take place within it' (1985, p.180). The emphasis is placed on the symbolic order – the sphere of how meanings are constructed – which implies that the social sphere can never be permanently fixed and will always be subject to contested meanings. Laclau and Mouffe stress the 'articulatory practices' which temporarily fix meanings by arresting the flow of differences to construct nodal points or privileged sites. Thus men or women – as nodal points in these terms – and their 'interests' or 'needs' rest not on biological differences, reproductive relations or sexual divisions of labour, but rather on the discursive practices that produce them. We can see that these approaches allow for a more fluid notion of the state, and potentially for the possibility of change rather than fixity.

3   An application of a Foucauldian perspective

It is commonplace in discussions of needs definition (Doyal and Gough, 1991) to attempt to establish notions of universality, to quantify needs and to establish how these can best be satisfied by social policy. Foucault's ideas provide an alternative approach. Here the question may be asked what notions of power, control, normalization and self-regulation are involved in producing the concept. Once the social is understood as the site where needs become politicized, contested and interpreted, then what is important are the processes by which certain needs are politicized and others are not. Needs can no longer be taken as given and simply waiting to be expressed and satisfied.

In the domain of needs feminists have generally argued that women should be treated differently from men in order to make up a 'deficit'. The assumption on which this approach was based was that, once women's needs (for child care, refuges and so on) had been met, they could enter the terrain of demands for equal treatment in the labour market or 'public life'. Women's needs were perilously situated in the more private domains of life. Needs discourse has been strategically deployed by feminists to win gains from the public purse, but women's needs have also always been in some sense marginal to the main game. In many cases women are constituted as victims or as 'lacking'.

Thus, just as in Foucauldian terms social policy is a highly normative discipline which constructs ideal models of society based on notions of social justice which disguise the concrete functioning of power, so it can be argued more specifically that gendered power relations are one such terrain. This power operates in subtle ways through the constitution of specific subjects such as the single parent, the battered wife and the girl in moral danger. These subjects become the focus of a whole range of practices wherein the modern forms of domination and repression are to be found. This is not to deny that there are women bringing up children on their own, nor that some women are battered. Feminists have, however, sometimes been unaware of the way in which these subjects are constituted as having inbuilt or essential attributes and defects which require certain kinds of intervention and surveillance. The social practices which are aimed at these subjects stem directly from the discourses which created them in the first place.

Need, then, is located within discourses of the private/public interface while at the same time producing these private/public distinctions. Thus, elderly people cared for at home by women for free are deemed not to have needs while those cared for in the public domain do. Women's need to be protected from violence is more clearly established and recognized in the public arena. This lack of protection actually in part constitutes the domestic for women. No claims for provisions and services based on need can have a neutral effect. Given that women have argued that they need special treatment as embodied subjects who bear and support children, who are vulnerable to men physically and so on, it has followed that women are disadvantaged in many terrains often designated as public and mainstream. Needs discourse has operated to provide women with all sorts of benefits and to shift back the boundaries of the domestic. But it has also confirmed women as 'lacking', marginal and powerless, as subjects to be regulated.

In public policy arenas need is defined according to bureaucratic procedures and regulations which define some people in – those who are deemed to be deserving – and other people – the undeserving – out. In Britain, where the major form of housing provision is owner-occupation, a household defined as in housing need according to local and central government housing policy may be eligible for public housing. Women are highly represented among those defined as in housing need. In the context of a society where public housing is a marginalized sector, this translates into women having a claim for housing only at the margins and not in the mainstream of owner-occupation – which has also, we must not forget, historically been a well-subsidized sector. Once in the public housing sector women find themselves subjected to practices of surveillance already referred to. This is not to suggest that public housing for women in housing need is not worth fighting for; the point is that, drawing on Foucault's ideas, we are led to see that such claims are not as neutral as we might have thought.

A social pathology discourse is sometimes evoked to imply that some individuals are to blame for their predicament and are therefore not worthy of assistance and not in need. In urban policy documents, categories of individuals are constituted in the discourses used and the categories deployed and these matter in terms of both how applicants see themselves and how they are seen by others. Perceptions in turn have effects on how people are treated by others. Thus, homeless legislation as defined in the Housing Act 1985 Part III and its successor, the Housing Act 1996 Part VII, is described by Cowan (1996) as encouraging a gatekeeper approach in that housing officers are required to exercise power in the form of discretion as to who is 'intentionally homeless' and who is not. Women who are victims of domestic violence are now exempted from being referred back to their former local authority for rehousing, although for some time after the first Homeless Persons Act's inception in 1976, in many areas such women were defined as 'intentionally homeless' because they supposedly had a home to return to. As a result of a White Paper suggesting that lone parents were jumping the housing queue, the duty under the former Act to provide permanent accommodation to homeless applicants was weakened to an obligation to ensure that suitable accommodation was made available for a minimum of two years. The discourse underpinning these changes is of homeless people as undeserving of permanent accommodation.

What we have seen from the foregoing discussion is that Foucault's focus on power as exercised and as constitutive of the social, of norms and of subjects provides a different way into understanding social policies and their effects. Further, once discourses are interrogated to see what assumptions are embedded within them, we can begin to see that what may appear as a benign or positive policy may also have complex and contradictory effects. It is not argued here that policies directed towards meeting women's needs are necessarily a 'bad thing'. Rather it is to point out that they create subject positions which may not be the ones desired in their initial formulation or intention.

Foucault's insights and their application to social policy can enable new ways of thinking and new strategies of intervention. The shift from grand theory or meta-narratives allows us to develop more specific analyses of particular policies at particular times, in the recognition that any one policy can have contradictory and unexpected effects. Foucault's view of power also allows us to see the workings of power in a variety of settings and as intricately connected to knowledge. In social policy terms the role of the expert and the professional in determining people's lives is at least as important as the social and economic structures in which people are situated. The attention to discourse makes us aware how crucial, amongst other things, written documents – such as laws and policy reports – are in constructing particular subject positions for particular individuals. And the emphasis on the interrelation of power and resistance gives agency back to people who are often constructed as powerless and as victims.

However, a Foucauldian approach to social policy has its problems. Central to Foucault's approach is his critique of universalism
and universal notions of justice, truth, equality and so on. Yet these
are the very cornerstones of social policy. In a famous debate with
Foucault in 1974, Noam Chomsky articulated a position with which
many advocates of a fair social policy system would agree. In his
view, in order to have a better society we need fixed and rational
standards for judging what constitutes a better and more just society
(Rabinow, 1986b). Yet, for Foucault, any attempt to construct universal notions of justice ignores the concrete functioning of power.
The very idea of justice, he argues,

> has been invented and put to work in different societies as an instrument
> of a certain political and economic power or as a weapon against that
> power. One can't, however regrettable it may be, put these notions
> forward to justify a fight which should overthrow the very fundaments of
> our society. (Foucault, 1974, p.187)

Foucault is not suggesting here that the idea of justice should not
be involved in political struggle, but that the basic metaphor is not
conversation but a battle (Rabinow, 1986a, p.6). Knowledge is implicated in this battle and can never be separated from power. This
position is illustrated in his involvement with an anti-prison group in
France (Macey, 1993, pp.257–89) whose principal aim was not to
promote the reform of prisons, but to obtain and disseminate information about prisons, giving prisoners the right to speak on their
own behalf about the specific practices which brought them into
conflict with the demands of power. Whatever the merits are of
arguing for the importance of the specific, the local and the particular, against the general, the overarching and the universal, Foucault's
insights have brought new ways of thinking about social policy
which have challenged earlier orthodoxies in provocative and useful
ways.

Note

This chapter draws much of its argument from joint work with Paddy Hillyard. See
Hillyard, P. and Watson, S. (1996) 'Post-modern social policy: a contradiction in
terms?', *Journal of Social Policy*, 25 (3), pp.321–46.

References

Bordo, S. (1988) 'Anorexia nervosa: psychopathology as the crystallization of culture', in
Diamond, I. and Quinby, L. (eds) *Feminism and Foucault*, Boston, MA, North Eastern
University Press.

Cameron, D. and Fraser, E. (1987) *The Lust to Kill: A Feminist Investigation of Sexual Murder*, Cambridge, Polity Press.

Cowan, D. (general ed.) (1996) *The Housing Act 1996: A Practical Guide*, Bristol, Jordans.

Donzelot, J. (1979) *The Policing of Families: Welfare versus the State*, London, Hutchinson.

Doyal, L. and Gough, I. (1991) *A Theory of Human Need*, London, Macmillan.

Foucault, M. (1974) 'Human nature: justice versus power', in Elders, F. (ed.) *Reflexive Water: The Basic Concerns of Mankind*, London, Souvenir Press.

Foucault, M. (1977a) *Discipline and Punish: The Birth of the Prison* (trans. A. Sheridan), London, Allen Lane.

Foucault, M. (1977b) 'An interview', *Radical Philosophy*, 16, pp.10–15.

Foucault, M. (1979) *The History of Sexuality, Volume 1: An Introduction* (trans. R. Hurley), London, Allen Lane.

Gough, I. (1979) *The Political Economy of the Welfare State*, London, Macmillan.

Laclau, E. and Mouffe, C. (1985) *Hegemony and Socialist Strategy: Towards a Radical Democratic Politics*, London, Verso.

Macey, D. (1993) *The Lives of Michel Foucault*, London, Vintage Books.

Poster, M. (1984) *Foucault, Marxism and History: Mode of Production versus Mode of Information*, Cambridge, Polity Press.

Pringle, R. and Watson, S. (1992) 'Constructing interests', in Barrett, M. and Phillips, A. (eds) *Destabilizing Theory*, Cambridge, Polity Press.

Rabinow, P. (1986a) 'Introduction', in Rabinow (1986b).

Rabinow, P. (ed.) (1986b) *The Foucault Reader*, Harmondsworth, Penguin.

Smart, B. (1983) *Foucault, Marxism and Critique*, London, Routledge.

5

Constituting Welfare Subjects through Poverty and Sexuality

Jean Carabine

Contents

---

1 Introduction

In considerations of the constitution of welfare subjects and criteria of eligibility to benefits, the relationship between discourses of poverty and discourses of sexuality has been left unexamined. Analyses of sexuality are rarely, if at all, included as either an integral or even a marginal part of work on historical or contemporary social policy work on poverty. This is not surprising given that the relationship between sexuality and social policy, as practice or discipline, is also largely ignored and under-researched (Carabine, 1996a). Historical analyses also have an important role to play in the wider project of developing theoretical frameworks and understandings of the relationship between social policy and sexuality (Carabine, 1996b).

This chapter considers the intersection of discourses of illegitimacy and unmarried motherhood and the relief of poverty in Britain during the early part of the nineteenth century. It does so through an analysis of the Bastardy Clauses of the New Poor Law Act 1834 and Assistant Commissioners' Reports (the term 'Commissioners' will be used to refer to all contributors to the Reports: see *Report from His Majesty's Commissioners* in the reference list). Of particular interest is how discourses of sexuality have been an important strand in determining eligibility and 'deservedness' for relief from poverty, particularly in the case of women, and how what I identify as the 'discourse of bastardy' played a significant part in constituting single, pregnant women and unmarried mothers (hereafter referred to as unmarried mothers) as undeserving welfare subjects in a particular and different way. Through the invocation of a negative discourse of female sexuality, such women became identified as morally corrupt welfare recipients. Through this, responsibilities and conditions were linked to rights and, by association, to social citizenship. The discourse of bastardy served to exclude unmarried mothers from welfare/benefits, and poor relief was used to penalize as well as to socially exclude them through stigmatization.

2 Understanding sexuality and social policy

Four different aspects – invisibility, normalization, constitutiveness and contestation – can be distinguished as central to understanding the relationship between sexuality and social policy. Invisibility refers, first, to the ways in which certain aspects of sexuality are invisible in social policy, particularly in policy-making and practice (see Carabine, 1992, 1995) and it also refers to the invisibility of sexuality as an analytical category within the 'discipline' of social policy, particularly when sexuality is very visible elsewhere (see Carabine, 1996b). Normalization refers to the role of social policy in defining and reaffirming heterosexuality as it is composed at any specific moment as acceptable and appropriate sexuality. Constitutiveness means that sexuality as discourse and knowledge – that is, what we know as the 'truth' of sexuality – is constituted through social policy. Contestation reflects how social policy is a focus for political action, a site where the 'truths' of sexuality are contested, challenged and changed (Carabine, 1996a, p.59).

Foucault has shown that through 'normalization' individuals are compared and differentiated according to a desired norm, and that this process produces homogeneity. It establishes the measure by which all are judged and deemed to conform or not. In his notion of 'normalization' Foucault did not conceive power as being imposed by one section, class or group of society on another. Rather he saw it as a dynamic of knowledge, practised and learned, which was dispersed around various centres of practice and expertise. Both social policy and sexuality can be understood as such centres of expertise and practice. We shall take sexuality first.

In *The History of Sexuality* (1990), Foucault investigates the ways in which sexuality has come to be seen and spoken of: the development of knowledges about sex, as a means of understanding the operations of power. For Foucault, sexuality is socially constructed and produced by effects of power and spoken of in terms of 'truths'. He argues that power is constituted through discourses (Foucault, 1990, 1991). Discourses are historically variable ways of specifying knowledges and truths, whereby knowledges are produced as 'truths', in this case about sexuality. Discourses function as sets of socially and historically constructed rules designating 'what is' and 'what is not'.

Dominant discourses of sexuality specify what sexuality is at particular moments in time. These knowledges or 'truths' tell us what is 'normal' and 'natural' sexuality whilst establishing the boundaries of what is acceptable and appropriate sexuality. Although what we know to be heterosexuality at any given time is historically, culturally and socially specific, subject to redefinition and transformation, it is heterosexuality that persists as the benchmark of 'normal' and 'natural' sexuality (see Carabine, 1992, 1996a, for a more detailed discussion).

In this way, ideas about heterosexuality become naturalized in commonplace thinking with the effect that heterosexual relationships are taken for granted as the norm. Social policy as practice and discipline develops within 'the social' and policy-makers, writers and analysts are also influenced by these common understandings about the nature of sexuality.

In relation to sexuality and social policy, normalization can be identified as operating in three main ways. First, in constituting appropriate and acceptable sexuality and, second, as operating in a regulatory capacity through which, not only is heterosexuality established and secured, but women's and men's bodies and sexuality are disciplined and controlled, albeit differently. This regulatory function can be seen to operate, explicitly through legislation and statutes and implicitly: (a) through normative assumptions about heterosexuality as 'normal' and natural assumptions which then inform the discursive content of social policy; and (b) through the linking of notions of eligibility to welfare services and benefits to ideas about appropriate and acceptable sexuality. However, the existence of such a regulatory function does not necessarily imply, nor lead to, successful regulation. Indeed, regulatory strategies are also often contested. Third, this normalization process produces both differentiating effects and has fragmented impacts, being variously regulatory, penalizing or affirmative in respect to different groups of women.

Normalizing ideas about appropriate sexuality then, explicitly inform and influence social policy, welfare practice and the terms of popular and political debate. For example, in 1988 Margaret Thatcher, the then British Prime Minister, spoke of the apparent problem of young, single girls who were deliberately getting pregnant in order to jump the housing queue and obtain benefits (*Guardian*, 23 November 1988). These ideas were more forcibly endorsed in the run-up to and during the 1993 Conservative Party Conference, when a series of swingeing attacks on single mothers were made. The message came through loud and clear that welfare benefits and housing should only be available to, by implication, 'respectable', married women. It was also believed that welfare worked as a perverse incentive to young girls to become pregnant.

Foucault's work and especially his concept of discourse can be used to interrogate, first, sexuality as a discourse which is constituted, amongst other things through social policy and, second, social policy as practice and discipline as one means by which sexuality itself is constituted. This shows not only that discourses of sexuality are 'played' through social policy as an effect of disciplinary power but also that sexuality discourses interact with and traverse other discourses central to welfare and social policy and in so doing are mediated by those discourses.

3 Discourse and sexuality: explaining sexuality

In order to analyse the 1834 New Poor Law through the lens of sexuality we need to understand what sexuality meant in the early part of the nineteenth century. In the eighteenth century, women had been viewed as sexually voracious and men as sexually passive (see Hitchcock, 1997; Laqueur, 1993). By the early nineteenth century this earlier understanding of sexuality had begun to shift towards what was to become the stereotypical notion and domestic ideal of Victorian female sexuality – the passive, pure and innocent woman. Central to the construction of this domestic ideal was '[t]he contradiction between a sexless, moralized angel and an aggressive, carnal magdalen' (Poovey, 1989, p.11). Not only was sexuality in a state of flux during this period but it was also in a state of crisis (Taylor, 1983, Ch. 9; Clark, 1995, Ch. 4) because 'rates of premarital sex, illegitimacy, and common law marriage soared' and because of '[c]lashing moral standards' among plebeians (Clark, 1995, p.42) and between them and the middle classes.

It was common practice, especially in rural areas, for conception to occur prior to marriage. Illegitimacy and common-law marriage were part of an 'alternative plebeian morality' and for many of the labouring classes 'premarital sex after a promise of marriage [w]as acceptable' (Clark, 1995, p.43; Laslett, 1977, p.128). Indeed, premarital pregnancy was seen as an important economic consideration in determining a woman's fertility (Weeks, 1989, p.60; Perkins, 1989, pp.182–3; Rendall, 1985, p.194). However, as a result of increasing industrialization, urbanization and economic insecurity, marriage did not always follow.

Mort (1987, p.37) identifies this period as one in which moral environmentalism was linked with a new construction of the sexual. Moral environmentalism represented a belief that sexual depravity, particularly of the urban poor, was the cause and result of urban decay, disease and squalor. This belief led to programmes of social intervention which sought both to discipline the urban poor and to educate them into appropriate regimes of cleanliness and morality. Mort identifies moral reform, with sexual reform as its central plank, as a key component of programmes aimed at disciplining the labouring classes. Invariably sexuality was negatively portrayed and the concern was with 'sexual immorality' as 'defined through the significations of dirt, disease, squalor, corruption and the political and cultural threat of an urban working-class populace' (Mort, 1987, pp.37–8).

Working-class men were represented as 'brutalized' by industrialized work and with their own inherent moral deficit placing them closer to nature. Working-class women, on the other hand, 'were both eroticized and condemned as immoral pollutants, the cause of the decline of whole communities and heralded as the agents of moral reform' (Mort, 1987, p.47). To Victorian Poor Law reformers, unmarried mothers were the negative embodiment of the emerging Victorian ideal of female sexuality, being perceived as sexually active, immoral and deceitful.

Mort (1987) maps out how during the 1830s health and morality became negatively conflated such that sickness and disease signified immorality among the urban poor and this was reflected in the way in which sexuality was constituted in and through medico-moral writings of the time. Examination of the New Poor Law Act reveals how this was also constituted through discourses that centred on poverty and welfare. Whereas in medico-moral discourses it is the unhealthy and immoral behaviour of the poor which is pivotal in a negative construction of sexuality, in the bastardy discourse it is poverty and immorality (female sexuality and female poverty) which are the key axes in negative constructions of female sexuality.

To illustrate this, first, the situation surrounding bastardy prior to the enactment of the 1834 Act will be outlined and the chief concerns of the Commissioners summarized. The chapter will then illustrate the ways in which a discourse of bastardy was created which took women as its central focus. It will be suggested that the discourse played a significant part in constituting unmarried mothers as undeserving welfare subjects. The final section explores what this analysis tells us about discourses of poverty.

4   1834 New Poor Law and Bastardy Clauses

The New Poor Law Act 1834 (or NPL) was an attempt to reduce the increasing costs of poor relief through the introduction of a centralized, more economical and more efficient but less generous system of relief. Central to achieving this aim were the principles of less eligibility, the workhouse and the work ethic. The Bastardy Clauses, an appendix to the main Report, were the outcome of the Commissioners' concerns about increasing illegitimacy and related increased demands for poor relief.

In the 1830s, under the old Poor Law, it was an offence to have an illegitimate child which neither parents were able to support (see Marshall, 1969, p.207). Prior to the 1834 NPL, both the unmarried mother and the reputed father of the illegitimate child were legally financially responsible for supporting the child and parents could be imprisoned if they failed to do so.

Where a woman was unable to support the child and sought poor relief, the parish would seek remuneration from the man. Those men unwilling or unable to pay maintenance, or to marry, were imprisoned for bad debt for up to three months. In the case of women the situation was different. If a woman was unable to pay and requested poor relief she could be imprisoned for a period of between six weeks and twelve months for the crime of being a lewd woman rather than for bad debt. In practice men rarely paid maintenance and often only as little as a fifth or a third was ever repaid, leaving the parish to foot the bill for the remainder. Women were seldom imprisoned for being a lewd woman and magistrates were reluctant to commit further, supporting the view of the Commissioners that single mothers were insufficiently punished for becoming pregnant.

Unhappy with the rising rates and costs of illegitimacy, the Commissioners sought to amend the existing bastardy laws through the Bastardy Clauses of the 1834 NPL. Not only did they believe the existing legislation dealing with bastardy to be ineffective, they were also convinced that the combination of the existing bastardy laws and poor relief provision was significant in encouraging women to have illegitimate children. Illegitimacy, like venereal disease at the beginning of the next century (see Bland, 1983), became both a metaphor and signifier of national immorality with pauper unmarried mothers as its personification. The Commissioners had three concerns in their focus on bastardy: support for illegitimate children; parish relief payments made to the mother; and the ineffective attempts to obtain maintenance payments from fathers.

5 Women and the discourse of bastardy

Whilst the Commissioners were clearly concerned with rising illegitimacy rates and increasing costs, attempts to obtain repayments from fathers, and the failure of the existing legislation to reduce or even stop illegitimacy, these aspects became expressed through the 'discourse of bastardy'. In this discourse women became the central concern and, consequently, concerns about increasing illegitimacy, costs and maintenance became expressed as an anxiety about female morality, and particularly women's sexual immorality, and women's power over men. A negative discourse of female sexuality and morality was thus produced.

In the operation of the discourse of bastardy five discursive strategies can be distinguished: the negative representation of unmarried mothers; the representation of men as victims of women's immorality; the absence of male responsibility; related to the first two, the association of unmarried mothers with immorality; finally, and dependent on the preceding strategies, the distinguishing between unmarried mothers and other recipients of poor relief on the basis of notions of deserving and undeserving. These interdependent discursive strategies are separated here for the purposes of clarity.

5.1 Negative representation of unmarried mothers

Discursively, the language used to describe unmarried mothers was moralistic, judgmental, critical and often damning. Unmarried mothers were characterized as lying, manipulative, irresponsible, promiscuous, sexually corrupt and as bad mothers. The Commissioners tell us, for example, that 'continued illicit intercourse has, in almost all cases, originated with the females' (Commissioners, 1971, p.94) and that 'the female in very many cases becomes the corruptor . . . the women . . . feel no disgrace' (Mr Richardson ibid., p.96). What was significant about this process of negative characterization was that it was restricted to women and rarely, if at all, extended to men. This strategy was further developed through the representation of women as predatory and men as victims and through the association of unmarried mothers with immorality.

5.2 Men as victims, women as predatory

Throughout the bastardy sections, men are generally presented as being at the mercy of women, as falling victim to their lying and immoral ways. The existing legislation is seen as placing them 'at the mercy of any abandoned woman' (Commissioners, 1971, p.198). Emotive language was used in which the men were spoken of as 'unfortunate persons' and 'innocent victims' (ibid., p.98) while 'whenever the mother was mentioned allusion was made to "vice"'. 'The language of the report was "The female is most to blame"' (Henry Philpotts, Bishop of Exeter, House of Lords, Hansard, 1834, 3rd series, vol. 25, cols 586–94, 28 July).

Men were perceived to be at the mercy of unmarried mothers, first, because they deliberately enticed men to have sex with them, and, second, because such women were believed to falsely swear men to be fathers for financial gain, and they were frequently thought to swear the richest men of the parish to be the putative father in order to secure a higher maintenance payment (Commissioners, 1971, pp.113A, 94, 98). Such claims were firmly denied in evidence provided to the 1844 Commission of Inquiry for South Wales into the Welsh Rebecca Riots (in Henriques, 1967, p.118, footnote). Third, it was believed, women took advantage of men's fear of being imprisoned by 'forcing' them to marry them (although parish officials played a large part in this).

5.3 Absence of male responsibility

Significantly, fatherhood is not presented as a responsibility which men should or even would want to embrace positively. Instead, it is presented as something foisted on men; as something they would not, and should not have to, choose. Missing is any explicit expectation that men should be financially responsible. Indeed, the Commissioners recommended that mothers should be held solely responsible for the support of their illegitimate children (18th Remedial Recommendation, Commissioners, 1971, p.196) and this was enacted in the 1834 Act. So that even when the Reports acknowledged that men failed to fulfil their legal financial responsibilities and often absconded, they were not presented in a negative light in the main report, nor were the men involved criticized. Men's non-payment of maintenance is taken for granted as an inevitable, if unsatisfactory, state of affairs.

This absence of responsibility is achieved through the positioning of men within the discourse of bastardy in a number of ways. The first is the absence of a discourse of male responsibility for their sexuality. This is reinforced by presenting men as the unfortunate victims of female sexuality. These two aspects combine to produce a notion of men's blamelessness for the rising costs of illegitimacy and increasing numbers of illegitimate children. Constituting men as the blameless party is operationalized through the language used to speak of men and through the absence of a moral discourse when speaking of them.

The language does not utilize discursive strategies which present men's behaviour as immoral, predatory or as undeserving. Whilst men's behaviour is not entirely condoned, condemnation is rare. The absolving of males from responsibility for their illegitimate offspring is further compounded by the presentation of bastardy as a burden to men and as profitable for women. Thus, '[t]o the men indeed it is a *burthen*' (Main Report, Commissioners, 1971, p.93; emphasis added) and 'often *grieviously unfair*' (Checkland and Checkland, 1974, p.36; emphasis added).

Finally, in suggesting that women falsely accused men of being the fathers of their children, it was men who were believed over women. This was so even when the evidence from the Reports showed that men were often the instigators or at least equal conspirators (see Captain Chapman quoted in Main Report, Commissioners, 1971, p.94). The Commissioners were reluctant to accept that two parties, the man and the woman, were involved in producing an illegitimate child.

Thus, women were presented as being guilty of perjury and characterized in ways which distinguished them from the men who were party to illegitimacy. Through this process of differentiation it was possible to treat the parties differently and different rights, responsibilities and punishments could be established, determined and allocated. Men, therefore, were not held to account whilst women were held responsible for both their own and men's sexuality.

5.4 Immorality and unmarried motherhood

The processes of differentiation and negative representation were strengthened by the association of unmarried mothers with immorality in the Reports. Claims are made that '[t]he charge of bastardies is accompanied by a very large share of mischievous and immoral consequences. Such mothers were presented as sexually immoral and lying, selfishly concerned with securing their own financial gain and as bad mothers' (see Mr Power's evidence, Commissioners, 1971, p.96 and Mr Wilson, Sunderland, Appendix A, ibid., p.136). Whilst it was common during this period to see fears being expressed about the morality of the labouring classes, it was women, and unmarried mothers in particular, who were specifically identified in the Reports.

Women were both immoral and guilty of exercising their immorality in ways which, with the support of the law, disadvantaged men. In short, in the eyes of the Commissioners the law gave women power, through their sexuality, over men; and the exercise of that power had a detrimental and undesired effect on women.

5.5   Deserving and undeserving recipients of relief

In the Reports the distinction between deserving and undeserving recipients of relief is repeatedly emphasized. In the Bastardy sections the Commissioners compared unmarried mothers with other recipients of relief, such as widows and the elderly, who were accepted as having an unquestioned and earned right to relief. Unmarried mothers were described as 'defrauding of the relief of the impotent and aged, *true poor of the same parish*' (Commissioners, 1971, p.92; emphasis in original) and as living in the lap of luxury in comparison to their neighbours, particularly in relation to widows. '[S]o the sum the woman receives with the whole of her children, and what the mother can earn, enables them to live as comfortably, or indeed more so, than most families in the neighbourhood' (ibid., p.95). Widows possessed an unquestionable right to poor relief by virtue of having been married – 'this was one of the many premiums on marriage' (ibid., p.196). After all, the 'unmarried mother had voluntarily put herself into the situation of the widow: she has voluntarily become a mother, without procuring for herself and her child the assistance of a husband and father' (George Taylor's Report, Commissioners, 1971, p.128). In contrast the unmarried mother earned her 'right' to poor relief through illicit intercourse. Enshrined in this is the notion of women's dependency on men, as other writers have noted (Thane, 1978; Ginsburg, 1979, pp.79–87) along with the privileging and normalization of marriage.

This device of comparing unmarried mothers against others and singling them out as undeserving of relief on the basis of their sexual behaviour and marriage status was employed to stigmatize them as a group and to punish them by marking them out as not eligible for relief. Through this discursive process their sexual behaviour became the means by which it was possible to deny them poor relief. In practice, post-1834, this meant that unmarried mothers were given poor relief but only through the workhouse. Here, it can be seen how ideas about appropriate and acceptable sexuality both inform eligibility and access to welfare and influence the *type* of welfare received.

Much of the discussion so far has been concerned with the discursive aspects of the Report and Act as they concerned unmarried mothers. Whilst it is difficult to determine how the Act impacted on the experiences of unmarried mothers as few, if any, personal accounts exist, through using a variety of sources it is possible to suggest how unmarried mothers were categorized and treated by welfare agencies. Evidence from the Webbs (Webb and Webb, 1910, pp.36–42) suggests that unmarried mothers were unlikely to receive poor relief except through the workhouse. Once in the workhouse a woman was further categorized as able-bodied or sick, a nursing mother or according to 'whether or not she was of "good character" or "dissolute and disorderly habits" or the mother of an illegitimate child' (Webb and Webb, 1910, p.43). Categorization had material effects for the women as it determined their diet, employment and any freedom which they might experience. An examination of Poor Law official circulars for the period 1840–51 (Poor Law Commission, 1840–1851) also supports the idea that unmarried women with children were treated punitively and harshly.

However, it should not be assumed that once in the workhouse women meekly accepted their position. There are accounts of women 'inmates' rioting and fighting and of attacking workhouse staff (see for example 'Workhouse sketches' (1861) published in The *Macmillan Magazine*). Some accounts present this as a case of 'women behaving badly' (see Longmate, 1974, p.162), but these actions could equally be interpreted as acts of resistance.

6 Constituting poverty and sexuality: the discourse of bastardy

The discourse of bastardy reveals concerns about wider issues of power and sexuality in society. For example, the discourse can be seen as a statement of the double standard of sexual morality, establishing men's freedom and right to exercise their sexuality without responsibility while regulating and controlling women's sexuality, defining their responsibilities and diminishing their rights.

The new discourse of bastardy can also tell us something about the gendered social relations of British society in the 1830s. I suggested above that the Commissioners were particularly troubled that the bastardy laws afforded women power over men. Whether this was the case or not does not concern us here; what is important is that subsequent legislation was based on the assumption that the bastardy laws gave women an unwarranted power over men. The discourse can, therefore, also be read as an expression of fears that society was under threat and being undermined by the existing bastardy laws and what we see in the Commissioners' concerns is a desire/attempt to reaffirm and reassert, albeit in new ways, a gender economy which had assumed the position of dominance. Thus, the discourse can also be understood as a means through which relatively new middle-class values impacted on working-class women. It also reveals something about the ways in which this occurred.

By the 1830s the middle-class ideal of the family had become firmly embedded in dominant English culture as the only proper and correct way to live (Hall, 1992, p.91). The evangelicalism of the period demanded a new national moralism aimed initially at the aristocracy but after the French Revolution this was extended to 'putting the houses of the poor in order' (Weeks, 1989, Ch. 2; Hall, 1992, p.79).

Central to achieving this new morality was the home, marriage and
the family, and women had a key role to play as 'moral regenerators
of the nation' (Hall, 1992, p.85). Hall identifies this as a part of an
ideology of domesticity through which ideas about appropriate
morality, social and sexual roles, and family were played. The symbolic significance of sexuality to this nineteenth-century ideology has
been identified by, for example, Weeks (1989) and Mort (1987). What
has been less apparent is the significance of the 1834 New Poor Law
and related reports in imposing middle-class values of female
sexuality, family and marriage on poor women. This is not to suggest
that working-class men and women indiscriminately adopted or even
accepted middle-class values. They did not, and thus struggles
against a particular gender order were also part of class struggle.

There was widespread hostility and opposition to the 1834 New
Poor Law, which was 'rejected by working people as a thoroughly
heartless attack on the comfort, dignity and customary rights of the
poor' (Dinwiddy, 1986, p.72). According to Henriques (1967) the
Bastardy Clauses were the most unpopular part of the 1834 Act.
Protests focusing specifically on the provisions contained in the
Clauses criticized them for dealing with women unfairly, operating a
dual standard of morality and for allowing men to seduce women
with impunity (see Henriques, 1967, p.112; 1979, cols 52–8; Brundage,
1978, p.538; Taylor, 1983, pp.201–4; Rendall, 1985, p.197). Indeed, the
Bastardy Clauses were also hotly debated in the House of Lords (see
Hansard, 1834, 3rd series, vol.25, cols 586–94, 28 July) and were only
just approved, by 93 votes to 82 (ibid., pp.1096–7, 8 August).

Other writers (Weeks, 1989; Mort, 1987) have identified how contemporary nineteenth-century concerns about morality and sexuality
can be interpreted as fears about the uncertainty, changing social
relations and changing social world that resulted from urbanization,
industrialization and rapid population growth. To middle-class
proto-Victorian society women's immorality symbolized wider social
ills and was emblematic of the breakdown of national morality and
the social order as a whole. Central to a new-found middle-class
morality were women as torch-bearers of both men's and the nation's
morality. Concerns about national morality and the possible collapse
of society were fuelled by fears about the deterioration of society as a
result of the increasing immorality of the labouring classes: this could
be witnessed in profligate families, population growth, overcrowd-
ing, dirt, disease and squalor and, of course, illegitimacy.

In mapping out the discourse we can discern the operation of
power, in the form of all-male Commissioners and others constructing
a selective, if not contested, 'truth' about women through the discourse of bastardy. Through this discourse a process of definition was
also enacted. Thus, single pregnant women and unmarried mothers
became defined, identified and characterized through social policy.

The poverty discourse of 1834 constituted men as breadwinners (Dean, 1991, p.96). In re-analysing this discourse, and specifically the discourse of bastardy, through the lens of sexuality we can see that unmarried mothers were constituted not only as dependent on men, but also as a social problem, sexually immoral and as dangerous and therefore undeserving of poor relief. The positioning of unmarried mothers, discursively at least, as 'other', constituted married motherhood as the norm of what was seen as appropriate and acceptable moral and sexual behaviour. Appropriate and acceptable sexuality was presented as either sexual relations within an economically viable marriage or celibacy until an economically viable marriage was possible. This became the 'norm' by which all women would be measured and judged to be moral or immoral, to be deserving, or undeserving, of poor relief. Therefore, for women their rights and respectability could only be successfully gained through a financially secure marriage or through celibacy. Unacceptable moral/sexual behaviour was to be punished, and eligibility to relief as a right denied. The influence of this discourse can be seen in later responses to unmarried motherhood right through to the early 1990s. Indeed, Carol Smart (1992, p.23) identifies the nineteenth century as a highpoint in the historic condemnation of unmarried mothers.

This has left us with a legacy of single unmarried mothers as stigmatized. This research shows that social policy played a significant role in this process. It has also left us with a legacy of differentiated gendered rights and responsibilities (see Williams, 1998). Men have not, until recently at least, tended to be the focus of social policy in this area. This is in part due to the way that male and female sexuality have traditionally been perceived and the operation of the sexual double standard.

6.1   What does it tell us about poverty?

Analysing the 1834 NPL and related Reports through the lens of sexuality reveals at least three important features, the first of which supports previous critiques (Novak, 1988; Ditch, 1991) that poverty discourses can be understood as a means of categorizing the poor into deserving with rights (the elderly, widows) and undeserving with duties and responsibilities. The second is that welfare discourses interact with and utilize other dominant discourses in society and that this works, in this example at least, to further categorize and divide the poor into deserving and undeserving. The research illustrates that the constitution of welfare subjects is the outcome of the interaction of multiple discourses which, whilst clearly powerful and influential, often bear little resemblance to individual experiences and 'realities'.

Third, this analysis also illustrates that poverty discourses were concerned with much more than simply poverty understood as insufficient material resources. Not only were other dominant discourses 'played through' poverty discourses but poverty discourses played a part in constituting those other dominant discourses. In this case ideas and discourses about sexuality, morality, gender relations, the family and marriage were embedded in poverty discourses. Correspondingly, poverty discourses became a means by which appropriate sexuality, gender relations, morality, the family and marriage were spoken about. This process, albeit historically specific, is also evident in contemporary analyses of social policy, as in the claim that teenage mothers deliberately became pregnant in order to obtain benefits and council housing (*Guardian*, 23 November 1988; Roseneil and Mann, 1996). As I have argued elsewhere (Carabine, 1996a), it is through social policy that sexuality is (in part) produced, but this is not a one-way process because what we know to be the 'truths' or knowledges of sexuality also constitute social policy in a specific way, a way which reflects the existing power/knowledge relations centred on sexuality, as well as other discourses, such as 'race', gender, politics and welfarism. Here, the intersecting axis of poverty discourses with sexuality has been highlighted, but further research would reveal other articulations with constructions of social order, not only in terms of gender, but class and, of course, 'race', ethnicity and nationality. What this analysis of the 1834 New Poor Law suggests is that in order to fully understand social policy discourses – their operation and their effects – we need also to look at their intersection with other dominant discourses in society.

References

Bland, L. (1983) '"Cleansing the portals of life": the venereal disease campaign in the early twentieth century', in Langan, M. and Schwarz, B. (eds) *Crisis in the British State, 1880–1930*, London, Hutchinson.

British Parliamentary Papers (various volumes and dates) *The Poor Laws*, Shannon, Ireland, Irish University Press.

Brundage, A. (1978) *The Making of the New Poor Law: The Politics of Inquiry, Enactment, and Implementation, 1832–1839*, New Brunswick, NJ, Rutgers University Press.

Carabine, J. (1992) 'Constructing women: women's sexuality and social policy', *Critical Social Policy*, Summer, 34, pp.24–37.

Carabine, J. (1995) 'Sexuality, politics and policy-making', in Wilson, A. (ed.) *A Simple Matter of Justice*, London, Cassell, pp.91–109.

Carabine, J. (1996a) 'Heterosexuality and social policy', in Richardson, D. (ed.) *Theorizing Heterosexuality*, Milton Keynes, Open University Press.

Carabine, J. (1996b) 'A straight playing field or queering the pitch? Centring sexuality in social policy', *Feminist Review*, 54, pp.31–64.

Checkland, S.G. and Checkand, E.O.A. (eds) (1974) *The Poor Law Report of 1834*, Harmondsworth, Pelican.

Clark, A. (1995) *The Struggle for the Breeches: Gender and the Making of the British Working Class*, London, Rivers Oram.

Dean, M. (1991) *The Constitution of Poverty: Toward a Genealogy of Liberal Governance*, London, Routledge.

Dinwiddy, J. (1986) *From Luddism to the First Reform Bill: Reform in England, 1810–1832*, Oxford, Blackwell.

Ditch, J. (1991) 'The undeserving poor: unemployed people, then and now', in Loney, M., Bocock, R., Clarke, J., Cochrane, A., Graham, P. and Wilson, M. (eds) *The State or the Market: Politics and Welfare in Contemporary Britain*, London, Sage.

Foucault, M. (1990) *The History of Sexuality, Volume 1: An Introduction* (trans. Robert Hurley), New York, Vintage Books. (First published in French, 1976; this translation first published 1978, Random House.)

Foucault M. (1991) *Discipline and Punish: The Birth of the Prison* (trans. Alan Sheridan), Harmondsworth, Penguin. (This translation originally published, 1977, London, Allen Lane.)

Ginsburg, N. (1979) *Class, Capital and Social Policy*, Basingstoke, Macmillan.

Hall, C. (1992) *White, Male, and Middle Class: Explorations in Feminism and History*, Cambridge, Polity Press.

Hansard Parliamentary Debates (1834) 3rd Series, volumes XXV, XXVI, London, Hansard.

Henriques, U.R.Q. (1967) 'Bastardy and the New Poor Law', *Past and Present*, 37, pp.103–29.

Henriques, U.R.Q. (1979) *Before the Welfare State: Social Administration in Early Industrial Britain*, London, Longman.

Hitchcock, T. (1997) *English Sexualities, 1700–1800*, Basingstoke, Macmillan.

Laqueur, T. (1993) 'Sex and desire in the Industrial Revolution', in O'Brien, P. and Quinault, R. (eds) *The Industrial Revolution and British Society*, Cambridge, Cambridge University Press.

Laslett, P. (1977) *Family Life and Illicit Love in Earlier Generations: Essays in Historical Sociology*, Cambridge, Cambridge University Press.

Longmate, N. (1974) *The Workhouse*, London, Temple-Smith.

Marshall, D. (1969) *The English Poor Law in the Eighteenth Century: A Study of Social and Administrative History*, London, Routledge, Kegan & Paul (first published 1926).

Mort, F. (1987) *Dangerous Sexualities: Medico-moral Politics in England since 1830*, London, Routledge & Kegan Paul.

Novak, T. (1988) *Poverty and the State*, Milton Keynes, Open University Press.

Perkins, J. (1989) *Women and Marriage in Nineteenth-century England*, London, Routledge.

Poor Law Commission (1840–51) *Official Circulars of Public Documents and Information*, New York, Augustus M. Kelly, 1970, vols VII–X.

Poovey, M. (1989) *Uneven Developments: The Ideological Work of Gender in Mid-Victorian England*, London, Virago.

Rendall, J. (1985) *The Origins of Modern Feminism: Women in Britain, France and the United States, 1780–1860*, Basingstoke, Macmillan.

Report from His Majesty's Commissioners on the Administration and Practical Operation of the Poor Laws with Appendix (A) Part 1: *Reports from Assistant Commissioners and Indices* (1834) in British Parliamentary Papers (1971) *Poor Laws*, vol. 8, Shannon, Ireland, Irish University Press.

Roseneil, S. and Mann, K. (1996) 'Unpalatable choices and inadequate families: lone mothers and the underclass debate', in Bortolaia Silva, E. (ed.) *Good Enough Mothering? Feminist Perspectives on Lone Mothering*, London, Routledge, pp.191–210.

Smart, C. (ed.) (1992) *Regulating Womanhood: Historical Essays on Marriage, Motherhood and Sexuality*, London, Routledge.

Taylor, B. (1983) *Eve and the New Jerusalem: Socialism and Feminism in the Nineteenth Century*, London, Virago.

Thane, P. (1978) 'Women and the Poor Law in Victorian and Edwardian England', *History Workshop*, 6, pp.29–51.

Webb, S. and Webb, B. (1910) *English Poor Law Policy*, London, Longmans, Green and Co.

Weeks, J. (1989) *Sex, Politics and Society: The Regulation of Sexuality since 1800*, London, Longman (first published 1981).

Williams, F. (1998) 'Troubled masculinities in social policy discourses: fatherhood', in Popay, J., Hearn, J. and Edwards, J. (eds) *Men, Gender Divisions and Welfare*, London, Routledge, pp.63–100.

6

Constructing Gendered and Racialized Identities: Young Men, Masculinities and Educational Policy

Ann Phoenix

'Definitions of children's needs in policy are always mediated by adults – more specifically by professional "experts". Parents or other adult carers are asked to speak on children's behalf.' (Saraga, 1998, p.139)

The topic of men and the associated concept of 'masculinity' are now, just about, on political and policy agendas. Of course in many ways this is not new; it is just that now politicians, policy-makers, social policy managers, and increasingly practitioners are naming men and masculinities as an object of concern. This might be as something that needs to be attended to, to be dealt with, to be treated as a problem, to be changed, to be defended, or even just to be talked about and debated. (Hearn, 1998, p.37)

1 Introduction

Much social policy is concerned with macrosocial analyses of welfare settlements. This chapter considers a more microsocial issue: boys' educational 'under-performance'. At the microsocial level, it is generally easier to see how policy definitions construct not only specific ways of understanding social problems, but also their associated subject positions and solutions. In doing so, those policies frequently claim to be addressing the needs of particular subjects while taking little account of the subjects' constructions of self and their social positioning. This is perhaps especially clear when children and young people are the subjects of policies since their 'needs' are frequently decided with little reference to their own views (Alderson, 1993; Saraga, 1998; Woodhead, 1997). Policies for children thus demonstrate the discursive constructions of children and childhood current at the time of enactment of legislation or, more locally, the devising of practices.

There is currently a great deal of cross-disciplinary interest in researching and theorizing children as active agents rather than passive objects of socialization (for example, Brannen and O'Brien, 1995, 1996; Mayall, 1999; James and Prout, 1997). In social policy, some of that interest has been fuelled by an engagement with the possibilities for new ways of thinking, heralded by the Children Act 1989 and by increasing interest in the United Nations Convention on the Rights of the Child (see Chapter 7 this volume). Despite this emergent concern with children as agents, much work on childhood and child development continues to treat children as largely undifferentiated. Yet it has been apparent, at least since the 1930s, that the processes of racialization, gendering and social class differentiation produce specific childhoods for children positioned differently within the social formation (see, for example, Clark and Clark, 1939, 1947). Recent research evidence demonstrates that children are differentially constructed and treated by adults on the basis of 'race', gender and social class (Gillborn, 1995; Ogilvy et al., 1990, 1992; Sonuga-Barke et al., 1993; Walkerdine, 1997; Walkerdine and Lucey, 1989). An understanding of children's and young people's agency must, therefore, include analyses of differences among them. Thus, while gender and 'race' are absent from many policy statements on children and young people, both are central to the construction of children as subjects of social policy. The area of boys' educational performance simultaneously renders both explicit, since masculinities are always racialized and expressed through a social class position (Back, 1996; Edley and Wetherell, 1995; Westwood, 1990) as well as through personal narratives.

This chapter aims to consider some of the contradictions that arise from the neglect of children's and young people's perspectives in educational policy. On the one hand, gender-, colour- and class-'blind' approaches have implicitly constructed the 'normal' child as white, middle-class and a boy (Walkerdine, 1988). On the other hand, attempts to remedy what are constructed as problems such as boys' educational 'underachievement' necessarily focus explicitly on boys. While some of these attempts do treat boys as gendered and gender as relational (for example Connell, 1996; Epstein et al., 1998; Mac an Ghaill, 1994; Salisbury and Jackson, 1996), few treat them as reflexive subjects who contribute to the construction of their own positioning.

This chapter argues that 'colour-blind' approaches and those which neglect children and young people's agency reproduce static and essentialist notions of children, 'race', ethnicity and gender which lead to piecemeal changes. For example, some schools and educational authorities have shifted from a focus on girls' educational 'underachievement' in comparison with boys to a concern with boys' 'underachievement' in comparison with girls without apparently questioning whether the comparisons themselves need to be interrogated. In addition, such approaches have assumed that 'race' and ethnicity are concepts relevant only to minority ethnic groups. The first part of this chapter briefly discusses current anxieties about boys' educational 'underachievement'. It then uses boys' accounts to demonstrate the importance of understanding boys' own investment in racialized, masculine identities and the difficulties in engagement with the educational process that this may pose for some. Such difficulties cannot be wished away simply by introducing changes to educational structures or delivery since they are a pervasive way in which boys themselves constitute racialized masculinities.

2 Crisis? What crisis?

The study of boys and masculinities is not new. Indeed, in 1978 McRobbie and Gaber (reprinted in McRobbie, 1991) argued that young women were generally omitted from studies which claimed to be of youth but were really of young men. Knowledge produced about young men was treated as if it pertained to all young people while implicitly being about masculinity. McRobbie (1991) and Griffin (1985) both conducted landmark studies of young women, designed to provide understandings of girls comparable to that about boys provided by Willis' (1977) study of white, working-class boys making the transition from school to work. However, one of the marked social changes in recent years has been a shift in the pronouncements made about boys and masculinities. A decade ago it was taken for granted that, even if specific groups of boys and young men were considered problematic (for example, working-class and/or black boys), this was neither a general problem nor a problem of masculinities. It is now difficult for people in Britain to fail to notice the newspaper articles, television programmes, research studies, government pronouncements and statements from educationists about problems with boys. The problems catalogued tend to centre on education, but also relate to issues of violence, criminality, uncertainties over relationships and identities, sexuality, employment and suicide.

Concerns have been voiced in many countries about figures that indicate that girls are now gaining more qualifications than boys (including in Australia, some Caribbean countries, Germany, Japan, New Zealand, Scandinavia, the United Kingdom, and the United States). Two decades ago, it was girls' educational performance which was more likely to be discussed as cause for concern in many of these countries – particularly among feminist educationists (Epstein et al., 1998). Suggested explanations for this change include:

- biological differences as a result of evolutionary psychology (Kenrick and Trost, 1993; Plomin, 1994);
- that girls' and women's successes in education and employment have been detrimental to boys (Weiner et al., 1997);
- that feminism has indirectly led to repression of boys' natural tendencies to boisterousness etc. in schools. According to this argument, in the light of changing economic circumstances where boys can no longer hope to get 'traditional men's jobs' in which they can demonstrate their masculinity it is important that this constraint be removed (Kryger, 1998);
- the absence of adult male role models in the classroom (Pollack, 1998);
- coursework-based curricula that privilege girls' preferred ways of working (Phillips, 1993);
- the higher incidence of low self-esteem amongst boys than girls (Katz and Buchanan, 1999);
- that boys' behaviour is simply problematic and needs to be changed (Jackson, 1998; Salmon, 1998);
- gendered practices that need to be interrogated as relational, contradictory and multiple in order to change educational practices productively for all students. We currently lack – but need – complex understandings of what it means to 'do boy' in specific contexts (Connell, 1996; Davies, 1997).

There is now a substantial literature which addresses the ways in which social problems are socially constructed rather than naturally arising (for instance, Seidman and Rappaport, 1986); the social problem of the 'underachievement' of boys is no exception. Indeed, there is currently some concern about the social construction of this issue on the part of feminist educators who have pointed to some critical

issues which arise from this debate. Thus selective choices of educational statistics for comparison; neglect of the fact that working-
class and black boys have always done badly, while the most
privileged boys have always done well; the romanticization of boyhood; the implicit blaming of girls, women teachers and feminists
and neglect of the fact that half of all girls in Britain do *not* gain five
grades A–C at GCSE have all been cited as difficulties in the social
construction of the underachievement of boys (Epstein et al., 1998;
Reed, 1999; Skelton, 1998; Yates, 1997).

In this context, it is salutary to remember that it has traditionally
been taken for granted that boys naturally do better educationally
than girls and that evidence which challenges this is easily over-
looked or reconstructed as evidence that girls lack innate ability
(Walkerdine, 1997):

> In his 1693 educational treatise *Some Thoughts Concerning Education* John
> Locke too was addressing boys' underachievements. He was concerned by
> young gentlemen's failure to master Latin despite spending years studying
> it. Locke attributed this failure to the practice, current at the time, of
> teaching Latin by grammar rules. By contrast, he noted, little girls learned
> French rapidly and successfully just by 'prattling' it with their governesses.
> It is not because Locke wanted to remark on little girls' cleverness that he
> mentioned their success at French. Rather, he meant his remarks to show
> just how easy it was to learn languages by the conversational method, the
> method he wanted to promote (against contemporary opinion) to teach
> boys Latin. (Cohen, 1998, p.21)

Two points arise from these relational constructions of girls and
boys. First, as in Locke's formulation, many still reduce the solution
to problems of boys' educational 'underattainment' to methods of
teaching. Second, the implicit assumption that there is a gendered
intellectual hierarchy in which boys should *naturally* do well still
affects teachers' perceptions of girls and boys. Valerie Walkerdine's
(1988) work on children learning maths indicates that many teachers
considered that girls only did well because they worked hard. Even if
boys were not doing so well, they were constructed as naturally
talented. Walkerdine argues that in teachers' constructions, the
natural child is implicitly a boy, active and rebellious, so that he does
not sit and learn quietly but is not sufficiently talented to succeed in
any other way. At the level of classroom practices and educational
policy, therefore, 'child-centred pedagogy' was actually 'boy-centred
pedagogy'. Michele Cohen (1998) terms this 'a habit of healthy
idleness', which is valorized by some teachers.

This implicit gendering of childhood is central to the understanding of gender and attainment and to disrupting the old certainties
that have continued, for centuries, to underpin educational policy

and practices. In addition it is crucial to consider the gendered subject positions that boys and girls occupy and the power relations associated with them in order to comprehend the constitution of gendered differences and boys' investments in particular versions of masculinity. Carmen Luke (1996) suggests that young women and young men are 'pedagogically formed', continually learning how to 'make the (gendered) self' in everyday life. The sections which follow use boys' narratives of masculinities in order to analyse the ways in which the gendered subject positions they occupy locate them in relation to educational attainment as well as differences between boys in their 'performances' of masculinities. Such differences potentially allow spaces for intervention and change in social policy and practices.

3 The intersection of popular/hegemonic masculinities and education for 11–14-year-old boys in London schools

This section uses preliminary data derived from qualitative analyses of interviews conducted with seventy-eight 11–14-year-old boys from different ethnic and social class backgrounds in twelve London schools. The interviews comprise part of a study on the narrative constructions of masculine identities among boys.[1]

3.1 Academic work as antithetical to popular/ hegemonic masculinity

Connell (1987, 1995) theorizes masculinity as an active project which is produced from both a personal trajectory and the social resources available. It is relational in a double sense in that it is constructed in relation to other men as well as in relation to women, and power relations are an integral part of its construction. Connell identifies five types of masculinity:

- hegemonic – which is the form of masculinity which comes to dominate others or to be seen as ideal;
- marginal – where men do not meet the hegemonic ideal, but are not persecuted or challenged;
- complicit – where men cannot fit the hegemonic ideal, but do not challenge it, and
- subordinate (e.g. gay men).

According to Connell, all men benefit from hegemonic masculinity, despite the fact that few can be said to fit into it. This is because society is organized so that men gain 'the patriarchal dividend'. For this reason, many men aspire to the hegemonic ideal and it is important to the fantasy lives of many, although it is often deliberately parodied, critiqued or undercut.

While Connell's formulation has been enormously helpful to those studying masculinities, the notion of hegemonic masculinity has recently been subjected to critique. In practice, it proves to be too imprecise to apply easily, particularly since it is not embodied by many (or any) men (Donaldson, 1993). This is partly because there is currently a plurality of hegemonic models (for example, both macho and 'new' men can be hegemonic: see Cornwall and Lindisfarne, 1994). Despite these problems, the notion of 'hegemonic' masculinity is useful to the understanding of the ways in which the boys, in the study which informs this chapter, agreed on the characteristics which were taken for granted as ideally masculine. The term 'popular/hegemonic' indicates this commonsense acceptance of what dominant masculinity looked like for the boys (i.e. which forms had cultural authority), while leaving open the possibility of its multiplicity and that boys could resist being positioned within it.

The boys interviewed in the study all produced accounts which identified the characteristics of popular/hegemonic masculinities. These constructions included being: different to girls (who were generally constructed in essentialist terms as the opposite of boys); good at sport, particularly football; 'hard'; attractive, cool and not focused on schoolwork:

Q: What kind of things make boys popular in your school?

Luke: Um . . . amongst boys or amongst girls or in general? [Q: Both really], um . . . amongst the people who are are like . . . *hardest*, or . . . who girls think or boys think are like *attractive* and things like that um . . . like if someone's *really good at football*, then people will think you're a really good footballer and they probably um . . . yeah that kind of thing people like . . . being the *best person*, the *best fighter* or *best runner*, things like that. [Emphasis added]

Q: So it's all tied up with sport then? Sporting ability and also hardness as well?

Luke: Yeah that kind of thing.

(*14-year-old white boy*)

Anil: We just all play basketball together . . . and most of the ones the ones at the top they play football . . . and . . . the bottom ones just stay [*laughter*] stay in the classroom and do homework . . . and play cards or something.

(*14-year-old Asian boy*)

Q: Talking about popularity I wondered how you described boys that are popular – are they good at particular things or are they outgoing?

Thomas: Umm [*hesitant*] . . . some people are popular, some like me don't really have any enemies because they stay out of things whenever there is an argument, they don't take sides but if they have to they just say I don't want to. Other people are *good at football* and *good at sports*, some people are *actually clever* and some people know how to *answer back* that's why they always answer back to the teacher and *try and look cool*, that's what popular people usually do. Some are just popular because they *are clever and aren't shy*. [Emphasis added]
(12-year-old white boy)

In most of the boys' accounts, it was clear that being 'clever' was antithetical to being popular. This fits with Mac an Ghaill's (1994) typification of 'Academic Achievers' who were considered effeminate by boys and teachers alike.

Q: Are some boys particularly popular? How do they get to be popular?
Nathan: Yeah, some are, I don't really know why, I'm not sure really. One boy's popular and he's good at football.
Q: Are there any other things that make boys popular?
Nathan: No not really, if they're good at something.
Q: What about if you are good at schoolwork, do you become popular?
Nathan: No, I don't think so. Like sport, if you are good at sport you become popular.
(12-year-old white boy)

Most boys did not consider themselves to possess the characteristics of popular/hegemonic masculinity. Judith Butler's notion of gender as performative is useful here. Butler (1990, 1995) suggests that gendered identities are created partly through gendered 'performance' (together with the suppression of possibilities which are not performed). The boys in this study were differentiated in terms of whether or not they performed any of the characteristics associated with popular/hegemonic masculinities. Regardless of whether or not they admired such characteristics, boys compared themselves with the 'hegemonic ideal' and justified their 'non-hegemonic' status in a variety of ways. However, although some boys were able to see that others were 'performing' popular/hegemonic masculinity, this did not allow them to recognize that hegemonic masculinity is itself illusory (unlike, for example, the young women described by Ussher, 1997). Instead, they continued to assume that there was a 'real', hegemonic masculinity, but that it was out of reach of most boys. Looking down on boys they saw as 'pretending' allowed them to continue 'jockeying for position' (Edley and Wetherell, 1997) in relation to hegemonic masculinities, while denying other boys' claims to hegemony. Very few boys reported themselves, or were reported, to be both popular and obviously good at schoolwork.

From their accounts, it is clear that the very constitution of popular/hegemonic masculinities positioned boys in contradictory ways in relation to schoolwork and that these positionings would not be amenable to change simply by changing educational policy. Boys' subjective positioning with regard to masculinity would also require to be addressed.

3.2   The racialization of popular/hegemonic masculinity

Studies of young men in multi-ethnic societies make it clear that masculinities are racialized. For example, research with British young people suggests that black young men of African-Caribbean descent are viewed in some ways as 'super-masculine'. They are constructed as possessing the attributes that are considered to be most masculine: toughness and authentically male style in talk and dress. Paradoxically, while they are feared and discriminated against because of those features, they are also respected, admired and gain power through taking on characteristics which militate against good classroom performance (Mac an Ghaill, 1988; Back, 1996). In the US context, Majors and Billson (1992) refer to this as 'cool pose' – an aggressive assertion of masculinity among African-American men that allows control, inner strength, stability and confidence in the face of adverse social, political and economic conditions. 'Cool pose' fits many of the characteristics associated with popular/hegemonic masculinity and is much admired by white and black men. It does, however, impose costs on those black boys and men who cannot deal with it as simply performance, but fear that others might consider that they do not really possess it. These costs lie in the suppression of motivation to learn and of emotional expressiveness.

Tony Sewell (1997) found that many of the 15-year-old black boys he studied were both positioned by others, and positioned themselves, as superior to white and Asian students in terms of their sexual attractiveness, style, creativity and 'hardness'. They were, however, contradictorily positioned.

> Black boys are Angels and Devils in British (and American) schools. They are heroes of a street fashion culture that dominates most of our inner cities. On the other hand they experience a disproportionate amount of punishment in our schools compared to all other groupings . . . This experience of being the darling of popular youth sub-culture and the sinner in the classroom has led to the formation of a range of behaviours. How do African-Caribbean boys in particular respond in a school that sees them as sexy and as sexually threatening? These responses are what I call masculinities. They are linked to how the boys perceive themselves as males and how others perceive them. (Sewell, 1997, p.ix)

In Sewell's study, boys' accounts indicated that masculinities were racialized in two ways: through differential treatment by, for example, teachers; and because black, white and Asian boys were considered to be differentially positioned in terms of 'hegemonic' masculinity.

In the study reported here, white, black and Asian boys particularly attributed the characteristics of popular/hegemonic masculinity to black boys. The following example is notable not only for the racialization of black boys as popular, but for the differential racialization of Asian boys as not popular – a racialization that was common among the boys in both the study I undertook with Frosh and Patman and Sewell's [1997] study.

> *Des*: Don't know, I think the black boys are more popular.
> *Q*: Are they?
> *Des*: Hmhm.
> *Q*: Why's that?
> *Des*: Don't know it's just . . . black boys seem to get friends easier . . . and they're more popular I suppose.
> *Q*: Yeah . . . they get friends more easy yeah.
> *Des*: Mm . . .
> [. . .]
> *Q*: But I was just wondering cos you said that black boys tend to be quite popular and I was wondering if it was the same with Asian boys . . . What about in your class, are Asian boys as popular as black boys?
> *Des*: No, I shouldn't think so.
> *Jason*: No.
> *Q*: They're not, no.
> *Des*: No.
> *Q*: . . . Why's that?
> *Des*: . . . Don't really know [*sigh*] . . . black boys um Asian boys just go round with . . . like who they want . . . but they don't they don't go out picking, they wait for them come to them . . . they've only got a few friends . . .
> *Q*: They've only got a few friends yeah?
> [. . .]
> *Q*: So you tend to go around – you're more likely to go around with black boys than Asian boys are you?
> *Graham*: . . . Yeah.
> *Q*: Wh-why is that do you think?
> *Graham*: . . . Probably cos like . . . sometimes you think not . . . you ain't you're not really popular an' . . . you know someone who is popular and you go and like try and hang around with them?
> *(Group interview with four white boys from Year 8 [12–13-year olds])*

Educational policies designed to have an impact on boys' educational attainment thus have not only to address boys' constructions of themselves in relation to popular/hegemonic masculinities, but also how these are racialized so that many boys from all ethnic groups desire the signifiers of 'cool pose', which include opposition to industriousness in the classroom.

4   Teachers as amplifying gendered/racialized intersections and reproducing racism

The racialization of masculinities extended to teachers' reactions to boys. That some teachers are racially discriminatory against black students, particularly boys, has been reported in many studies (for example, Connolly, 1995; Mac an Ghaill, 1988; Sewell, 1997; Wright, 1992). In this study, however, much resentment was expressed against teachers for their perceived discrimination against boys in general and – in ethnically mixed schools – particularly black boys.

For some boys, this perception of unfairness bolstered their opposition to teachers and to getting on with their work. It is, of course, difficult to untangle narratives of fairness. It has, for example, repeatedly been found in work on racialization and racisms that white people who produce racist discourses often justify them on the grounds that they have been treated unfairly by or because of black people who, they argue, are really the ones who are prejudiced (e.g. van Dijk, 1993; Cohen, 1997; Hewitt, 1996). There has also long been research which demonstrates how easy it is for teachers and boys to be convinced that girls are getting a disproportionate amount of attention when teachers are giving equal attention to girls and boys (e.g. Spender, 1983; Stanworth, 1983). It may also be the case that current talk of a 'crisis' in boys' attainment leads some well-motivated teachers to deal more firmly with boys than they otherwise would. Such issues are integral to considerations of boys and education since narratives such as those presented below produce an ethos where it is assumed that gendered equality is not encouraged in the mixed classroom, and that women teachers are especially culpable. These discourses, in themselves, have consequences which require attention and analysis.

That these discourses are further reaching than the boys who produce them is illustrated by the fact that, in some mixed gender group interviews, girls also argue that boys are treated unfairly in comparison with girls and that this is particularly the case for black boys. The group interview quoted below is from 13-year-olds attending a mixed private school. The group consisted of two white girls, one black girl, one Asian boy, one black boy and two white boys.[2]

> *Black girl:* . . . A lot of them tend to be sexist as well [*Q*: Sexist are they?] . . .
> They give the boys harder punishments. Like they book them in
> Saturday . . . The girls they would just be 'don't do it again'.
> *Q*: Oh really? Does that happen yeah?
> *Boy:* Yeah. It's like in my maths. Suppose like one boy comes late, for
> registration and um the teacher goes like, come and see me after school
> and like five minutes later the girl could come even later and like she
> doesn't even notice her.

White girl: No, but like the girls like usually apologize and I think the girls are usually more polite to the teachers.

White girl 2: The girls are usually politer. I find in this school that . . .

Black girl[?]: And then one teacher, I'm not going to say which one, they call all the boys by their second names and all the girls by their first names . . .

Q: What do you think of that?

Two girls: It's annoying and also [*inaudible*]. It's stupid. I think it's a way of disciplining them though.

Black boy: My teacher calls everybody else by their first name and he keeps calling me by my second.

Q: Right . . . does he call all the boys by their second name?

Black boy: Some boys who he doesn't like. He calls them by their second, but all the others, he calls by their first.

Q: Right.

Black boy: It's so annoying.

Black boy: Once I got into trouble for talking in class and then the teacher give . . . gave me a detention and then the girl owned up and said it was her talking, but he never gave her a detention.

Black girl: No, but another thing is that does come back into race though, because like you're the only black boy in your class.

Black boy: I know yeah!

[*A lot of joint giggling continues at the start of the next turn.*]

Black girl: No, no seriously, like, no seriously, like certain things like, there's this black boy in my class and there's this other white boy, they're always, like, like they're always in trouble together. The both of them and one of them was allowed to go on a trip, the other wasn't and this one who wasn't was actually black, you know. [*Q*: – Right] – I don't know why that is cos that's sexism and racism put together.

White girl: There's a group, yeah in our class and um they don't do anything and it's like black boys and white boys and some half-castes and there's um one black boy in it and um like they all do the same things, but he's the one who's been threatened to be expelled and stuff, but no one else has. He's the one who has been threatened and all the others haven't and um.

Black girl: The mixed race one has though.

Black boy: Oh yeah, it's like the other boy in my class.

[*All talk together – inaudible.*]

White boy: If a boy does something wrong like once, the teachers hold the reputation and they get, they're like they're the ones that get in trouble all the time, even if it's not them.

Q: Oh do they! Have you got a reputation?

White boy: No.

Q: Have you got a reputation from any teachers? Have you got – sounds as if you've got a reputation with some teachers.

Black boy: What to get in trouble? – Yeah, some teachers just keep blaming it on you. Like there's a new teacher who's just come in, Miss — my form tutor and I always get in trouble even though I don't do nothing. It's like I go to pick up my bag and she says 'sit back in your seat' and when somebody else is talking, I get in trouble for it. [*Q*: Right] Cos I know she doesn't like me, cos once, there was me and there was another boy and we both didn't hand in our homework and she gave me a detention and the boy said he lost it and she believed him, so he was allowed to hand his homework in tomorrow, but I got a detention and I handed mine in tomorrow as well.

Addressing black masculinities as collective responses in a racist culture, Sewell (1997) found that many of the 15-year-old black boys he studied resented being 'othered' by teachers, being perceived as threatening and being picked upon for no other reason they could see than because they were black. However, for some, the knowledge that teachers were afraid of them was a source of power and an incentive to perform in ways which signified threat.

It is difficult to disentangle the factors that start the process of what comes to be reported as unequal treatment. Nonetheless, it is clearly unsatisfactory that boys (and black boys in particular) should feel that they are subjected to discriminatory treatment which, in mixed schools, is also sometimes noted by girls. Teachers, to a large extent, play important parts in what Connell calls 'schools as agents in the making of masculinities' (1996, p.213). A serious consideration of how boys come to occupy their current positions in education requires both more work on teachers' discourses of sexism and racism and recognition that boys are not passively inscribed in the educational process, but are agents within it.

5 Educational policy and changing masculinities

The findings of this study of 11–14-year-old boys indicate that constructions of popular/hegemonic masculinity are pervasive in their accounts. This masculinity is characterized by toughness, footballing prowess and resistance to teachers and education. These characteristics are commonly found in studies of masculinities and are ones that are particularly ascribed to black boys of African-Caribbean descent. Few of the boys in this study considered that they themselves exemplified hegemonic masculinity. However, whether or not they admired such characteristics, boys compared themselves with the 'hegemonic ideal' and justified their 'non-hegemonic' status in a variety of ways. Whichever positions they took in relation to masculinities, therefore, they contributed to a continuing focus on popular/hegemonic masculinity as the cultural ideal within schools. The elements which constitute hegemonic masculinity gave many boys an investment in not being seen to do schoolwork. The converse of this was that those boys who wished to identify with their school's academic values were subject to social disapproval from their male peers. Few managed to be both popular and overtly academically successful.

However, although this has not been the focus of this chapter, boys' constructions of their masculine identities were not unitary. Most boys demonstrated some contradictions in their accounts. These contradictions, together with some boys' dissatisfaction that masculinities are currently constructed as problematic allow some space for disruption of stereotypic masculinities. They also contribute to the dynamism of gendered practices and identities and to tensions around gendered identifications – all of which suggest that there may be possibilities for change in boys' educational performance in ways which do not vilify girls or women for boys' educational performance.

It is important, however, for educational policies to be based on an understanding of many boys' attraction to, desire for, or inability to ignore the characteristics constructed as central to popular/hegemonic masculinities which are counterposed to being seen to work in school classrooms. While changes in boys' educational attainment are dependent on shifts in boys' narratives of masculinity, such changes will also require an environment in which black (and other minority ethnic groups) and white boys are able to feel that they are fairly treated in their schools and not subjected to sexist or racist discrimination. Many of the boys in the study expressed resentment against what they perceive to be teachers' preference for, and favouritism towards, girls. This perceived bias was, in ethnically mixed schools, reported by boys and girls, black and white, to be racialized. Black boys, it was argued, were punished more, and treated less leniently, than were white boys.

These findings demonstrate both the importance of treating boys as active agents in the construction of their educational experiences and as differentiated – both in their positioning in relation to popular/ hegemonic masculinities and in their wider social positioning. It is unproductive to consider changes in educational policies without addressing the intersections of gender, racialization and social class.

Notes

1 ESRC grant number L129251015. The study is jointly conducted with Stephen Frosh and Rob Pattman (who did all the interviews) and is in the Economic and Social Research Council programme on childhood for 5–16-year-olds. It consists of group interviews followed by two individual interviews with each boy.

2 Thanks to Aisha Phoenix for transcribing this passage.

References

Alderson, P. (1993) *Children's Consent to Surgery*, Buckingham, Open University Press.

Back, L. (1996) *New Ethnicities and Urban Culture: Racisms and Multiculture in Young Lives*, London, UCL Press.

Brannen, J. and O'Brien, M. (eds) (1995) *Childhood and Parenthood*, London, Institute of Education.

Brannen, J. and O'Brien, M. (eds) (1996) *Children in Families: Research and Policy*, London, Falmer.

Butler, J. (1990) *Gender Trouble*, Cambridge, Polity Press.

Butler, J. (1995) 'Melancholy gender/refused identification', in Berger, M., Wallis, B. and Watson, S. (eds) *Constructing Masculinity*, London, Routledge.

Clark, K. and Clark, M. (1939) 'The development of consciousness of self and the emergence of racial identity in Negro preschool children', *Journal of Social Psychology*, 10, pp.591–9.

Clark, K. and Clark, M. (1947) 'Racial identification and prejudice in Negro children', in Newcomb, T.M. and Hartley, E.L. (eds) *Readings in Social Psychology*, New York, Henry Holt.

Cohen, M. (1998) '"A habit of healthy idleness": boys' underachievement in historical perspective', in Epstein, D., Elwood, J., Hey, V. and Maw, J. (eds) (1998) *Failing Boys? Issues in Gender and Achievement*, Buckingham, Open University Press.

Cohen, P. (1997) *Rethinking the Youth Question*, London, Routledge.

Connell, R. (1996) 'Teaching the boys: new research on masculinity, and gender strategies for schools', *Teachers College Record*, 98 (2) pp.206–35.

Connell, R.W. (1987) *Gender and Power: Society, the Person and Sexual Politics*, Cambridge, Polity Press.

Connell, R.W. (1995) *Masculinities*, Cambridge, Polity Press.

Connolly, P. (1995) 'Boys will be boys? Racism, sexuality and the construction of masculine identities among infant boys', in Holland, J. and Blair, M. (eds) *Equality and Difference: Debates and Issues in Feminist Research and Pedagogy*, Clevedon, Multilingual Matters.

Cornwall, A. and Lindisfarne, N. (eds) (1994) *Dislocating Masculinity: Comparative Ethnographies*, London, Routledge.

Davies, B. (1997) 'Constructing and deconstructing masculinities through critical literacy', *Gender and Education*, 9 (1), pp.9–30.

Donaldson, M. (1993) 'What is hegemonic masculinity?', *Theory and Society*, 22, pp.643–57.

Edley, N. and Wetherell, M. (1995) *Men in Perspective: Practice, Power and Identity*, London, Prentice-Hall.

Edley, N. and Wetherell, M. (1997) 'Jockeying for position: the construction of masculine identities', *Discourse and Society*, 8 (2), pp.203–17.

Epstein, D., Elwood, J., Hey, V. and Maw, J. (eds) (1998) *Failing Boys? Issues in Gender and Achievement*, Buckingham, Open University Press.

Gillborn, D. (1995) *Racism and Antiracism in Real Schools: Theory, Policy, Practice*, Buckingham, Open University Press.

Griffin, C. (1985) *Typical Girls*, London, Routledge.

Hearn, J. (1998) 'Troubled masculinities in social policy discourses', in Popay, J., Hearn, J. and Edwards, J. (eds) *Men, Gender Divisions and Welfare*, London, Routledge.

Hewitt, R. (1996) *Routes of Racism*, London, Centre for Multicultural Education, Institute of Education.

Jackson, D. (1998) 'Breaking out of the binary trap: boys' underachievement, schooling and gender relations', in Epstein et al. (1998).

James, A. and Prout, A. (eds) (1997) *Constructing and Reconstructing Childhood: Contemporary Issues in the Sociological Study of Childhood* (2nd edn), London, Falmer.

Katz, A. and Buchanan, A. (1999) *Leading Lads*, London, Topman.

Kenrick, D. and Trost, M. (1993) 'The evolutionary perspective', in Beall, A. and Sternberg, R. (eds) *The Psychology of Gender*, New York, Guilford Press, pp.159–73.

Kryger, N. (1998) 'Teachers' understanding and emotions in relation to the creation of boys' masculine identity', in Katz, Y. and Menezes, I. (eds) *Affective Education: A Comparative View*, London, Cassell.

Luke, C. (1996) 'Introduction', in Luke, C. (ed.) *Feminisms and Pedagogies of Everyday Life*, New York, State University of New York Press.

Mac an Ghaill, M. (1988) *Young, Gifted and Black: Student Teacher Relations in the Schooling of Black Youth*, Milton Keynes, Open University Press.

Mac an Ghaill, M. (1994) *The Making of Men: Masculinities, Sexualities and Schooling*, Buckingham and Philadelphia, Open University Press.

McRobbie, A. (1991) *Feminism and Youth Culture: From 'Jackie' to 'Just Seventeen'* (collected papers), Basingstoke, Macmillan.

Majors, R. and Billson, J. (1992) *Cool Pose: The Dilemmas of Black Manhood in America*, New York, Lexington.

Mayall, B. (1999) 'Children and childhood', in Hood, S., Mayall, B. and Oliver, S. (eds) *Critical Issues in Social Research: Power and Prejudice*, Buckingham, Open University Press.

Ogilvy, C., Boath, E., Cheyne, W., Jahoda, G. and Schaffer, H.R. (1990) 'Staff attitudes and perceptions in multi-cultural nursery schools', *Early Child Development and Care*, 64, pp.1–13.

Ogilvy, C., Boath, E., Cheyne, W., Jahoda, G. and Schaffer, H.R. (1992) 'Staff–child interaction styles in multi-ethnic nursery schools', *British Journal of Developmental Psychology*, 10, pp.85–97.

Phillips, A. (1993) *The Trouble with Boys: Parenting the Men of the Future*, London, Pandora.

Plomin, R. (1994) *Genetics and Experience: The Interplay between Nature and Nurture*, Newbury Park, CA, Sage.

Pollack, W. (1998) *Real Boys: Rescuing our Sons from the Myths of Boyhood*, New York, Henry Holt.

Reed, L. Raphael (1999) 'Troubling boys and disturbing discourses on masculinity and schooling: a feminist exploration of current debates and interventions concerning boys in schools', *Gender and Education*, 11 (1), pp.93–110.

Salisbury, J. and Jackson, D. (1996) *Challenging Macho Values*, London, Falmer.

Salmon, P. (1998) *Life at School: Education and Psychology*, London, Constable.

Saraga, E. (1998) 'Children's needs: who decides?' in Langan, M. (ed.) *Welfare: Needs, Rights and Risks*, London, Routledge/The Open University.

Seidman, E. and Rappaport, J. (eds) (1986) *Redefining Social Problems*, New York, Plenum.

Sewell, T. (1997) *Black Masculinities and Schooling: How Black Boys Survive Modern Schooling*, Stoke on Trent, Trentham Books.

Skelton, C. (1998) 'Feminism and research into masculinities and schooling', *Gender and Education*, 10 (2), pp.217–27.

Sonuga-Barke, E., Minocha, K., Taylor, E. and Sandberg, S. (1993) 'Inter-ethnic bias in teachers' ratings of childhood hyperactivity', *British Journal of Developmental Psychology*, 11, pp.187–200.

Spender, D. (1983) '"Telling how it is": language and gender in the classroom', in Marland, M. (ed.) *Sex Differentiation and Schooling*, London, Heinemann.

Stanworth, M. (1983) *Gender and Schooling*, London, Hutchinson.

Ussher, J. (1997) *Fantasies of Femininity: Reframing the Boundaries of Sex*, Harmondsworth, Penguin.

van Dijk, T. (1993) *Elite Discourse and Racism*, London, Sage.

Walkerdine, V. (1988) *The Mastery of Reason*, London, Routledge.

Walkerdine, V. (1997) *Daddy's Girl: Young Girls and Popular Culture*, London, Macmillan.

Walkerdine, V. and Lucey, H. (1989) *Democracy in the Kitchen*, London, Virago.

Weiner, G., Arnot, M. and David, M. (1997) 'Is the future female? Female success, male disadvantage and changing gender patterns in education', in Halsey, A.H., Brown, P. and Lauder, H. (eds) *Education, Economy, Culture and Society*, Oxford, Oxford University Press.

Westwood, S. (1990) 'Racism, black masculinity and the politics of space', in Hearn, J. and Morgan, D. (eds) *Men, Masculinities and Social Theory*, London, Unwin Hyman.

Willis, P. (1977) *Learning to Labour*, Aldershot, Gower.

Woodhead, M. (1997) 'Psychology and the cultural construction of children's needs', in

James, A. and Prout, A. (eds) *Constructing and Reconstructing Childhood: Contemporary Issues in the Sociological Study of Childhood* (2nd edn), London, Falmer.

Wright, C. (1992) *Race Relations in the Primary School*, London, David Fulton.

Yates, L. (1997) 'Gender equity and the boys' debate: what sort of challenge is it?', *British Journal of Sociology of Education*, 18 (3), pp.337–47.

7

Children as Welfare Subjects in Restructured Social Policy

Sharon Pinkney

Contents

1 Introduction

This chapter seeks to explore the complex representations of children as welfare subjects in social care. Children cut across all sites of welfare: education, health, housing, social care, income maintenance, youth justice and so on. Issues of children's 'voice', visibility and participation are becoming increasingly important. As an undifferentiated group, children differ from the other groups involved in the struggles for recognition such as those formed around inequalities on the basis of 'race', gender, class or disability. These latter groups articulated a series of challenges to the dominant social relations of welfare that were partly about changing the terms on which they were recognized as an official policy category. Children, on the other hand, had already been constituted as a centrally included category within social policy so the issues of visibility, participation, 'voice' and representation are different.

Social policies reflect the forms of representation and normative assumptions about the family and consequently about children. Within modern western societies children are perceived as vulnerable, dependent and in need of protection. Children have rights though these are highly circumscribed by adults, in particular by parents. Some children are also seen as being in need of control (Fox Harding, 1997) or in 'need' of the care that a ('normal') family should provide. In all of these representations of children, 'the family' is the framing presence in social policy. In particular the traditional, heterosexual family is seen as the best, most 'natural' place to bring up children. This family is also constructed as a place where the state should have limited powers of intervention. Social policies do not protect children from violence, poverty, marginalization, bullying or harassment. On the contrary, the legislation, policies and practices relating to children contain contradictory messages – on the one hand, constructing children as being in 'need' of protection and support but, on the other, allowing smacking and corporal punishment.

I will use a social constructionist framework to explore the issues relating to children within a restructured social care. The idea of 'new welfare subjects' has been used to capture the ways in which diverse groups of people from a range of subordinated and marginalized social positions have challenged the terms of their inclusion in the social settlement of the Keynesian welfare state (Lewis, 1998). The framework of social constructionism allows us to investigate the ways in which people are 'made up' into specific types or categories of people. Subjects are constituted during the course of their lives as they move in and out of a series of complex and interlocking relationships and spheres. The relations are both material and discursive. The subject can also be a status or position within a discourse. In this context children can be subjects of the discourse: for example, they can be constituted as in 'need' of protection, within social work discourses and legislation. Alternatively, they can be constructed as needing autonomy, as in some of the children's rights literature. Within both of these examples 'children' becomes the category at the centre of the discussion and policy formation. Being a subject also means being subjected to the discourses which claim to be the 'truth' and 'common sense'. In this way children become subjected to the institutional practices which emerge as normative within the discursive field. Lastly, subjects have identities which are associated with a sense of belonging to a particular group or category. Children have often been identified as a single category, a unified homogeneous mass and in this construction they become essentialized subjects. In this chapter I examine the legislation and institutional practices that have emerged in relation to specific categories of children.

Children as imagined and symbolic subjects are often used as a legitimizing image or representation for social policies. Within this framework, children are invested with the idea of hope for the future. The child achieves the status of an icon who is innocent of knowledge, agency and accountability. The outcome is that the 'child' has ethical claims on the adults who make laws and control things. In this account the child becomes a stand-in for a complicated set of anxieties and desires about national identity (Berlant, 1998). In the British context, this imaginary and essentialized 'child' is invariably white and middle-class and becomes the focus of national struggles. Within this chapter I will argue that children are not a homogeneous group but are differentiated social subjects.

While new social movements have challenged the conception and delivery of welfare to groups who were marginalized on the basis of differences such as social class, gender, 'race' and disability, the arguments relating to children have been less prominent. One of my arguments is that the normative images of childhood, which have become embedded within social policies, have helped to silence the violence, marginalization and poverty which large numbers of children experience.

The key examples from social care practice I focus on are the contradictions, challenges and opportunities implicit within the Children Act 1989 (England and Wales). This legislation attempts to bring together competing perspectives on children by focusing on those who are constructed as being either in 'need' or at 'risk' and then establishes a framework of support and intervention based upon these constructions. The second example examines some of the issues around the politics of participation in relation to children who are either 'looked after' within local authority care or the subjects of statutory investigation because of 'risk of significant harm'. The relations of power between adult and child, abuser and abused, professional and 'client' serve to problematize the current models of participation available to children in these contexts. Both the legislative changes introduced with the Children Act and the subsequent restructuring of Social Services Departments (SSDs) help us to understand how children are constructed and positioned as welfare subjects. Before looking in more detail at these two examples, I will briefly outline the framework within which social care services for children operated in the late 1990s.

1.1 Key factors shaping social care for children in the 1990s

These can be summarized as following, but it is worth noting that they represent a paradoxical convergence of New Right and new social movement critiques of welfare practice alongside aspects of the restructuring of social welfare.

- A move away from state provision towards private, family, voluntary and charitable provisions. This shift in the balance of the mixed economy of welfare was part of the increasing marketization of welfare between the late 1970s and early 1990s (Langan and Clarke, 1994).
- A general change in the aims, purpose and values of welfare, as a result of New Right influence on Conservative government policies during the 1980s and 1990s. One of the key transformations has been increased managerialism within welfare services. Managerialism involves both increased 'management consciousness' within organizations that deliver welfare, and a change in the field of relationships between welfare organizations and the public, private and voluntary sectors, as well as between organizations and their users (Newman, 1998).
- The critique of the role of social workers and an undermining of their professionalism and autonomy. In part the critique emerged in response to child abuse inquiry reports during the 1980s where social workers were criticized for either over- or under-intervention.
- Increasingly fragmented and specialized children's services. In part this can be seen to be a result of the critique of social workers during the 1980s as well as a response to more complex legislative frameworks.
- Linked with some of the above are changes in the discourses of social work. The language of social work has changed as social workers become care managers and 'clients' become 'customers'. These changes reflect wider shifts towards customer discourses in welfare and increased marketization (Clarke, 1998; Pinkney, 1998; see also Chapter 19 this volume).
- New social movements have challenged the way in which services within welfare are thought about, negotiated and delivered. These challenges came from those groups of people who were marginalized within the conception, planning and delivery of social services. These include service user groups, such as the disability movement and HIV-positive groups, the social work profession itself, and academics. These challenges have been described as part of the 'new social movements' which, taken together, constitute the social basis for new forms of transformative and emancipatory political and social change (Oliver, 1990; Williams, 1992). These perspectives help us to understand the emergence of a 'settlement', or temporary and unstable accommodation, between competing conceptions of the relationships between the 'new welfare subjects' and the state.

2 Mapping the field: competing perspectives on children

There have been various attempts to classify the different positions and perspectives regarding children. It is possible to trace at least four competing perspectives. These can loosely be termed: the children's rights; the New Right; child protection/state paternalism; and the parents' rights perspectives. In practice these perspectives are much more complex and fluid and will often overlap. The issues outlined earlier regarding children as welfare subjects need to be kept in mind within this section because they are central to understanding the perspectives. The additional and related point to consider is whether the perspectives assume that children have agency or whether they are being constructed as passive victims.

- *Children's rights perspectives*. These perspectives perceive the central issues to be children's lack of control and autonomy, coupled with a belief that children should have equality with adults in relation to rights, obligations and responsibilities. Generally, children are being viewed as active subjects who should have the right to self-determination and freedom from adult authority and control. These perspectives implicitly deny that childhood is a special stage of development which is clearly distinct from adulthood and results in vulnerability or the need for protection (Holt, 1975; Franklin, 1986). Although the child is being constructed as an active subject here, much of the literature constructs children in ways which are essentialist. The assumption is that 'the child' needs more rights and autonomy, but the literature tends to talk of children in undifferentiated ways. The other interesting point is the manner in which the literature largely constructs the world of adult rights in the same way – the assumption being that 'others' such as women and black people have managed to achieve rights unproblematically. I would want to argue that the sphere of rights for adult groups is far from unfinished.
- *The New Right perspective*. The main argument here is that state intervention into the family should be kept to a minimum. Privacy is highly valued and parents' civil liberties are often emphasized. Patriarchal authority is a particular feature of this perspective, with power invested in adults (males) within families. There is some affinity with the children's rights perspective above in that both oppose state intervention (Morgan, 1995; Goldstein et al., 1979). Here the child is constructed largely as a passive subject and the phrase 'children should be seen and not heard' would be a good example of the normative view of children which is implicit within these perspectives.

- *State paternalism and child protection perspective.* Here the state is viewed as the 'good parent', who replaces the 'poor/inadequate' parent. State professionals and experts are invested with considerable powers to intervene to protect children. The focus is on the child's right to adequate nurture and care. The child is viewed as an essentially dependent, vulnerable, passive subject in need of state protection (Kellmer Pringle, 1986). The child is not being viewed as a subject with agency within this construction.
- *Parents' rights perspective.* This approach favours biological birth families and sees that the role of the state should be to offer support to 'poor/inadequate' parents. The perspective acknowledges class, poverty and deprivation as the key explanatory factors in child abuse and neglect (Holman, 1980). The child subject would be marginalized within this perspective with the key emphasis being on the rights of parents, not children. Consequently it is parents and not children who are assumed to have agency here.

These competing perspectives on children are important and the repercussions and echoes from them can be seen to run through the legislation and practice within social care. It would be reasonable to say that some of the perspectives are temporally specific and as a result have dated somewhat. The children's rights perspective for example, is largely the result of a period of community activism and 'left' anti-statist libertarianism during the 1960s and 1970s. Similarly, the perspectives are much more fluid than they appear in this brief presentation. The state paternalism perspective has become much more complex, with social workers adopting competing positions. Some individuals and organizations within SSDs align themselves with a children's rights rather than the state paternalist perspective.

On closer scrutiny we can see the complexities and convergences of the perspectives more obviously. Much recent work has emphasized the importance of hearing what children say and of treating children and young people with respect. Alongside this there is an acknowledgement that children can be vulnerable because of size and age, so at times they will be in 'need' of protection. The important point here is that the children's rights perspective was developed largely as a result of the 'devastating neglect of children's own opinions which has characterized much of the welfarist approach' (Eekelaar, 1992, p.229).

2.1 The United Nations Convention on the Rights of the Child

The United Nations Convention on the Rights of the Child sets out state obligations to children within four broad categories: survival rights, developmental rights, protection rights and participation rights. The first three categories have been less problematic than the fourth area, participation rights, which I will examine in more detail later. The Convention contains an emphasis on welfare and autonomy, protection and liberation. Freeman (1995) argues that it is the first international document to state explicitly that children have a right to a 'voice' within processes affecting their lives. In relation to the four perspectives identified earlier, the Convention can be viewed as closest to the children's rights perspective, with its emphasis on children's rights to autonomy, respect, participation and 'voice'.

The United Kingdom ratified the Convention in 1991 although subsequent monitoring of the UK's performance was highly critical.[1] Eekelaar (1992) analysed the Convention, and concluded that childhood should not be viewed as an end in itself, stressing instead the connection between childhood and later development into adulthood. He argued for 'dynamic self-determination' (1992, p.43) which involves 'optimally positioning children to develop their own perceptions of their wellbeing as they enter adulthood' (ibid., p.58). The Convention has been viewed as useful by some who advocate a children's rights perspective, because it provides a means of applying moral pressure to governments and raises the profile of the arguments in favour of children's rights and liberation. It is clear, though, that on its own it will not bring about the dramatic changes required to create the possibilities for a politics of recognition that embraces children.

Since 1981 Norway has employed an ombudsperson specifically for children's rights. This was the first independent government spokesperson in the world appointed to protect the rights of children. Flekkoy (1991), who formerly held this post, has pointed out that viewing children as both vulnerable as well as needing autonomy is a positive step forward. The idea of a children's commissioner is a similar initiative that has gained momentum and looks likely to be supported within the United Kingdom.

3 State responses: social work with children

It is possible to explore the tensions between the different perspectives and the internal limits of each by looking at the relatively small group of children – well under 1 per cent in England at any one time (Fox Harding, 1997, p.3) – who enter the public care system each year. This group of children represents the biggest challenge in relation to arguments about children's rights. They are likely to have been victims of abuse and neglect and the arguments about protection and vulnerability as well as children's participation, 'voice' and autonomy will be sharpest here. Before looking at children and participation, it is necessary to examine the way in which the legislation constructs children as subjects who are either 'in need' or 'at risk'. It is also possible to view the way in which the competing perspectives outlined above are 'played through' within the legislation.

3.1   The Children Act 1989 (England and Wales)

The Children Act 1989 was introduced after almost two decades of fierce criticism of social work as well as growing unease within social work itself about its role and responsibilities in relation to work with children, in particular work relating to child protection. The Children Act can be viewed as a mixed bag. On the whole it has provided a clear legislative framework for intervention; it has also reasserted that children's 'needs' should be paramount. The construction of children's 'needs', rights and risks was to be negotiated in complex ways, largely by adults. One of the assumptions within the legislation was that the position of children could be safeguarded by a combination of welfare professionals and parents/carers. The Act was viewed positively by many social workers as a comprehensive and coherent piece of legislation which provided a legal framework for the protection and promotion of the interests and welfare of children. Some went further and argued that it amounted to a 'children's charter'. Given this generally positive reception it is worth examining in some detail.

Some of the key principles of the legislation are as follows:

- The interests and welfare of the child should be paramount.
- There is an assumption of minimal intervention, which became known as the 'no-order principle'. What this meant in practice was that a court order, such as a supervision or care order, should not be sought unless thought to be absolutely necessary and where voluntary agreements for work with the family had been tried and failed.
- The child's 'race', religion, language and culture should be taken into account when assessing or making a placement for a child.
- Proceedings should be implemented in a more timely fashion. This arose from criticisms that long delays in providing assessments for care proceedings had caused additional stress to the child and family concerned, which could in turn prejudice the welfare of the child.

It became possible to use the Act to remove the perpetrator of abuse from the home, rather than the child. This development could be viewed as a small victory for feminist and children's rights perspectives, which had argued that removing the child amounted to blaming the victim. The Children Act (Scotland) 1995 is more explicit in that it has 'an exclusion order' which could be used to exclude alleged abusers from the child's family home.

Even from this brief examination of some of the principles underpinning the Children Act, it is possible to trace the threads of earlier criticisms of social work and see the way in which they have manifested themselves within the legislation. The principle of the child's interests being paramount reminds us of earlier criticisms from the Jasmine Beckford Inquiry report that the child's needs had been lost sight of in the focus on the parents (London Borough of Brent, 1985). The children's rights perspectives would view this as a victory in that it does put the position of the child at the centre. Within the 'no-order principle' some of the criticisms of social work raised within the Cleveland Inquiry emerged. This included the criticism that social workers had misused their powers and been too quick to seek legal orders (Secretary of State for Social Services, 1988; Pinkney, 1998). This principle could be viewed as a small victory for parents' rights perspectives in that it challenges the authority of social workers and seeks to curtail their powers. The tension between children's and parents' rights perspectives is reflected and carried within the Children Act. The legislation does not resolve the dilemma for social workers seeking to strike a delicate balance between promoting the rights of the child and protecting the rights of the parents.

The criticisms of social work, as in other areas of welfare, are contested. It is interesting to examine the way in which some criticisms emerged as more dominant and influential in shaping social work with children, whilst others were either lost or silenced within the same legislation. One way of viewing this is to examine the legislation's more permissive features alongside its obligatory features. This involves comparing those elements to which SSDs should have due regard, such as the 'race', religion, language principle, with those elements which it is statutorily obliged to take into account, such as the child's interests being paramount: or, to put it another way, exploring the tension between child support and child protection.

3.2 Children in need vs. child protection

A major debate has emerged in the UK about how policy and practice for child protection and child support can be integrated. Increasingly the tension between the two areas is being played out through policymakers, managers and practitioners in social care. The Children Act 1989 provided a clear framework for child welfare in the widest sense, including protection, prevention and support services. In the early years of implementation, however, it became a source of some concern that 'children in need' were generally not receiving services which were considered either adequate or desirable.

The Children Act can be viewed as seeking to strike a delicate balance between promoting support services for families with 'children in need' and providing child protection services for children deemed to be at risk of abuse. Some have suggested that the Act reflects rather than resolves many of the inherent contradictions of social policy, particularly as it relates to children and families. While the Act provides a clear legislative framework, it cannot resolve many of the underlying conflicts between the 'state', the 'family' and the individual parent or child (Jack and Stepney, 1995). Saraga (1998) has argued that how the needs of children are defined, and which children are seen to require welfare provision, are socially constructed, varying historically and according to socioeconomic circumstances. Under the Act, the definition of 'children in need' is left up to the discretion of each local authority and this results in wide geographical variations.

This distinction between support and protection crucially impacts upon resources, and the criticism has often been made that children in need are neglected as resources are channelled into child protection instead. Contrary to the spirit of the Children Act 1989, 'children in need' have at times to be identified as being at risk of 'significant harm' before they qualify for services at all. The Department of Health (1993) commissioned research which focused on SSDs' response to 'children in need' and the findings show that generally they were experiencing problems in giving any priority to referrals outside of the child protection area. In the authorities examined, child protection 'cases' were talked of as the 'core business'. The demand-led context, general defensiveness and safeguarding meant that staff found it difficult to meet the needs of 'children in need' if they were not deemed to be at risk of 'significant harm'. Social workers felt they sometimes had to accentuate parts of the 'children in need' case to ensure that they qualified for support services. This raises interesting issues about the prioritization and categorization of 'need' and how professionals and service users work with them.

Public spending constraints have meant that there has been a tendency towards narrowing definitions of risk and need. Social workers often argued that the threshold of risk, particularly in relation to child protection, had constantly been raised. Competition for scarce resources resulted in preventive and supportive work being devalued, in a culture where performance targets, measurement of outcomes, and the demand for greater efficiency militate against the style of work which, by its very nature, is difficult to quantify in this way. The dilemmas facing social workers in providing services to 'children in need' as well as child protection have not gone unnoticed.

In 1994 the Audit Commission report, *Seen but not Heard: Coordinating Community Child Health and Social Services for Children in Need* was published. This document, together with the Department of Health report, *Child Protection: Messages from Research* (1995), informed an agenda for change, particularly in shifting the balance between child protection and support. Both of these reports were highly significant in shaping the future for child welfare services. The research was interpreted as support for the idea that most social work intervention is wasteful of resources and those resources could be more usefully employed in offering support to families and children. The report *Progress through Change* from the Social Services Inspectorate (1996) echoed the message of the previous research which called for a shift away from child protection to a more preventive and supportive approach. One of the concerns voiced by the SSI report was that organizational change often meant that the voice of the 'client' was sometimes lost (*Guardian*, 10 July 1996). It is unclear within the report whether the 'client' being referred to is the child or the parent(s).

3.3   Children and participation

The final area I want to consider is the idea of participation within welfare services. Generally, this is an issue that gained momentum throughout the 1980s and 1990s and is now being widely applied. We have already seen how the UN Convention sets out the state's obligations towards children under four headings, one of these being participation rights for children. An evaluation of participation within social care services would need to consider whether the participation is real, in the sense that the child or young person is able to participate fully and affect decisions and outcomes.

The idea of 'participation' itself can be problematized in that it has come to mean 'everything and nothing' (Croft and Beresford, 1996, p.175). During the 1980s two distinct approaches to user involvement in welfare services developed. The first was the consumerist approach, embedded within New Right visions of welfare. This approach constructs rights as enshrined within documents such as citizen's charters and complaints procedures which are central to this consumerist discourse. The second approach was more social democratic and came about as a result of the challenge of the new social movements. This approach views rights within a citizenship framework (see Chapter 22 this volume). These two approaches offer competing versions of participation. The social democratic version inspires more optimism about participation which is meaningful and active, but I will argue that neither approach, on its own, will progress genuine participation for children and young people within child protection/care decision-making. The changes within the organizational culture, attitudes, practices and policies would need to be extensive before children could be viewed as autonomous participative subjects within a citizenship model of welfare.

Meetings, such as child protection case conferences, and reviews of children and young people within the 'looked after' system, have been highlighted as a site for potential participation of children and young people in formal settings where important decisions are made regarding their lives. Children within the public care system have the right to attend meetings, case conferences and childcare reviews regarding themselves. In practice this right is under-utilized and children and young people often find it difficult to participate for a number of reasons. Needless to say, simply being present at a meeting does not amount to genuine participation.

Before looking at some of the obstacles to participation, it is important to set the context by outlining briefly the frameworks within which these meetings take place. The meetings are statutory reviews, case conferences and core-group meetings held to make decisions, recommendations and care plans regarding children who are deemed 'at risk' or who are being 'looked after' within local authority care. The meetings are formal: a senior professional from within social services usually chairs them. They are attended by a wide range of other professionals including (head)teachers, health visitors, medical practitioners, education social workers, residential or field social workers, family centre staff, legal representatives and others from various agencies involved with the child or family. In addition, parents will be encouraged to attend and they may bring along support people. This makes the list of those attending long and the numbers of people involved large. These meetings are often experienced by professionals as intimidating and difficult.

Nineteen ninety-one saw the publication of one of the key documents, which has shaped work with children and their families. *Working Together* (Department of Health, 1991) focused on the area of inter-agency co-operation in child protection and became central in providing guidance and advice on multi-agency working and decision-making within social work. This document provided a framework for social work to be one of a number of key organizations involved in decision-making in the child protection arena.

The difficulties and tensions created by inter-agency working should not be underestimated. These tensions are often played out in child protection case conferences, which are the formal arenas for decision-making in child protection. Each professional enters this arena with a different background, training, organizational structure, supervision, experience and interest in the child or family. Moreover, these differences may be compounded by the diverse organizational structures of the participants' agencies. Such differences often lead to tensions and conflict, which in themselves may detract from the interests of the child and be a barrier to the child's participation in this important decision-making setting.

This makes the issue of preparation for these meetings an important one and social workers are required to prepare the child and ascertain their wishes and feelings beforehand. In this way the child's perspective is often negotiated via welfare professionals who are empowered to act 'in the child's best interest'. This raises many dilemmas and the conflict inherent within the social workers' role at these meetings is a complex one to negotiate.

Discussions of participation have often ignored the dimensions of power in the child protection arena. The circumstances which lead to the child being involved in such a meeting are often those of abuse and/or neglect. To assume participation of children and young people in these circumstances, within such intimidating and difficult meetings, is, at the least, naive. Croft and Beresford (1996) argue that participation has sometimes been used to legitimize the actions of the state, particularly in the childcare/protection arena. New models of participation therefore need to take account of structural and institutional inequalities among the participants in childcare decision-making arenas as well as power differences between children and adults, abusers and abused, professional and 'client' and so on.

Voluntary organizations such as Childline, Who Cares? Trust and the Children's Legal Centres have been at the forefront of arguing that children need to have a stronger 'voice' and representation within children's services. Many of these organizations have developed a children's rights critique of current welfare services for children within the public care system. The arguments for a children's ombudsman/commissioner have also developed out of the citizenship and social welfare movement's critiques of welfare. Unfortunately these developments have been marginalized and the voluntary organizations themselves have been vulnerable to fluctuations in funding and changes in political administration at the local or national level. For example, the Children's Legal Centre opened in 1979 with the aim of promoting the full participation of children and young persons in decisions affecting their lives. In 1995 the Centre was closed due to funding problems and, although later reopened, it had to become more modest in its aims.

4 Conclusion

To some extent children are 'new subjects' within a reconstructed welfare state. The terms of their subordinated inclusion within welfare construct them in ways that are essentialist, homogeneous and imaginary. These constructions of children as dependent and vulnerable, 'in need' of protection and so on, serve to obscure the issues of the lack of representation of children and young people's 'voices' within social care services. This is despite some attempts to give greater emphasis to the views of children in social care. A politics of recognition would embrace the diverse perspectives of children, rather than ignoring, silencing, patronizing or making assumptions about their imaginary needs. Making children audible within social policy and social care services would require profound changes in the thinking, structure and organization of services to children and families.

As the brief example of participation showed, it is not enough simply to state that children may attend decision-making meetings about themselves; the changes required to facilitate children's representation would require wider-reaching changes than this. An analysis of power and inequality is an essential starting-point for these debates. The Children Act 1989 was used as an example to illustrate how policy-makers have regarded children's rights as paramount, although in practice this has often been undermined. Although the Children Act has been hailed by some as a victory for children's rights, the brief examination here has shown that complex and competing perspectives relating to children are embedded within it. The ambivalence of the state towards the rights and needs of children was also illustrated by the example of the United Nations Convention on the Rights of the Child which has been flaunted within the UK. In places it is possible to see some small advancement in the rights of children, although my general conclusion is that, overall, children are still not full welfare subjects in a citizenship sense. Rather, their position is one of subordinated inclusion within social welfare provision.

Note

1 The main criticisms of the committee set up to monitor progress with implementation of the Convention were that in the UK no mechanism for assessing the impact of policies on children had been put into place, insufficient resources were allocated, and most powerfully that the extent of child poverty negated the rights of the children affected (the Rowntree Trust estimates that one in three children within the UK is currently being raised in poverty). The committee also queried the generally low level of benefits and the withdrawal of benefit from 16- and 17-year-olds. The committee criticized the building of secure training centres for 12–14-year-old offenders as well as the non-prohibition of physical punishment within private schools and within the home.

References

Audit Commission (1994) *Seen but not Heard: Coordinating Community Child Health and Social Services for Children in Need.*

Berlant, L. (1998) *The Queen of America Goes to Washington City: Essays on Sex and Citizenship*, Durham, NC, Duke University Press.

Clarke, J. (1998) 'Consumerism', in Hughes, G. (ed.) *Imagining Welfare Futures*, London, Routledge/The Open University.

Clarke, J., Cochrane, A. and McLaughlin, E. (eds) (1994) *Managing Social Policy*, London, Sage.

Croft, S. and Beresford, P. (1996) 'The politics of participation', in Taylor, D. (ed.) *Critical Social Policy: A Reader*, London, Sage.

Department of Health (1991) *Working Together under the Children Act 1989: A Guide to Arrangements for Inter-agency Co-operation for the Protection of Children from Abuse*, London, HMSO.

Department of Health (1993) *Definition, Management and Monitoring of Children in Need*, London, HMSO.

Department of Health (1995) *Child Protection: Messages from Research*, Dartington Social Research Unit, HMSO.

Eekelaar, J. (1992) 'The importance of thinking that children have rights', in Alston, P., Parker, S. and Seymour, J. (eds) *Children, Rights and the Law*, Oxford, Clarendon Press.

Flekkoy, M.G. (1991) *A Voice for Children: Speaking Out as their Ombudsman*, London, Jessica Kingsley and UNICEF.

Fox Harding, L. (1997) *Perspectives in Child Care Policy* (2nd edn), London and New York, Longman.

Franklin, B. (ed.) (1986) *The Rights of Children*, Oxford, Blackwell.

Freeman, M.D.A. (1995) 'Children's rights in a land of rites', in Franklin, B. (ed.) *The Handbook of Children's Rights: Comparative Policy and Practice*, London and New York, Routledge.

Goldstein, J., Freud, A. and Solnit, A. (1979) *Beyond the Best Interests of the Child*, New York, The Free Press.

Holman, B. (1980) *Inequality in Child Care*, Poverty Pamphlet 26, London, Child Poverty Action Group.

Holt, J. (1975) *Escape from Childhood: The Needs and Rights of Children*, Harmondsworth, Penguin.

Hughes, G. and Lewis, G. (eds) (1998) *Unsettling Welfare: The Reconstruction of Social Policy*, London, Routledge/The Open University.

Jack, G. and Stepney, P. (1995) 'The Children Act 1989 – protection or persecution? Family support and child protection in the 1990s', *Critical Social Policy*, 43, Summer.

Kellmer Pringle, M. (1986) *The Needs of Children: A Personal Perspective*, London, Hutchinson (3rd edn, first published 1974).

Langan, M. and Clarke, J. (1994) 'Managing in the mixed economy of care', in Clarke et al. (1994).

Lewis, G. (1998) '"Coming apart at the seams": the crises of the welfare state', in Hughes and Lewis (1998).

London Borough of Brent (1985) *A Child in Trust: Report of the Panel of Inquiry Investigating the Circumstances surrounding the Death of Jasmine Beckford*.

Morgan, P. (1995) *Farewell to the Family?* London, Institute of Economic Affairs, Health and Welfare Unit.

Newman, J. (1998) 'Managerialism and social welfare', in Hughes and Lewis (1998).

Oliver, M. (1990) *The Politics of Disability*, London, Macmillan.

Pinkney, S. (1998) 'The reshaping of social work and social care', in Hughes and Lewis (1998).

Saraga, E. (1998) 'Children's needs: who decides?' in Langan, M. (ed.) *Welfare: Needs, Rights and Risks*, London and New York, Routledge/The Open University.

Secretary of State for Social Services (1988) *Report of the Inquiry into Child Abuse in Cleveland*, Cmnd 412, London, HMSO.

Social Services Inspectorate (1996) *Progress through Change: The Fifth Annual Report of the Chief Inspector*, SSI/DOH 1995/6, London, HMSO.

Williams, F. (1992) 'Somewhere over the rainbow: universality and diversity in social policy', in Manning, N. and Page, R. (eds) *Social Policy Review 4: The Public Sector in the 1980s*, Glasgow, Social Policy Association.

8

Social Policy and the Body

Julia Twigg

1 Introduction

This chapter addresses the relevance of the new theorizing about the body for social policy. It starts with a brief overview of the burgeoning field of work on the body, exploring where it came from and its main theoretical concerns. It then turns to the relationship of this literature to social policy, arguing that the subject has been slow to incorporate its perceptions. The reasons for this are twofold: negative, rooted in a defensive posture, and positive, based on certain key values within the social policy tradition. Finally, it suggests briefly some of the ways in which a social policy of the body may now be emerging.

2 The literature on the body

The current interest in the body and embodiment encompasses a range of themes and theoretical concerns. All start, in some degree, from a dissatisfaction with the dominant rationalistic account that has characterized the social sciences from their inception in the eighteenth century. Sociology and the social sciences in general are part of the post-Enlightenment project of modernity that privileges the rational, controlled and abstract over the disordered, uncontrolled and concrete. In this process emotions and the body have been relegated to a secondary status and a discredited (and, as we shall see, gendered and sometimes racialized) set of categories. Drawing on the legacy of Descartes and his radical separation of mind and body, the dominant tradition of social science has been that of the rational actor. This is particularly strongly so in relation to economics and certain traditions of political theory, but it has been true of much sociology and social policy also. Here the body is conceptualized as external to the actor, something to be managed or transcended, but not itself the subject of sociological analysis. Sociology, in its struggle to establish its intellectual territory and throw off the spectre of biological reductionism, engaged in a distancing exercise in which the field of the social was secured and established by means of excluding the biological and handing that over to the territory of science. The price of this exercise of disciplinary definition, Turner argues, was the exclusion from sociological analysis until recently of the lived body and its concerns (Turner, 1984, 1991; Williams and Bendelow, 1998).

The particular emphasis and value placed on theory and theorizing within sociology has also tended to exclude the body. As Morgan and Scott point out, theory and theorizing occupy a privileged position within sociology. Undertaken by the grand *masters* (the emphasis is intended) of the discipline, it is associated with abstraction and distance from everyday practices (Morgan and Scott, 1993). Bodies are things to be transcended or ignored. This legacy continues today even within writing about the body, so that current theorizing often maintains a distance from its subject and presents the body in a peculiarly disembodied way.

The most sustained challenge to these emphases came initially from feminism. Feminism early focused on the ways in which women's bodies were controlled and manipulated within patriarchy, exploring a range of issues from abortion and reproductive rights, through rape, pornography and the wider commodification of women's bodies, to dieting and the imposition of beauty ideals (Davis, 1982; hooks, 1982; Hull et al., 1982; Bordo, 1993; Martin 1987; Smart, 1989). A series of social institutions – medicine, religion, marriage, the law – were implicated in the control of women through the control of their bodies. As Walby and others have argued, one of the more profound ways in which patriarchy operates is through the control of the body (Walby, 1990).

Feminism has also drawn attention to the way in which women are presented in culture as more embodied than men, in some senses as representing the body itself. Feminist writers have explored how this has been used to justify exclusionary practices in employment, education, and public life generally. Women are reduced to their bodies, confined within the matrices of sexuality and reproduction. Women's bodies have traditionally been presented negatively in culture as lesser, and in some sense pathological, compared with the male norm: fluid, soft, weak, uncontrolled and leaky compared with the hard, strong, defined, contained bodies of men. Women are caught in a set of dichotomies in which they represent the devalued, unmarked, silenced categories of nature, the body, emotions, in contrast to culture, the mind, reason (Jordanova, 1989).

Malestream sociology reflected and endorsed this negative account. The feminist project has therefore been a dual one: to bring the body back in, but in such a way that its truths and experiences are valued not repressed. Feminism has sought a fuller, more satisfactory account of being than the over-rational, controlled and limited one presented in the dominant analytic tradition. In doing so it has opened up the possibilities of exploring men's experiences of embodiment too (Connell, 1995). Initially this literature focused on issues of violence, aggression and sexuality, especially gay sexuality; but, as Morgan argues, there is a need to go beyond this 'over-phallusized' picture of men, and to explore the bodies, not just of athletes and soldiers, but dons and bishops also (Morgan, 1993).

The critique of the dominant tradition has also opened up the field of emotion (James and Gabe, 1996; Bendelow and Williams, 1998; see also Chapter 9 this volume). This occupies an uncertain position in relation to the sociology of the body. Some feelings – desire, anger – seem to belong naturally in this territory; others – amusement, boredom – less obviously so. The difficulty lies in the mind/body divide, for emotions lie at the heart of this vexed subject. As many commentators remark, we both *are* and *have* our bodies, and literature about the body and embodiment has struggled with the legacy of Cartesian dualism (Williams and Bendelow, 1998).

Recent sociological work on emotions has tended to concentrate on their deployment in social life, particularly in work. Hochschild's account of flight attendants was a path-breaking study, and her characterization of emotional labour has been extended in fields such as hospice work, nursing and care work generally (Hochschild, 1983; James, 1989; Lawler, 1991). Here the issues are less those of the body itself than the role of emotion in social life, though it should be noted that many of the areas where emotional labour is of central significance are also ones where body work and body care are involved. Once again gender is the key. Definitions of 'women's work', both paid and unpaid, are often rooted in ideas of an essential women's nature – more emotional, more concerned with the bodily – so that the link between body work and emotion is maintained in the person of the woman worker.

Not all in sociology and social theory have accepted the dominant rationalistic paradigm, and Turner identified an oppositional tradition which he traces from Nietzsche through Schopenhauer and Marcuse in which the body, identified as the seat of desire, irrationality and sexual pleasure, provides the basis for a critique of capitalist rationality (Turner, 1991). The most powerful current influence in this – broadly conceived – tradition is Foucault.

The body for Foucault is not natural or neutral but created and reproduced through discourse. Foucault sets out to map the history of bodies and the effects of power on them, a territory he terms 'bio-power'. Through this, bodies are defined, ordered and controlled. One of the ways it operates is through 'dividing practices', techniques whereby populations or categories of person are created by dividing them off from others: the isolation of lepers or the confinement of the poor or mad are examples. Dividing practices are often given a physical or spatial expression through separate buildings, different categories of ward, subdivisions of the institution. Fundamental to the operation of disciplinary institutions like the prison, the asylum, or the Poor Law institution is the ordering of bodies within them (see Chapter 5 this volume). Such institutions constrain and control the bodies of inmates. Bentham's panopticon is the paradigm of disciplinary technique, offering the organization of space and human beings in a visual order that lays bare the structures of power. Surveillance is continuous and all are caught in the machine, even the one who watches (Foucault, 1973, 1977, 1979; Rabinow, 1984; Merquior, 1985; Sheridan 1980).

Knowledge for Foucault is a form of power. Thus in parallel with the emergence of dividing and exclusionary institutions, we observe the rise of scientific classifications that order mental diseases, that provide taxonomies of the poor, or elaborate types of sexual deviance. By the application of such systems of knowledge, particular populations or groups are defined and created. Through the collection of data and statistical techniques, 'norms' are created against which individuals can be judged and classified. Anomalous individuals or populations are then made subject to corrective or therapeutic technologies

The terms in which such schemes are elaborated and applied are often overtly humane, full of the rhetoric of humanitarian reform and progress. It is part of Foucault's aim to show that progressive and enlightened responses are just as much expressions of power as more openly repressive ones. Foucault thus overturns the account given of medicine, or the treatment of the insane, or the growth of sexual toleration and freedom as unambiguously progressive, and substitutes a darker account in which the development of the modern age represents not enlightenment and progress but new and different forms of repression – ones in which the disciplinary forces are no longer external and physical but internalized in systems of thought and the practices that support them. Disciplinary techniques are not simply imposed by institutional structures but exist in forms of self-formation, applied by individuals to themselves, using such techniques as confession, self-interrogation, therapy, the exercise and control of the body. Often these processes of self-development are mediated by another – a priest, a therapist, a personal trainer.

Foucault's work on sexuality has been particularly influential on the literature on the body. Much current work on sexuality starts from him and the critique of essentialism – the idea that sexuality and the body can be understood in terms of an unchanging biology that is transcultural and transhistorical. New work, particularly under the influence of Queer Theory, emphasizes instead how both sex and gender are discursively produced, thus undermining the earlier feminist distinction between the two: all is now gender (Butler, 1993). Sexualities – the plural is significant – are socially constructed; and this has opened up political space for the critique of heterosexuality as ideology.

In many ways these post-modern approaches represent a more radical version of the social constructionism that has long been the dominant paradigm in medical sociology. Social constructionism – the idea that medical knowledge does not represent neutral facts, but is socially constructed and thus reflects social and cultural categories and power relations – has been a powerful tool of analysis, but it is increasingly subject to criticism within medical sociology where its account is seen as philosophically inadequate to deal with the full complexities of the body and embodiment. This has gone in parallel with a disquiet at the disembodied nature of much theorizing about the body – the sense of paradox that in focusing so much on the body and its discursive construction, we have lost sight of its fundamental material existence.

New interest in the body has also revived earlier work that had explored these issues, though not directly under that label. The anthropological tradition represented by Mauss, Firth, Turner and Douglas has always retained an interest in the body and its symbolism (Mauss, 1973; Firth, 1973; Turner, 1969; Douglas, 1966, 1973). Goffman, working in a different mode, is similarly sensitive to the ways in which bodies operate in the interactionist order, exploring how we use and interpret our or other people's physical presence (Goffman, 1959). Elias presents a historical account of the imposition of restraint on the body through the growing internalization of rules of conduct and modesty in relation to, for example, eating, posture and bodily privacy (Elias, 1978).

Lastly, interest in the body has itself been fuelled by a perception that under conditions of post-modernity, the body assumes new significance, becoming as Shilling and others have argued central to self-identity (Shilling, 1993; Featherstone, 1991; Synnott, 1993). The privatization of meaning consequent on the decline in a religious world-view and the shift to consumption values means that people seek meaning at the individual level, in and through their bodies. The body becomes a project to be worked upon. There is thus an active concern with techniques of management and regimes of well-being that link the bodily and the spiritual, exemplified in alternative medicine and linked to New Age forms of spirituality. Within consumer culture the body becomes a vehicle for pleasure, display and self-expression (Featherstone, 1991). Media and advertising erode the old restraints and promote the new pleasures of purchase and consumption. With this has come an extension of the commodity form into more and more of social life, including the experience of the body. Consumer culture is preoccupied with perfect bodies, spread through glamorized representations of advertising and the increasing dominance of the visual image in culture. This hedonism has its ascetic side, and we see in parallel the development of regimes of mortification and denial (dieting, exercising) and discourses of purification and restraint, though largely in the modern context used to pursue consumerist rather than religious goals.

3 The body and social policy: resistances and rejections

How does this literature on the body relate to social policy? To a large extent, social policy seems to have remained untouched by these concerns, at least at the conscious level. So far, there has been no social policy of the body – though, as we shall see, one may be in the process of forming. Although certain fields of social policy have taken on aspects of this theorizing, the response is fragmentary. There has been no wholehearted embrace. Why is this? I will propose two sets of reasons: the first negative, rooted in a defensive posture; and the second positive, rooted in criticism of the literature on the body from the perspective of key values within social policy. Let us start with defensive unease.

The problem is that social policy both as a discipline and as a set of practices is itself implicated in many of the processes that are subject to the critique of this literature. We only have to list the primary topics of Foucault's analysis – the prison, the clinic, the Poor Law institution, the asylum – to see how they represent in historical form the central subjects of social policy. They map clearly on to a familiar institutional definition of the subject. Social policy as a discipline is also part of the emergence of the social sciences in the nineteenth century with their systems of classification, their use of dividing practices to define and separate out categories of persons or sub-groups of the population, their deployment of statistical techniques to establish norms and with them define deviance. Though all the social sciences are implicated in these practices, it is clear that social policy, with its orientation to public issues and commitment to informing and improving public interventions, is most heavily so. The world of humanitarian effort and of professional expertise that Foucault unmasks is very much the world of social policy.

Now it is not the case that this inheritance has remained unchallenged or unexplored within social policy. The radical tradition within the discipline has been particularly concerned to expose the ways in which social policy has been used as a mechanism of class-, gender- or 'race'-based power. The rule of experts, the construction of 'social problems', the interventions in people's lives for their own or society's good have increasingly been subject to scrutiny and critique. But I think a certain unease does remain. Social policy is about informing practice. It does aim both to know the social world and to improve it, and this ameliorative emphasis places it firmly in the sights of the Foucauldian critique.

A second way in which social policy is implicated is through its discourse. The discourse of social policy is heavily rationalistic; indeed in some of its manifestations, it epitomizes the dominant account referred to at the start of this chapter that theorizing around the body and embodiment has sought to challenge. Social policy is a multidisciplinary subject (though perhaps most heavily influenced by sociology) in which economics occupies an important and prestigious, though often unremarked, place. Of all the social sciences, economics is most wedded to rationalistic modes of thought; and the individual rational actor remains at the heart of economic theory. The impact of health economics both in the policy world and the academy, and of parallel developments in the economics of welfare, have acted to reinforce these modes of thought in the discipline.

The impact of managerialism, which has been widespread in public agencies since the 1980s, has reinforced these tendencies. Indeed, when we refer to some of the ways in which theorizing about the body does have relevance to social policy, it is the dominance of managerialist accounts in, for example, community care that has helped obscure the fact that most care work at the front line is body work.

Lastly, the location of social policy in relation to government and policy-makers affects the nature of its discourse. Social policy as a discipline is committed to making a difference rather than simply presenting an analysis. This means that it must talk to government and policy-makers in terms that they understand and endorse. Inevitably this means reflecting back the language and problematics of policy-makers. Much research in social policy is funded by government, and this further acts to reinforce the discourses of policy-makers within the discipline.

4   A better-based critique?

Are there also, however, good reasons for resisting this new theorizing, ones that are less defensive and better based? I will start with the question of tone, though I am not sure on which side of the divide of negative and positive resistances this properly lies. Work on the body is characterized by a relentlessly voguish tone. Cyborgs, female body-builders, transsexuality, internet sex: these are the stuff of journals like *Body and Society*. In fact all these subjects encapsulate important theoretical issues, but the preoccupation with them does convey a sense of fashionability that can seem at odds with the moral seriousness of social policy. Social policy has always been a meat-and-potatoes sort of subject, and this down-to-earth character is ill at ease with style-oriented approaches.

More seriously, a second resistance lies in the lack of empirical referent for much of this theorizing – what Bury describes as its 'frustratingly "data free" character' (Bury, 1995). Social policy is a strongly empiricist subject, rooted in the investigation of facts and the collection of data. Though often criticized as a weakness – including by me – this is also a source of its strength. Its concrete, down-to-earth qualities, its demand for evidence, act as useful antidotes to looser forms of theorizing. Work on the body needs the empirical strand that social policy provides.

What I am less sure about is whether there is a more deeply rooted theoretical difference here. Some at least of the theorizing about the body takes a more radical post-modern approach to the nature of knowledge, ultimately regarding all attempts to know the social world as doomed: all we can know are forms of discourse, and these are endlessly changing, fluid, evanescent. Our own accounts are simply another version of these. Though all in social policy would – I think – accept that facts never speak for themselves and that all descriptions are theory-laden, few would be happy with the radical relativism of some post-modern approaches. The thoroughgoing application of such an epistemology denies the relevance and indeed possibility of empirical work. This is not something that social policy as a discipline can, I think, incorporate. Taylor-Gooby goes further and sees such intellectual trends as acting as ideological smokescreens, hiding from view significant social developments, and masking changes in the distribution of power in society (Taylor-Gooby, 1994).

5   The negativity of the bodily

It is also possible to ask whether the focus on the body contains its own negativities and whether these should lead us to be chary of accepting the new body emphasis too easily. I will explore this in relation to disability and age.

A central plank in the politics of disability has been the wish to get away from an oppressive obsession with the bodies of disabled people – their failure, their dysfunctionality – and seek instead the social causes of disability (Oliver, 1990; Morris, 1993; see Chapter 3 this volume). An emphasis on the bodily potentially demeans disabled people, presenting them as the rejected 'other' of the freak show, subject to the prurient, pitying gaze of dominant society. Disabled women in particular have written of the distress and anger caused by being the subject of a voyeuristic speculation on what is 'wrong' with their bodies (Morris, 1993; Lonsdale, 1990). Much of the power of the social model of disability, associated with the work of Oliver, Finkelstein and others, comes from its capacity to transcend the bodily, to go beyond a narrow focus on impairment, and assert that the problem lies elsewhere in the surrounding social structure.

In a similar way, social gerontology has been concerned to combat the excessive focus on the body and its decline that is characteristic of the bio-medical model which dominates both professional and popular accounts of ageing. The political economy approach substitutes an account that shows how many of the features and problems of old age arise out of the structural position of older people, in particular the impact of social and economic factors that result in many older people being poor, isolated, lacking in material resources, socially excluded. These, rather than bodily decline, are the causes of their difficulties. The task is to get away from an oppressive focus on the bodies of older people, and see instead the structural constraints they face (Townsend, 1986; Walker and Phillipson, 1986).

Negative images of bodily decline are as central in the operation of ageism, as they can be in racism. The most offensive insults are body-based, and they rest on the widespread use of the bodily in culture to denigrate and demean. One of the persistent criticisms of the literature on the body is its over-abstract, etherialized character. Part of the reason for this lies in the deeply held convention that to present the bodily is to be in some sense demeaning of the person; and the dematerialized account arises from a desire to steer clear of these negativities. A brief example from my own research illustrates the problem. I was writing about a very disabled, elderly woman living at home. A person of great courage and enterprise, she was forced to live her entire life on her bed. This meant that if care workers failed to arrive for some hours or even days, she was forced not just to eat, sleep and live, but also excrete in the bed, and I wrote a sentence to that effect. After I had done so, reading it through I thought: I cannot write that. It is too exposing. It leaps from the page and dominates the whole account. To refer to someone excreting, even using that slightly clinical term, is to expose and lessen. But how otherwise could I write about my topic, which is the management of the body and the denial of the bodily in community care?

In my view it *is* possible in these cases to explore issues around the body without falling into the trap of endorsing oppressive accounts. It is possible in large measure to present an enlightening and beneficial account of age or disability that draws on theorizing about the body. For example, recent work on older women has carried over feminist critiques of the ways in which women are identified as 'Body', or in which their status is defined in terms of the attractiveness or fertility of their bodies, into the analysis of the negative presentation of older women or of the menopause (Martin, 1987). Other accounts have begun to use more phenomenological approaches to explore older people's experiences of embodiment (Osberg, 1996).

In a similar way new theorizing around impairment had put back on to the agenda issues that were excluded by the dominance of the social model. As Hughes and Paterson (1997) have recently argued, the social model, by looking only at disability, consigned the bodily (in the form of impairment) to the theoretical shadows, or worse the realm of bio-medicine, leaving large parts of the subjective experience of disabled people invisible and untheorized. New work by Shakespeare (1994), Hughes and Paterson (1997) and others has begun to explore the possibilities of using post-structuralist and phenomenological approaches to the body to develop a sociology of impairment. This would allow an analysis of the disabled body, but not in the oppressive, reactionary form of early work.

I say *in large measure* because I think that certain approaches in the field – notably those that draw on Foucault – remain more recalcitrant. I would like to give the example here of some work by Lee-Treweek (1996, 1998) exploring the residential home, and I should emphasize that it is work that I greatly admire and have been influenced by. Lee-Treweek's account is one that presents the processes of care in Foucauldian terms of manipulation and domination in which body work is central. Reading it made me uneasy. There is something about the very account and the terms used in it that seems like an abuse in itself. Just to talk of surveillance, panopticonization and the management of bodies is to denature and depersonalize. The language of interpretation has itself taken the processes further down the line. The account itself seems to have become part of the oppression, just as the account Miller and Gwynne gave back in the 1970s of the lives of the disabled people in the Cheshire Home in terms of the passage to social death reinforced their oppression, though in that case the result was an outburst of anger and challenge to the research from the subjects (Miller and Gwynne, 1972; Campbell and Oliver, 1996). It is hard to see how such accounts could survive the incorporation into them of the views and perspectives of the elderly residents. It seems to me that it is only possible to apply a thoroughgoing Foucauldian analysis by suppressing those. Social policy, by contrast – in its aspirations at least – contains a strong value orientation towards listening to and taking seriously the subjectivities of those on the receiving end of care.

This in turn raises the larger issue of the latent sadism of Foucauldian-influenced accounts. Inscribing, disciplining, ordering: the discourse is heavy with sadistic objectification. Though this aspect is often obscured by the way it is embedded within a radical critique, it is what makes it exciting as well as repellent, and it is central to its academic and wider appeal.

A final difficulty relates to the nature of power in Foucault's work. Power in Foucault is continuous and anonymous. It is not exercised by one group over another; rather it is pervasive through society, and all are caught in its web. This is deeply unsatisfactory from the social policy point of view. I have criticized earlier social policy for its managerialist and governmental focus and for the dream of the rule of neutral, rational experts that underlies this. But social policy also contains a more radical tradition, one that is very much concerned to explore the power dynamics of society. Questions of distribution, equity, justice are central to it, and these cannot be explored without considering the role of social divisions and the operation of power within society. Who exercises power over whom and in whose interests? Exploring the ideologies that mask the realities of power is a central part of the subject. The Foucauldian vision of power as discursive and anonymous is at odds with this.

6 An emergent social policy of the body?

What might a social policy of the body look like? We can start by noting that its elements already exist. As Lewis and her colleagues comment, the irony of the relative absence of the body from social policy is that: 'the body in diverse forms is central to [its] practices . . . Disabled bodies, "ethnic" bodies, children's bodies, sexualized bodies, old bodies, bodies in need, bodies in danger, bodies at risk are all at the heart of social policy' (Lewis et al., 2000).

We already have some emergent examples of the field. Nettleton and Watson's *The Body in Everyday Life* (1998) and Davis' *Embodied Practices* (1997) take forward a range of empirical work that links the body to the concerns of social policy. Lupton's *Food, the Body and the Self* (1996) contains important insights for the development of the social politics of food. Lawler's *Behind the Screens* (1991) with its emphasis on body work has transformed our understanding of nursing. Saraga's edited collection *Embodying the Social* (1998) makes links between embodiment and issues of 'race', disability and sexuality. Lewis, Hughes and Saraga outline how welfare practices are themselves constitutive of the body, and how welfare subjects are embodied through and in the contested discourses of social welfare (Lewis et al., 2000). My own work on the provision of bathing and personal care for people living in the community also takes the body as central to its problematic, locating the provision of intimate care in the dynamics of exposure, boundaries and power, and suggesting ways in which the management of the body is central to the analysis of community care, though this is something that the managerialist cast of much writing on the subject has obscured (Twigg, 1999, 2000). The scope for future work in the area is considerable.

7 Conclusion

The last ten years have witnessed a great explosion of work on the body across the social sciences and humanities. The intellectual sources of this are diverse, though much has been located in a post-structuralist paradigm. In general, social policy has been slow to develop this area, and I have suggested some of the reasons – good and bad – why this is so. Though it is a literature that needs to be interrogated with a degree of scepticism, it has, I believe, a great deal to offer social policy, containing the capacity to open up large areas of the subject that are currently locked away, hidden from analytic view. Bodily themes resonate through the subject matter of social policy. They deserve to do so openly.

References

Bendelow, G. and Williams, S.J. (eds) (1998) *Emotions in Social Life: Critical Themes and Contemporary Issues*, London, Routledge.
Bordo, S. (1993) *Unbearable Weight: Feminism, Western Culture and the Body*, Berkeley, CA, University of California Press.
Bury, M. (1995) 'The body in question', *Medical Sociology News*, 21 (1), pp.36–48.
Butler, J. (1993) *Bodies that Matter: On the Discursive Limits of 'Sex'*, London, Routledge.
Campbell, J. and Oliver, M. (1996) *Disability Politics: Understanding Our Past, Changing Our Future*, London, Routledge.
Connell, R.W. (1995) *Masculinities*, Cambridge, Polity.
Davis, A.Y. (1982) *Women, Race and Class*, London, The Women's Press.
Davis, K. (ed.) (1997) *Embodied Practices: Feminist Perspectives on the Body*, London, Sage.
Douglas, M. (1966) *Purity and Danger: An Analysis of the Concepts of Pollution and Taboo*, London, Routledge & Kegan Paul.
Douglas, M. (1973) *Natural Symbols: Exploration in Cosmology*, Harmondsworth, Penguin.
Elias, N. (1978) *The History of Manners, Volume 1: The Civilising Process*, Oxford, Blackwell.
Featherstone, M. (1991) 'The body in consumer culture', in Featherstone, M., Hepworth, M. and Turner, B.S. (eds) *The Body: Social Process and Cultural Theory*, London, Sage.
Firth, R. (1973) *Symbols: Public and Private*, London, Allen & Unwin.

Foucault, M. (1973) *The Birth of the Clinic: An Archaeology of Medical Perception*, London, Tavistock.

Foucault, M. (1977) *Discipline and Punish: The Birth of the Prison*, London, Allen Lane.

Foucault, M. (1979) *The History of Sexuality, Volume 1: An Introduction*, London, Allen Lane.

Goffman, E. (1959) *The Presentation of Self in Everyday Life*, Harmondsworth, Penguin.

Hochschild, A. (1983) *The Managed Heart: The Commercialization of Human Feelings*, Berkeley, CA, University of California Press.

hooks, b. (1982) *Ain't I a Woman? Black Women and Feminism*, London, Pluto.

Hughes, B. and Paterson, K. (1997) 'The social model of disability and the disappearing body: towards a sociology of impairment', *Disability and Society*, 12 (3), pp.325–40.

Hull, G.T., Scott, P.B. and Smith, B. (eds) (1982) *All the Women Are White, All the Blacks Are Men, But Some of Us Are Brave*, New York, Feminist Press.

James, N. (1989) 'Emotional labour: skill and work in the social regulation of feelings', *Sociological Review*, 37 (1), pp.15–42.

James, V. and Gabe, J. (eds) (1996) *Health and the Sociology of the Emotions*, Oxford, Blackwell.

Jordanova, L. (1989) *Sexual Visions: Images of Gender in Science and Medicine between the Eighteenth and Twentieth Centuries*, Hemel Hempstead, Harvester Wheatsheaf.

Lawler, J. (1991) *Behind the Screens: Nursing, Somology and the Problem of the Body*, Melbourne, Churchill Livingstone.

Lee-Treweek, G. (1996) 'Emotion work, order and emotional power in care assistant work', in James, V. and Gabe, J. (eds) *Health and the Sociology of Emotions*, Oxford, Blackwell.

Lee-Treweek, G. (1998) 'Women, resistance and care: an ethnographical study of nursing auxiliary work', *Work, Employment and Society*, 11 (1), pp.47–63.

Lewis, G., Hughes, G. and Saraga, E. (2000) 'The body of social policy: social policy and the body', in McKie, L. and Watson, N. (eds) *Organizing Bodies: Institutions, Policy and Work*, Basingstoke, Macmillan.

Lonsdale, S. (1990) *Women and Disability: The Experience of Physical Disability among Women*, Basingstoke, Macmillan.

Lupton, D. (1996) *Food, the Body and the Self*, London, Sage.

Martin, E. (1987) *The Woman in the Body*, Milton Keynes, Open University Press.

Mauss, M. (1973) 'Techniques of the body', *Economy and Society*, 2, pp.70–88.

Merquior, J.G. (1985) *Foucault*, London, Fontana.

Miller, E. and Gwynne, G.V. (1972) *A Life Apart: A Pilot Study of Residential Institutions for the Physically Handicapped and the Young Chronic Sick*, London, Tavistock.

Morgan, D. (1993) 'You too can have a body like mine: reflections on the male body and masculinities', in Scott and Morgan (1993).

Morgan, D.H.J. and Scott, S. (1993) 'Bodies in a social landscape', in Scott and Morgan (1993).

Morris, J. (1993) *Independent Lives? Community Care and Disabled People*, Basingstoke, Macmillan.

Nettleton, S. and Watson, J. (1998) *The Body in Everyday Life*, London, Routledge.

Oliver, M. (1990) *The Politics of Disablement*, Basingstoke, Macmillan.

Öberg, P. (1996) 'The absent body: a social gerontological paradox', *Ageing and Society*, 16 (6), pp.701–19.

Petersen, A. and Brunton, R. (eds) (1997) *Foucault: Health and Medicine*, London, Routledge.

Phillipson, C. and Walker, A. (eds) (1986) *Ageing and Social Policy: A Critical Assessment*, Aldershot, Gower.

Rabinow, P. (1984) *The Foucault Reader: An Introduction to Foucault's Thought*, Harmondsworth, Penguin.

Saraga, E. (ed.) (1998) *Embodying the Social: Constructions of Difference*, London, Routledge.

Scott, S. and Morgan, D. (eds) (1993) *Body Matters: Essays on the Sociology of the Body*, London, Falmer Press.

Shakespeare, T. (1994) 'Cultural representations of disabled people: dustbins for disavowal', *Disability and Society*, 9 (3), pp.283–99.

Sheridan, A. (1994) *Michel Foucault: The Will to Truth*, London, Tavistock (first published 1980, Routledge).

Shilling, C. (1993) *The Body and Social Theory*, London, Sage.

Smart, C. (1989) *Feminism and the Power of Law*, London, Routledge.

Synnott, A. (1993) *The Body Social: Symbolism, Self and Society*, London, Routledge.

Taylor-Gooby, P. (1994) 'Postmodernism and social policy: a great leap backwards?', *Journal of Social Policy*, 23 (3), pp.385–404.

Townsend, P. (1986) 'Ageism and social policy', in Phillipson and Walker (1986).

Turner, B.S. (1984) *The Body and Society: Explorations in Social Theory*, Oxford, Blackwell.

Turner, B.S. (1991) 'Recent developments in the theory of the body', in Featherstone, M., Hepworth, M. and Turner, B.S. (eds) *The Body: Social Process and Cultural Theory*, London, Sage.

Turner, V.W. (1969) *The Ritual Process: Structure and Anti-structure*, Harmondsworth, Penguin.

Twigg, J. (1999) 'The spatial ordering of care: public and private in bathing support at home', *Sociology of Health and Illness*, 21 (4), pp.381–400.

Twigg, J. (2000) *Bathing, the Body and Community Care*, London, Routledge.

Walby, S. (1990) *Theorizing Patriarchy*, Oxford, Blackwell.

Walker, A. and Phillipson, C. (1986) 'Introduction', in Phillipson and Walker (1986).

Williams, S.J. and Bendelow, G. (1998) *The Lived Body: Sociological Themes, Embodied Issues*, London, Routledge.

9

Social Policy and the Emotions

Paul Hoggett

1   A limited construction of the subject

One of the criticisms of 'traditional' social policy, perhaps first coherently made by Fiona Williams (1989), was that it was blind to the nature of the subject it necessarily assumed; blind, for example, to the gendered or racialized nature of this subject. However, this criticism has now become so widely accepted that it is unwittingly in danger of becoming a new orthodoxy in which the human subject in post-modern social policy is apprehended only in its socially constructed form (Gribbins, 1998; O'Brien and Penna, 1998).

In contrast, I wish to argue that there are certain aspects of our nature as human beings which are as constitutive of 'the social' as they are constituted by it. In this chapter I am particularly concerned to explore our nature as emotional beings. Such an exploration seems appropriate now for a number of reasons. For one thing I am struck by the way in which the embodied and emotional nature of the subject is rapidly emerging as a key theme within our sister discipline, sociology (Craib, 1995, 1997; Hochschild, 1983; Shilling, 1997;

Bendelow and Williams, 1998; Williams, 1998a, 1998b). More personally, as someone with a background in mental health who is now undertaking a psychotherapy training, I have long felt perplexed and frustrated by the seeming inability of the social sciences to move beyond what seem to be rationalist models of the human subject.

Let me begin by summarizing what seem to me to be some of the key problems with social constructionist approaches to social policy. First, by emphasizing the discursive construction of subjects, selves and identities such approaches are in danger of providing us with 'over-socialized' (Shilling, 1997) accounts. In their most extreme form such accounts lead one to assume that the laws of nature apply only to the non-human world. This is an anthropocentric view which separates us from the nature in ourselves (our body, our psychological capacities, etc.) (Benton, 1991). This is not to say that such accounts provide us with no way of bringing the body into view, but it is a socially constructed body that is presented, one preoccupied with the way in which society inscribes its disciplinary codes upon a passive corporeality.

Second, such approaches tend to privilege cognition and language above emotion and affect. By marginalizing emotion we end up with a strangely one-sided view of human relations. For example, it is as if racism or sexism were simply ways of linguistically positioning another or imposing particular narratives upon them. In contrast, in everyday life, we do find ourselves talking about 'racist sentiments' and it is but a short step from here to begin to glimpse the way in which powerful flows of destructive affect can have a profound impact upon social life. If we are to stick with the idea of discourses, then we must begin to recognize the affective as well as cognitive dimension of such phenomena.

Third – and this flows from the two previous criticisms – social constructionist accounts of the subject (ones that Shilling, 1997 suggests include post-structuralist and Foucauldian perspectives) provide us with no adequate way of theorizing agency. Leonard (1997) tries to reconcile his Foucauldianism with his activism by resort to the writings of the late (but not yet deceased) Foucault where the power/resistance dyad is developed. As Thompson (1998) notes, given Foucault's earlier preoccupation with the ubiquitous and determining nature of power the reappearance of the determining subject in Foucault's final works seems rather dramatic. Not only dramatic but rather unsatisfactory. For the subject which is now posited, exists in a world lacking in intersubjectivity and it is therefore a predatory subject which 'regards all others merely as objects, to be used in whatever way necessary to achieve its own ends' (Thompson, 1998, p.142). The best that can be hoped for is the achievement of a certain symmetry in power relations, what Foucault describes as an 'agonism': 'a relationship which is at the same time reciprocal incitation and struggle' (Foucault, 1982, p.222). However, this provides us with an impoverished grasp of agency, one in which the creative potential of the human being is only ever invoked in relation to struggle with the other.

Leonard (1997, p.145) is aware of the limitations of a purely Foucauldian perspective and notes the way in which it so easily leads to a substitution of (impotent) intellectual critique for social critique. In his final chapter he can be found searching for a subject whose agency is more concrete and embodied than discourse theory allows for when he speaks of the importance of hope, anger and rage in the development of resistant forms of solidarity (ibid., p.162). But agency does not only come to us in acts of resistance. As passionate beings we are also capable of imagination, play and the externalization of internal capacities. This is absent from Foucault's reactive notion of the subject.

2   The affective subject

It is my view that social policy needs a subject in which mind and body, reason and passion, self and other, agent and object are held simultaneously in mind without splitting one from the other. As Craib (1997) points out, there is not only something Cartesian in the proliferation of binaries that otherwise results, there is also something psychotic about this split way of thinking.

Shilling (1997), in his review of alternatives to the dominant over-socialized view of the subject, provides a number of useful lines of thought. One approach is to draw attention to the importance of the body and the embodied subject in social science (see Chapter 8 this volume). A second approach, one that Shilling (1997) locates in critical realism, grounds our personhood in a pre-social 'body plus consciousness'. For Archer (1995) such a consciousness not only provides the ground for perception, discrimination and judgement but also for a universal sense of selfhood, the 'I' who exists as a psychical, physical and spiritual person. Craib (1997), drawing on the work of Mead (1934), notes how this referent, 'the non-socialized source of creativity and originality' (p.3) was later marginalized by interactionist appropriations of Mead's work. Within feminist political theory Jessica Benjamin (1994), in argument with Judith Butler, makes a similar point when insisting that the 'I' is not a grammatical fiction. As she notes, whilst it may be true that the subject is split, it is even more true that there must therefore be some kind of subject that engages in splitting.

In this chapter I wish to develop the 'body plus consciousness' perspective in a particular direction towards what Simon Thompson calls an 'affective ontology' (personal communication). At the heart of this position is the idea that we are all, irrespective of culture, emotional beings, that the body is the original site of the affects and emotions, and that these saturate consciousness. Furthermore I would concur with Williams (1998b) and others that there exist some basic emotions or what might be called emotional universals. According to Williams these basic emotions, 'rooted in our biological make-up and shared among all human beings as embodied agents . . . are endlessly elaborated, like colours on a painter's palette, across time and through culture' (p.750).

I would suggest such basic emotions are best thought of in terms of affect, something that exists on the boundary between the psyche and the soma. With affect quantitative considerations are dominant, whereas with emotion the qualitative dimension is much more important. Emotions therefore involve thought; moreover they are always directed towards some kind of object or person. As Williams (1998a) notes, like power, emotions are fundamentally relational. Affect on the other hand is much more free-flowing, more of an unbound energy. Furthermore, whilst the emotions are central to our nature as embodied and sensual beings they are rooted in affects whose 'excessive' nature constantly overflows the boundaries of the single body. It follows that there can be no group without emotion; emotions lie at the heart of the solidarities and divisions which make up group life. Indeed, in the work of the psychoanalyst Wilfred Bion (1961, 1970), the group and its emotions become the key to understanding the individual; it is as if the psyche, our inner world, is itself structured like a simple society (Hoggett, 1998).

This intimate connection between physical and psychical life, between the group and the individual, has much to offer any project of rethinking social policy. This is because it points toward a holistic vision for the aims and indeed processes of policy, a social policy which aims at meeting the emotional as well as physical needs of human beings.

3 The relational basis of our higher needs

In rethinking the welfare state we are inevitably drawn to the question of what needs should be addressed by a welfare society. Both Giddens (1994) and Fiona Williams (in Chapter 22 of this volume) raise the question of whether existing models of welfare need to go beyond purely redistributive strategies which address our basic needs towards a wider and more inclusive purview of human capacities which include questions of identity and well-being.

From its inception, the welfare state addressed the five great issues – want, disease, squalor, idleness and ignorance – which, with the exception of ignorance, were concerned with our physical needs.

It has paid lip-service to well-being and prevention whilst devoting its resources (often inadequately) and its thinking to the acute and immediately pressing difficulties that people have faced. To my mind this connects to a wider assumption that social policy is designed primarily to address social problems (Spicker, 1995). But well-being can only be thought of as a problem with some difficulty. Moreover well-being refers to the totality of an individual's social relations. As the user movement within mental health insists, what we require is a service that can adopt a holistic approach to integrated subjects rather than one adapted to specialized, professional interventions aimed at 'objects'.

Because physical needs primarily require material resources for their satisfaction, the primary concern of the post-war welfare state was with the fair and efficient allocation of these resources. The social democratic tradition in the UK has been intimately linked to this redistributive vision, to questions of 'who gets what?' Yet it was not this vision that drew me into working in the welfare state in the early 1970s. Like many others I found the social democratic vision inherently limiting. Not just because it assumed that distribution could be tackled within capitalism but, more importantly, because it seemed blind to the necessity of transforming social relations. It was as if the quality of life were merely a matter of the quantity of material goods (the size of the 'social wage' as it was put in those days) rather than something which was also concerned with the nature of social relations – in households, between sexes and generations, in neighbourhoods, in factories and indeed within the welfare institutions themselves. Yet it is the nature of these social relations which determines the extent to which our emotional needs are satisfied.

What are our emotional needs and what kinds of social arrangements contribute to their satisfaction? Honneth (1995) adopts Winnicott's psychoanalytic perspective when arguing that the core of the subject is built upon the recognition derived from a 'good enough' experience of parental love and understanding. His phrase 'good enough' draws our attention to the paradox that a good enough environment is also one that will fail the child just enough to facilitate the development of its autonomy. It provides the ontological security, the stable and secure sense of being, which enables the subject to move on in new struggles for self-respect and self-esteem. Without this sense of being, one Giddens (1991) following Erickson (1959) refers to as 'basic trust', the individual lacks any experience of an internal community. The alternative is a life of unbearable aloneness, one portrayed vividly in studies such as that conducted by James Glass (1989) of people who have been categorized as 'psychotic'.

Thus, the concept of 'well-being' provides a core principle around which a new vision of positive welfare could be organized. We could think of it as a meta-level principle which probably underlies a number of the 'good enough principles for welfare' that Fiona Williams develops (in Chapter 22 of this volume), specifically inter-dependence, care, bodily integrity and ontological (as opposed to social) identity. A secure sense of being provides the basis for doing and relating. With this foundation, interdependence becomes possible; without it, social relations become a continuing agonistic struggle. Bodily and psychical integrity, freedom from physical and emotional violence, are central to the development of our being. Traumatized subjects are haunted by a past which casts its shadow over all assertions of agency, in the worst case leaving them doomed to repeat past injuries in future encounters: as we now know, so many abusive fathers were themselves once abused children.

4   Development towards interdependence

As Barnes and Walker (1996) note, empowerment is not just about involvement in policy decisions which affect your life, it is about increasing personal powerfulness in all aspects of life. The concept of human development includes the idea of empowerment but goes beyond it. It is equivalent to a concern for the full development of human powers and capacities – moral, expressive, cognitive and spiritual. If this reminds some readers of the early Marx, the Marx of the *Economic and Philosophical Manuscripts*, I have no problem with this. Nor do I have any regrets if this sounds 'sixtiesish'. The unfashionableness of such ideas is perhaps epitomized by the 'New' Labour government which seems intent on convincing its citizens that the only source of value comes from paid work, no matter how alienating and exploitative this may be, and that the only form of dependence that can be welcomed is dependence upon the vagaries of an unregulated labour market. In contrast, DIY culture (McKay, 1998) is one of the clearest repudiations of this restricted sense of what it means to be human that we have in Britain today. As *Squall* (1995),[1] the mouthpiece of 'sorted itinerants', used to put it in its editorial statement, this is a culture 'standing for diversity, com-munity and respect. To give fair voice to those who have none, have gone hoarse, or are frightened to speak. To battle for a better environment – countryside, urban and psychological.' There is a paradox at the heart of the struggle for development which DIY culture recognizes, for to discover your power you have to have respect for limits, including your own. We need each other. A simple idea, but how strongly we rail against it, how hard our narcissistic culture finds this prospect. A society which has no sense of tragedy, pain or disappointment is dangerous. Its power is based upon the denial of its relations of interdependence with the other and on a denial of limits, including those provided by nature itself.

Even within the debates in social policy around the theme of empowerment one senses a reluctance at times to speak of our need for each other and our obligation towards each other. For example, there is a danger that we collude with that wider cultural orientation, one cultivated so assiduously by Thatcherism, which sees all public service workers primarily as a kind of enemy within, blindly pursuing their own interests under the guise of serving others. Such rhetoric connects to deeply held and often unconscious impulses within all of us which foster a ruthless attitude towards those such as teachers, nurses and carers on whom, at times, we all depend. As Winnicott (1945) once noted, at the very beginning our love for our mother is ruthless. It is as if the mother has no existence beyond her relationship to the child. Only later do we develop a capacity for concern for the mother (other), understanding her(him) as a separate being with her(his) own needs, i.e. as a person who deserves respect.

It has become too easy to denigrate public sector workers as if they were all simply bearers of discourses of domination, agents of the disempowerment of service users rather than actors also caught within the inherently contradictory logics of care and control, equity and rationing, and empowerment and exploitation (Foster and Hoggett, 1999). Public sector workers and service users face each other in a relationship of conflictual interdependence. There are real tensions between the needs of these two groups which cannot simply be ducked, for by doing so we collude with that rhetoric of consumer sovereignty which has been used to assault the British workforce for two decades. If the value of interdependence is to lie genuinely at the heart of a new vision of welfare then the idea of mutual respect between workers and users must be one of its programmatic objectives. Such respect can only be generated through a process of open and, at times, conflictual argumentation in which each side is drawn towards an acceptance of the abuse and wilful misunderstanding which it sometimes inflicts upon the other. For this to begin, people need to speak up and make their voices heard, even though there is a risk that they may get some things wrong. In social policy such a process of argumentation is only now beginning (Ungerson, 1997; Morris, 1997).

5 A 'democracy of the emotions'

Giddens (1991, 1994) has usefully drawn our attention to the way in which processes of detraditionalization have impacted upon our most intimate relations. As a consequence, roles such as 'husband', 'wife', 'partner', 'child' and so on have lost something of their 'given' nature and have become things which can be changed and shaped. Choice of partner, and the possibility of 'un-choosing' a partner, has brought more of an element of equality into our intimate relations (one is no longer stuck with an abusive partner 'till death do us part') and has also provided the basis for the flowering of a huge variety of household forms.

Giddens' phrase 'a democracy of the emotions' is also a pertinent way of describing recent developments in the praxis of democracy within the public sphere. The new social movements, perhaps particularly the women's movement, have brought a reflexivity into the practice of democracy itself. How people organize themselves in struggle, how people engage in dialogue in public spaces: these issues have become questions of choice and reflection no less than our intimate relations. At the heart of this development has been a reconceptualization of the relationship between means and ends. The idea that the nature of the means was unproblematic, or wholly justified by the ends, was replaced by the idea that the means should prefigure the ends. This early notion of prefiguration became developed by the peace and direct action movements of the 1980s and 1990s into a concern for 'process' (Schlosberg, 1995), that is, a concern to develop ways of organizing which struggled to be as inclusive, open and reflexive as possible (Touraine, 1981).

Within political theory this trend finds its fullest expression in the work of Iris Marion Young (1996) in her critique of deliberative democracy. The concept of deliberative democracy arises from the work of Habermas (1979) and specifically his argument that the development and extension of forms of non-strategic and non-instrumental dialogue – 'the free and unconstrained public deliberation of all about matters of public concern' (Benhabib, 1994) – was the best hope for critical forms of radicalism at the close of twentieth-century capitalism. In the UK such ideas underpin the movement for democratic renewal around constitutional reform, devolution, the empowerment of local government and the democratization of welfare. There is, however, a rationalism about deliberative democracy which is disturbing. The preoccupation with arguing and 'the force of the better argument' finds expression in the idea of writers such as John Elster (1998) that arguing is intrinsically connected to rationality; its content is impartial and disinterested; its style is calm and unflustered. In contrast, Young (1996) argues that such speech-forms are themselves exclusionary. By privileging the agonistic and disembodied voice, the more 'excited and embodied' voices of women, cultural and other minorities are devalued. Young advocates what she calls a 'communicative democracy' which is as open as possible to a plurality of speech forms including greeting, rhetoric and story-telling.

As both Young (1996) and Schlosberg (1995) point out, the new social and direct action movements insist that we should not have to leave our feelings behind when we enter deliberative spaces in the public sphere. Forums must be created in which people can bring their group identities, their particular experiences and their own forms of expression knowing that they will be treated with the same respect as the educated, white and male voice through which government still largely speaks.

6 Coming to voice

The privileging of certain kinds of speech forms makes it difficult for excluded groups to speak in their own voice. The concept of 'voice' is central to democratic theory (Hirschmann, 1970). It indicates the vital role that argument, dissent, protest and other forms of political action play in the public sphere. People only begin to become politically powerful when they find their voice. This is described vividly by bell hooks (1989). As she puts it, 'for women within oppressed groups who have contained so many feelings – despair, rage, anguish – who do not speak, as poet Audre Lorde writes, "for fear our words will not be heard or welcomed", coming to voice is an act of resistance' (hooks, 1989, p.12).

Coming to voice is, above all, about finding words for experience. Not any words, certainly not the words of the 'other' which may deaden or mystify that experience, nor even the words of the well-meaning but privileged ally who attempts to speak for you. As Croft and Beresford (1998) note, one of the paradoxes of the post-modernist turn in social policy is the way in which the experience of the service user is reinterpreted and restructured in academic debate so that users find themselves represented in another's privileged speech. Again, to cite hooks,

> I see how many of the people who are writing about domination and oppression are distanced from the pain, the woundedness, the ugliness. That it's so much of the time just a subject – a 'discourse' . . . I say remember the pain because I believe true resistance begins with people confronting pain, whether it's theirs or somebody else's, and wanting to do something to change it. (hooks, 1989)

One of the crucial ways in which oppression works is by denying people access to the words which would give meaning and expression to their experience. All of us, sometimes, are lost for words. We sense something is wrong or unjust but we feel alone. Maybe the rest of the group thinks differently or maybe we feel impotent when faced by another who is so much more articulate than ourselves (a number of senior academics spring to mind). Now think of the black child in an all-white school, or the woman tormented by voices in her head when being interviewed by a psychiatrist, or the learning-disabled teenager struggling to have his sexual feelings taken seriously. To be lost for words is to be left with experience that you have no way of symbolizing. Such forms of 'symbolic abolition' foreclose dialogue: 'foreclosure consists in not symbolizing what ought to be symbolized . . . it is a "symbolic abolition"' (Laplanche and Pontalis, 1973, p.168). What you are left with is pain and nowhere to put it, nothing but a broken and restricted language which cannot hold it. This is why Iris Marion Young refers to the 'excited and embodied' voices of the excluded. For some people have to speak their pain through their body or through actions. This is an unbearable explosive pain that 'reasonable people' shrink from. As hooks (1989) notes, if such pain is to be heard, the audience needs to learn to listen in new ways.

7   Containing emotion in institutions

If pain cannot be given words, if anger, fear or despair cannot be given voice, then it gets somatized or, worse, it gets projected on to the other. These are both ways in which affect is mapped unreflexively on to the body or person of self or other. In a similar way, affect gets somatized on to the body of the group or organization.

Bion (1962) speaks of the containment of affect, of emotional experience. For Bion the relationship between container and contained is *the* fundamentally constitutive relationship upon which the fate of human development revolves. If this relationship is a symbiotic one then experience is contained in a way which leads to thought and development. Imagine a young child on her first day at school. If her fears can be recognized and accepted by those around her, if she can in this way feel understood, then school can be a place in which learning from experience occurs. But if she finds no adequate containment of her fears they will be lodged inside her, finding expression in dreams, in tears which seem to have no foundation, in withdrawal or aggression towards her peers. Here her environment contains affect by suppressing it, forcing it back inside. Bion calls this relationship between container and contained parasitic, one which leads to the impoverishment rather than enrichment of self and other.

In a classic study of trainee nurses in a large London teaching hospital in the late 1950s, Menzies (1960) examined what happened when public sector workers and those for whom they cared were trapped in an institution which lacked any means of respecting emotional experience. As Menzies noted, hospitals are places where raw emotional experience is constantly evoked in patients, relatives and staff. Fear of dying and pain, disgust at processes of bodily decay and disease; humiliation, abandonment and the constant chronic uncertainty of the patient's life, all of these are the currency of hospital life. Despite this, Menzies found that the nursing profession at that time was organized largely on the basis of the denial of emotional experience, both of the patient and the nurse. As a consequence, the organization of nursing within the hospital acquired the characteristics of what Menzies called a 'social defence system'. It was as if systems, rules and procedures had been designed primarily either to prevent any form of emotional contact between nurses and patients or to suppress the feelings which were inevitably evoked when these defences were broken through. Menzies catalogued in great detail the elements of this perverse social system which ranged from the 'Taylorized' 'task list' method of organizing nursing which prevented any forms of nurse–patient contact, to the constant emphasis on 'professional detachment', to the culture of depersonalization that characterized the ward. Rigid hierarchies, the delegation of responsibility upwards (nurses would be punished for taking initiative) and a culture of blaming were additional elements of the system, the effects of which were not only deleterious for patient care but also ensured that the most emotionally mature trainees were the least likely to finish their training successfully. Attempts have been made to develop more holistic approaches to nursing care over the last three decades, particularly through the slow diffusion of the concept of 'primary nursing' (Pearson, 1988). However, Menzies' findings still have a strong resonance with the experience of nursing today (Aspinwall and Hoggett, 1998).

Institutions, then, can become organized systems of defence against anxiety. Painful affects become mapped on to the body of the institution; they become part of its fabric, like a fine corrosive vapour which penetrates everywhere. Procedures, regulations, even the physical fabric of buildings and rooms, come to contain traces of suppressed affect. This is what happens if words are not available to give meaning to emotional experience but are used to suppress and foreclose it.

As bell hooks (1989) notes, any emancipatory project (such as the regeneration of a welfare society) must always be in touch with the pain – the rage and anguish of the excluded as much as the fear and despair of the vulnerable. In contrast, the post-war welfare state seemed partly designed to separate society from this pain, to keep it out of sight, locked away in asylums, residential homes for children and the elderly, in special schools or covered up by organizational systems which did their best to separate workers from the emotional life of the service user. Much of this still goes on today. Charters of residents' rights and quality inspectorates can only gesture towards people's relational needs when care workers, including qualified nurses, are paid £5.50 per hour. The panoply of performance monitoring and management systems which developed in the 1990s has provided a new means of separating workers from the lived experience of users. The detailed documentation of virtually everything that is done or planned to be done for clients, patients or pupils which is now embodied in care or curriculum planning documents, assessments and reviews, patient records, monitoring reports etc. is fast becoming a vast simulacrum, a deceptive substitute, for real contact. The point is that such documentation is not designed to promote emotional contact, dialogue and learning but to enable the organization to look *as if* it is doing these things. Appearance has become inextricably confused with reality or, semiotically speaking, the system of signification (the documentation) has become a thing in itself, masking rather than revealing actual social relations of welfare.

8   Care and justice

It seems that we have been able to talk with some confidence about the positive value of care only quite recently in social policy. It is as if we have been so concerned to examine the social construction of care, the penetration of care by power, its gendered nature and so on, that we lost the courage to say that, despite all this, care has value. In this sense the feminist reappropriation of care (Bowden, 1997) has been a long time coming. The tragedy has been that for much of the last two decades the ethic of care and the ethic of justice have stood opposed to one another, as if the legitimate anger which always lies at the root of the struggle for social justice would be contaminated or corrupted by any talk of love, care or compassion. Yet each, in their own way, is essential to the development of solidaristic ties. For whereas justice finds its object in the universal stranger, care 'begins with a self who is enmeshed in a network of relations with others' (Kittay and Meyers, 1987), relations of give and take with the familiars on whom we depend and who depend on us in turn.

Let us be clear. Ours is primarily a society that does not care. It elects governments that do not want to pay for care, indeed make a virtue of lowering taxes rather than properly funding welfare services and paying care workers. It perpetrates euphemisms such as 'care in the community' and forces more and more of the work of care back on to women who are simultaneously put under pressure to engage in waged work. It has tolerated regimes of abuse in homes for children and elderly people under the name of care. It has colluded with and furthered the development of forms of professionalization which have disempowered service users under the name of care. Despite all this, care survives. It survives in households and friendship networks; it survives in hospices and therapeutic communities; it survives in the work of home care assistants and nurses. And because care survives, people enjoying such care can become strong, strong even in death and decay.

Power saturates all social relationships. All of us, every day, engage in some relationships in which we have power over others –

as professionals, as family members, as political activists and as self-help group members. We are enmeshed in discourses which embody relations of power both at work and at home. If, however, we conclude that power inevitably leads to domination and that agency is only possible through resistance to domination, then most of us may as well pack up and leave the stage. Surely the point is that the power we all have can be used for good effect or for ill. We can use the power that resides in our personal qualities and our skills and experiences to help other people. Otherwise why would people want to become parents, or teachers, or nurses? This is simple stuff and I feel angry at having to say it out loud. And, of course, we mess it up. We mess our kids up. But we often also help them find the strength to overcome the damage we have done to them.

Note

1 *Squall* was a magazine that came out of the DIY movement and covered travellers' issues, road protests, squats, raves and suchlike. Its last known address was 'Squall@phreak.intermedia.co.uk'.

References

Archer, M. (1995) *Realist Social Theory*, Cambridge, Cambridge University Press.

Aspinwall, K. and Hoggett, P. (1998) *Leading With Care: Report of the Collaborative Inquiry on the Johnson and Johnson/King's Fund Nurse Leadership Programme*, London, King's Fund.

Barnes, M. and Walker, A. (1996) 'Consumerism versus empowerment: a principled approach to the involvement of older service users', *Policy and Politics*, 24 (4), pp.375–93.

Bendelow, G. and Williams, S. (eds) (1998) *Emotions in Social Life: Critical Themes and Contemporary Issues*, London, Routledge.

Benhabib, S. (1994) 'Deliberative rationality and models of democratic legitimacy', *Constellations*, 1 (1), pp.26–52.

Benjamin, J. (1994) 'The shadow of the other (subject): intersubjectivity and feminist theory', *Constellations*, 1 (2), pp.231–54.

Benton, T. (1991) 'Biology and social science: why the return of the repressed should be given a (cautious) welcome', *Sociology*, 26, pp.225–32.

Bion, W. (1961) *Experiences in Groups*, London, Tavistock.

Bion, W. (1962) *Learning from Experience*, London, Heinemann.

Bion, W. (1970) *Attention and Interpretation*, London, Tavistock.

Bowden, P. (1997) *Caring: Gender-sensitive Ethics*, London, Routledge.

Craib, I. (1995) 'Some comments on the sociology of the emotions', *Sociology*, 29, pp.151–8.

Craib, I. (1997) 'Social constructionism as a social psychosis', *Sociology*, 31, pp.1–15.

Croft, S. and Beresford, P. (1998) 'Postmodernity and the future of welfare: whose critiques, whose social policy?', in Carter, J. (ed.) *Postmodernity and the Fragmentation of Welfare*, London, Routledge.

Elster, J. (ed.) (1998) *Deliberative Democracy*, Cambridge, Cambridge University Press.

Erickson, E. (1959) *Identity and the Life Cycle*, New York, International University Press.

Foster, D. and Hoggett, P. (1999) 'Change in the Benefits Agency: empowering the exhausted worker', *Work, Employment and Society*, 13 (1), pp.19–39.

Foucault, M. (1982) 'Afterword: the subject and power', in Dreyfus, H. and Rabinow, P. (eds) *Michel Foucault: Beyond Structuralism and Hermeneutics*, Brighton, Harvester.

Giddens, A. (1991) *Modernity and Self-Identity: Self and Society in the Late Modern Age*, Cambridge, Polity Press.

Giddens, A. (1994) *Beyond Left and Right: The Future of Radical Politics*, Cambridge, Polity Press.

Glass, J. (1989) *Private Terror/Public Life*, Ithaca, NY, Cornell University Press.

Gribbins, J. (1998) 'Postmodernism, poststructuralism and social policy', in Carter, J. (ed.) *Postmodernity and the Fragmentation of Welfare*, London, Routledge.

Habermas, J. (1979) *Communication and the Evolution of Society*, Boston, MA, Beacon Press.

Hirschmann, A. (1970) *Exit, Voice and Loyalty*, Cambridge, MA, Harvard University Press.

Hochschild, A. (1983) *The Managed Heart: The Commercialisation of Human Feeling*, Berkeley, CA, University of California Press.

Hoggett, P. (1998) 'The internal establishment', in Bion Talamo, P., Borgogno, F. and Merciai, S. (eds) *Bion's Legacy to Groups*, London, Karnac Books.

Honneth, A. (1995) *The Struggle for Recognition: The Moral Grammar of Social Conflicts*, Cambridge, Polity Press.

hooks, b. (1989) *Talking Back: Thinking Feminist, Thinking Black*, London, Sheba. (First published Boston, MA, South End Press, 1988.)

Kittay, E. and Meyers, D. (eds) (1987) *Women and Moral Theory*, Totowa, NJ, Rowman & Littlefield.

Laplanche, J. and Pontalis, J.B. (1973) *The Language of Psycho-Analysis*, London, Hogarth.

Leonard, P. (1997) *Postmodern Welfare: Reconstructing an Emancipatory Project*, London, Sage.

McKay, G. (1998) *DIY Culture: Party and Protest in Nineties Britain*, London, Verso.

Mead, G.H. (1934) *Mind, Self and Society*, Chicago, University of Chicago Press.

Menzies, I. (1960) 'Social systems as a defence against anxiety', *Human Relations*, 13, pp.95–121.

Morris, J. (1997) 'Care or empowerment? A disability rights perspective', *Social Policy and Administration*, 31 (1), pp.54–60.

O'Brien, M. and Penna, S. (1998) *Theorising Welfare*, London, Sage.

Pearson, A. (ed.) (1988) *Primary Nursing*, London, Croom Helm.

Schlosberg, D. (1995) 'Communicative action in practice: intersubjectivity and new social movements', *Political Studies*, 43, pp.291–311.

Shilling, C. (1997) 'The undersocialised conception of the embodied agent in modern sociology', *Sociology*, 31, pp.737–54.

Spicker, P. (1995) *Social Policy: Themes and Approaches*, Hemel Hempstead, Prentice-Hall.

Squall (1995) No.10, Summer.

Thompson, S. (1998) 'The agony and the ecstasy: Foucault, Habermas and the problem of recognition', in Ashenden, S. and Owen, D. (eds) *The Shadow of Difference: Habermas, Foucault and Political Theory*, London, Sage.

Touraine, A. (1981) *The Voice and the Eye: An Analysis of Social Movements*, Cambridge, Cambridge University Press.

Ungerson, C. (1997) 'Giving them money: is cash a route to empowerment?', *Social Policy and Administration*, 31 (1), pp.45–53.

Williams, F. (1989) *Social Policy: A Critical Introduction*, Cambridge, Polity Press.

Williams, F. (2000) *New Principles for Welfare*, Cambridge, Polity Press.

Williams, S. (1998a) '"Capitalising" on the emotions? Rethinking the inequalities in health debate', *Sociology*, 32, pp.121–39.

Williams, S. (1998b) 'Modernity and the emotions: corporeal reflections on the (ir)rational', *Sociology*, 32, pp.747–69.

Winnicott, D.W. (1945) 'Primitive emotional development', in Winnicott, D.W. (1975) *Through Paediatrics to Psycho-Analysis*, London, Hogarth.

Young, I.M. (1996) 'Communication and the other: beyond deliberative democracy', in Benhabib, S. (ed.) *Democracy and Difference*, Princeton, NJ, Princeton University Press.

10

Class and Social Policy

Gerry Mooney

<table>
<tr><td colspan="3">Contents</td></tr>
<tr><td>1</td><td>Introduction</td><td>156</td></tr>
<tr><td>2</td><td>The contested meaning of class</td><td>158</td></tr>
<tr><td>3</td><td>The marginalization of social class in social policy</td><td>161</td></tr>
<tr><td>4</td><td>Class effects and social policy</td><td>164</td></tr>
<tr><td>5</td><td>Rethinking social policy: the contribution of class analysis</td><td>167</td></tr>
<tr><td colspan="2">References</td><td>168</td></tr>
</table>

1 Introduction

Class is both central and marginal to social policy. The main aim of this chapter is to explore this claim, a claim which, at first reading, is not only apparently paradoxical, but also appears to belie the existence of a long tradition of concern with social class differences and inequalities in British social policy writing and research and which arguably assumed something of a renewed vigour in the late 1990s.

Class 'matters' to social policy in a myriad of ways: it continues to be a major factor in, for instance, the structuring of health inequalities, in educational attainment, in relation to housing and health provision, and it underpins the distribution of poverty and economic inequality in modern capitalist societies. We will examine some aspects of these 'class effects' in section 4. In the main, studies of these inequalities and aspects of social policy tend to utilize the notion of class in a rather descriptive way. Important as such studies are, particularly in relation to the valuable empirical evidence which they generate, this chapter argues for something more than class as a mere descriptive tool. Class here is employed as an analytical category, as a means of exploring

unequal class relations. Erik Olin Wright employs this in his examination of poverty in the United States:

> adding a class analysis perspective to the analysis of poverty is not just
> adding another variable to a laundry list of factors in a multivariate model.
> It changes the way we think about the political dynamics at stake in
> attempts to do something about the problem. Specifically, since a class
> analysis of poverty argues that there are significant numbers of privileged
> people with a strong, positive material interest in maintaining poverty,
> significant advances towards reducing poverty in the United States must
> place the problem of power and struggles over power at the centre of the
> political agenda. (Wright, 1995, p.99)

Wright's argument is no less applicable to our understanding of
poverty and social policy issues in the United Kingdom. Using class
in a relational sense should be a central feature in any attempt to
rethink social policy. This enables us to comprehend both the class
nature of the state and the reproduction of class inequalities in and
through social policy. This view of class is one which is currently
unfashionable and stands starkly against much contemporary theorizing on social policy (see section 3 below). While I think it is fair to
say that the majority of those researching and publishing in the very
broad and diverse field of 'social policy' see class as important in the
restricted descriptive sense, class as agency – a collective agency
central to shaping and/or resisting policy developments – is largely
absent from the social policy literature (cf. McCarthy, 1989; Pierson
1992; George and Miller, 1994). There appears to be a widespread
reluctance to use class in this second, more dynamic way, and this
comment from Michael Cahill's *The New Social Policy* is indicative of
the predominant usage of class in contemporary social policy:

> Class is important in the distribution of life chances. Clearly social class
> matters in relation to education, health and housing and many people are
> aware of the differential advantages enjoyed by people from different class
> locations. But it is social class as an organizing principle, as a unifying
> concept which is in sharp decline. (Cahill, 1994, p.18)

In this chapter we will explore some aspects of class inequalities as
they relate to particular areas of social policy, focusing primarily on
health and educational inequalities. From this we move to consider
arguments from a Marxist perspective which assert the centrality of
class as both a social division and an agent of change. Before turning to
a consideration of these questions, we need to clarify two issues of
definition. First, 'social policy' as used here is not defined in a narrow
sense as solely concerned with the policy process or policy outcomes,
but with the generalized social context within which policies are

developed and implemented; second is the thorny issue of what we mean by 'class'.

2 The contested meaning of class

In a relatively short chapter such as this there is little space to do justice to the ongoing debate which surrounds class, both as a useful concept within the social sciences in general, and social policy in particular, and as a fundamental division within contemporary society. To say that class is a subject of much controversy does little to convey the intensity of the argument which envelops class theorizing (for discussions of this see Crompton, 1998; Lee and Turner, 1996).

There are many different definitions and meanings of class. Broadly speaking, however, class as an analytical device is a way of making sense of a person's economic position and the inequalities that this may generate. Generally, class divisions refer to people's socioeconomic circumstances, whether in the labour market or in the production process. While material/economic factors are crucial in the structuring of class inequalities, class also refers to wider differences in power, social position and life chances in general.

Within this more general understanding of class, it is possible to separate out more specific notions of class and the social dynamics that the term signals. Thus, in the social policy literature class tends to be understood in three main ways: as emerging from exploitative production relations; as economic position and as occupational status. Let us now briefly consider each.

The idea of class as exploitation is primarily associated with Marxist theorizing. For Marxists, class is essentially a relationship between groups of people who have identifiable positions within the entire system of social production (Croix, 1981; Gubbay, 1997). Class is objectively defined: the key determinant of class under capitalism is whether or not one is forced to sell one's labour-power in order to survive. As Ferguson and Lavalette point out, for Marxists this definition of the working class 'includes the vast majority of the population within modern societies – whether they perceive themselves to be part of the working class is, at this level, immaterial' (1999, p.35).

For Marxists, the exploitative nature of capitalist production relations forms the basis of class oppression in all its forms. Thus for Smith:

> even in the richest societies in the world . . . the working class (defined objectively) still experiences oppression. Oppression takes many forms: regressive taxation policies; inferior schools; substandard or inaccessible medical care; the prevailing ideologies . . . the list goes on. Oppression is . . .

a product of a system based upon the rule of a tiny majority at the expense of the vast majority . . . oppression is endemic to capitalism. (Smith, 1994, p.40)

The basic building-blocks of Marxist approaches to the study of social and welfare policy are evident here, with the emphasis upon class oppression and upon the class basis of the modern state as reflected in, for example, the social policies it generates and implements, as representing competing class interests. What is important for Marxists is the distinction between class as an objective factor or – as Marx and Engels put it – class *in* itself, and class *for* itself, that is subjective factors (Marx and Engels, 1983, p.211). For those writing in the classical Marxist tradition, both objective and subjective factors are necessary for the development of class consciousness: that is, people's awareness of their own and others' class position. The development of full class consciousness, which was pivotal in Marx's theory of working-class struggle and revolution, could only emerge through class solidarity and collective action (see Lavalette, 1997; Mackintosh and Mooney, 2000). Thus, there is a dialectical interplay of structure and agency. It is the intersection of consciousness with position that produces a working class as a collective agent of change, reflecting Marx's dictum that people make history but not in circumstances of their own choosing.

The centrality of class as an agent of (historical) change within Marxist perspectives is absent from the second major tradition of class analysis which is derived from a Weberian theoretical framework. Like Marx before him, Max Weber recognized that ownership or non-ownership of property was a central aspect of class divisions. This, however, was only one dimension of the shared set of economic circumstances that constituted classes. For Weber:

> We may speak of a 'class' when (1) a number of people have in common a specific causal component of their life chances, in so far as (2) this component is represented exclusively by economic interests in the possession of goods and opportunities for income, and (3) is represented under the conditions of the commodity or labour markets. (Gerth and Mills, 1948, p.181)

Instead of the Marxist emphasis upon two main antagonistic classes – the owners of capital (or the bourgeoisie) and the wage-labourers (or proletariat) – in the Weberian perspective there is a large number of classes within society. Weberians not only stress differences between classes but divisions *within* classes, for example between skilled and unskilled workers, between professional and non-professional groups, or between salaried and waged workers. Different class groupings have distinctive economic and status positions, measured primarily in relation to labour market position and differential access to consumption resources, such as housing and health provision. Thus, some social classes will enjoy better 'life chances' than others, meaning that they will have relatively privileged opportunities for education, health, housing, employment and levels of income.

Weber is credited with highlighting forms of social stratification other than those of class, particularly in relation to status divisions. For Weberians, unlike Marxists, status differences, that is different amounts of prestige, are often more potent than class as the basis of social action and social division. Importantly, for Weberians, non-class-based divisions such as status can undermine class divisions and thereby represent an independent dimension of social stratification.

So these are two very different meanings and understandings of the same notion, class. While theorists working in both traditions have continued to refine, rework and debate the relative merits of these approaches, there is little doubt that despite some attempts to integrate Marxist and Weberian models, the contrasts between them continue to be more pronounced than any similarities which may exist. At the basis of this are their very different approaches to the study of society itself and their sharply contrasting methodologies.

While there are other models of social class, much of contemporary social science and social policy class theorizing derives from the foundational approaches of Marx and Weber. However, there is a third approach that has been heavily used in social policy research, which relies upon occupational measures of class. Conventional classifications here range from social class I to V or VI, to the differentiation of people as class A, B, C and so on. Occupational measures of class have also been to the fore in social policy research conducted by governmental and commercial agencies. Class in this sense is a useful social indicator and has been employed in a diverse range of ways to account for differences in voting patterns, health inequalities, geographical concentrations of poverty, housing patterns and employment opportunities, through to take-up of health services and variations in educational performance.

Despite the obvious attractiveness of this type of approach there are widely acknowledged difficulties in using occupational measures. Apart from the difficulty in accounting for the class position of those who are unemployed, such measures ignore the ways in which the structures of class, in terms of either production or market relationships (and gender, 'race' and age differences also), structure employment patterns. A further difficulty is that occupational measures cannot provide any evidence of capital or wealth ownership. Arguably the most important limitation of occupational measures is that while they often reflect some kind of gradational, hierarchical ordering of occupations, with professional and managerial categories always located higher than unskilled manual jobs for instance, there is little sense of class as a relational category. In other words, class relationships, exploitative or otherwise, are absent from this understanding of class.

Marxist and Weberian approaches offer competing explanations of class divisions, though in my view the explanatory power of the Marxist model is more potent. In this model class is not used as a descriptive category, or in a theoretically agnostic way as it often is in Weberian and other non-Marxist accounts (Goldthorpe and Marshall, 1992), but as an important analytical device employed to make sense not only of economic-based divisions, but of the social totality of capitalist society itself. Class plays a considerably more restricted role in the Weberian tradition but nonetheless many Weberians continue to see class-based divisions as key aspects of the wider system of social stratification (Marshall et al., 1988; Marshall, 1997).

3   The marginalization of social class in social policy

One of the key developments within British social policy analysis over the past twenty to thirty years has been the major contribution of feminist and anti-racist writers to an understanding of the discourses and practices which underpin social and welfare policy both in Britain and in other welfare regimes. These have been instrumental in questioning the dominant Fabian tradition in post-war social policy (which was primarily about social 'administration') that social policies operated in the 'best interests of society as a whole'. In the late 1980s and early 1990s writers such as Fiona Williams (1989) and Norman Ginsburg (1992), among others, rightly highlighted the marginalization of gender and 'race' in British social policy. Ginsburg further claimed that class was also 'fading out of academic fashion':

> There remains a huge antipathy to using and operationalizing the concept of 'class' in policy analysis, presumably for fear of its Marxist connotations. Yet, in Britain above all, class (using whatever definition) is manifestly fundamental to the social structure and therefore to analysing the functioning and impact of the welfare state. (Ginsburg, 1992, p.189)

Despite the centrality of class in shaping Britain's social structure, with relatively few exceptions (cf. Ginsburg, 1992; Jones and Novak, 1999; Ferguson and Lavalette, 1999; Lavalette and Mooney, 2000; Novak, 1988; Saville, 1983), class has largely faded from social policy's theoretical agenda. Even in a number of the textbooks produced in the mid- to late 1990s class is conspicuous by its absence (see, for example, Alcock et al., 1988; Ellison and Pierson, 1998). In both the Alcock, Erskine and May, and Ellison and Pierson student readers for example, while, rightly, there are chapters devoted to 'gender and social policy' and to '"race" and social policy', class does not receive similar treatment. In other books class is given the briefest of mentions. This is not an argument against social policy theorizing and writing on gender and 'race'/racisms, but an attempt to highlight that class has largely slipped from focus. Ironically, the demise of class in much of the social sciences during the past two decades has been accompanied by a reclaiming of the notion from those on the political right. This is evidenced by the widespread usage of discourses of 'the underclass', a diverse *de-classed* grouping of welfare 'dependants', lone parents and other 'marginalized' social categories (see Morris, 1994). What factors have contributed to this 'eclipse' of class?

In the British academy for much of the 1980s and 1990s class analysis, particularly of the Marxist variety, has been under attack. This is true not only of social policy, but also of much of the social sciences in general. In part this is due to a wide-ranging critique of Marxist ideas from an increasingly influential post-modernist and post-structuralist literature (see Laclau and Mouffe, 1987; Chapter 4 this volume).

Post-structuralists and post-modernists rejected the idea central to Marxism that there are *objective* economic interests, which lead to class-based solidarity. Interests are seen more in 'post-Marxist' theorizing as contingent and discursive (for more on this see Crompton, 1998; O'Brien and Penna, 1998).

The rejection of class as a meaningful notion was, of course, not simply a product of this new theorizing but part and parcel of a longer critique and rejection of Marxist thinking within the social sciences. In 1989, for example, Ray Pahl, a leading British sociologist, could claim that 'class as a concept is ceasing to do any useful work for sociology' (1989, p.194) while Pakulski and Waters (1996) went further to argue that class is dead.

For both post-modernists/post-structuralists and Weberian thinkers alike, Marxism as a perspective was guilty of reducing all social phenomena to economic relationships and was, as a result, economically reductionist, incapable of theorizing and explaining non-class-based forms of social stratification (see Gubbay, 1997 for a rebuttal). Marxism was further presented as an approach that was overwhelmingly concerned with social structures at the expense of human agency. As Ferguson and Lavalette (1999) argue, such a representation is perhaps true of Marxism in its Stalinist variants, where class as agency was absent, but is at best a caricature of the classical Marxist tradition with its stress on the complex interplay of structure and agency and its rejection of reductionist thinking. Indeed it is worth noting that critics of Marxism almost always portray its most vulgar forms.

It is widely argued that class has been undermined as a result of a diverse range of interrelated social, economic, political and cultural developments. These have been widely discussed elsewhere (Westergaard, 1995; Lee and Turner, 1996; Crompton, 1998; Edgell, 1993; Jones, 1997) and only the briefest of discussion is possible here.

Claims about the dissolution and fragmentation of class divisions have tended to rely upon occupation-based measures in studies of the relationship between class and voting patterns, and on labour market changes, particularly a decline in manual blue-collar occupations and the rapid growth of white-collar, service-based employment. The emergence and spread of new types of 'flexible', 'post-Fordist' systems of production and labour markets accompanied these shifts in occupational structure. Such changes for many commentators were reflected in a decline in the 'traditional' working-class and work-based class identities, often centred upon single-class communities such as coal-mining, textiles and shipbuilding. These structural changes undermined, it was claimed, mass membership of organizations such as trade unions, the Labour Party and work-based social and political associations. Yet other structural changes were seen as leading to increasing individualism and the rising importance of consumption and lifestyles as a source of identity are said to have replaced work-based class identities. Thus, it is argued, the 'old certainties' of social class have been eroded.

The slump in blue-collar manual employment and the rise of service jobs represented for many social scientists, particularly, but not exclusively, those working within the Weberian tradition, a vindication that Marxist claims about the inevitability of class polarization, that is, a sharpening of class divisions, were inadequate and mistaken. Thus, a decline in the working class and growth in the middle class was posited as one of the key social structural changes in recent decades, a claim taken up by the New Labour leadership in the late 1990s and by its key thinkers such as Anthony Giddens (1998).

However, all too often the restructuring of class relations has been confused with the end of class, in particular the end of the working class. Undoubtedly the industrial working class is much smaller than twenty or thirty years ago but then the 'industrial' working class was never the working class in its entirety and as a category it cut out groups of workers, both female and male, black and white, who were not employed in manual and 'smokestack' industries. Further, such claims also neglect the fact that many white-collar workers, particularly those engaged in the delivery of health, education and other welfare services, now see themselves as working class in ways which were almost inconceivable in the 1950s and 1960s. Additionally, proponents of the various 'end of class' theories have little to say about the continuing existence and reproduction of wealth, privilege, power and dominance at the top of the social scale (cf. Westergaard, 1995).

Many different but related arguments and debates are compressed here and space does not allow for a detailed exploration of such claims. It is important, however, to recognize that what we have here are contested claims: different interpretations of social and economic change; interpretations which rely not only upon different meanings of class but on sharply divergent class theorizations.

To conclude, it should be clear that class is a contested notion with different meanings and the subject of ongoing debate surrounding its utility, and validity as a means of understanding social inequality and social divisions within contemporary society. An appreciation should also have been gained of some of the main conceptual and analytical weaknesses which tend to characterize 'end of class' theorizing. In the remaining sections, the discussion focuses on class in relation to particular aspects of social and welfare policy, and on the ways in which writers working within a broad Marxist framework have employed class as a category in their analyses of social policy in capitalist societies. The chapter concludes by making a case for a class analysis of social policy as a contribution to rethinking social policy.

4 Class effects and social policy

The marginalization of class in social policy theorizing in the 1980s and 1990s stands in contrast to its role in previous generations of social policy analysis. In the late 1950s, for example, Richard Titmuss (1987) was already arguing that the distribution of welfare was favouring the middle classes over the working classes, a claim repeated in many subsequent studies, while the 'rediscovery of poverty' debate in the 1960s drew attention to the existence of a sizeable grouping in the population whose needs were not being addressed by welfare and social policy provision. However, it was not until the 1970s that Marxist theorists in particular employed a notion of class as a central means of critiquing the welfare state, in a very different way from Titmuss and others before him. From this period feminist and anti-racist theorists emphasized the extent to which the social policies characteristic of the post-war welfare settlement both reflected and imposed dominant values about the perceived position of women and black people within society. These arguments helped to broaden social policy as a field of enquiry and analysis. Marxists were also instrumental in this phase of widening and rethinking social policy analysis, (cf. O'Connor, 1973; Gough, 1979).

The starting-point for Marxist analysis was the argument that welfare and social policies are *state* policies and, as such, are committed to the maintenance and reproduction of capitalist social relations. While 'class', or at least certain limited understandings of class, were part and parcel of the Beveridgean welfare state, Marxists argued that class inequalities had not been reduced nor had there been a significant redistribution of resources to the working class. Further, state policy interventions worked to compound and reproduce class inequalities in health provision, in educational attainment and so on. Thus social policies reflect and uphold the divisions of exploitation and oppression within capitalism, and reflect assumptions not only about the role of 'the family' and women in society, but also of the role of labour and the drive for profit.

While this generation of Marxist theorizing was guilty of neglecting the gendered and racialized assumptions which were central to the Beveridgean welfare state, they can also be attacked – somewhat ironically, given the thrust of Marxism – for the absence of class as agency and the marginalization of class struggle in their analyses. In essence the major focus of these accounts of social welfare has been on the structural inequalities that exist within modern societies, the role of social policies in promoting or sustaining ideological hegemony and on the contribution of such policies to the maintenance of society. Such a focus reflects the historical influence of Fabianism on social policy thinking in Britain.

Marxist and many non-Marxist theorists alike, especially those working within a Weberian understanding of class, stress the continuing existence of structural class-based inequalities in their critiques of social and welfare policy. Let us briefly focus on two areas of social policy that have been the subject of considerable research to highlight this: the links between class and health and between class and education. Again these rely mainly upon occupational class schemata but nonetheless the empirical evidence that they generate has been used to defend the concept of class and class analysis from its critics. Indeed John Westergaard (1995), one of the most vociferous defenders of the Marxist notion of class, argues that class has been declared dead or dying when its significance and effects have become sharper. Westergaard focuses on the deepening of income and wealth inequalities and the growth of poverty in the 1980s and 1990s to make his point, but the salience of class is all too evident in other forms.

Inequalities in health and educational outcomes have long been highlighted as key indicators of class inequality. The close relationship between class membership and patterns of morbidity and mortality has long been a concern of social policy analysis and has been well established through research, some of it government-sponsored. Notable here was the Black Report, first published in 1980. It concluded that:

the poorer health experience of the lower occupational groups applied at all stages of life . . . The class gradient seemed to be greater than in some comparable countries . . . and was becoming more marked. During the twenty years up to the early 1970s . . . the mortality rates for both men and women aged 35 and over in occupational classes I and II had steadily diminished while those in IV and V changed very little or had even deteriorated. (Townsend et al., 1988, p.2)

Within one month of being elected in May 1997 the Labour government appointed Sir Donald Acheson to chair an 'Independent Inquiry into Inequalities in Health'. Its subsequent report, which focused on health inequalities in England and Wales, showed that while death rates have fallen for all social groups since the late 1970s, there has been a sharpening of differences in life expectancy between social classes. In the 1970s, for example, death rates among men aged 16–65 were almost twice as high for those in unskilled occupations (social class V) as for those in professional groups (class I). By the 1990s this gap had increased to almost three times higher (Acheson, 1998, p.11). In the late 1980s the death rates for men in semi-skilled and unskilled categories were 68 per cent higher than among those in classes I and II, and among women 55 per cent higher, an increase from 53 and 50 per cent respectively in the late 1970s. Such figures, stark as they are, are compounded by inequalities in life expectancy and in the incidence of ill-health (see Scambler and Higgs, 1999, for a discussion of these).

In relation to differences in educational attainment and outcomes, class is again a clear factor. Again there is a long tradition of social scientific research on education and class inequalities. In his study of the relationship between class and educational achievement, Furlong argues that despite the significant economic, social and political changes which have characterized recent decades, class-based social divisions remain 'central to an understanding of educational outcomes and the advantages of the middle classes have largely been preserved throughout a period of rapid change in education and the labour market' (Furlong, 1997, p.69).

Furlong also notes, however, that there appear to be some signs of a weakening of class differences among young women, highlighting the complex interplay of class-based and non-class-based social divisions.

Nevertheless the dominant picture which emerges from studies of social inequalities in contemporary Britain is of a deepening of class divisions. While such studies still see class inequalities as a central feature of contemporary British society, they are limited in their emphasis and reliance upon empirical measures of class, particularly occupational classifications. Such inequalities cannot be fully understood without a 'strongly relational' class schema (Gubbay, 1997).

Thus, in relation to the distribution of risk factors for health, Scambler and Higgs argue that these can only be adequately

> comprehended in terms of an adequate theory of class relations – necessarily incorporating analyses of power, contradictory or incompatible class interests, and so on . . . Stated more generally, in as far as those risk factors that contribute to the production of health inequalities can only be properly explicated in terms of their embeddedness in class relations, so can their reproduction. (Scambler and Higgs, 1999, p.289)

It is the emphasis on class as relational which allows us to transcend the limitations of descriptive or 'weakly relational' measures of class and to employ class as an explanatory tool to make sense of those processes which reproduce and reinforce class disparities.

5   Rethinking social policy: the contribution of class analysis

It seems rather odd to be making a case that class is important to social policy at a time when the available empirical evidence, despite its pitfalls, overwhelmingly points to a widening and deepening of occupational social class inequalities in health, income and other aspects of welfare during the 1980s and 1990s. This period also witnessed a strengthening of class differences within and amongst some minority ethnic groups and amongst women but again, as Westergaard has argued, the denial of class is often most potent in periods when class divisions are at their sharpest.

In this chapter you have come across a particular argument about social class, an argument derived from a Marxist perspective. It is an argument that makes claims, contested claims, not only about class and social policy but also, crucially, about the wider social totality. This type of approach stands against much of the thrust of recent social policy/welfare writing which has tended to separate 'welfare' off almost as a discrete area of social activity. Instead it is argued that only by locating social policy within this totality do we begin to develop a comprehensive and adequate understanding of its dynamics and relations, and class analysis is an invaluable tool in this process. This is *not* to argue that non-class-based forms of oppression are simply reducible to the functioning of capitalism but to argue that they take their present form in ways which are mediated by the wider (and complex) social totality of modern capitalist society. So this is not an argument to diminish the importance of divisions of gender or 'race' for our understanding of social policy, but to bring class back in. To understand class as agency not simply structure; to see that class is, above all, exploitative and relational; and to utilize class as an analytical and explanatory notion, not a mere descriptive device.

Let us return to the claim made at the start – that class is both central and marginal to social policy. What has been argued here is that class is central to our understanding of social policy and while class is recognized as an important social division and source of inequality within much of the social policy literature, the importance accorded to it has diminished to some extent in recent times, especially in analytical terms. There had been a slippage in the use of class in the 1980s and 1990s in that it had been deployed primarily as a descriptor of influences on social policy, and as an effect of policies, with reliance upon narrower occupational schemata of various kinds. The notion of class as an objective economic relation and class as a 'collective agency', which may have a role in shaping and/or resisting policy developments is, at the very least, marginalized in the literature. As Miliband points out, 'class analysis is largely *class struggle* analysis' (1989, p.3). In a 1996 Gallup survey over 80 per cent of those surveyed believed that there was a class struggle taking place in modern Britain. For the past one hundred years and more, class struggles in Britain have been a major influence on social and welfare policies, from struggles over the Poor Law in the mid-nineteenth century, the Clydeside rent strikes in the period from 1915 to the early 1920s which hastened in state housing provision, through to the fight against the 'poll tax' in the late 1980s and the ongoing struggles against workfare policies and privatization strategies in their many forms in the 1990s (see Lavalette and Mooney, 2000; Mizen, 1998).

Arguably a new welfare settlement has been in the making in the late 1990s. There is little sign that class inequalities, on any criteria, are being addressed. Indeed class has been almost totally removed from the current social policy lexicon. In 'New' Labour's attempt to identify a 'third way', the end of class divisions is confirmed, while in the plethora of debates and policies concerned with 'social exclusion', class is almost completely absent.

The idea advanced in this chapter is that the recognition of class as a central agency, shaping and recreating the world, can help us to understand social policy, the nature of welfare provision, and struggles over both, in modern capitalist societies. While this may be an unfashionable idea in some quarters, through a focus on class relations we can begin to explore social policy as part of a wider social totality, as part and parcel of the relations and processes of exploitation and oppression.

References

Acheson, D. (1998) *Independent Inquiry into Inequalities in Health*, London, HMSO.
Alcock, P., Erskine, A. and May, M. (eds) (1988) *The Student's Companion to Social Policy*, Oxford, Blackwell.

Cahill, M. (1994) *The New Social Policy*, Oxford, Blackwell.

Croix, G. de Ste (1981) *Class Struggle in the Ancient Greek World*, London, Duckworth.

Crompton, R. (1998) *Class and Stratification* (2nd edn), Cambridge, Polity Press.

Edgell, S. (1993) *Class*, London, Routledge.

Ellison, N. and Pierson, C. (eds) (1998) *Developments in British Social Policy*, London, Macmillan.

Ferguson, I. and Lavalette, M. (1999) 'Social work, postmodernism, and Marxism', *European Journal of Social Work*, 2 (1), pp.27–40.

Furlong, A. (1997) 'Education and the reproduction of class-based inequalities', in Jones (1997).

George, V. and Miller, S. (eds) (1994) *Social Policy: Towards 2000*, London, Routledge.

Gerth, H. and Mills, C.W. (eds) (1948) *From Max Weber*, London, Routledge.

Giddens, A. (1998) *The Third Way*, Cambridge, Polity Press.

Ginsburg, N. (1992) *Divisions of Welfare*, London, Sage.

Goldthorpe, J.H. and Marshall, G. (1992) 'The promising future of class analysis: a response to recent critiques', *Sociology*, 26, pp.381–400.

Gough, I. (1979) *The Political Economy of the Welfare State*, London, Macmillan.

Gubbay, J. (1997) 'A Marxist critique of Weberian class analysis', *Sociology*, 31 (1), pp.73–89.

Jones, C. and Novak, T. (1999) *Poverty, Welfare and the Disciplinary State*, London, Routledge.

Jones, H. (ed.) (1997) *Towards a Classless Society?* London, Routledge.

Laclau, E. and Mouffe, C. (1987) 'Post-Marxism without apologies', *New Left Review*, 166, Nov./Dec., pp.79–106.

Lavalette, M. (1997) 'Marx and the Marxist critique of welfare', in Lavalette, M. and Pratt, A. (eds) *Social Policy: A Conceptual and Theoretical Introduction*, London, Sage.

Lavalette, M. and Mooney, G. (eds) (2000) *Class Struggle and Social Welfare*, London, Routledge.

Lee, D.J. and Turner, B.S. (1996) *Conflicts about Class*, London, Longman.

McCarthy, M. (1989) *The New Politics of Welfare*, London, Macmillan.

Mackintosh, M. and Mooney, G. (2000) 'Identity, inequality and social class', in Woodward, K. (ed.) *Questioning Identity: Gender, Class, Nation*, London, Routledge/The Open University.

Marshall, G. (1997) *Repositioning Class*, London, Sage.

Marshall, G., Newby, H., Rose, D. and Vogler, C. (1988) *Social Class in Modern Britain*, London, Hutchinson.

Marx, K. and Engels, F. (1983) *Collected Works*, volume 6, Moscow, Progress Publishers.

Miliband, R. (1989) *Divided Societies*, Oxford, Oxford University Press.

Mizen, P. (1998) '"Work-welfare" and the regulation of the poor: the pessimism of post-structuralism', *Capital and Class*, 65, pp.35–53.

Morris, L. (1994) *Dangerous Classes*, London, Routledge.

Novak, T. (1988) *Poverty and the State*, Milton Keynes, Open University Press.

O'Brien, M. and Penna, S. (1998) *Theorizing Welfare*, London, Sage.

O'Connor, J. (1973) *The Fiscal Crisis of the State*, London, St James Press.

Pahl, R. (1989) 'Is the emperor naked? Some questions on the adequacy of sociological theory in urban and regional research', *International Journal of Urban and Regional Research*, 13 (4), pp.709–20.

Pakulski, J. and Waters, M. (1996) *The Death of Class*, London, Sage.

Pierson, C. (1992) *Beyond the Welfare State*, Cambridge, Polity Press.

Saville, J. (1983) 'The origins of the welfare state', in Loney, M. et al. (eds) *Social Policy and Social Welfare*, Milton Keynes, Open University Press.

Scambler, G. and Higgs, P. (1999) 'Stratification, class and health: class relations and health inequalities in high modernity', *Sociology*, 33 (2), pp.275–96.

Smith, S. (1994) 'Mistaken identity – or can identity politics liberate the oppressed?', *International Socialism*, 62, pp.3–50.

Titmuss, R. (1987) 'The irresponsible society', in Abel-Smith, B. and Titmuss, R.M. (eds) *The Philosophy of Welfare: Selected Writings of R.M. Titmuss*, London, Allen & Unwin.

Townsend, P., Whitehead, M. and Davidson, N. (1988) *Inequalities in Health: The Black Report and the Health Divide*, Harmondsworth, Penguin.

Westergaard, J. (1995) *Who Gets What?* Cambridge, Polity Press.

Williams, F. (1989) *Social Policy: A Critical Introduction*, Cambridge, Polity Press.

Wright, E.O. (1995) 'The class analysis of poverty', *International Journal of Health Services*, 25, pp.85–100.

11

From the KWNS to the SWPR

Bob Jessop

1 Introduction

This chapter considers selected aspects of welfare state restructuring in Britain and certain other advanced western capitalist economies. More specifically it identifies some major shifts in the functions, the scale and modes of delivery of the state's involvement in securing the economic and social conditions for capital accumulation. It explains these shifts in terms of some general economic, political and sociocultural changes in advanced capitalist societies and their implications for economic and social policies. My analysis has three implications for issues relevant to this volume: the relation between changes in social and economic policy; how the territorial scale on which social policies are designed and implemented has changed in line with the re-scaling of the economic and political systems; and the changing balance between market, state and civil society in social policy delivery. In particular, I argue that, relative to the earlier post-war period, social policy is becoming more closely subordinated to economic policy; it is acquiring increasingly important supra- and sub-national dimensions; and its delivery has been subject to a partial rollback of the state in favour of market forces and civil society.

Unfortunately a brief chapter requires a one-sided, over-simplified approach. This does not imply that social policy can be explained only through capitalism's changing dynamic nor that given policy changes always have identical causes or follow the same course. Rather, this chapter aims to reveal aspects of welfare that other accounts overlook. In particular it illuminates Claus Offe's paradoxical claim that 'while capitalism cannot coexist *with*, neither can it exist *without*, the welfare state' (1984, p.153; emphasis in original).

2   The Keynesian welfare national state

An important step in clarifying Offe's paradox is to typify the welfare state that he claims is both necessary to and incompatible with capitalism. This is the form that became dominant in north-western Europe, North America, Australia and New Zealand during the 1950s to 1970s in conjunction with a specific economic growth dynamic. It can be described in ideal-typical terms as the Keynesian welfare national state (or KWNS). Each term in this fourfold construct highlights *distinctive* features of the KWNS and ignores any *generic* properties it may share with other types of capitalist welfare regime. One can also compare other types of capitalist welfare regime with the KWNS and/or with each other in terms of their own distinctive features on these four dimensions.

This fourfold schema derives from features of capitalism as a mode of production. The first dimension refers to the state's distinctive roles in securing conditions for profitable private business. This is the field of economic policy. It is important because market forces alone cannot secure these conditions and must be supplemented by non-market mechanisms. The second dimension refers to the state's distinctive roles in reproducing labour power individually and collectively over various time spans of the life course and across generations. This is the field of social policy. It matters because labour power is a fictitious commodity. For, although it is bought and sold in labour markets and may add value in production, it is not itself directly (re)produced within and by capitalist firms with a view to private profit. Labour power enters the market economy from outside. This poses economic problems as regards its individual and collective suitability to capital's needs and its own survival in the absence of a secure income or other assets; social problems regarding social inclusion and cohesion; and political problems regarding the legitimacy of state intervention in this area. The third dimension refers to the primary scale on which economic and social policies are decided – even if they are underpinned or implemented on other scales. This is significant

Table 11.1 *The Keynesian welfare national state*

1 Keynesian	=	Full employment
		Closed economy
		Demand management
		Infrastructure
2 Welfare	=	Generalized norms of mass consumption
		Welfare rights
3 National	=	Relative primacy of national scale
4 State	=	Market and state form mixed economy
		State corrects 'market failures'

because economic and social policies are politically mediated and the primary scales of political organization may not coincide with those of economic and social life. Finally, the fourth dimension refers to the primary mechanism, if any, for supplementing market forces in facilitating capitalist profitability and reproducing labour power. This matters because the state is just one mechanism through which attempts are made to overcome market failures and inadequacies. Both capitalism's overall dynamic and the nature of the wider society depend on the particular mix of mechanisms.

The KWNS will now be defined on these four dimensions. First, in promoting the conditions for the profitability of private capital, the KWNS was distinctively *Keynesian* in so far as it aimed to secure full employment in a relatively closed national economy and to do so primarily through demand-side management. Likewise, in reproducing labour-power as a fictitious commodity, the KWNS's *welfare* orientation was distinctive in so far as it tried: (a) to generalize norms of mass consumption beyond male workers earning a family wage in Fordist sectors in order that all full national citizens and their family dependants share the fruits of economic growth (and thereby also contribute to effective domestic demand); and (b) to promote forms of collective consumption favourable to mass production and mass consumption. Thus, its economic and social policies were linked to economic and social rights attached directly or indirectly to citizenship of a national territorial state – whether this citizenship was based on descent, acculturation, naturalization, political tests, or some other criterion (on different types of national state, as opposed to nation-state, see Jessop, 1999a). The KWNS was *national* in so far as the national territorial state was mainly responsible for developing and guiding Keynesian welfare policies. Local and regional states acted mainly as relays for policies framed at the national level; and the various international regimes established after the Second World War were mainly intended to restore stability to national economies and national states. And the KWNS was *statist* in so far as state institutions (on different levels) were the chief complement to market forces in the post-war 'mixed economy' (see Table 11.1).

3   Recent and continuing changes in welfare regimes

This section notes four general trends in welfare restructuring and assesses their overall significance. The first trend is a shift from Keynesian aims and modes of intervention to Schumpeterian ones; the second is a shift from a welfarist mode of reproduction of labour-power based on the *rights* of worker-citizens *qua* citizens to welfare benefits to a workfarist mode based on the *obligations* of worker-citizens *qua* workers to support themselves as far as possible through integration into the labour and other markets. The third is a shift from primacy of the national scale in economic and social policy-making to a post-national framework in which no scale is predominant; the fourth is a shift from the state's primacy in compensating for market failures to more networked, partnership-based economic, political and social governance mechanisms. These trends can be considered separately. Indeed, both severally and in combination, they have developed quite differently in different societies. Nonetheless the trends can be synthesized into a general claim that a shift is occurring from a Keynesian welfare national state (KWNS) to a Schumpeterian workfare post-national regime (SWPR).

All four changes are closely connected to attempts to solve difficulties in the economic growth dynamic that characterized the KWNS societies. This growth dynamic involved a virtuous circle of mass production–mass consumption that produced growing prosperity in the increasingly integrated American and north-west European post-war economies. The connection between these changes and the crisis of this 'Atlantic Fordist' system does not imply that they are entirely explicable in terms of a transition to an emerging post-Fordist regime. This economic crisis is better seen as a critical contextual factor for struggles to define the nature and depth of crises allegedly affecting the KWNS itself – especially regarding whether or not these crises can be resolved only by developing a new form of welfare regime. Some further factors shaping the development of the SWPR will be considered in the next section.

The ideal-typical Schumpeterian workfare post-national regime can be described as follows. First, regarding its functions for capital, the SWPR is *Schumpeterian* in so far as it tries to promote permanent innovation and flexibility in relatively open economies by acting on the supply side and to strengthen as far as possible their competitiveness. Second, regarding social reproduction, the SWPR can be called (perhaps infelicitously and at the risk of misunderstanding) a *workfare* regime in so far as it subordinates social policy to the demands of labour market flexibility and economic competitiveness. This includes efforts to cap or reduce the social wage considered as a cost of production. Third, the SWPR can be termed *post-national* in so

Table 11.2 *Schumpeterian workfare post-national regime*

1 Schumpeterian	=	Innovation and competitiveness
		Open economy
		Supply-side policies
2 Workfare	=	Subordinates social to economic policy
		Puts downward pressure on 'social wage'
		Attacks welfare rights
3 Post-national	=	Relativization of scale
4 Regime	=	Increased role of governance mechanisms
		to correct market and state failures

far as the increased significance of other spatial scales and horizons of action renders the national territorial state less important as a 'power container'. This can be described as a 'relativization of scale' compared to the primacy of the national in the KWNS. Finally, regarding policy delivery, the SWPR can be termed a *regime* to highlight the increased importance of non-state delivery mechanisms in providing state-sponsored economic and social policies (see Table 11.2).

The SWPR ideal-type derives from recent trends in those capitalist economies that developed some form of KWNS. Like all ideal-types, it involves one-sided accentuation of empirically observable features to construct a logically possible social phenomenon. This does not imply that examples of the SWPR exist in pure form nor that any movement along its different dimensions occurs evenly in pace or degree. What exist are more complex, path-dependent mixes of types – alloyed with various incidental and accidental features. Nonetheless welfare regimes can be compared through ideal-types to identify differences within and across economic spaces, states or societies and to guide research into welfare reform. The evidence shows significant variation in efforts to identify and solve problems of the KWNS. It involves neither unidirectional movement nor multilateral convergence across all national regimes. Indeed, alternative trajectories with different end-points and different patterns of 'conservation–dissolution' of past features can be identified on all four dimensions.

4   Contextualizing the changes

The KWNS experienced a multidimensional crisis in the 1970s and 1980s. This had various general economic, political and sociocultural causes. The timing, incidence and forms of the crisis in specific cases were also shaped by more conjunctural factors. The latter include the outcome of struggles over how best to interpret these crises, assess their significance, and derive policy conclusions from these diagnoses.

Economically, the KWNS was undermined by the increasing opening of national economies and their resulting interpenetration through a variable mixture of extraversion, inward investment and an expanding international division of labour. This weakened the 'taken-for-grantedness' of the national economy as an object of economic management and reduced the effectiveness of Keynesian policies. In addition, regional and local economies were increasingly held to have their own specific problems. These could be solved neither by the usual national macroeconomic policies nor by standardized KWNS industrial and/or regional policies formulated by the central state. Other economic factors weakening the KWNS included the challenges posed by lower-waged, export-oriented East Asian economies; changes in the overall organization and dynamic of the economy (often summarized as the emergence of post-Fordism); and the feminization of the labour-force, with its impact on the family form and the family wage which had played key roles in the KWNS.

Overall, these changes made it harder for the state to manage its national economy *as if* it were closed (as it had done, for example, in relying on demand management) and so prompted an interest in, and a shift towards, more supply-side intervention. This could be limited to neo-liberal, supply-side measures or extended to include tailor-made measures targeted at specific sectors and/or places. There was also an increasing emphasis on flexibility in manufacturing and services (including the public sector) based on new technologies (especially micro-electronics and information and communication technologies) and more flexible forms of organizing production. There was growing concern with competitiveness *vis-à-vis* other economies. This has created political openings for attacks on social welfare in so far as critics emphasize its fisco-financial costs rather than its contribution to economic performance.

Politically, the KWNS was undermined by several phenomena. These include: growing political resistance to taxation and the emerging stagnation–inflation; crisis in post-war compromises between industrial capital and organized labour; new economic and social conditions and attendant problems that cannot be managed or resolved readily, if at all, through continuing reliance on top-down state planning and/or simple market forces; growing resentment about the bureaucratism, inflexibility and cost of the welfare state as it continued to expand during the late 1960s and 1970s; and the rise of new social movements which could not be easily integrated into the post-war compromise.

Socially, the KWNS was undermined by two emerging trends in civil society. The first is a weakening of the sense of national identity and solidarity that had shaped the KWNS in its formative period and helped to sustain the coalition behind it. The second trend involves changes in the more specific values, social identities, and interests associated with the welfare state. This is associated with rejection of the social democratic and/or Atlantic Fordist commitment to a class-based redistributive politics; a pluralistic identity politics and 'politics of difference' that emphasizes mutual respect, authenticity and autonomy; increased concern for personal empowerment rather than for the bureaucratic administration of legal rights, monetized entitlements and uniform public services; and expansion of the so-called 'third' sector, which supposedly operates flexibly outside of the framework of pure markets and the bureaucratic state (but often in close conjunction with them as a 'shadow market' and 'shadow state'). These shifts have fragmented the KWNS coalition of forces, led to demands for more differentiated and flexible forms of economic and social policy, and led to concern with ensuring *lifetime* access to the benefits of a restructured welfare regime (such as life-long learning).

5   Forms of SWPR

I now consider four ideal-typical strategies for moving to the SWPR: neo-liberalism, neo-corporatism, neo-statism and neo-communitarianism. The prefix 'neo-' indicates that there are important discontinuities with the liberal, corporatist and statist variants of the KWNS linked to Fordism and/or their contemporary communitarian alternatives. While specific economic, political and intellectual forces are often closely identified with one or other response, the types are best seen as poles around which different solutions could develop. Each has contrasting implications for economic and social policy in the emerging SWPR. Individual mixes depend on institutional legacies, the balance of political forces, and the changing economic and political conjunctures in which different strategies are pursued.

Neo-liberalism is closely associated with leading international economic bodies (such as the OECD, IMF and World Bank) and is the preferred strategy in the USA and Britain. It aims to promote a market-led process of economic and social restructuring. For the public sector, it involves privatization, liberalization and imposition of commercial criteria in the residual state sector; for the private sector, it involves deregulation and a new legal and political framework to offer passive support for market solutions. This is reflected in government promotion of 'hire-and-fire', flexi-time and flexi-wage labour markets; growth of tax expenditures steered by private initiatives based on fiscal subsidies for favoured economic activities; measures to transform the welfare state into a means of supporting and subsidizing low wages as well as to enhance the disciplinary force of social security measures and programmes; and the more general reorientation of economic and social policy to the private sector's 'needs'. These measures are linked to disavowal of reciprocal social responsibilities in favour of managerial prerogatives, market forces and a strong state. Neo-liberals also support free trade and capital mobility. They expect innovation to follow spontaneously from the freeing of individual entrepreneurs and workers to seize market opportunities in a state-sponsored enterprise culture.

Neo-corporatism involves a negotiated approach to restructuring by private, public and third sector actors and aims to balance competition and co-operation. It is based on a shared understanding of the linkages between private economic interests and social accords in securing the stability of a socially embedded, socially regulated economy. This system differs from Fordist corporatism with its mass production, its co-operation between big business, mass unions and interventionist state, and its concerns with full employment and stagflation. Neo-corporatist arrangements reflect the diversity of policy communities and networks relevant to innovation-driven growth and the increasing heterogeneity of labour-forces and labour markets. In an emerging SWPR these arrangements are also more directly and explicitly oriented to innovation and competitiveness. They extend beyond business associations and trade unions to include policy communities representing functional systems (such as science, health, education); and policy implementation becomes more flexible through the extension of 'regulated self-regulation' and public–private partnerships. Corporatist arrangements may also become more selective (for example, excluding some entrenched industrial interests and marginal workers, integrating some 'sunrise' sectors and privileging core workers); and, reflecting the greater flexibility and decentralization of key features of the post-Fordist economy, the centres of neo-corporatist gravity move toward firms and localities at the expense of centralized macroeconomic concentration. Moreover, whether at local, national or supra-national level, states use their resources to support decisions reached through corporatist negotiation rather than pursue more autonomous, proactive, neo-statist initiatives. Compliance with state policies is voluntary or else depends on actions taken by self-regulating corporatist organizations endowed with public status.

Neo-statism involves a market-conforming but state-sponsored approach to economic and social restructuring whereby the state seeks to guide market forces in support of a national economic strategy. This guidance involves the state's deployment of its own powers of imperative co-ordination, its own economic resources and activities, and its own knowledge bases and organizational intelligence. Compared with the KWNS, however, there is a changed understanding of international competition (see the Appendix for an explanation). This is a Schumpeterian view based on dynamic competitive advantage rather than one oriented to Ricardian static comparative advantage or a Listian conception of dynamic growth based on catch-up investment in a protected, mercantilist economy. Neo-statist policies involve a mixture of decommodification, state-sponsored flexibility, and other state activities aimed at securing the dynamic efficiency and synergistic coherence of a core productive economy. This is reflected in an active structural policy that sets strategic targets relating to new technologies, technology transfer, innovation systems, infrastructure, and other factors affecting international competitiveness broadly understood. The state also favours an active labour market policy to reskill the labour force and to encourage a flexi-skill rather than flexi-price labour market. It guides private–public partnerships to ensure that public as well as private interests are served. Whilst the central state retains a key strategic role in these regards, it also encourages parallel and complementary activities at regional and/or local levels. However, its desire to protect the core technological and economic competencies of its productive base is often associated with neo-mercantilism at the supra-national level.

Neo-communitarianism is a fourth strategic variant of the SWPR. Compared with the other three variants, it represents a more decisive break with the KWNS. For, whereas there were liberal, corporatist and statist variants of Atlantic Fordism, the latter's growth dynamic actually undermined the sort of social economy favoured by communitarians (Carpi, 1997). In contrast, the Fordist crisis and emerging post-Fordist economy both offer considerable scope for its expansion. Neo-communitarian strategies emphasize the contribution of the 'third sector' and/or the 'social economy' (both located between market and state) to economic development and social cohesion and the role of grassroots (or bottom-up) economic and social mobilization in developing and implementing economic strategies. They also emphasize the link between economic and community development, notably in empowering citizens and community groups; the contribution that greater self-sufficiency can make to reinserting marginalized local economies into the wider economy; and the role of decentralized partnerships that embrace not only the state and business interests but also diverse community organizations and other local stakeholders. The neo-communitarian strategy focuses on less competitive economic spaces (such as inner cities, deindustrializing cities, or cities at the bottom of urban hierarchies) with the greatest risk of losing from the zero-sum competition for external resources. Against the logic of a globalizing capitalism, the social economy prioritizes social use-value. It aims to redress the imbalance between private affluence and public poverty, to create local demand, to reskill the long-term unemployed and reintegrate them into an expanded labour market, to address some of the problems of urban regeneration (for example in social housing, insulation and energy-saving), to provide a different kind of spatio-temporal fix for small and medium enterprises, to regenerate trust within the community and to promote empowerment. This involves co-ordinated economic and social strategies across various scales of action and, ideally, a minimum income guarantee – whether as citizens' wages, basic income, or carers' allowances.

6 Amplification and qualification

This section amplifies and qualifies my arguments. The first amplification concerns the discursive and material constitution of objects of economic management and social policy. The KWNS and SWPR involve more than a simple shift in the form of external intervention into 'the' economy: they are actually premised on different notions of the economy as an object of intervention and a redrawing of its boundaries. Keynesianism rests on the construction of a relatively closed national economic space understood in terms of a problematic relationship between demand and supply as mediated through state control over national money and credit. Schumpeterian policies are premised on an open entrepreneurial economic space understood in terms of a competitive search for 'super-profits' deriving from permanent innovation and flexible responses to economic challenges with the primary problem being the promotion of an enterprise-friendly sociopolitical environment. Welfare and workfare likewise refer to very different objects of social policy. Welfare policies are premised on rights attached to national citizenship and, in many cases, on stable 'traditional' family structures and the gender relations they authorize. In line with the Keynesian–Fordist model, the social wage is seen as a source of domestic demand rather than as a cost of production. Workfare policies are premised on mobile workforces, active integration into labour markets, and a wider range of domestic arrangements. In addition, in the Schumpeterian–post-Fordist model, the social wage is viewed as a cost of international production and thus subject to downward pressure to promote competitiveness.

The national character of the KWNS was premised on the socially and politically constructed coincidence (and structured coherence) of a national economy–sovereign state–national society. This permitted the primacy of the national scale in economic and social reproduction. The SWPR's post-national character results from the decomposition of this nationally centred structured coherence. This is reflected not only in the greater significance of globalization, triadization, regionalization, transnational urban networks, cross-border regions and so on, but also in the state's denationalization (or 'hollowing out') as specific state powers and capacities are moved upwards, downwards and sideways. It is also related to the partial decomposition of hegemonic national identities due to the emergence of more multi-ethnic and/or multicultural societies and the rise of more differentiated, multi-tiered political loyalties with the crisis of the national territorial state. It is also linked to the internationalization of economic and social policy in key respects (cf. Deacon, 1996) and its decentralization to lower levels of government.

The state's role in the mixed KWNS economy is premised on a particular model of the capitalist economy that limits its principal modes of co-ordination to market and plan, exchange and hierarchy. What this model constructed as 'market failure' had to be solved by reinvigorating market forces and/or through compensatory state action. Partnership's role in the SWPR is tied to the (re)discovery of self-organizing networks as an alternative to market and plan. Networking is considered particularly appropriate to the multi-tiered, multi-spatial and multi-temporal co-ordination problems associated with the emerging post-Fordist political economy since it promises greater flexibility and involves a wider range of stakeholders in decision-making and implementation.

Let me now qualify the one-sided presentation of the preceding arguments, which was intended to highlight differences between the KWNS and SWPR. For there are also obvious continuities between past and present welfare regimes – whether these are simple continuities or involve complex 'conservation–dissolution' effects. In general we can expect greater continuities in those areas of economic and social policy that are less directly implicated in international competitiveness, permanent innovation and flexible labour markets. Thus, to give just one example, more effort will go on actively integrating the young unemployed and single parents into a Schumpeterian workfare system than on the retired or long-term carers of the disabled or elderly. Conversely, more emphasis will be put on reducing the public costs of caring for the disabled or retired – reflected in the widespread, politically concerted 'fiscal panic' about the future burden of pensions and long-term medical care for the elderly and the associated attempts to increase the private funding of pensions and health care.

There are also some important counter-trends to the four trends discussed above. First, following the recent Asian crisis, its spread to Russia, Norway and Brazil, and the growing calls for a 'new financial architecture', there has been growing interest in Keynesianism on a macro-regional basis (notably among the newer social democratic governments in mainland Europe). This suggests that some commitments associated with the KWNS may have 'jumped scales' (i.e. been displaced to other levels). Second, although welfare rights tied to national citizenship are under attack from some advocates of welfare reform, this is being countered by interest in regional or even global policies directed against 'social dumping'. There is also an increased commitment to human rights regardless of national citizenship – a commitment which still lacks teeth and which has not stopped hostility to 'economic migrants' who allegedly threaten to destabilize fragile labour market compromises. Third, although post-national policy-making and implementation have expanded through the denationalization of the state and the internationalization of policy regimes, national states have gained an increased importance in inter-scalar articulation, that is in modulating the transfer of powers across scales and in struggles to shape the new international policy regimes in national interests (including an interest in social cohesion). Fourth, although there has been a shift from government to governance (or from the mixed economy to the 'negotiated econ-omy'), states on various levels are reasserting their powers of 'meta-governance', i.e. their claim to shape the context and conditions under which public–private partnerships, private interest govern-ment, or regulated self-regulation operate.

7 Conclusions

I now return to the three social policy issues identified in the intro-duction. First, in so far as social policy concerns the reproduction of labour-power as a fictitious commodity, it varies with changes in economic growth dynamics and associated policies. The opening of national economies makes it harder to pursue social policy in isolation from economic policy and this encourages efforts to subordinate social to economic policy – or, at least, to co-ordinate these policy fields more effectively. The concern for international competitiveness, innovation, enterprise and flexibility challenges KWNS social policy oriented to full employment, generalized mass consumption, and social redistribution via collective consumption. Instead the emphasis turns to creating enterprising, flexible economic subjects; privatizing the public sector or moving to private–public partnerships to create market and network opportunities; and actively integrating citizens into the labour market as far as possible. Increasing global competition also encourages treatment of the social wage more as a cost of inter-national production than a source of domestic demand. This leads to attacks on rights (considered as a stock of future entitlements) without obligations and to downward pressure on all forms of social expendi-ture. Against these neo-liberal tendencies that are so destructive of the KWNS, some form of social policy is still required to compensate worker-citizens for flexibility and adaptability and support them in the face of a turbulent global environment.

Second, in so far as social policy is politically mediated and the territorial scale of politics alters (in part due to shifts in economic space), the design and implementation of social policies will be re-scaled along with the re-scaling of the economic and political systems. The shift from the primacy of the national to a post-national policy-making framework is significant here. Supra-national agencies such as the EU, World Bank, International Labour Organization, OECD and IMF, as well as international NGOs, are getting more heavily involved in social policy-making; and there is an enhanced role for local, regional and cross-border states. National states in turn play a key role in inter-scalar management. Third, in so far as states as well as market forces are held to fail as mechanisms for social reproduction, interest grows in the contribution to social policy of alternatives such as networks, partnerships and self-organization. This also involves new forms of government monitoring of social policy and its outcomes.

Finally, I want to suggest the following solution to 'Offe's paradox'. On the one hand, capitalism (in its Atlantic Fordist form) did co-exist with the welfare state (in its KWNS form) for an extended period. Eventually the Fordist growth regime and its KWNS mode of regulation became mutually contradictory. This prompted a search for new economic and social bases for capital accumulation; and this involved a partial dismantling of the KWNS. In this sense the emerging post-Fordist accumulation regime cannot co-exist with the KWNS. However, this search process also involves a search for new forms of state intervention that might help to resecure conditions for profitability and the reproduction of labour-power. One could perhaps call this a simple restructuring of the welfare state but emphasizing the continuity of state economic and social policy in this way actually hides as much as (if not more than) it reveals. For, as argued above, the core organizational principles of the KWNS are being superseded by those of the SWPR. This has several possible forms (as did the KWNS) and is associated with a rich and wide range of re-visionings of a new 'welfare society'. One should certainly not regard the neo-liberal workfare state favoured by Margaret Thatcher and John Major (and taken as the starting-point for New Labour's 'Third Way') as the only option.

References and further reading

Carpi, J.A.T. (1997) 'The prospects for the social economy in a changing world', *Annals of Public and Co-operative Economics*, 68 (2), pp.247–79.

Deacon, B. (1996) *The Globalization of Social Policy*, London, Sage.

Jessop, B. (1993) 'Towards a Schumpeterian workfare state? Preliminary remarks on post-Fordist political economy', *Studies in Political Economy*, 40, pp.7–39.

Jessop, B. (1999a) 'Reflections on the (il)logics of globalization', in Olds, K., Kelly, P., Kong, L., Yeung, H.W. and Dickens, P. (eds) *Globalization and the Asia Pacific: Contested Territories*, London, Routledge, pp.19–38.

Jessop, B. (1999b) 'Narrating the future of the national economy and the national state? Remarks on re-mapping regulation and re-inventing governance', in Steinmetz, G. (ed.) *STATE/CULTURE: State-Formation after the Cultural Turn*, Ithaca, NY, Cornell University Press, pp.378–405.

Jessop, B. (2000) 'Restructuring the welfare state, reorienting welfare strategies, re-visioning the welfare society', in Greve, B. (ed.) *What Constitutes a Good Society?* Basingstoke, Macmillan.
Offe, C. (1984) *Contradictions of the Welfare State*, London, Hutchinson.

Appendix: Concepts of competitiveness

The idea of competitiveness is conceptually ambiguous and politically controversial. There are many ways to define and measure it; and current policy debates indicate the political issues at stake. These points are related. For competitiveness is a discursively constructed notion with obvious strategic implications both economically and politically: different notions entail different forms of political action with different effects on the competitive positioning of firms, sectors, regions and nations as well as on the balance of political forces within and beyond the state.

The *Ricardian* account, named after David Ricardo, an early English political economist, stresses the importance of static comparative advantages and/or relative prices. Thus competitiveness depends on exploiting the most abundant and cheapest factors of production in a given economy (e.g. land, raw materials, labour, capital, enterprise) and exchanging products embodying these factors for products from other spaces with different factor endowments. Ricardian competitiveness depends on static efficiency in the allocation of resources to minimize production costs with a given technical division of labour and on the assumption that current economic conditions will continue.

The *Listian* account is named after Friedrich List, a nineteenth-century German political economist. It suggests that a national state can develop infant industries or services which are not based on abundant or cheap factors of production provided that it rejects free trade in favour of protection, state support and state guidance of the economy. This implies that international competitiveness depends on growth efficiency in the allocation of resources among *already available* processes and products in terms of the likely impact of their (re-)allocation on economic growth and on the ability to protect infant industries from premature competition from more advanced firms or economies.

The *Schumpeterian* account is named after Joseph Schumpeter, a twentieth-century Austrian political economist. It suggests that competitiveness depends on developing the individual and collective capacities to engage in permanent innovation – whether in sourcing, technologies, products, organization or marketing. These capacities extend beyond the narrow economy to include a wide range of extra-economic factors. Thus Schumpeterian competitiveness depends on dynamic efficiency in allocating resources to promote *innovations* that will alter the pace and direction of economic growth and enable the economy to compete more effectively.

The *Keynesian* approach is less concerned with international competitiveness because it assumes a relatively closed national economy. Nonetheless one can derive a view about competitiveness from it – that full employment of resources (including labour) will enhance efficiency by reducing unit costs of production, facilitating the realization of economies of scale, and reducing the welfare costs of maintaining underemployed labour power. Moreover, if full capacity utilization leads to inflation, its effects can be compensated by devaluation.

12

New Approaches to Comparative Social Policy: the Changing Face of Central and Eastern European Welfare

Lynne Poole

Contents

1   Introduction

If we look at the history of the comparative study of social welfare, we can recognize the importance of recent developments in the discipline: in short, and perhaps rather crudely, we have seen a shift from a focus on 'welfare effort' or levels of social expenditure as a percentage of GDP (Wilensky, 1975) to different models or regimes of welfare (Titmuss, 1974; Mishra, 1981; Therborn, 1987; Esping-Andersen, 1990; Liebfried, 1993). Notwithstanding the strengths of these latter approaches relative to earlier methods of comparative social policy, they do not address the gendered nature of welfare regimes. In particular they neglect the relationship between paid and unpaid work and the informal provision of welfare (see Chapters 1 and 2 this volume respectively and Langan and Ostner, 1991).

As part of the recent developments in social and cultural theory, feminists have begun to rework orthodox comparative typologies in order to incorporate a recognition of the importance of women's unpaid work and the mixed economy of welfare provision (Langan and Ostner, 1991; Lewis, 1992, and Chapter 2 this volume; Orloff, 1993; Sainsbury, 1996). And, whilst there has been rather less work in this area, some comparative social policy commentators are beginning to explore the ways in which welfare experiences are structured by 'race' as well as class and gender (Pierson, 1991; Baldwin-Edwards, 1991a, 1991b; Ginsburg, 1992, 1994; Williams, 1995). For example, Baldwin-Edwards (1991b) attempts to identify 'national policy regimes' within the EU in relation to the rights of migrants and the position of illegal immigrants. In doing so, he roots his discussion in the wider context of EU transnational policies and the status of EC and non-EC migrants under EU law. Williams (1995) goes further, highlighting the ways in which even gendered typologies have tended to ignore the dimension of 'race'/ethnicity and arguing for their inclusion, not simply as an add-on, but in such a way as to fully integrate what she terms the '"race"/ethnicity logic'. These developments are all welcome and have served to enrich the debates about welfare and its future, in Western Europe in particular. However, when we come to consider the case of Central and Eastern European welfare (in this context referring to the welfare of Poland, the Czech and Slovak Republics, Hungary, Romania and Bulgaria), both in the state socialist period prior to 1989 and in the light of more recent developments, we find that whilst modelling has been attempted, it has been limited in its application for a number of reasons.

2   The limits of orthodox comparative typologies

First, commentators have tended to draw on the work of Esping-Andersen (1990), adapting his 'three worlds of welfare capitalism', and concluding that the most likely outcome of social policy transformation will be the development of variants of these models. This is despite the fact that it is still unclear what future lies ahead for post-state-socialist societies. Indeed, there is no historical precedent for the shift from state socialism to capitalism. Given the legacies of the past and the current global context of the transformation process, there can be no guarantee of a 'westernized' outcome (Bryant and Mokrzycki, 1994). It is, then, rather ironic that it is Esping-Andersen himself who has argued that the application of typologies of western welfare regimes may not be appropriate to the region, at least in the shorter term when Central and Eastern Europe is being used as a 'virtual laboratory of experimentation' (Esping-Andersen, 1996, p.267) – a kind of practice circuit for new social policies which have potential for a restructured and possibly residualized welfare in the West.

Second, there has been a tendency to ignore the question of how key social divisions structure the population's experience of welfare. For example, commentators have drawn on the more orthodox gender-blind approaches developed in 'western' comparative social policy (see for example, Mishra, 1981; Gotting, 1994; Standing, 1996), and in doing so have ignored recent developments in the feminist comparative literature, as well as wider questions of inclusion and exclusion. Deacon (1992) recognizes these limitations and goes some way towards incorporating the social divisions of both gender and 'race'/national identity into his tentative comparative framework. He also recognizes that given the complex legacies of state socialism and the severe problems facing policy-makers in the region, Central and Eastern European governments may draw on alternative approaches to welfare provision – in particular, the authoritarian regimes of South America or Japanese and South East Asian models (Deacon, 1992).

Third, whilst there may well be *some* mileage in drawing on the typology of western regimes, as illustrated by Deacon's work, we can identify a number of other practical difficulties that have to be faced when trying to think through social policy transformation in Central and Eastern Europe, all of which relate to the fact that we are studying a region that continues to be in severe flux.

In a period of rapid and often contradictory change in all spheres of life it is difficult to develop a clear picture of the situation at any given point in time. Of course, it is true that constant change characterizes all societies to some extent, but it is the degree and breadth of that change, coupled with the tendency for reform at the economic, political, social, cultural and administrative levels at one and the same time, that marks Central and Eastern Europe out as a special case. We can illustrate this by summarizing the main changes seen across the region throughout the 1990s. These are as follows: democratization, with the introduction of parliaments and free elections; the development or redevelopment of legislatures, executives, constitutions and political pluralism; the marketization of the economy and privatization, marking a significant shift away from centralized command economies; a rejection of what has been termed Marxist-Leninist ideology; the restructuring of welfare characterized by the demise of the state-led, work-based model and a diversification of policy and provision broadly along more western lines; and the activating of civil society (see Holmes, 1997; White et al., 1998). In recognizing the breadth of change, but taking care not to overstate the extent of change to date nor its evenness across the region, we can suggest that identifying an appropriate model of welfare which will retain its relevance in all cases as the transformation process advances is highly problematic.

In a period of continued 'crisis' – economic, social, cultural and political – trying to separate the more substantial, long-term social policy changes from the ad hoc, temporary arrangements that have been thrown up as a reaction to acute crises, is almost impossible even at this juncture, ten years after the beginnings of the formal transformation process.

As Williams (1992) notes in relation to the 'western' experience of welfare reform, it is difficult to get an overall picture of the state of welfare in Western Europe, given the diversity of policy responses to common social, economic and demographic changes (see also Taylor-Gooby, 1996). If this is the case in Western Europe, the same is certainly true in the East. There, too, policy responses have differed despite broadly similar social, economic and political forces at work. In addition, it is not possible to identify a unifying ideology which will give us clues about the future direction of welfare policy: ideological divisions exist not only at the national and regional levels, but, as Deacon et al. (1997) highlight, both between and within the international agencies involved in the area. Developing a useful Central and Eastern European model of welfare is thus fraught with difficulties.

More generally, the focus of comparative typologies tends to be on the questions of 'how much welfare?' and 'how is welfare delivered?' (Bonoli, 1997). Adding in a third dimension around the question of 'who provides?' helps to broaden our focus in useful ways, not least by incorporating issues relating to the informal provision of welfare. Nevertheless it does not fully solve the problem. As Taylor (1996) argues, an approach which includes an analysis of the balance between the state and the market misses the essential point that exclusions result whether welfare is state collectivist or market oriented – as the history of Central and Eastern Europe as much as that of Western Europe demonstrates. The issue of social power is neglected in this type of approach. In particular, there is no recognition of the unequal power relations that underscore both state collectivist and market-oriented welfare, nor is there any recognition that both embody exclusionary processes.

These problems or dilemmas may explain the general dearth of literature which attempts to theorize social policy change in its entirety. The focus has tended to be on more manageable issues and confined areas of study (see for example, Deacon et al., 1997 and Standing, 1996). That is not to deny the importance of such work, which represents a lifeline for the social policy teacher faced with a plethora of sources about 'doing business' in Central and Eastern

Europe, making the region a safe place for capital, and how to westernize social policy priorities and provision in the region (Barr, 1994).

What I want to argue is that we need to move beyond the work of western typologists, for all the reasons outlined above (see also Lewis, 1998a), if we are to develop a fuller understanding of social policy transformation in Central and Eastern Europe and thus systematically analyse:

1   in what ways social difference is constructed, represented and understood by powerful actors at a national, regional and international level who are exerting an influence in the region;
2   which social divisions and problems are seen as the concern of policy-makers and why;
3   the impact dominant welfare discourses have on the shape of welfare policies pursued by the state;
4   how, to what extent and in what ways questions of gender inequality, racialization, able-bodyism and heteronormativity, *as well as* class, are being addressed, reproduced and reinscribed in newly emerging policies;
5   who stands to win and lose as a result of the welfare priorities and practices that are beginning to emerge.

Perhaps not surprisingly, feminist writers have provided us with a useful body of work on which to build. Their work has explored the changing position of women in Central and Eastern Europe in relation to processes of transformation across a range of spheres (see for example, Corrin, 1992; Rai et al., 1992; Einhorn, 1993; Funk and Muellar, 1993), as well as providing us with an analysis of women's experiences under state socialism (Buckley, 1981, 1989; Molyneaux, 1981, 1985; Einhorn, 1993). All of these commentaries provide us with valuable insights into the assumptions, processes and practices of these regimes in relation to gender, and women in particular.

3   Feminist approaches to studying Central and Eastern European welfare policy and provision

So how exactly have feminist writers improved on the gender-blind approaches to studying Central and Eastern European societies in general, and social policies in particular? Whilst it is tempting to explore some of the key contributions to our understanding of women's experiences of welfare in the region in some detail given the richness of the material, this would take us beyond the remit of this chapter. For our purposes, it is sufficient to offer two examples of that contribution – one which focuses on the situation prior to the 1980s and one which takes as its starting-point the beginning of the trans-formation process.

3.1 Superwomen and the double burden: the great worker-mother

Many feminists writing about women's experiences prior to 1989 have focused on the concept of the double burden and have high-lighted the ways in which dominant ideas about the 'natural' role of women were retained under state socialism, but with an inadequate theorization of women's liberation – based on participation in the production process or paid work – bolted on. What women were left with was a situation in which they could choose neither the role of worker nor of mother on its own, but were forced to combine them – leading to the construction of 'the great worker-mother' (Molyneaux, 1981, 1985; Corrin, 1992; Rai et al. 1992; Einhorn 1993). These studies enabled a deconstruction of the often contradictory discourses around women that existed prior to 1989. In turn, they enabled social policy analysts to untangle what on the face of it looked like an incongruous set of contradictory family policies and explain the subordinated inclusion of women in the production process, which resulted in either their continued dependence on men and the state for material assistance and support services of dubious quality or, in the case of single parents, the constant threat of increased poverty.

3.2 Women in the face of change: a 'new' womanly mission

Several feminist writers have similarly begun to explore the ways in which women are more recently being returned to the private sphere. Their status as workers has been marginalized, in part a result of the reworking of dominant ideas about the 'proper' or 'natural' role of women. This is itself a response at least in part to acute economic crisis and societal disintegration, though in some notable cases other factors are implicated, not least the increased official legitimation of religion, for example in Poland. This shift in the 'official' discourses of the family, reproduction and the role of women is captured by the following quotation from Gorbachev's *Perestroika*:

> Engaged in scientific research, working in construction, in production and in services, women no longer have enough time to perform their everyday duties at home – housework, the upbringing of children and the creation

of a good family atmosphere. We have discovered that many of our problems – in children's and young people's behaviour, in our morals, culture and in production – are partially caused by the weakening of family ties and slack attitudes to family responsibility . . . we are now holding heated debates . . . about the question of what we should do to make it possible for women to return to their purely womanly mission. (Gorbachev, 1987, p.117)

This is a rather old quote now but one which illustrates the shifts in the dominant discourses of womanhood that have been, and continue to be, evident not only in post-Soviet society but across the region as a whole (Einhorn, 1993). Indeed, alarmingly, though perhaps not surprisingly, some women have found reason to celebrate this process of reconstructing women's 'natural' role in society and subsequently repositioning them firmly back into the private sphere in so far as it relieves them of the double burden they carried in the era of state socialism (Rai et al., 1992).

However, in exploring these shifting discourses we must take care not to suggest that all women across the region, irrespective of class position or other axes of differentiation, share one universal experience. On the contrary, Szalai (1998) agues that the effects of societal transformation and the discourses which serve to legitimize them – for example in relation to unemployment and poverty – are not necessarily gendered in straightforward ways. She goes on to show how certain groups of Hungarian women have managed to carve out a new public role for themselves by building on the informal economy that existed to boost poor state services at the community level prior to 1989. So, whilst many of the working-class women engaged in industrial mass production under the old regime have become part of the 'new poor', some have managed to gain limited employment providing services for better-off households as work-based, state provision shrinks. Yet other sections of the female population, mostly drawn from the majority ethnic group, have become engaged in managing the 'new poor' (which also includes older people and the Roma population), offering social-work-type services on a part-time, subcontractual and temporary basis and working for newly emerging community-based NGOs (non-governmental organizations). As Szalai highlights, the fortune of this latter group of women is 'bound up with the misfortune of their clients' (1998, p.11).

For our purposes, the key point to emphasize here is that a concern to examine the shifting discourse of gender roles and the sexual division of labour helps us to understand how gender differences are represented and understood by powerful national and international actors in the region and analyse the impact that these emerging discourses have on shaping social policies. (See Deacon et al., 1997 and Cochrane, 1998 for a discussion of the role of global actors and the forces of globalization, and Gower, 1993 and Winters, 1995 for a discussion of the EU as a regional actor.) But, as the example above illustrates, we also need to untangle the complex relationship between shifting discourses and the restructuring processes of transformation, and their diverse impact on sections of the highly differentiated population. Only in this way can we begin to assess the extent to which questions of gender inequality, for example, are being reworked, reproduced and reinscribed in policy, in both old and new ways.

So, notwithstanding the usefulness of some of these commentaries, many of them, when taken on their own, furnish us with only a partial view of developments in the region in relation to social divisions and inequality. My argument is, first, that this is in part a result of an approach that does not tend to recognize the diversity between women – the differentiated gendered subject (see Chapter 1 this volume). Second, and very closely related, I want to argue for an approach which not only takes on board gender inequality but also allows us to focus on class inequality, racialization, able-bodyism and heteronormativity, whilst also recognizing that the social constituencies which these processes produce are internally differentiated. In this way we can begin to explore the range of divisions through which people's lives are constituted in post-state socialist Central and Eastern Europe, and how they are structured by social relations of power and inequality (Williams, 1992). As Szalai's (1998) study suggests, women's experience can be seen to be highly variable once we incorporate the divisions of 'race' ethnicity, age and class. In contrast, studies focusing on the experience of the Central and Eastern European Roma population, both pre- and post-1989, have shown how social policy and the wider processes of transformation have reproduced particular social divisions in more similar ways across the time period, though the degree of exclusion may now be more marked (Crowe and Kosti, 1991; Kalibova et al., 1993; Barany, 1994; Fonseca, 1996; Pickles and Smith, 1998).

4   A new approach to studying social policy in transformation?

O'Brien and Penna (1998) argue that post-structuralist theory – with its rejection of the concept of the universal subject, its adoption of a deconstructionist approach and its focus on power/knowledge systems – calls for an analysis of competing welfare discourses, their social and political origins and the ways in which dominant ideas shape and institutionalize notions of rights, responsibilities and duties around constructions of normality and need. It has at its heart a recognition that individuals cannot be reduced to the status of universal subject – be that in relation to class, gender or 'race' – as their lives are constituted by a number of axes of difference (Fraser, 1997). Moreover, at different times and in different circumstances, different aspects of our identity will be centred, depending on the particular power/knowledge relationships that are to the fore.

This approach, then, can be usefully applied to the study of trans-formative social policy in Central and Eastern Europe. However, we need to take care not to draw on these developments in social and cultural theory in such a way as to marginalize the dimension of class. Again drawing on Fraser (1997), we can recognize that group identity does not fully supplant class interest as a point of political mobil-ization and that the cultural domain does not fully supplant issues of exploitation as a focus of claims of injustice. These co-exist and, whilst the demise of state socialism in some senses took class off the agenda, despite the fact that state socialism had rather little to do with equality and solving the problem of class and material poverty, the problem of class divisions and material inequality has not been solved anywhere, East or West. Indeed, in Central and Eastern Europe where workers regularly mobilize in protest at growing levels of poverty and unemployment, often alongside women and older people, there is a need to 'decentre' – but not reject – the relevance of class divisions. In doing so, we can recognize the 'cross-cutting axes of difference' through which people's lives are constituted (Fraser, 1997, p.13), not least those around nationality and religion, both of which are increas-ingly relevant in Central and Eastern Europe. It is to the application of these new approaches to the study of social policy that we now turn, foregrounding the 'race' dimension and exploring the processes of racialization at work and their consequences.

4.1   Completing the picture: racialized subjects in Central and Eastern Europe

Racialization can be defined as a set of social processes by which people are divided into discrete categories on the basis of physical variations or cultural practices and subsequently assumptions are made about them as a result of this categorization (Lewis, 1998b). Crucially, 'racial' differences are seen as an essential characteristic – they are perceived to be natural as opposed to arising out of social processes. In turn this essentialism is used to legitimize processes of 'othering'. Our bodies, or any culturally perceived sign, can act as a boundary signifier to divide the population into 'us' and 'them' (Yuval-Davis, 1997, p.47).

Throughout the state socialist era, processes of racialization in both the Soviet Union and the nations of Central and Eastern Europe were evident. For example, in the USSR under the leadership of Stalin, Jews were constructed as 'the other', a threat to the state socialist project and the Soviet identity. As such they were subjected to the policies of assimilation (Pinkus, 1988). A 'standardized, homogeneous centrally sustained culture' was imposed on all minority groups (Zaslavsky, 1993, p.32) and this, coupled with the Russification of all spheres of life, resulted in the formal subordination of non-Russian national identity and religion, with grave consequences. By the late 1930s many Jews, as well as non-Russian national minorities, were to become victims of the purges, accused of Trotskyism, nationalism and involvement in Zionist plots. Indeed, a significant section of the Jewish population 'disappeared' by not registering their Jewish identity in population censuses while others sought to emigrate or relocate to the Middle East, where they had been promised territorial autonomy, in order to escape the cultural and religious restrictions placed upon them. In the period after the Second World War in particular, the Soviet press, controlled by the party-state apparatus, began to intensify the racialization of the Jewish population, constructing elaborate stereotypes (Pinkus, 1988, pp.151–4) and inciting racial hatred. Events in Poland in the 1960s illustrate similar racializing processes at work in Central Europe. Here, too, there was an intensification of anti-Jewish propaganda, which led to violent anti-Semitism and the eventual expulsion of Polish Jews from the country.

However, it has perhaps been the Roma populations who have been commonly constructed as the most racialized and disadvantaged group of people under the rule of state socialism (for example, see Barany, 1994; Roma Rights, 1997). As an absolute 'other' historically, Romany people across the region have been blamed for the social ills of society and denied the social rights of citizenship granted those deemed to be 'of' the nation.

Both of these examples serve to illustrate the ways in which nation, 'race'/ethnicity and religion have been used as boundary signifiers to divide the population of Central and Eastern Europe. More recently, with the collapse of the state socialist system and the obvious strains of transformation, the pathologization of social difference has become even more visible as processes of racialization are reworked in the context of national renewal. Nationalism and religion have re-emerged across the region, only this time – with the demise of Soviet domination – they have become powerful forces. New national-based elites have sought not only to defend their newly won independence and control over their own systems of national government, but also to redefine what it means to be part of the nation in 'racial' and ethnic terms. This has resulted in the continued racialization and exclusion of the Roma, and of also those deemed to be 'non-indigenous' peoples: to give two examples, both the Slovaks living in the Czech Republic, and the Russians living in Central and Eastern Europe but outside of the Russian Federation, have also been constructed as 'other'. This reproduction of social divisions, in both old and new ways, has resulted in three broad types of response. Some have stayed in the region and have struggled to create opportunities for themselves despite their marginalization, for example in newly emerging labour markets. Some have begun to organize themselves, finding their collective voice and calling for autonomy or even secession, in an effort to win the right of self-determination as their states are reconstructed as nations (Yuval-Davis, 1997, p.76). Yet others have fled the newly emerging regimes, creating significant movements of people across the continent. The Slovakian Romanies are one example of this latter trend, arriving on the south coast of Britain in the late 1990s and seeking asylum from persecution. Here they have also been constructed as an undeserving group of 'bogus asylum-seekers', encouraged to come here by their own national governments in search of economic opportunities. They have been labelled 'benefit tourists' and, as such, have been denied assistance and subjected to racist abuse, harassment and at times expulsion. Constructed as a threat to our 'fragile' welfare system, itself based on discourses of belonging and nationhood, the Roma are seen as a challenge to Britain's own project of 'national renewal' championed by Tony Blair. Indeed, under his leadership the New Labour government introduced the Asylum and Immigration Bill in 1999 which limited the assistance available to such asylum-seekers to food vouchers and small monetary payments for essential travel expenses. Many of the additional forms of assistance will thus become discretionary where they are retained at all. Plans to disperse asylum-seekers around the country have also been developed.

It is interesting to note the parallels in Russia, where Russians returning to the Federation in this period of continued 'crisis' are seen as an additional threat to the national renewal agenda as incomers with their own needs and demands (Jordan, 1998).

Recent developments arising out of the complex transformation process have, then, led not only to the intensification of old exclusions but also to the construction of new racialized subjects who have their own specific experiences of exclusion and marginalization. However, these complex processes of definition and redefinition and their outcomes have also raised questions about the organization of welfare elsewhere in Europe. The movement of people across national boundaries clearly represents a transnational challenge to nationality as a basis for welfare (see Chapter 11 this volume; Williams, 1995; Jordan, 1998). And, despite the rise of transnational organizations and institutions, not least the European Union, there is currently little evidence to suggest that they represent a solution (Liebfried, 1993; Hantrais, 1995; Jordan, 1998). In addition, any progress in this area will be self-limiting and partial, as the first wave of enlargement eastwards will not offer the same opportunities for the populations of those countries which are excluded from the list of new member-states. The threat of what has been termed 'Fortress Europe' illustrates these limitations. For example, Hantrais (1995) notes the active development of rights of freedom of movement for migrants within EU borders, but goes on to highlight the growing controls over non-EU immigration, particularly at the level of member-states. Similarly, Clarke and Cochrane (1993) focus on the EU's concern to maintain high levels of employment and welfare across member-states, whilst excluding those from outside. These exclusionary processes obviously have significant implications for those Central and Eastern European states that fail to get admitted, and hence for migrants from this part of the region who are seeking opportunities within the borders of the EU. Roberts and Bolderson (1999) explore the ways in which EU member-states disentitle such migrants from social security benefits, either entirely or partially, and point to the use of residency, nationality and asylum-seeker status criteria in order to achieve these ends. In doing so, they also highlight the work of Robinson (1996) which places the development of increasing controls in the context of growing migration from the Balkans.

This part of the discussion has illustrated the ways in which discursive practices and material injustices and inequalities, in part arising out of the transformation process itself (Deacon, 1992; Standing, 1996), work to position particular groups of people within society and structure their experiences of the transformation in specific ways. The notion of constructing a welfare state for 'the nation', assumed to be ethnically homogeneous, fails to capture these exclusionary processes and does not acknowledge the exclusive notion of 'the people' at the heart of such constructions. An underdeveloped, not yet finished set of citizenship rights looks set to go on excluding significant numbers of people in a plethora of different ways, as shown by the experiences of women and 'racial'/ ethnic minority groups. Indeed, it seems likely that Central and East European citizenship will continue to be mediated through and dependent on 'membership of a specific ethnic, "racial", religious or regional collectivity' (Yuval-Davis, 1997, p.91). Particular groups of people will continue to be socially positioned in relation to their class and gender, age, sexual orientation and able-bodiedness. However, the limitations of the emerging systems of social welfare in the region are often not presented in this way. On the contrary, national governments, regional and international actors frame the difficulties largely as ones of affordability – claiming that there is no alternative. Where difference is recognized as a criterion for assessing entitlement, differences are constructed as 'natural' through the use of an essentialist approach. It is thus the task of critical social policy commentators to uncover the complex social processes at work. We need to concern ourselves with both the structure of society and power relations *and* the production of meaning, rather than displacing one with the other (Phillips, 1997). This gives rise to an approach which has at its heart a recognition that material economic injustice has a cultural dimension, and vice versa; in order to redistribute effectively and inclusively we need to recognize difference and diversity. Only if we analyse *all* of these dimensions then, and begin to work around the ideas of both structure and culture, can we begin to understand more fully:

1 developments that are taking place and choices that are being made in the region;
2 the impact they have across the social spectrum, and not just in terms of class divisions, at different times and in different situations;
3 how we can struggle against an exclusive welfare system in another setting altogether – that of Central and Eastern Europe – at a time when the world economy is going into recession (Bryant and Mokrzycki, 1994), and the shifting discourses of welfare in the West have resulted in what has been termed the 'individualization of the social' (Ferge, 1996). Both of these realities are being used to legitimize the elevation of economic policy over social policy and the residualization of state welfare, something which rather ironically characterized the state-socialist period.

5 Conclusion

In this chapter I have argued that the question of *how* we approach the study of social policy is of central importance. Moreover, I have highlighted the ways in which the recent development of post-structuralist theory, coupled with a recognition of what has been termed the 'cultural turn' (Clarke, 1998), have enabled us to reassess how we explore welfare relations, processes and practices. In particular, these recent developments have challenged old or orthodox approaches to the study of social policy, calling for the development of a new methodology which expands the concerns of social policy commentators to include a recognition that the field of social policy is socially constructed (Saraga, 1998). Consequently we have seen an increasing concern to explore and explain:

• how social problems and social differences are socially constructed;
• how dominant discourses around social difference are reworked over time;

- how these discourses shape social policy;
- how resultant social policies structure people's experiences of welfare.

However, this concern has been largely limited to the study of Western Europe and the United States. In contrast I have argued that the increased influence of post-structuralism and a growing focus on processes of social construction and the discursive sphere should not be confined to the study of social policy in Western Europe. On the contrary, these recent developments in social and cultural theory can enrich the study of social policy in transformation in Central and Eastern Europe too. The challenge now is to develop an integrated approach to studying the region: an approach which emphasizes the continued relevance of social class, but places it alongside other social divisions; an approach which accepts the limitations of an undifferentiated analysis which centres on a single dimension of difference; and an approach which combines a concern with the material conditions of people's lives and inequality with those discursive processes which help to structure our experiences of welfare in both Eastern and Western Europe.

References

Baldwin-Edwards, M. (1991a) 'Immigration after 1992', *Policy and Politics*, 19 (3), pp.199–211.

Baldwin-Edwards, M. (1991b) 'The socio-political rights of migrants in the European Community', in Room (1991).

Barany, Z.D. (1994) 'Nobody's children: the resurgence of nationalism and the status of gypsies in post-communist Eastern Europe', in Serafin, J. (ed.) *East-Central Europe in the 1990s*, Oxford, Westview Press.

Barr, N. (1994) *Labour Markets and Social Policy in Central and Eastern Europe: The Transition and Beyond*, Oxford, Oxford University Press.

Bonoli, G. (1997) 'Classifying welfare states: a two dimensional approach', *Journal of Social Policy*, 26 (3), pp.351–72.

Bryant, C.G.A. and Mokrzycki, E. (eds) (1994) *The New Great Transformation*, London, Routledge.

Buckley, M. (1981) 'Women in the Soviet Union', *Feminist Review*, 8, Summer, pp.79–106.

Buckley, M. (1989) *Women and Ideology in the Soviet Union*, Brighton, Harvester.

Carter, J. (ed.) (1998) *Postmodernity and the Fragmentation of Welfare*, London, Routledge.

Clarke, J. (1998) 'Coming to terms with culture'. Paper presented at the SPA conference, University of Lincolnshire and Humberside, 14–16 July.

Clarke, J. and Cochrane, A. (eds) (1993) *Comparing Welfare States: Britain in International Context*, London, Sage/The Open University.

Cochrane, A. (1998) 'Globalization, fragmentation and local welfare citizenship', in Carter (1998).

Corrin, C. (1992) *Superwomen and the Double Burden*, London, Scarlett.

Crowe, D. and Kosti, J. (eds) (1991) *The Gypsies of Eastern Europe*, New York, Armonk.

Deacon, B. (ed.) (1992) *The New Eastern Europe: Social Policy Past, Present and Future*, London, Sage.

Deacon, B., Hulse, M. and Stubbs, P. (1997) *Global Social Policy*, London, Sage.
Einhorn, B. (1993) *Cinderella Goes to Market: Citizenship, Gender and Women's Movements in East Central Europe*, London, Verso.
Esping-Andersen, G. (1990) *Three Worlds of Welfare Capitalism*, Cambridge, Polity Press.
Esping-Andersen, G. (ed.) (1996) *Welfare States in Transition*, London, Sage.
Ferge, S. (1996) 'The changing of the welfare paradigm: the individualization of the social'. Paper presented at the SPA conference, Sheffield Hallam University, 16–18 July.
Fonseca, I. (1996) *Bury Me Standing: The Gypsies and their Journey*, London, Vintage.
Fraser, N. (1997) *Justice Interruptus: Critical Reflections on the 'Postsocialist' Condition*, London, Routledge.
Funk, N. and Muellar, M. (eds) (1993) *Gender Politics and Post-Communism*, London, Routledge.
Ginsburg, N. (1992) *Divisions of Welfare*, London, Sage.
Ginsburg, N. (1994) '"Race", racism and social policy in western Europe', in Ferris, J. and Page, R. (eds) *Social Policy in Transition*, Aldershot, Avebury.
Gorbachev, M. (1987) *Perestroika: New Thinking for Our Country and the World*, London, Collins.
Gotting, U. (1994) 'Destruction, adjustment and innovation: social policy transformation in East and Central Europe', *Journal of Social Policy*, 4 (3), pp.181–200.
Gower, J. (1993) 'EC relations with Central and Eastern Europe', in Lodge, J. (ed.) *The European Community and the Challenge of the Future*, London, Pinter.
Hantrais, L. (1995) *Social Policy in the European Union*, Basingstoke, Macmillan.
Holmes, L. (1997) *Post-Communism: An Introduction*, Cambridge, Polity Press.
Jordan, B. (1998) *The New Politics of Welfare*, London, Sage.
Kalibova, K., Haisman, T. and Gjuricova, J. (1993) 'Gypsies in Czechoslovakia: demographic developments and policy perspectives', in O'Loughlin, J. and Wusten, H. van der (eds) *The New Political Geography of Eastern Europe*, London, Belhaven Press.
Langan, M. and Ostner, M. (1991) 'Gender and welfare', in Room (1991).
Lewis, G. (1998a) 'Same place, different culture?: thinking welfare through the post-colonial'. Plenary address delivered at the Social Policy Association Conference, Lincoln, 14 July.
Lewis, G. (1998b) 'Welfare and the social construction of "race"', in Saraga (1998).
Lewis, J. (1992) 'Gender and the development of welfare regimes', *Journal of European Social Policy*, 2 (3), pp.159–73.
Liebfried, S. (1993) 'Towards a European welfare state', in Jones, C. (ed.) *New Perspectives on the Welfare State in Europe*, London, Routledge.
Mishra, R. (1981) *Society and Social Policy: Theories and Practices of Welfare*, Basingstoke, Macmillan.
Molyneaux, M. (1981) 'Socialist societies old and new: progress towards women's emancipation', *Feminist Review*, 8, Summer, pp.1–34.
Molyneaux, M. (1985) 'Family reform in socialist states: the hidden agenda', *Feminist Review*, 21, Winter, pp.47–64.
O'Brien, M. and Penna, S. (1998) *Theorizing Welfare: Enlightenment and Modern Society*, London, Sage.
Orloff, A.S. (1993) 'Gender and the social rights of citizenship: the comparative analysis of gender relations and welfare states', *American Sociological Review*, 58 (3), pp.303–28.
Phillips, A. (1997) 'From inequality to difference: a severe case of displacement?', *New Left Review*, 224, pp.143–53.
Pickles, J. and Smith, A. (eds) (1998) *Theorizing Transition: Political Economy of Post Communist Transformations*, London, Routledge.
Pierson, C. (1991) *Beyond the Welfare State*, Cambridge, Polity Press.

Pinkus, B. (1988) *The Jews of the Soviet Union: The History of a National Minority*, Cambridge, Cambridge University Press.

Rai, S., Pilkington, H. and Phizacklea, A. (eds) (1992) *Women in the Face of Change: The Soviet Union, Eastern Europe and China*, London, Routledge.

Roberts, S. and Bolderson, H. (1999) 'Inside out: migrants' disentitlements to social security benefits in the EU', in Clasen, J. (ed.) *Comparative Social Policy: Concepts, Theories and Methods*, London, Blackwell.

Robinson, V. (1996) *Redefining the Front Line: The Geography of Asylum Seeking in the New Europe*, cited in Roberts and Bolderson (1999).

Roma Rights (1997) 'Roma: persecution in the East', in *Race and Class*, 39 (1), pp.100–6.

Room, G. (ed.) (1991) *Towards a European Welfare State?* Bristol, SAUS.

Sainsbury, D. (1996) *Gender, Equality and Welfare States*, Cambridge, Cambridge University Press.

Saraga, E. (ed.) (1998) *Embodying the Social: Constructions of Difference*, London, Routledge/The Open University.

Standing, G. (1996) 'Social protection in Central and Eastern Europe: a tale of slipping anchors and torn safety nets', in Esping-Andersen (1996).

Szalai, J. (1998) 'Conflicts of gender and class: paradoxes of women's changing situation in post-1989 Hungary'. Paper presented at the Women and Recognition Struggles conference in Stockholm, 7–11 November.

Taylor, D. (1996) 'Citizenship and social power', in Taylor, D. (ed.) *Critical Social Policy: A Reader*, London, Sage.

Taylor-Gooby, P. (1996) 'The response of government: fragile convergence', in George, V. and Taylor-Gooby, P. (eds) *European Welfare Policy*, Basingstoke, Macmillan.

Therborn, G. (1987) 'Welfare state and capitalist markets', *Acta Sociologica*, 30, pp.237–54.

Titmuss, R. (1974) *Social Policy: An Introduction*, London, George Allen & Unwin.

White, S., Batt, J. and Lewis, P.G. (eds) (1998) *Developments in Central and East European Politics*, London, Macmillan.

Wilensky, H.L. (1975) *The Welfare State and Equality: Structural and Ideological Roots of Public Expenditure*, Berkeley, CA, University of California Press.

Williams, F. (1992) 'Somewhere over the rainbow: universality and diversity in social policy', in Manning, N. and Page, R. (eds) *Social Policy Review 4*, Glasgow, Social Policy Association.

Williams, F. (1995) 'Race/ethnicity, gender and class in welfare states: a framework for comparative analysis', *Social Politics*, Summer, pp.127–59.

Williams, F. (1996) 'Feminism, postmodernism and the question of difference', in Parton, N. (ed.) *Social Theory, Social Change and Social Work*, London, Routledge.

Winters, A. (1995) 'The European Community: a case of successful integration?', in DeMelo, J. and Panagariya, A. (eds) *New Dimensions in Regional Integration*, Cambridge, Cambridge University Press.

Yuval-Davis, N. (1997) *Gender and Nation*, London, Sage.

Zaslavsky, V. (1993) 'Success and collapse: traditional Soviet nationality policy', in Bremmer, I. and Taras, R. (eds) *Nations and Politics in the Soviet Successor States*, Cambridge, Cambridge University Press.

13

A World of Difference? Globalization and the Study of Social Policy

John Clarke

1 Introduction

Globalization poses some rather difficult questions for the study of social policy, not least because of the way in which it disrupts the 'national' focus of attention within social policy. Social policy tends to be studied in relation to national welfare states or welfare systems. Even comparative social policy has been centred on comparisons between different national welfare states or systems. Globalization – and the transnational processes and relationships associated with it – represents a significant challenge to this conventional formulation of the object of study in social policy. At the same time, the encounter between globalization and social policy produces other difficulties. One concerns the character and direction of globalization itself since it is a much disputed concept (see, *inter alia*, Hirst and Thompson, 1999; Jameson, 1998; Jessop, 1998; and Massey, 1999). In this chapter I will be trying to take account of different understandings of globalization, because they raise difficult questions about social welfare. For these purposes, I think it is worth distinguishing three sets of differences in conceptualizations of globalization.

The first divergence concerns whether globalization is viewed as a distinctive process or as an effect of other economic, social and political processes. The former sees globalization as a causal process – a political, economic and cultural dynamic that has remade the geographical or spatial order of the world into a new configuration. Globalization, in this view, has consequences for other social arrangements, including the claim that it has undermined the system of post-war welfare states in advanced capitalist countries. The alternative view treats globalization as a result of other processes. It describes a new alignment of regions, nations and transnational interrelationships which are the effect of diverse economic, political and cultural dynamics. For example, Jessop argues that:

> Globalization is generally better interpreted as the complex resultant of many different processes than as a distinctive causal process in its own right. It is misleading to explain specific events and phenomena in terms of the process of 'globalization', pointless to subsume anything and everything under the umbrella of 'globalization' and unhelpful to seek to link anything and everything to 'globalization' as if this somehow conveys more insight than alternative rubrics could. (Jessop, 1998, p.1)

The second line of difference in views of globalization concerns whether it is treated as a linear development, unfolding in one clear and distinctive direction, or is viewed as a combination of contradictory tendencies and potentials. The former involves a view of globalization as a fairly homogeneous process in which the increasing mobility of capital, investment, trade and information dissolves outmoded barriers, boundaries and ways of life in the construction of a 'new world order' (and is accompanied by a 'global culture'). The alternative view sees the condition of globalization as marked by unevenness, contradictions and tensions. Thus economic and political realignments have spatially differentiated impacts, remaking places, nations and regions in different ways and reorganizing their relationships. These processes are also seen to have contradictory consequences, both homogenizing and diversifying cultural forms, for example, or undercutting the centrality of nation-states while being accompanied by an intensification of nationalism and nation-forming.

These sets of views of globalization intersect with a third type of difference. Here globalization is either understood as a sort of apocalyptic or epochal change, or as a cluster of partial, uneven and unfinished tendencies. The former treats globalization as a major shift in which all the major dimensions of human life have been remade in the creation of a 'new world order', such that old understandings, habits and ways of thinking are increasingly inappropriate or redundant. The latter suggests that the geo-political realignments are still 'in process' – marked by the break-up of some old configurations, the persistence of others, and attempts to fix new patterns, hierarchies and relationships.

The above are fairly crude sketches of what are complex sets of arguments about the nature of globalization and the ways of theorizing it in the social sciences. Nevertheless, they are sketches that may help us to explore the intersection of globalization and social policy in this chapter. How globalization is viewed is significant for thinking about the implications for social policy. In what follows, I have drawn out different aspects of globalization (emphasizing different sorts of dynamics) and examined the questions that they raise for the study of social policy. In keeping with this book's concerns, I have tried to pose the question: 'what sorts of rethinking of social policy are provoked by looking at globalization?'

There is, however, one more introductory issue that needs to be addressed. It concerns how social policy is understood in this meeting with globalization. For the most part, the 'welfare states' or 'welfare regimes' that have been discussed in the context of globalization are very narrowly conceived. Like conventional comparative social policy, such discussions treat social policy as denoting the large income transfer programmes linked to unemployment, illness and retirement (and their fiscal bases). Such a view ignores the extensive efforts to explore how welfare policies and practices are implicated in the production or reproduction of complex forms of social differentiation and inequality (see, for example, the argument in Cochrane, 1993). Viewing welfare systems as income transfer machines (which may be geared by different sorts of cogs) delivers a narrow and economistic view of social policy, even if it makes quantified comparison easier. One purpose of this chapter is to insist that the encounter between globalization and social policy should not retreat from the broader understandings of social welfare that other processes of 'rethinking social policy' have created.

2 Globalization and political economy

Globalization has been predominantly conceived of as an economic process or, at least, as a process whose primary driving forces are economic ones. At its heart can be found the greater mobility of capital, investment, production processes and the new forms of technology (particularly information technology) that enable this increased spatial freedom. With the dissolution of the Communist bloc, the world is increasingly envisaged as a single integrated market, in which deregulation works in the service of 'free trade'. These processes have called into question the role of nation-states, national governments and their public spending programmes (including social welfare spending) in a number of ways.

First, there has been for some time a clear 'business agenda' (Moody, 1987), in which corporate capital has articulated its demand for 'business-friendly environments' (geo-political places with low tax, low regulation and low-cost labour). Such demands have been enforced by 'capital flight' – the reality or threat of relocating investment, industrial and commercial processes elsewhere. Second, such concerns have been installed as 'global economic wisdom' in a variety of supra-national organizations and agencies, such as the International Monetary Fund, World Bank and the World Trade Organization (see Deacon et al., 1997). Their policies, often under the rubric of 'structural adjustment programmes', have tended to reinforce a vision of minimalist or *laissez-faire* government, centred on reducing levels of public spending and borrowing. Third, there has been a consistent and international thread of political support for this vision of a global world of free trade. Neo-liberal political ideology has been unevenly influential but its effects have been particularly strong in Anglophone states (the UK, USA and New Zealand, for example). There are, however, risks attached to taking neo-liberal ideology at its word. New Right governments may have talked about 'rolling back the state', but they have also used the state (and public expenditures) to create and enforce the conditions of 'free' markets and 'flexible' labour forces (see, for example, Jessop, 1998 and Chapter 11 in this volume). Indeed the same can also be said of some of the supra-national organizations referred to above.

This changing political economy has implications for the way in which welfare states are viewed. The most pessimistic and apocalyptic view is that the new global economy has sounded the death knell for the developed (Western European) welfare state. Policies of economic and social management are not sustainable by national governments in the face of deregulated capitalism. John Gray, for example, has argued that:

> Bond markets have knocked away the floor from under post-war full employment policies. No western government today has a credible successor to the policies which secured western societies in the Keynesian era . . . Social market systems are being compelled progressively to dismantle themselves, so that they can compete on equal terms with economies in which environmental, social and labour costs are lowest. (Gray, 1998, p.92)

There are reasons for treating such accounts of the end of the welfare state with some caution. One concerns the comparative evidence for welfare state decline or retrenchment. A number of studies have highlighted continuing divergences in national welfare states, despite evidence that international pressures on national governments are increasing. For example, Esping-Andersen and his colleagues conclude that 'global economic competition does narrow policy choice' but that 'standard accounts are exaggerated and risk being misleading. In part, the diversity of welfare states speaks against too much generalization' (1996, p.2). This, then, points to a second variant within the political economy approach to globalization and social welfare. While accepting the shifting economic alignment towards greater global integration, such studies indicate the continuing importance of national politics and institutional arrangements for choices over the shape, direction and character of welfare policies:

> There are additional reasons why we should not exaggerate the degree to which global forces overdetermine the fate of national welfare states. One of the most powerful conclusions in comparative research is that political and institutional mechanisms of interest representation and political consensus-building matter tremendously in terms of managing welfare, employment and growth objectives. (Esping-Anderson, 1996, p.6)

This concern to retain a conception of political capacity or agency is shared by other writers. For example, Hirst and Thompson (1999) take a more sceptical view about both the extent of economic globalization and the degree to which it constrains or determines national politics of welfare. They have argued that

> Welfare states are coming under intense pressure on costs and types of services for a variety of reasons – ageing population, high rates of family break-up, rising costs and complexity of health care, and increasing diversification and professionalization of services – and of these reasons the openness of the national economy to external shocks is neither the principal one nor a new factor. (Hirst and Thompson, 1999, p.46)

They go on to suggest that 'Globalization has not eliminated the scope for extensive welfare, and even within the constraints of the EU, states have clear options if they have the political resources' (ibid., p.51).

There are, then, substantial differences of opinion about the scale and consequences of economic realignment. Nevertheless, these arguments share a common view of the globalization/social welfare encounter as being a matter of understanding the relationship between the economy and national welfare states. Globalization might also make us more attentive to the diversity of the politics and forms of social welfare. Social welfare is the focus of expansionist as well as retrenchment policies, as countries of the South look to create or expand public health and welfare provisions (even in the face of neo-liberal wisdom). Not all of these political tendencies centre on the state, however; many involve non-governmental organizations and other social actors in welfare systems. In section 4 I will return to some of the problems of focusing on the nation-state/welfare state in studying social policy.

A number of writers have presented a different view of the relationship between economic constraints and political agency in relation to existing welfare states. For example, Hay argues that it is important to examine 'the extent to which the parameters of the politically possible are circumscribed *not* by "harsh economic realities" and "inexorable logics" of competitiveness and globalization, but by *perceptions* of such logics and realities and by what they are *held to entail*' (1998, p.529). I will return to this issue in section 5. This argument forces us to think about globalization as a double entity: a condition or set of processes in the world and a discourse about the state of the world that attempts to make its image of the world come true in practice.

For studying social policy, the political economy aspect of globalization raises a number of questions. I want to emphasize three at this point:

1   To what extent do contemporary economic processes and relationships undermine post-war welfare settlements in western capitalist societies?
2   What is the interaction between economic and political processes in the contemporary reconstruction of social welfare?
3   Do political economy approaches take too narrow a view of welfare states and systems – both in terms of how social policy is understood and in terms of the nation-state/welfare state focus of attention?

3   Globalization and social-cultural dynamics

Perhaps the most significant point of overlap between political, economic and social-cultural aspects of globalization is the issue of inequality. Most analysts seem certain that globalization is associated with new or deepened patterns of inequality: between regions, between countries, between places within countries, and between and within different groups of people. In the first instance, this is primarily related to socioeconomic inequalities – the unequal distribution of wealth and income. The new economic and political relationships of globalization are bound up with shifting configurations of rich and poor. Some of these involve the reinforcement or intensification of existing patterns of inequality – between North and South, or between those in and out of work, or between gender groups, for example. Others involve the creation of new patterns as places, industries, occupations and regions rise and fall. Sassen suggests that one of the features of the new global economy is that the intensity of inequalities has deepened: the economic (though not necessarily geographical) gaps between rich and poor have increased (for example Sassen, 1998, p.xxxiii). However, inequality is not just a matter of income and wealth. The new economic relationships have also been accompanied by the uneven distribution of other sorts of resources – information, access to formal political power and, not least, mobility.

In a context where 'free trade' and the 'free movement of capital' have been distinctive features of the new arrangements, the mobility of people is a more complex matter. People who wish to move in search of new places, new possibilities and new economic opportunities or labour markets are likely to find themselves confronted by national and regional borders, barriers and regulations. Massey suggests it is important to grasp the duality of processes affecting the movement of people internationally:

> International migration does, of course, continue, but it is reduced and hedged about, controlled . . . Moreover, what international migration remains is clearly segregated between the rich, those with skills and/or money to invest on the one hand, and who can move with relative ease, and the poor and unskilled on the other, against whom the barriers are raised. (Massey, 1999, p.13)

She argues that these barriers to mobility (such as the closure of borders to 'economic migrants') mean we should not overstate the fluidity of people, places and cultures in globalization. Although labour migration plays a significant part in the remaking of some economic regions, intensified controls on immigration and asylum elsewhere have tried to slow the movement of people. Such spatial unevenness is a characteristic condition of globalization – rather than the image of a uniform or homogenized world order (see also Gibson-Graham, 1996, pp.126–45). Both material inequalities and issues about geographical mobility cross-cut the field of social policy. In the case of inequalities, the old social democratic imagery of egalitarianism and redistribution has been internationally displaced by a combination of neo-liberal justifications for the necessity of inequality (as economic motivation) and more corporatist concerns with forms of social exclusion. On the other hand, the issue of migration is increasingly constructed as a 'social policy problem' in political discourse. Migrants are represented as a threat to services and benefits ('exploiting' welfare provision or being 'benefit tourists'). They give rise to awkward questions about citizenship status, membership of the 'welfare community' and entitlements to welfare (Morris, L., 1998). They are categorized using vocabularies that echo traditional social policy distinctions between the 'deserving' and 'undeserving' poor, for example in the distinction between 'genuine refugees' and 'economic migrants'.

It is important to reflect on these forms of inequality, marginalization and exclusion in relation to social policy. Material or socioeconomic inequalities tend to be equated with particular conceptual categories or approaches, such as distinctions between rich and poor, or ideas of class divisions. In current debates within social policy, these are often counterposed to approaches that have foregrounded other social divisions – for instance those based on the constitution of gendered and racialized difference. These are sometimes framed as a division between a 'politics of recognition' and 'politics of redistribution' (see, for example, Taylor-Gooby, 1996; Taylor, 1998; Ellison, 1999; Chapters 10, 20, 22, this volume). In this chapter I do not expect to be able to resolve these arguments, but I do want to note a view that the analysis of inequality and (im)mobility should not be split in this way. The unequal distribution of wealth and income flows through a variety of social categories that make a difference to the place of individuals. People do not exist one-dimensionally: as 'labour', as 'black people', as 'women' or as 'disabled people'. Rather they all bear multiple identities, although the relative significance and consequences of specific identities may change. To put it another way, 'poor people' are rarely just poor. The construction of gender positions (and responsibilities), aged positions, racialized positions and en/dis-abled positions shapes who ends up as poor. Similarly, the constructed social identities of different groups shape their capacities for mobility – as the occupants of 'business class', as 'tourists', as 'genuine refugees', as 'unwanted dependants' and as 'economic migrants'.

There are other connections between globalization and social policy implied here. The mobility of people and cultures, particularly to the major metropolitan centres or 'global cities', makes more visible the tensions around the relationship between the categories of nation, 'race', people and culture. For much of the twentieth century, it has been assumed that these categories are more or less equivalent: the nation = the people = a racial group = a way of life. Globalization does not mean the sudden arrival of 'others' who disrupt the purity and stability of the 'race/nation' equation. However, its forms of cultural and social mobility have made the long-running tensions and the lack of fit between these categories more evident and more politically charged. Globalization's forms of mobility include, of course, the commercial exploitation of cultural diversity itself. Sassen registers some of these social and cultural dynamics in suggesting that, 'The large western city of today concentrates diversity' (1998, p.xxx). At the same time, it is important to pay attention to relations of dominance and subordination within such social and cultural diversity.

Challenges to the normative order of social policy (and its naturalizing conceptions of difference) have been a consistent and

significant line of attack on the limitations of the social democratic or
Keynesian welfare states in the West (see Chapter 22 this volume). In
part, these issues have been centred on the limitations of, and
unequal access to, (national) citizenship (Lewis, 1998a). But they have
also raised more transformative possibilities for welfare policy and
practice in which issues of culture and identity have been central
themes (see, for example, Lowe, 1997; Ross, 1998). However, this
compressed diversity is itself a focus of significant political conflict.
Categories of 'race', 'culture' and 'nation' have become intense sites
of resistance to the cultural and social politics of diversity. Moreiras
has argued that

> Neoracism is the sinister counterpart to the cultural politics of difference
> that the immigrant imaginary and other nonimmigrant but nevertheless
> subaltern social groups, generally invoke as their emancipatory banner.
> Neoracism works in effect as the mirror image of identity politics, that is,
> as an identity politics of the dominant . . . (Moreiras, 1998, p.98)

Neither these issues nor the struggles around them are simply
matters of 'globalization'. But the processes of realignment of people,
cultures and identities within and beyond nation-states have underlined the constructed and contingent nature of 'citizenship'. At the
same time, movements and institutions operating beyond the nation-
state have provided resources and means for challenging the constructed, contingent and unequal forms of national citizenship.

What issues are raised for the study of social policy from exploring these social and cultural dynamics associated with globalization?
I would suggest the following as starting-points:

1   What forms of inequality are emerging, and what existing forms
    are changing, in the economic, social and cultural processes
    associated with globalization?
2   How can the analysis of forms and dynamics of inequality
    engage with the complex and cross-cutting lines of social differ-
    entiation?
3   What forms of inequality are being addressed in, or excluded
    from, social welfare policies?
4   How can analysis deal with both the substantive content of
    citizenship rights or entitlements and the contested construction
    of citizenship itself?

4   Globalization and institutional realignment

The issue of the nation-state exemplifies the problems of generalizing
about globalization. There have been claims that globalization has

undermined, reduced the significance or limited the decision-making capacity of the nation-state. From the standpoint of social policy, such claims have recurrently seemed premature or inaccurate. The nation-state continues – at least in the established capitalist economies – to be the major focus for the politics, policies and practices and provision of social welfare. As we have seen, Esping-Andersen suggests that 'global competition does narrow the field of domestic policy choice' (1996, p.2). This may be the dominant conception of the significance of globalization – the view that more open economies, in a more internationally competitive system, reinforced by global institutions such as the World Bank, change the conditions of national economic and social policy-making. However, there are other questions about the relationship between the national and the global that are significant for social policy.

For good reason, social policy has tended to operate with the idea of the nation-state as a central element in its field of analysis (though this does not mean that it has always been formalized as an explicit concept: see Clarke, 1996). In western capitalist societies, welfare has been predominantly organized in and through the nation-state. Globalization is associated with processes that dislocate the apparent unity of the phrase 'nation-state', forcing some space between the two terms such that nation and state cannot be assumed to be coterminous. 'Nations' have become increasingly unstable and contested entities, most obviously in the post-Soviet era in Europe. Nations have been both dismembered and remade (Sassen, 1998). They have been constructed as geographically bounded places, as sets of people, and as inherited, or even repressed but recovered, ways of life or cultures. Borders have been both weakened and reinforced (for example, within and around the European Union). At the same time, the welfare state and other public services became the focus for anti-statist politics as the New Right embarked on its mission to free capital, markets and the 'people' from the state as the incarnation of socialism.

This is both less and more than suggesting that globalization has undermined or displaced the nation-state. It is *less* because my argument here is about processes that contribute to dislocations or 'unsettlings' in the connection of nation and state (see also Hughes and Lewis, 1998). It is *more* because it opens up a sense of different potential axes of conflict within and beyond the nation and the state. Jessop (1999; and Chapter 11 in this volume) has pointed to the complications of geo-political *scale* in globalization. He refuses the simplifying 'global or local' framework in favour of tracing the differentiated flows of power, resources, capacities and decisions between local, subnational, national, regional and global levels. In this analysis, the nation-state does not disappear but is placed within more complex sets of scalar relationships and processes.

In the context of social policy, it may be worth pursuing further these disturbances around the nation/state alignment by looking at the relationships between 'nation-state' and 'welfare state'. These phrases denote central institutional formations in which the nation/ state, and welfare/state have been constructed as stable linkages (see also Clarke et al., 1998, p.3). However, the stability or unity of the phrase 'welfare state' can no longer be assumed, given that 'welfare' has been one of the central (if not the main) focal points of New Right politics in the 1980s and 1990s. The shift towards 'welfare pluralism', 'mixed economies of welfare' and the organizational dismemberment of the public sector in the USA and UK means that we need to think of each of the terms – welfare, nation and state – as being the focus of separate, if overlapping, sets of political conflicts. It is also important to recognize the ways in which the 'welfare state' as an institutional form is not the only way in which public or social welfare can be organized, produced and provided. The diversity of existing (and desired) forms of organizing welfare imply a need to conceptualize 'welfare regimes' as composed of more than just the state or the market, or even the state, market and the family (see, for example, Mayo, 1994). The existence of various forms of voluntary, associational, community-based or non-governmental organizations involved in struggling for welfare and in providing welfare in different places poses significant analytical problems for the study of social policy.

At the same time, the meaning, scope and scale of 'welfare' is being contested and renegotiated in many national contexts, with the USA in the vanguard of the search for the 'end of welfare' (see, *inter alia*, Mink, 1998). While 'welfare' in the US context has been narrowly equated with AFDC (Aid for Families with Dependent Children) rather than any wider concept of social welfare, it is clear that other public programmes are also under threat (for instance, in proposals to privatize social security). In a variety of ways, the integrity of the nation has become contested – in terms of citizen membership, in terms of constitutional arrangements, in terms of geographical, political and cultural boundaries and in terms of the permeability of such boundaries to migration. At the same time, the role, scope and scale of the state has been under constant challenge, particularly but not exclusively, from the New Right since the late 1970s. The effect has been growing uncertainty about what the state can and should do; about what government can be trusted to do; and about what the public can afford to have the state do. We have seen efforts to 'reinvent' government and the organization of services to the public – sometimes identified as a shift from 'government' to 'governance'. 'Public services' can no longer be assumed to refer to both services *to* the public and services located *in* the public sector, given moves towards a more 'mixed economy of welfare' (Rao, 1996). Clarke and

Newman (1997, pp.22–33) have argued that it is important to trace both the shift towards other agencies of provision and the new means by which multiple providers are tied by financial and performance management systems into a field of 'dispersed' state power. The difficulty is to grasp how such processes may involve both 'welfare pluralism' and new forms of state power or control 'at a distance' (Hoggett, 1996).

These issues about the remaking of nation, state and welfare mean that we must think of globalizing processes as uneven: not homogenizing the world but reworking the relationships between its parts. For social policy, this means thinking geographically (or even geo-politically) in ways that go beyond the conventions of comparative studies. Comparative studies have internationalized social policy by comparing several national welfare states or welfare regimes (for example, Cochrane and Clarke, 1993; Esping-Andersen, 1990). Globalization creates a need to move beyond an analysis which primarily draws out the ways in which 'it's different here' towards a recognition that even 'here' is itself conditional and unstable (Lewis, 1998b). For social policy, the 'here' has typically been understood as the bounded and stable space of the nation-state (as welfare state). Globalization invites us to think about the contingent nature of those boundaries and the institutional stability of the nation-state. We can no longer take for granted the nation-state/welfare state complex as the basic object of study.

So what questions might these processes of institutional realignment pose for the study of social policy? I would suggest three main areas:

1   Which of the processes and relationships that traverse or cut across the nation-state have implications for social policy?
2   In what ways are the institutional settlements of nation-state and welfare state becoming dislocated?
3   What changes are there in both the meaning of, and the means of providing, social welfare?

5   Globalization as discourse

I want to return to an earlier issue – the view that 'globalization' needs to be treated as a discourse. It may be helpful to explore how the dominant public and political representations of globalization as an economic and social process form a distinctive discourse. It is a discourse that lays claim to a distinctive knowledge – about economies and their dynamics and about their consequences. This discourse of globalization has drawn considerable strength from the revival of neo-classical economics as the dominant world-knowledge:

the one that knows the 'real' or 'hard facts' about life. In this guise, economics stands for the 'basic' knowledge against which other disciplinary knowledges are judged to be secondary or even superficial. This view of the role of 'harsh economic truths' has had an impact on the study of social policy and on the public politics of welfare. It has underpinned the anti-statist and pro-market direction of many critiques of welfare. It has provided the vocabulary for transforming political debate about welfare choices into a matter of surrendering 'what we can no longer afford' and it has elevated 'good fiscal housekeeping' to a major performance target of each nation-state, organization and service worker. It has attempted to drown political conflict through its claims to demonstrate the existence of the 'natural' rates of unemployment and taxation. In all these respects, the rise of neo-classical economics has been aligned with the attempted naturalization of a neo-liberal economy: the presentation of it as the only possible – and the necessary – form of social organization.

Doreen Massey has delineated the main dimensions of this conception of globalization. She stresses the need to treat a discourse not just as the representations, words and connections that form a field of knowledge, but also as a socially embedded or institutionalized construction of the world:

> the imagination of a globalization in terms of unbounded free space chimes all too well with that powerful rhetoric of neo-liberalism around 'free trade'. It is a pivotal element in a powerful, political, fully-fledged discourse. It is a discourse which is produced in the countries of the world's North. It is a discourse which has its institutions and its professionals – the IMF, the World Bank, the World Trade Organization, Western governments. It is a discourse which is normative; and it is a discourse which has effects. (Massey, 1999, p.10)

As Massey and others have argued, such constructions have enabled the powerful (in economic and political terms) to represent themselves as powerless in the face of the new global 'realities'. Despite this, they usually manage to act to intensify this dominant mode of globalization. The new global economy is selectively represented in this dominant discourse. Its positive features (dynamism, innovation, flexibility and so on) are stressed over its disruptions, its intensification of inequalities, its chaotic contradictoriness, and its profound instabilities (see Gray, 1998). These 'problems' tend to be passed off as either temporary interruptions of normal service or merely a developmental phase before 'mature' globalization. At the same time, globalization is appropriated as a legitimizing narrative to frame more specific projects. Clarke and Newman have argued that there is a discursive 'cascade of change' from the global to the local:

The narrative descent from the global to the local constructs equivalences between different entities. In this globalized environment, nations, corporate bodies and individuals are seen to face the same challenges and have the same objectives (survival or success). Global change has created the conditions in which nations must compete against each other, organizations must compete for markets and resources, and individuals must compete for jobs, income and security. These equivalences rest on a naturalizing assumption about the universality of 'being enterprising'. Individuals, organizations and nations share common impulses or drives and these should not be blocked or repressed. (Clarke and Newman, 1997, p.48)

This narrative enables specific changes to be constructed as essential and irresistible by locating them as the necessary adaptation to new global realities. This narrative form is deployed in both organizational change strategies and in political programmes. It is important to re-emphasize that its power rests significantly on the capacity to effect a closure around *this* globalization as the only, the necessary, the desirable and the irresistible form of globalization. It must try to make alternatives silent, invisible or simply the stuff of utopian fantasies ('not real' and 'not realistic'). Nevertheless, the processes contributing to globalization have always been more than this neo-liberal vision. New conditions of, and possibilities for, social, political and cultural mobilization are also part of the 'new world order'. They may be uneven, contradictory and unfinished but they outrun the simplifying assumptions of globalization understood as the world of free trade.

6   A tentative conclusion?

Globalization poses new questions for the study of social policy. Minimally, it means paying attention to economic, social and political processes that lie beyond the geo-political confines of the nation-state which have consequences for the direction and organization of social welfare. Globalization also means having to rethink some of the basic conceptual framework of social policy itself, exploring the ways in which the trinity of nation, state and welfare are being remade. Finally, globalization implies looking at established questions within social policy in new ways. The status of citizenship, the relationships between economic and social policies, the intersections of inequalities, social problems and social policies, the role of social welfare in reproducing or redressing forms of inequality and the forms of conflict over the state and welfare do not become irrelevant because of globalization. However, we have to find ways of thinking about them that take account of the shifting scales (from local through to global), processes and relationships that globalization implies. In this rethinking of old questions and exploration of new ones, it is vital to resist the temptation to view 'globalization' as a causal force. Such a view treats social policy (or changes in social welfare) simply as the effect or product of globalization. If we keep in mind the argument of Held and his co-authors that 'Globalization is not a singular condition, a linear process or a final end-point of social change' (1997, p.258), it becomes possible to treat the intersection of globalization and social policy as a focus for active 'rethinking'.

References

Clarke, J. (1996) 'The problem of the state after the welfare state', in May, M., Brunsdon, E. and Craig, G. (eds) *Social Policy Review 8*, Canterbury, Social Policy Association.

Clarke, J. and Newman, J. (1997) *The Managerial State: Power, Politics and Ideology in the Remaking of Social Welfare*, London, Sage.

Clarke, J., Hughes, G., Lewis, G. and Mooney, G. (1998) 'Introduction', in Hughes, G. (ed.) *Imagining Welfare Futures*, London, Routledge/The Open University.

Cochrane, A. (1993) 'Comparative approaches and social policy', in Cochrane and Clarke (1993).

Cochrane, A. and Clarke, J. (eds) (1993) *Comparing Welfare States: Britain in International Context*, London, Sage/The Open University.

Deacon, B. with Hulse, M. and Stubbs, P. (1997) *Global Social Policy*, London, Sage.

Ellison, N. (1999) 'Beyond universalism and particularism: rethinking welfare theory', *Critical Social Policy*, 19 (1), pp.57–85.

Esping-Andersen, G. (1990) *The Three Worlds of Welfare Capitalism*, Cambridge, Polity Press.

Esping-Andersen, G. (ed.) (1996) *Welfare States in Transition: National Adaptations in Global Economies*, London, Sage in association with UNRISD.

Gibson-Graham, J.K. (1996) *The End of Capitalism (As We Knew It): A Feminist Critique of Political Economy*, Oxford, Blackwell.

Gray, J. (1998) *False Dawn: The Delusions of Global Capitalism*, London, Granta Books.

Hay, C. (1998) 'Globalization, welfare retrenchment and "the logic of no alternative": why second-best won't do', *Journal of Social Policy*, 27 (4), pp.525–32.

Held, D., Goldblatt, D., McGrew, A. and Perraton, J. (1997) 'The globalization of economic activity', *New Political Economy*, 2 (2), pp.257–77.

Hirst, P. and Thompson, G. (1999) *Globalization in Question: The Myths of the International Economy and the Possibilities of Governance* (2nd edn), Cambridge, Polity Press.

Hoggett, P. (1996) 'New modes of control in the public service', *Public Administration*, 74, pp.9–32.

Hughes, G. and Lewis, G. (eds) (1998) *Unsettling Welfare: The Reconstruction of Social Policy*, London, Routledge/The Open University.

Jameson, F. (1998) 'Preface', and 'Notes on globalization as a philosophical issue', in Jameson and Miyoshi (1998).

Jameson, F. and Miyoshi, M. (eds) (1998) *The Cultures of Globalization*, Durham, NC, Duke University Press.

Jessop, B. (1998) 'Reflections on globalization and its (il)logics' in Olds, K., Kelly, P., Kong, L., Yeung, H.W. and Dicken, P. (eds) *The Logic of Globalization*, London, Routledge.

Jessop, B. (1999) 'Globalization and the nation state', in Aronowitz, S. and Bratsis, P. (eds) *Rethinking the State: Miliband, Poulantzas and State Theory*, Minneapolis, MN, University of Minneapolis Press.

Lewis, G. (ed.) (1998a) *Forming Nation; Framing Welfare*, London, Routledge/The Open University.

Lewis, G. (1998b) 'Same place, different culture?: thinking welfare through the post-colonial'. Plenary address to the Social Policy Association Conference, Lincoln.

Lowe, L. (1997) *Immigrant Acts: On Asian American Cultural Politics*, Durham, NC, Duke University Press.

Massey, D. (1999) 'Imagining globalization: power-geometries of time-space', in Brah, A., Hickman, M. and MacanGhaill, M. (eds) *Future Worlds: Migration, Environment and Globalization*, London, Macmillan.

Mayo, M. (1994) *Communities and Caring: The Mixed Economy of Welfare*, London, St Martin's Press.

Mink, G. (1998) *Welfare's End*, Ithaca, NY, Cornell University Press.

Moody, K. (1987) 'Reagan, the business agenda and the collapse of labour', in Miliband, R. et al. (eds) *The Socialist Register 1987*, London, Merlin.

Moreiras, A. (1998) 'Global fragments: a second Latinamericanism', in Jameson and Miyoshi (1998).

Morris, L. (1998) 'Legitimate membership of the welfare community', in Langan, M. (ed.) *Welfare: Needs, Rights and Risks*, London, Routledge/The Open University.

Morris, M. (1998) *Too Soon, Too Late: History in Popular Culture*, Bloomington, IN, Indiana University Press.

Rao, N. (1996) *Towards Welfare Pluralism: Public Services in a Time of Change*, Aldershot, Dartmouth.

Ross, A. (1998) *Real Love: In Pursuit of Cultural Justice*, London, Routledge.

Sassen, S. (1998) *Globalization and Its Discontents: Essays on the New Mobility of People and Money*, New York, The New Press.

Taylor, D. (1998) 'Social identity and social policy: engagements with postmodern theory', *Journal of Social Policy*, 27 (3), pp.329–50.

Taylor-Gooby, P. (1996) 'In defence of second-best theory: state, class and capital in social policy', *Journal of Social Policy*, 26, pp.171–92.

14

Decriminalizing Criminology

John Muncie

1 Introduction

This chapter explores the implications for criminology when its key referent – 'crime' – is subjected to a series of critical deconstructions. Historically such an endeavour is in its infancy – probably no more than thirty years old. It has taken two major forms:

- broadening the subject matter of criminology away from a sole reliance on those injurious acts defined as such by the criminal law – theft, burglary, criminal damage and so on – in order to establish that a vast range of *harms* – sexism, racism, imperialism, economic exploitation and so on – could and should be included as the focal concern of an area of study called criminology (Schwendinger and Schwendinger, 1970);
- recognizing that 'what is crime' rests crucially on the power to define and the power to police certain 'transgressions' whilst ignoring or giving little attention to others. The key problematic for criminology then becomes not crime nor criminal behaviour, but social order and how that order is produced and struggled over (Shearing, 1989).

Both approaches lead us to ask some quite fundamental questions. What things constitute the proper domain of criminology? Can criminology do these things and still remain distinctively criminological? Or, is it better conceived as a branch of sociology or political science?

2 Crime-ology

First we must consider how criminology reached this precarious state of affairs. Traditionally the discipline has defined itself around two rationalizing discourses: the search for the causes of crime and the devising of methods and means for its control. Up to the 1960s positivism maintained that if we looked hard and long enough we would be able to 'discover' crime in a range of physiological, psychological, economic or structural predeterminants. The criminogenic condition could then be treated by designing interventions to alter individual behaviour either through medicine or psychiatry or by opening up new opportunities for community development. As Shearing (1989) has aptly described it, this endeavour can best be described as *crime-ology*. However, these agendas were to come under sustained attack.

By the 1960s and 1970s an emergent radical criminology developed two key counter-propositions:

- If criminology restricts itself to questions of cause/remedy it becomes an adjunct of government or at best a think-tank to develop policy and advance the interests of particular political constituents. It needs to sever all such institutional ties if it is to have any independent academic credibility.
- Crime cannot be identified simply by focusing on known offenders. These are but one element of the 'problem of crime' and only capable of identification following a series of social constructions involving the power to formulate criminal laws, police targeting, courtroom discretion, media representations and so on. As such, crime has no independent existence. Rather what criminology can and should study are processes of criminalization: how certain harmful acts/events come to be defined and recognized as 'crime' whilst others do not.

As a result it became commonplace in radical circles to assert that the end of criminology was imminent. A century of searching for the causes of crime and of devising methods for its control had seemingly come to a dead end. We were no nearer establishing causation than we were in effecting any reduction in crime rates. Nothing seemed to work. So the emergent wisdom of the 1970s urged us to concern ourselves more with new developments in social, political and legal theory, rather than being burdened with inconclusive empirical projects. However, this foundational critique took place against the political backdrop of a resurgence in popular law and order politics and authoritarianism. Its critical edge became lost within the resuscitation of criminology in a myriad of reactionary, realist and reformist guises. As law and order politics swept through the political landscape of the 1980s criminology was rejuvenated, focusing once more on untangling causes and formulating effective measures of crime management, rather than working to contest and disrupt its rationalizing agenda.

A resurgent radical right revived a neo-classical vision of criminality as voluntaristic – as a course of action willingly chosen by wicked, calculating individuals lacking in self-control. In policy circles a burgeoning administrative criminology argued that all that could be realistically hoped for was to implement pragmatic means aimed at reducing the opportunity for crime and to manage crime through situational preventative measures. Managerial efficiency (what works at some times in some places), cost-effectiveness (what works cheaply) and pragmatic risk assessment have become its defining principles (see Chapter 15 this volume). Simultaneously, a left realism was convinced that the problem of crime was growing out of control and that once more its causes needed to be established and theorized. Left realists also thought that in tandem with the exploration of the causes of crime, a social justice programme needed to be initiated to tackle social and economic inequalities under the rubric of 'partnerships' and 'inclusive citizenship'. In these ways, by the 1980s criminology's historic project to find cause and cure once more achieved ascendancy: an ascendancy that continues to be reflected in a host of new criminology departments in higher education, a succession of academic/practitioner conferences and a burgeoning academic press (Muncie et al., 1996). At the end of the century, criminology – as crime-ology – never seemed so vital and flourishing. Where, however, does this leave the radical critique of the 1960s and 1970s: as an historical anomaly in the history of the discipline or as a vital point of resistance and theoretical renewal?

3 Beyond legal definitions of crime

Contrary to the orthodoxy prevailing among many criminologists, theoretical development has far from come to a standstill. There remains an important body of deconstructionist knowledge – originating in no small measure from a European school of abolitionism – which continues to move beyond the essentialist signifiers of crime, criminality and criminal justice to facilitate the production of new critical insights and alternative visions of justice (De Haan, 1990; Steinert, 1986; Bianchi, 1986; van Swaaningen, 1997). Nowhere is this more clearly seen than in the telling reminder that realist and administrative criminologies are trapped within a state and legally defined notion of 'crime'. As abolitionists had established in the 1980s, if our concern with crime is driven by fears for social stability, personal safety and social justice, then we may be well advised to look beyond 'crime' to discover where the most dangerous threats and risks to our person and property lie.

Poverty, malnutrition, pollution, medical negligence, domestic violence, corporate corruption, state violence, genocide, human rights violations and so on all carry with them more widespread and damaging consequences than most of the behaviours and incidents that currently make up the 'crime problem'. In the 1940s Sutherland's (1949) pathbreaking work on white-collar crime had introduced a definition of crime based on such concepts as *'injury* to the state' and 'socially *harmful'*. In the 1970s radical criminologists advocated a deepening of the criminological agenda to include racism, sexism and economic exploitation. In many respects this important debate was foreclosed by the growing hegemony of realist approaches. Despite this it is a debate that remains unfinished. Indeed it took until the 1990s for numerous harms to begin to be accepted as legitimate issues for criminological inquiry (Muncie and McLaughlin, 1996). Questions of human rights denial have begun to enter the agenda, not simply through extending conceptions of 'what is crime?' but by recognizing the legal transgressions routinely committed by those wielding political and economic power and their ability to deny or conceal the harms they unleash under the protection of the law (Cohen, 1993). In a similar vein it has taken some twenty years of feminist enquiry to have it acknowledged that violence, danger and risk lie not just on the streets or in the corridors of power, but in the sanctity of the home (see Chapter 16 this volume). Recognizing male violence and opening up the vexed question of 'violent masculinities' has the potential to disrupt the narrow and myopic concerns of much of what currently is understood to be the 'crime problem' (Segal, 1990; Campbell, 1993).

In other areas, too, we can witness a partial emergence of 'hidden crime' on to a mainstream agenda. The murder of Stephen Lawrence and the unrelenting campaign by his family to expose police and judicial racism catapulted racial violence and intimidation to the forefront of issues to be addressed by all law enforcement agencies in the late 1990s. State crime in the form of illegal arms dealings, genocide and torture has been consistent front-page news following successive wars in the Balkans and the establishment of the War Crimes Tribunal in The Hague. A long campaign against the trans-portation of live animals from Britain to Europe has drawn the issue of animal rights into a crime discourse, as has a recognition of the culpable negligence of tobacco and food companies in knowingly marketing unsafe and life-threatening substances. It has also become increasingly likely that we will find numerous aspects of social policy (in particular housing policy and youth homelessness) and environmental policy (in particular road-building and pollution) being described within a crime discourse. In itself this deepening of the criminological agenda has once more forced a reconceptualization of the proper domain of criminology.

This reimagining of crime and criminology has also been made possible by the eventual arrival of post-modernist perspectives in criminological discourse and the insistence that a recognition of the limited and limiting nature of the discipline can only be overcome by constantly questioning and stretching established boundaries. In the early 1990s a post-modern criminological imagination – emanating to no small degree from feminism – had warned that criminology would remain forever narrow and self-justifying unless it began to deconstruct its key taken-for-granted referents (crime, criminality, deviance and so on). Foucault's (1977) identification of a multiplicity of power relations and his questioning of the ability of any totalizing or meta-theory (Marxism, for example) to answer all questions was also pivotal. A growing disenchantment with a priori claims to the 'truth' cast doubt on all the rational and modernist intellectual movements of the past. As a result, post-modernist perspectives opened up a vital space in which reflexive knowledge of the entire criminological enterprise could be excavated (Smart, 1990). For some this has meant not only the abandonment of 'crime', but also a rejection of all grand theory and the prioritization of a wide variety of disparate and subjective positions. The sensitizing concepts of difference, diversity and localism have slowly filtered into the margins of the criminological domain. It is through such deconstructionism that the possibility of subjugating the concept of crime to that of social harm has once more been raised.

4   Recoding crime as social harm

In a harm-based discourse the concept of 'crime' remains important only in so far as it alerts us to relations of power embedded in social orders which generate a whole series of social problems for their populations but of which only a selected few are considered worthy of criminal sanction. A conception of crime without a conception of power is meaningless. The power to render certain harmful acts visible and to define them as 'crime', whilst maintaining the invisibility of others (or defining them as beyond criminal sanction), lies at the heart of the problem of working within notions of 'the problem of crime'. Notions of 'crime' offer a peculiarly blinkered vision of the range of misfortunes, dangers, harms, risks and injuries that are a routine part of everyday life. If the objective of criminology is to reveal such misfortunes, risks and harms then this narrow conception of 'crime' has to be rejected. So the first stage in decriminalizing criminology (or in decentring crime as its sole justification and object of inquiry) is to recognize that any number of damaging events are far more serious than those that make up the 'crime problem'. Moreover, many of these incidents (such as petty theft, shoplifting, recreational drug use, vandalism, brawls, anti-social behaviour) would not seem to score particularly high on a scale of serious harm. Despite this it is often these 'minor' events that take up much of the time and preoccupation of law enforcement agencies and the criminal justice system.

Conversely, the risk of suffering many of those crimes defined by the state as 'serious' would seem negligible compared to such everyday risks as workplace injury and avoidable disease. As many textbooks conveniently remind us but then seemingly forget, the risk of homicide is far less than that of terminal disease or of being struck by lightning and we are more likely to suffer accidental injury than theft. Yet why are we generally more afraid of crime than of other more pertinent threats to our personal safety? Questions such as these were first raised by Sutherland (1949) and then by the Schwendingers (1970), but the concept of social harm has never seriously been incorporated into criminology. Steinert (1986) refers to 'troubles', Hulsman (1986) to 'problematic events', Pepinsky (1991) to the 'violent refusal of democratic behaviour' and whilst De Haan (1990) talks of crime as social harm he never closely interrogates the concept. He is ultimately persuaded to argue that there is no solution to the problem of defining crime. It will always carry with it a set of contestable, epistemological, moral and political assumptions (De Haan, 1990, p.154).

By the mid-1990s critical theorists in the US (Henry and Milovanovic, 1994, 1996) had developed a *constitutive criminology* in which crime was defined as the 'power to deny others'. Crime was characterized as taking two major forms: harms of reduction and harms of repression. Harms of reduction refer to situations when an offended party experiences some *immediate* loss/injury because of the actions of others. Harms of repression refer to situations when power is used to restrict *future* human potential aspirations, and development. These concepts of harm are primarily used to bring a wide range of hidden crimes into the centre of the agenda and to reveal how certain harms, far from being condemned, are legitimized by the activities of various legal and social institutions. This is particularly the case in those 'crimes' – sexual harassment, racial violence, hate crime and so on – which threaten human dignity (Tifft, 1995) and often seem to be lacking in legal status or are given scant attention by law enforcement agencies. However, what has remained unclear is how far the recoding of crime as harm is capable of challenging and overthrowing legal definitions. As Nelken (1994a) has argued, campaigns to extend the criminal label so that it includes new forms of injury continually run the risk of reinforcing the concept of crime even when it is seemingly being attacked. On a different front Matthews and Young (1992) have maintained that such deconstructions are so relativist and value-laden that they become inoperable. They also encourage nihilism and cynicism. Moreover, they lament that by removing the principal object of criminology (crime) the subject is dissolved into larger *essentialist* disciplines such as sociology.

In response Henry and Lanier (1998) have put the case for an integrated definition of crime which recognizes the legally defined and the legally ignored, the serious and the trivial, and the visible and the obscured. Using the analogy of light refracting through a prism they recognize that what counts as crime is forever contingent and changing. Nevertheless, such a model which integrates crime and harm still tends to depend on crime as its starting-point. What would happen if instead we began an analysis with social harm? (See section 6.)

5   Recoding criminal justice as social justice

In parallel, the redefining of crime as harm opens up the possibility of dealing with pain, suffering and injury as conflicts and troubles deserving negotiation, mediation and arbitration rather than as criminal events deserving guilt, punishment and exclusion. As Bianchi (1986) argued, crime should be defined in terms of tort and dispute. Criminal law should be replaced by reparative law. Such a discourse is less concerned with controlling, preventing and punishing and more with enabling, empowering and restoration. Questions of crime control are subordinated to those of a wider social justice agenda in which governments and the wider community recognize disadvantage, difference and diversity and acknowledge that they have a responsibility for enhancing personal and social development. Whilst a concept of harm encourages conceptions of victimization as ubiquitous, it enables recognition of its most damaging forms beyond those which are currently recognized by media, law and the state. Perceptions of seriousness frequently reveal the differential value placed on human life, depending on social status and position within the hierarchy of power. On this basis, for example, the deaths of Princess Diana and the TV presenter Jill Dando are somehow assumed to be more serious than the regular and continuing murders experienced by Nationalist and Loyalist communities in Northern

Ireland. Moreover, a concept of harm enables injury to be addressed by a wide variety of social responses and without necessarily evoking or extending the penetration of the criminal justice system. De Haan captures much of this spirit in the concept of redress. The concept has an extensive set of formal definitions and meanings from 'to put right, repair, rectify something suffered or complained of' to 'correct, amend, reform or do away with a bad or faulty state of things' (cited by De Haan, 1990, p.158). For De Haan it opens the door to dealing with social problems or conflicts (such as crime) through neighbour-hood rather than criminal courts and in pursuance of compensation or reconciliation, rather than retaliation or blame allocation:

> To claim redress is merely to assert that an undesirable event has taken place and that something needs to be done about it. It carries no impli-cations of what sort of reaction would be appropriate; nor does it define reflexively the nature of the initial event . . . It puts forth the claim for a procedure rather than a specific result. Punitive claims already implied in defining an event as a 'crime' are opened up to rational debate. (De Haan, 1990, p.158)

The aim, as Cohen (1994) has also described, is to integrate, rather than exclude; to reduce or, if possible, abolish deliberately inflicted pain; to seek restoration rather than retribution.

6 Towards a series of multiple replacement discourses

To do justice to such visions the discipline may well need (yet again) to reconsider its connection to those self-fulfilling and self-justifying versions of criminology (particularly when they appear as criminal justice studies) that currently occupy the political and policy main-stream. Working within established discourses of crime and criminal justice necessarily closes the door to any imaginative rethinking. So it remains the case that important work will always need to be done in exposing the ways in which these knowledges of 'crime', criminal justice and criminology are built and activated. However, this should not preclude the search for a series of discursive frames that are capable of registering the fragmented complexities of our subject matter and of opening up the possibility of challenging alternatives (Muncie, 1998).

Harm can signify a host of material and emotive negativities – from notions of pain to fear, insecurity, violation, grief, powerless-ness, dispute and transgression – as well as the prevailing discourse of crime. The task is to subject each of these signifiers to a process of deconstruction. What we require now is not just a deconstruction of crime but a deconstruction of the concept of social harm. In turn this may necessitate the development of a psycho-sociology of injury, a psycho-sociology of exclusion and so on, rather than something necessarily called *criminology*. It would force a recognition that our subject matter is inherently unstable. Whilst legal wrongs provide the clearest focus, already notions of incivility (anti-social behaviour), malpractice (corporate/political corruption), risk (likelihood of committing future crimes) and violation (of human rights) are circulating on the margins of criminal definition and policy formulation. In themselves these 'new' signifiers – emanating from the right and left of the political spectrum – alert us to the ongoing struggle over what is the proper constitution of 'crime'. For those on the right the identification and control of 'incivility' is a clear priority, whilst for those on the left the redefinition of corporate malpractice as crime would allow such perpetrators to face the same (or enhanced) criminal justice consequences as are endured by 'ordinary criminals'. The danger, of course, may be that the drawing of such 'non-crimes' into the centre of criminology will lead to the criminalization of all 'undesirable behaviour' by the criminal justice mainstream and herald its further penetration into all matters of conflict resolution. For example, notions of community safety were first promoted as a means of liberalizing crime prevention policy; now they have been appropriated by New Labour as a means of targeting the 'anti-social' and used to justify all manner of punitive interventions from curfews to custody. From an abolitionist perspective these emergent discourses do not challenge that of 'crime', but become appropriated by it because they continue to fail to recognize the multi-faceted nature of harm (see Table 14.1).

It should be noted, too, that whilst the concept of harm is clearly capable of broadening criminology's horizons and radically unsettling its traditional agenda, it continues to operate within a discursive frame of the negative. However, when we acknowledge that harm is not only a source of fear but also a source of *fascination* and *entertainment*, we are faced with a quite different set of possibilities. Any cursory glance at television programme listings, the contents of mass circulation newspapers or the shelves of fiction in bookshops will confirm the extent to which an audience perceives crime not just as a social problem but as a major source of amusement and diversion. The way in which we enjoy violence, humiliation and hurt casts doubt on the universal applicability of harm as always connoting trouble, fear, loss and so on. For participants, too, the pleasure in creating harm, or doing wrong or breaking boundaries is also part of the equation and needs to be thought through. Part of such a task is already present in a *cultural criminology* which uses everyday existences, life histories, music, dance and performance as databases to discover how and why certain cultural forms become criminalized

Table 14.1 *Deconstructing social harm*

	Discourse	Discursive frame
Established	Crime	Criminal justice
	↑	↑
Emergent	Incivilities	Social policy/community safety
	Malpractice/negligence	Regulation
	Risk	Risk assessment/management
	Violation	Human rights
Absent/marginal	Exclusion	Restoration/inclusion
	Loss/damage	Compensation
	Dispute	Conflict resolution/mediation
	Troubles	Redress
	Fear	Trust
	Powerlessness/insecurity	Empowerment
	Injury/pain/hurt	Healing
	Grief/loss of the past	Reconciliation/mourning/memory
	Recognizing pleasure	
Absent	Doing 'wrong'	Desire/excitement
	Difference	Tolerance
	Transgression	Delight/display
	Dis-respect	Drama
	Dis-order	Carnival
	Resistance	Celebration

(Presdee, 2000). The intention, as Ferrell and Sanders (1995) have argued, may be to expand and enliven criminology, but when pushed to its logical conclusion it is also quite capable of breaking the boundaries of the discipline. Much of this work is also in its infancy. Katz (1988), for example, has talked of the 'seduction of crime' in which disorder becomes in itself a 'delight' to be sought after and savoured. Presdee (2000) captures this sense of the interrelationship of pleasure and pain through the notion of 'crime as carnival'. Carnival is a site where the pleasure of playing at the boundaries is clearly catered for. Festive excess, transgression, the mocking of the powerful, irrational behaviour and so on are all temporarily legitimized in the moment of carnival. Breaking rules is a source of joy, of humour, of celebration. Many acts that might otherwise be considered criminal are temporarily tolerated. In such acts as SM, raving, joy-riding, recreational drug use, reclaim the streets parties, computer hacking, gang rituals and extreme sports, Presdee finds enduring fragments from the culture of the carnival. Moreover, as Thornton's (1995) study of 1990s youth club cultures found, there is a continual and shifting exchange between the boundaries of acceptability and illegality, between subcultural authenticity and media manufacture, between moral panics about deviance and the celebration of rule breaking by the subcultural participants themselves. All such instances suggest we need to push deeper and deeper to capture the full meaning of social harm. Certainly notions of crime have a place here, but one subjugated to, and set against, a multiple series of replacement discourses incorporating transgression, dis-respect, disorder and resistance, as well as loss, injury, troubles and so on. Such discourses themselves may also suggest a new sociology of deviance based on difference and 'otherness' (van Swaaningen, 1999, p.23). Once more the discursive frame necessary to recognize these elements needs to shift not just from criminal justice to social justice, restoration, reconciliation and so on, but to delight, drama, tolerance, celebration and the pursuit of jouissance (see Table 14.1). Significantly, too, as we move from established discourses of harm to those that are absent, the constitution of the subject shifts from 'individual offender' to 'collective victim', whilst in a discourse of pleasure new visions of the subject as collective 'innovator or celebrator' are raised.

To date, criminology's greatest and recurring limitation is that it allows dominant and state-defined conceptions of crime to run its agenda. This remains perhaps the biggest hurdle to be cleared in the search for a series of self-reflexive replacement discourses in which transgression might be understood without reference to crime, harm reduced without recourse to criminalization, and social justice achieved without recourse to criminal law. Yet such reconceptualizations and reframings remain important because they alone allow for a reimagining of criminology which would enable it to break free of its obsession with legal wrongs and prioritize such alternative goals as trust, redress, dialogue, tolerance, empowerment and celebration.

In 1890 Topinard, writing in the *Athenaum*, expressed his dislike for the term 'criminological anthropology' to describe the then fledgling science of crime and criminality. He reluctantly suggested using the term 'criminology' instead, 'until a better term can be found'. Over a century later that search seems even more urgent and necessary.

References

Bianchi, H. (1986) 'Pitfalls and strategies of abolition', in Bianchi, H. and van Swaaningen, R. (eds) *Abolitionism: Towards a Non-Repressive Approach to Crime*, Amsterdam, Free University Press.

Campbell, B. (1993) *Goliath: Britain's Dangerous Places*, London, Methuen.

Cohen, S. (1993) 'Human rights and crimes of the state: the culture of denial', *Australian and New Zealand Journal of Criminology*, 26 (2), pp.97–115.

Cohen, S. (1994) 'Social control and the politics of reconstruction', in Nelken (1994b).

De Haan, W. (1990) *The Politics of Redress*, London, Unwin Hyman.

Ferrell, J. and Sanders, C.R. (eds) (1995) *Cultural Criminology*, Boston, MA, North Eastern University Press.

Foucault, M. (1977) *Discipline and Punish*, London, Allen Lane.

Henry, S. and Lanier, M.M. (1998) 'The prism of crime: arguments for an integrated definition of crime', *Justice Quarterly*, 15 (4), pp.609–27.

Henry, S. and Milovanovic, D. (1994) 'The constitution of constitutive criminology' in Nelken (1994b).

Henry, S. and Milovanovic, D. (1996) *Constitutive Criminology: Beyond Postmodernism*, London, Sage.

Hulsman, L.H.C. (1986) 'Critical criminology and the concept of crime', *Contemporary Crises*, 10 (1), pp.63–80.

Katz, J. (1988) *Seductions of Crime: Moral and Sensual Attractions in Doing Evil*, New York, Basic Books.

Matthews, R. and Young, J. (1992) 'Reflections on realism', in Young, J. and Matthews, R., *Rethinking Criminology: The Realist Debate*, London, Sage.

Muncie, J. (1998) 'Deconstructing criminology', *Criminal Justice Matters*, 34, pp.4–5.

Muncie, J. and McLaughlin, E. (eds) (1996) *The Problem of Crime*, London, Sage/The Open University.

Muncie, J., McLaughlin, E. and Langan, M. (eds) (1996) *Criminological Perspectives: A Reader*, London, Sage/The Open University.

Nelken, D. (1994a) 'Reflexive criminology?', in Nelken (1994b).

Nelken, D. (ed.) (1994b) *The Futures of Criminology*, London, Sage.

Pepinsky, H. (1991) *The Geometry of Violence and Democracy*, Bloomington, IN, Indiana University Press.

Presdee, M. (2000) *Cultural Criminology and the Carnival of Crime*, London, Routledge.

Schwendinger, H. and Schwendinger, J. (1970) 'Defenders of order or guardians of human rights', *Issues in Criminology*, 7, pp.72–81.

Segal, L. (1990) *Slow Motion: Changing Masculinities, Changing Men*, London, Virago.

Shearing, C. (1989) 'Decriminalising criminology', *Canadian Journal of Criminology*, 31 (2), pp.169–78.

Smart, C. (1990) 'Feminist approaches to criminology or postmodern woman meets atavistic man', in Morris, A. and Gelsthorpe, L. (eds) *Feminist Perspectives in Criminology*, Milton Keynes, Open University Press.

Steinert, H. (1986) 'Beyond crime and punishment', *Contemporary Crises*, 10 (1), pp.21–38.

Sutherland, E.H. (1949) *White Collar Crime*, New York, Holt, Rinehart & Winston.

Thornton, S. (1995) *Club Cultures*, Cambridge, Polity Press.

Tifft, L. (1995) 'Social harm definitions of crime', *The Critical Criminologist*, 7 (1), pp.9–13.

van Swaaningen, R. (1997) *Critical Criminology: Visions from Europe*, London, Sage.

van Swaaningen, R. (1999) 'Reclaiming critical criminology', *Theoretical Criminology*, 3 (1), pp.5–28.

15

Crime Control, Social Policy and Liberalism

Kevin Stenson

1 Introduction

This chapter describes the growing political salience of issues of crime control in liberal democracies. It distinguishes three broad strategies of crime control that have crystallized in recent years: punitive sovereignty, which attempts to regain control of public places from perceivably disorderly groups; target-hardening and actuarial justice, which try to reduce the opportunities for crime and apply the logic of risk assessment and management to crime and criminals; and community security strategies, which try to link crime control to efforts to defend affluent neighbourhoods and regenerate decaying and disorderly localities. They operate in a variety of hybrid forms at local levels.

The chapter goes on to distinguish Marxist and broadly Foucauldian theories (termed here the 'governmentality school') which try to explain these changes. The main concerns of the former are the new regulatory forms that buttress the evolution towards a new service and high-tech capitalist economy. The second approach is more radically *political*. Its main concerns are the shifting forms of rule traversing older boundaries between statutory, voluntary and commercial institutions in liberal polities. In this perspective, domains such as the economy, the state, the social and the sphere of policing and criminal justice are seen as politically constituted and differentiated. With the decline of social modes of government characteristic of the welfare state and the rise of targeted, partnership-based strategies of crime control and community regeneration, the boundaries between crime control and older policy fields defined as 'social policy' and 'economic policy' are blurring. However, a central theme in liberal modes of government is the struggle for sovereign control by agencies of the law and state over geographical territory and perceivably disorderly populations at local level. This concern has been neglected by theorists of governmentality. The analysis of sovereignty offers potential for bridge-building between Marxist and governmentality schools. The chapter concludes by identifying key tensions in the struggle for sovereignty through crime control in liberal polities.

2   Prioritizing crime control

Issues of crime control have steadily ascended the agendas of the liberal democracies in the last twenty years (Stenson, 1991; Downes and Morgan, 1997). The roots of this lie in the US administration of Richard Nixon in the early 1970s, which replaced the rhetorical 'War on Poverty' with a 'War on Crime'. This created a discursive template from which subsequent politicians in both Democrat and Republican camps deviate at their peril. Margaret Thatcher's successful election campaign of 1979 imported US law and order rhetoric which has since become a salient feature of political discourse in the Anglophone democracies, and is now rapidly spreading to other advanced societies (Taylor, 1998). In the economically advanced world the neo-liberal assault on what was perceived to be the overreach of the tax-funded central state, municipal authorities and welfare services has been applied with greatest force in the Anglophone countries. This assault included the advocacy of market-based mechanisms for supplying human needs and the importation of managerial disciplines into the remaining public sector agencies (Clarke and Newman, 1997). These policy shifts have interacted with the effects of increasing global interdependence of markets, mobility of capital and the related decline of large-scale traditional industries, employing males. The latter are giving way to new, high-tech and service-based industries which favour more educated and female labour forces. These changes are associated with chronically high unemployment among less educated males, focused in poor inner-city neighbour-hoods and outer peripheral areas of social housing. They are also viewed by some commentators as associated with a newly patho-logized image of violent, anti-social and misogynistic masculinity, enraged at its inability to adapt to the needs of the new (official) economy (Campbell, 1993).

The new salience given to crime control is, in part, driven by the increasing public concerns about fear and risk in both public and private spaces. In a variety of ways these policy shifts and deeper changes in governmental rationalities and political economy are held by commentators to be criminogenic. They range, *inter alia*, from the greater opportunities for white-collar and organized crime, resulting from the neo-liberal bonfire of 'red tape' regulations, to property crime associated with high unemployment, to the growth of drug-based and other illegal economies in the desolate urban zones created in the wake of the collapse of manufacturing industry, to the incivilities associated with homelessness and under-occupied and alienated young people and all those deemed to be 'other' to the mainstream population (Wilson 1987; Stenson, 1991; Croall, 1992; Bailleau, 1998; Taylor, 1998). In addition, the increasing social power of feminism and anti-racist and gay rights movements has helped to spotlight hitherto neglected fields of crime such as domestic violence, rape, paedophilia and racist and homophobic violence (Bowling, 1998). They are accompanied by growing anxiety over the impact of people fleeing from war and poverty into the advanced societies.

3   Hybrid strategies of crime control

The new governmental focus on law and order is manifested in three strands of policy and practice that operate in uneasy tension with each other and in differing combinations in the various jurisdictions. While the policy templates are disproportionately manufactured in the USA, there is increasing international intellectual traffic conveyed by exchanges between academics, civil servants and politicians (Stenson, 1998a). This involves a lively import/export trade in ways of conceptualizing policy issues and solutions to them. It should be remembered that these policy strategies represent tendencies at work against the backcloth of the everyday operations of the complex field of institutions of policing, crime prevention and criminal justice. In the liberal democracies these differentiated but functionally inter-dependent institutions of crime control are usually described optim-istically as 'systems' of policing and criminal justice (Davies et al., 1995). Their mandated tasks involve the management of those who may be likely to transgress, or who have transgressed, the criminal codes. Yet, given the awesome density and complexity of these institutions in most modern societies, it would be misleading to imagine that individual governments can easily effect change in a simple mechanistic, top-down fashion.

With this caveat in mind, first, it is possible to identify the broad strategy of *punitive sovereignty*. This approach, in alliance with business interests, aims to regain control over public spaces for those deemed to be 'respectable' citizens/consumers. One of the goals of punitive sovereignty is to recover the means for the majority of the population to enjoy the public spaces and opportunities for consumption, assembly and interaction that underpin a liberal democracy. It is manifested in so-called zero tolerance policing, first developed in New York, and other strategies to improve the 'quality of life' for 'respectable' folk by clearing the homeless, drug offenders, muggers, prostitutes, pimps, burglars and other petty criminals from the streets (Kelling and Coles, 1996; Ferrell, 1996; Stenson, 1999, 2000). The criminal justice dimension of this strategy is manifested, for example, in the tendency to increase mandatory minimum sentences for more serious offences, particularly burglary and offences involving violence. This was first made apparent in California's 'three strikes and you're out' laws and related escalating imprisonment rates that cannot be explained simply in terms of variations in the official crime rates. It is also evident in the increasing use of the death penalty in the USA (Zimring and Hawkins, 1997; Simon, 1996). Similarly, it is manifested in the dramatic international expansion in provision of both state and commercial prisons.

Second, there are *target-hardening*, or situational crime prevention strategies; they are premised on the notion that most offenders are rational actors. These strategies aim to reduce opportunities for offending through locks, bolts, environmental redesign (Cornish and Clarke, 1986; Clarke, 1997), use of CCTV and – at the extreme end of the continuum – the concept of the fortified gated community with twenty-four-hour security (Davis, 1993). This approach eschews attempts to deal with root causes of crime prevention and it is in tension with those conservative policies that advocate the need to uphold authority with the profligate use of imprisonment. There is a broad affinity between target-hardening and tendencies at work in the criminal justice systems, where older concerns with the allocation of 'just deserts' or with using criminal justice as a vehicle to reform offenders have been giving way to pragmatic risk management approaches. The principal goal of what has been characterized as the 'new penology' of *actuarial justice* is to contain or manage the problems of crime through the use of an actuarial logic: assessing and managing in the most efficient and cost-effective ways the risks posed by offending (Feeley and Simon, 1994). The range of approaches making up target-hardening and actuarial justice has had a considerable international impact on mainstream policy-making and, as such, has transformed technical, administrative, criminological theory into a governmental tool of key significance (Stenson, 1996, 1999).

Third, *community security* approaches involve a *turn to the local.* They echo the newly fashionable emphasis, internationally, on social crime prevention, community/restorative justice, mediation and problem-solving community policing (Brazemore, 1998; Clear, 1998). They involve attempts to foster greater community responsibility for the security and insurance of businesses, homes and neighbourhoods, through Neighbourhood Watch and other forms of citizen action, though these local strategies tend to work more effectively in more affluent areas. They also revive and update older ambitions to tackle the deeper social and economic causes of crime. The modern templates for these approaches were built on traditional models of urban regeneration and crime prevention programmes and became increasingly attractive to policy-makers internationally. These were developed in the 1980s in those cities in the USA that had suffered most heavily from deindustrialization.

Eschewing 'big government', macroeconomic and social interventions to alleviate social dislocation, these operate largely at local levels. Weeding out 'criminogenic' people and environmental conditions, these strategies and technologies aim to seed and foster stronger, informal family and community controls and virtuous spirals of economic and social regeneration. In the UK this has been manifested in a plethora of urban regeneration and crime prevention schemes since the mid-1980s (European Forum for Urban Security, 1994; Hope, 1995; Bureau of Justice Assistance, 1997; Crawford, 1997; Hughes, 1998; Stenson and Watt, 1999). These approaches are usually legitimized by a rhetoric that advocates the social inclusion of marginalized groups in the economic and social mainstream. It is not always clear to what extent strategies under this heading share similar premises to the first approach: that is, to exclude and punish those deemed to be 'other' in relation to the majority of 'decent' folk in the targeted neighbourhoods (Davis, 1993). In addition, this shift may embody a widening of the net of social control, creating new forms of dependency (Cohen, 1985). Furthermore, as the experience of legislation in the US and UK requiring information about the whereabouts of paedophiles to be disseminated to local populations has shown, this turn to the local can, unwittingly, foster new forms of vigilantism (Johnston, 1996; Simon, 1998). This is the often unacknowledged downside of the policy emphasis on empowerment and devolution of responsibility. This phenomenon, while democratic in a majoritarian sense, can strike at the heart of the values of liberal tolerance for minorities, the weak and the damaged.

4 Neo-Marxist explanations

Despite the survey of change outlined above, there is no theoretically neutral way to describe the increasing governmental focus on crime control. Some of the most influential interpretive frameworks for making sense of these changes offer broadly Marxist or neo-Marxist accounts (see Chapter 11 this volume; Crowther, 1999). There is not the space to make finely grained distinctions between the various alternative Marxist models, so here I emphasize the common, recurrent features. They highlight the causal significance of political-economic processes: the drive for capital accumulation; the progressive subordination of local economies to the logic of an integrated and globalized capital market and the leading corporations; and the consequent growth of social and economic inequality and conflict. They also highlight the role of the state: the complex of public institutions that, while claiming to act in the public interest, are seen to act disproportionately to secure the interests of capital and the social classes and institutions that benefit most from it. Agencies of crime prevention, policing and criminal justice are seen as core components of the state.

This narrative of change focuses on the struggle to create new regulatory frameworks to buttress the emerging high-tech and service-based capitalist economy in the advanced societies (Hay, 1996). This is seen as being achieved through attacking the power of labour, privatization, downsizing of workforces, deregulation, promoting labour 'flexibility', part-time working and the creation, therefore, of insecurity of employment, low wages and, perhaps unwittingly, the growth of illegal economies. These allegedly 'criminogenic' conditions have, it is argued, required an enormous expansion in the commercial security industry. There is also a reliance on the police and criminal justice to regulate the effects of neo-liberal market reforms, and the rapid reconstruction of state powers and institutions at national, local and (nascent) international levels, in order to secure hopefully unchallengeable frameworks for the production and circulation of commodities (Jefferson, 1990; Muncie et al., 1995; Coleman and Sim, 1998). The apparent redistribution of powers and responsibilities to locally based agencies and community groups masks a strengthening of centralized fiscal and administrative powers (McLaughlin and Muncie 1994; Clarke and Newman, 1997).

Initiated at national and local levels by secretive and often informal 'partnership' groups of decision-makers and resource gatekeepers in the public, commercial and voluntary sectors, these developments include: social and professional networks of civil servants, corporate chiefs, senior police officers, urban managers, health, welfare and justice professionals and representatives of security firms. These networks, scarcely accountable to democratic scrutiny, develop and manage complex mixtures of the crime control strategies previously outlined. In some countries, such as the UK, a steering role has been retained by government ministers and expert senior civil servants in the central ministries (Stenson, 1996). These developments, while manifest in many of the advanced societies in varying combinations, are likely to be particularly visible in cities with large poor and unemployed populations such as Liverpool and Los Angeles (Davis, 1993; Coleman and Sim, 1998).

Central players in the new governing alliances include the major retailing chains, who within Marxist and neo-Marxist theory are viewed as having a strong interest in promoting the values of consumerism and excluding perceivably impecunious and disruptive groups from high streets, shopping malls and city centres. For these players, urban regeneration, crime control and community safety require the construction of safe, clean, graffiti-free spaces, under blanket surveillance, for capital investment and the spectacle of conspicuous consumption. This is in contrast to strategies which would emphasize, for example, the expression of youthful identities, the protection of women from male violence, minorities from racial attack or the consumer from profiteering and the tainting of food and water supplies by producers contemptuous of regulatory safeguards (Ferrell, 1996; Coleman and Sim, 1998).

It is important to note that although the dominant theme of this interpretive model hinges on notions of class domination, while retaining the same logic of explanation, sub-themes have emerged which recognize the co-existence of other forms of domination: that is, that the police and criminal justice agencies which support capitalism also support a dominant gender and racial order, helping to reproduce the subordination of women and sexual, 'racial' and ethnic minorities (Cook and Hudson, 1993; European Commission, 1996).

5   Governmentality perspective and liberal government

By contrast with Marxist narratives, the bias in my perspective, inspired by the later work of the French philosopher Michel Foucault (1991), is to highlight not capitalism, viewed as an economic system, but the centrality of transformations in human governance in broadly liberal democratic societies. This perspective has a political focus and the capitalist market and the state are *not* accorded any particular explanatory, causal privilege. They are seen as political constructions: differentiated spheres of social relations produced by liberal modes of government. In addition, my analysis has an explicitly normative basis, favouring the production of knowledge that will help to safeguard and extend liberal values, and provide checks and balances on tyranny, which can develop from the political left as well as from the right (Stenson, 1998b). Hence, the analysis of the increasing centrality of crime control is developed through an investigation of the changing nature of liberal democratic rule, broadly conceived (Foucault, 1991; Barry et al., 1996). These changes involve not just the governmental activities of the public statutory agencies but also a host of agencies and networks beyond the state (Rose and Miller, 1992; Stenson, 1999).

6   Government, governmentality and governance

One of the key insights of the Foucault-influenced perspective employed here is that policy strategies are not just responses to external social problems. Rather, the 'problems' they address are given shape and recognition by the emerging policy discourses, in which academic theories and research can play a critical role (Stenson, 1991). Hence, crime control strategies embody power/knowledge (Foucault, 1977). These embody reflections on the arts of government. They forge new ways to make populations thinkable and measurable for the purposes of liberal government – what Foucault described as *governmentality* (Foucault, 1991; Stenson 1991, 1998b). This is a gloss for a series of processes through which populations, often at the level of the nation-state, but also on local and international spatial scales, are categorized, differentiated and sorted into hierarchies. The everyday processes of public *government*, the exercise of publicly financed and organized power, are underpinned by censuses, official and academic surveys of social problems in myriad forms. These do not simply describe the world, they also create – in this policy field – their own regimes of what count as the accredited 'truths' about the nature, causes and remedies for crime (Foucault, 1977; Stenson, 1991).

However, these public forms of government are part of a larger sphere of *governance*. Without according any theoretical privilege to the role of public agencies, I use it here in its broadest sense to refer to the more or less rational means to shape human conduct, by trying to structure the field of constraints and possibilities within which action takes place (Gordon, 1991). Governance ranges from self-governance to the governance of family life, to the governance of commercial firms, voluntary associations and religious organizations, to attempts by international organizations such as the IMF to govern the world economy (Shearing, 1996). Political scientists have argued that with the fiscal crises facing national welfare states from the mid-1970s and with the anti-state rhetoric and practice of neo-liberal administrations since that time, the nature of public government has changed significantly – indeed has been reinvented (Osborne and Gaebler, 1996). With privatization of public assets and governmental functions and the introduction of commercial disciplines into the public services, there has been a redistribution of the tasks of government, in welfare and crime prevention. The new governmental forms cross the boundaries of the statutory, commercial and voluntary sectors and include the involvement of active citizens' groups of various kinds.

7 The social logic of government

The governmentality narrative about the growing salience of crime control locates it as part of the shift away from welfarist policies and practices and challenges the view that these shifts can be understood principally in terms of changes in the economy and the state (Rose and Miller, 1992; Stenson, 1999). Governing in the name of the social – which underpinned the policies of welfare states in the high period between 1945 and 1980 – attempts to foster social solidarity, hence providing an effective underpinning for the operation of markets (Rose, 1996; Stenson, 1998b, 1999). The aims of social government include the goals and technologies of redistributive social justice, tutelage of the poor into the perceived norms of acceptable citizenship (Donzelot, 1979) and the use of actuarial technologies of risk-sharing. The pool of risk-sharers ultimately encapsulates the citizens of the state and protects against crime, unemployment, sickness, old age and the other risks associated with the minimally regulated play of markets (Donzelot, 1991). 'Social' policies, operating with universalist criteria for service provision, were associated with the development of a differentiated institutional apparatus for the delivery and co-ordination of the major social services (Stenson and Watt, 1999). The social logic of government fosters the differentiation of 'social' policies and a 'social' sphere from the 'economic' sphere of economic/ contractual relations. However, this should not be conceived of simply as the operation of official agencies, since the 'social' creates a field of possibilities for recipients of social services to try to set their own agendas. Moreover, differentiation of a field of 'social policy' was assisted, in part, by the academic disciplines of social policy and other social sciences that conceptualize the 'social' as a separate domain of investigation. This established an academic division of labour that led to a relative uninterest by social policy experts in issues of crime control (Hill, 1996; Crowther, 1999).

8 Policing and criminal justice as a separate sphere

The social logic of government thus also facilitated the differentiation of police and criminal justice agencies as possessing a relatively distinct domain of objects and concerns, serviced academically by criminology and penology. This was, to a degree, buffered both from market pressures and also, to some extent, from naked political pressures. In the sphere of policing and criminal justice, at the core of liberal orders there have been attempts to create buffers between central state authority and the work of the courts and the police and, more broadly, a differentiation between these functions and social policy, even if in the margins there may have been attempts to use criminal justice as a vehicle of social reform and rehabilitation (Garland, 1985). In the UK the long traditions – since 1829 – of 'policing by consent' and constabulary independence were seen as bulwarks of democratic freedom from central state tyranny. These traditions became central to the legitimation of the British model of policing by consent (Reiner, 1992; Stenson, 1993).

In most countries of continental Europe, up until 1945, police and justice agencies had suffered from a long association with the absolutism and oppression of the old police states, absolutist and authoritarian regimes (Mawby, 1990). This led, in the post-war period, to the creation of systems of policing and justice that at least maintained the appearance of being governed, not by politicians, but by the rule of law and codes of professional and administrative rationality (Lacey and Zedner, 1995). Hence, in different liberal, democratic jurisdictions, hierarchically structured policies and systems to control crime and provide justice operated within relatively secure and predictable funding streams and through accredited bodies of expertise. They were seen as spheres of policy and practice, distinct from executive government and from the whims of national or local, populist opinion or pressure – the spectre of mob justice or lynch law.

With the rise of neo-liberal modes of government and the decline of social government since the late 1970s, this differentiated institutional sphere of crime control and criminal justice has become less distinct from other spheres of government and from aspects of social policy. Hence, the demand for 'partnership' between agencies of government threatens to breach the buffers and boundaries between these domains. Indeed, in this narrative, the social is now on the wane or even dying. Within this view, the fostering of social solidarity is no longer accorded priority as an end in itself (Rose, 1996). Broad, inclusive, national notions of the risk-sharing collectivity give way to smaller, risk-sharing collectivities (O'Malley, 1992; Stenson, 1993; Rose, 1996). Businesses and local communities are encouraged to be more self-reliant or enrolled in the tasks of crime prevention and other tasks of government, since there is decreasing confidence in the ability of the central state to provide effective security for the generality of citizens. State and local state agencies are encouraged to target their interventions towards those 'communities', social groups and neighbourhoods that are seen as manifesting high levels of criminal and other modes of social risk to themselves and to the well-being of other groups and interests (O'Malley and Palmer, 1996; Stenson, 1996, 1998a; Garland, 1996).

A number of criticisms can be made of the 'decline of the social' narrative. First, while governing in the name of the social may have generic features recognizable internationally, governmental practices have varied considerably in national, regional and local settings and operate in hybrid forms with other logics of government (Esping-Andersen, 1990; Stenson and Factor, 1995; Zedner, 1995; Lacey and Zedner, 1995; Stenson, 1998b). In Britain there has, until the recent neo-liberal era, been a particularly rich tradition of local independence, the use of discretionary powers and 'community'-based policing and crime prevention (Johnston, 1992). Second, despite the arguments about needing to focus on government operating in non-state agencies, many of the recent key initiatives, for example with respect to crime prevention, originate in central state ministries (Stenson, 1996).

Furthermore, it is possible, for example in the UK, to see state initiatives like the New Deal for Communities (1998) and the provisions of the Crime and Disorder Act 1998 as embodying a reformulation of holistic social strategies. This works through attempts to create pluralistic, 'joined up', partnership policy strategies (Stenson and Watt, 1999). Yet this new holism reinforces the blurring of the boundaries of crime prevention and control, urban regeneration and other fields of social policy. Examples of integrated crime reduction strategies can range from 'early interventions' to support effective parenting, to anti-truanting initiatives and youth services, to environmental redesign to reduce opportunities for crime (Bright, 1998). Youth work, in particular, has been transformed and legitimized increasingly under the label of crime prevention (Stenson and Factor, 1994). This has led commentators to argue that there has been a recoding of large elements of social policy under the heading of crime control: 'the criminalization of social policy' (Crawford, 1997; Stenson and Watt, 1999).

9   Sovereignty

While the boundaries between criminal justice and the social have become more porous, the contested struggle for sovereignty remains a central thread within liberal governing practices. This is particularly so where there are fierce contests locally for dominance over territory for criminal and many other purposes. Sovereignty is here conceived not as the functioning of a ready-made state, but rather as a set of technologies of rule – usually operating in hybrid interaction

with other technologies – employed in the struggle to control geographical territory (Foucault, 1991; Stenson, 1998b, 1999). The concern
with bringing the writ of sovereign law, backed by the coercive
apparatus of the state, to the rookeries of the poor in the nineteenth
century has its modern counterpart in attempts to regain control over
perceivably disorderly housing estates and the illegal economies
which sustain them. State agendas of government must compete with
multiple formal and informal agendas of governance in a liberal
social order (Stenson, 1996, 1998b, 1999). Moreover, the 'death/
decline of the social' narrative also, perhaps, overemphasizes the
historic role of welfare practices within criminal justice and under-
estimates the continuity of harsh sovereign controls (Scraton, 1987).
The concern with (state) sovereign technologies of control remains a
strength of the neo-Marxist approaches (Grimshaw and Jefferson,
1987). This is so even if their conception of the range of alternative
modes of governance is somewhat selective and exaggerates the
extent of and potential for 'resistance' to central state authority.

Hence sovereignty should be given greater prominence within
governmentality research. Yet sovereignty is not simply the crude
exercise of coercive power; it operates now within the framework of
governmentality. In addition to a focus on local, problem-solving
partnership-based crime prevention and policing initiatives, there is a
growing emphasis on developing technologies that map patterns of
crimes and crime opportunities, providing local policy-makers and
residents with more finely grained data. These enable authorities to
create, monitor and evaluate crime reduction and urban redevelopment measures and also signal a growing concern with the relation
between crime and deprived, 'excluded' populations and neighbourhoods, a concern now officially inscribed in EU social policy (Bottoms
and Wiles, 1996; Graham and Bennett, 1995; Levitas, 1996). This,
in the language of this body of theory, lies at the core of governmentality: the means whereby populations are made thinkable and
measurable for the purposes of government.

10 Conclusion: policing a new sovereignty?

We are witnessing and contributing to nothing less than a fundamental rethinking of the nature of liberal government itself in an age
of accelerating, profound social, economic and political changes. The
struggle to bring government to perceivably ungoverned areas and
populations remains a central connecting thread within liberal government, particularly given the sharp growth in material inequalities
since the 1970s at every spatial level. There are, however, two central
contradictions that lie at the heart of the reconstituting modes of
liberal rule. First, the apparent decline of the nation-state and the

redistribution of some sovereign powers to other authorities, for example at a European level, can create a crisis of jurisdiction and legitimation. In the EU context, as yet, no stable transcendent European state fills the vacuum left by the erosion of the sovereign powers and symbolic authority of nation-states. Nevertheless, the struggles between communal groups at local levels over territorial dominance and by statutory agencies to maintain sovereign control over territory continue. We are witnessing a fracturing of levels of sovereignty from the local to the national and the international levels, albeit with diverse temporalities. The second key contradiction of the governmental shift towards local and communal modes of government is a tension over the transcendent nature of sovereign power. The mandate of statutory agencies to intervene locally is secured by notions of sovereign law, which must be legitimized in terms of supra-local, transcendent social collectivities.

Only thus can the police and urban managers – as required in the UK by the Crime and Disorder Act 1998 – acquire the practical legitimacy to act as brokers between communal groups in conflict, whose norms may be at variance with each other and with wider legal norms. Yet to the extent that the police and other statutory agencies become involved with local communal groups in partnership schemes, they risk compromising the illusion of transcendence and impartiality which underpins sovereignty (Stenson and Factor, 1994; Stenson, 1999). The attempt to enforce what may be seen as discriminatory powers in defence of sectional interests may create a proliferation of alternative strategies of governance by various minorities through criminal, political, religious and other modes of organization, resulting in escalating spirals of resistance against sovereignty itself. The problem of sovereignty is likely to remain enduringly central for liberalism, rather than becoming an archaic leftover from the past. It seems that the price paid for the entrepreneurial and individualistic consumerist freedoms of the majority is a growing reliance on sovereign powers used to contain the recalcitrant and disaffected minorities (Valverde, 1996).

Note

I would like to thank Chris Crowther for help in the preparation of this chapter.

References

Bailleau, F. (1998) 'A crisis of youth or of juridical response?' in Ruggiero (1998).
Barry, A., Osborne, T. and Rose, N. (eds) (1996) *Foucault and Political Reason*, London, UCL Press.
Bottoms, A. and Wiles, P. (1996) 'Crime and policing in a changing social context', in

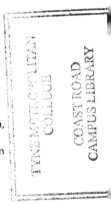

Saulsbury, W., Mott, J. and Newburn, T. (eds) *Themes in Contemporary Policing*, London, Policy Studies Institute.

Bowling, B. (1998) *Violent Racism, Victimization, Policing and Social Context*, Oxford, Clarendon Press.

Brazemore, J. (1998) 'Assessing the citizen role in community sanctioning: restorative and community justice dimensions'. Paper delivered to the Conference of the American Society of Criminology, Washington, DC, 11–14 November.

Bright, J. (1998) 'Preventing youth crime', *Criminal Justice Matters*, 33, Autumn, pp.15–17.

Burchell, G., Gordon, C. and Miller, P. (eds) (1991) *The Foucault Effect: Studies in Governmentality*, Hemel Hempstead, Harvester Wheatsheaf.

Bureau of Justice Assistance (1997) *Revitalizing Communities: Innovative State and Local Programmes*, Washington, DC, US Department of Justice.

Campbell, B. (1993) *Goliath: Britain's Dangerous Places*, London, Methuen.

Clarke, J. and Newman, J. (1997) *The Managerial State*, London, Sage.

Clarke, R. (ed.) (1997) *Situational Crime Prevention: Successful Case Studies* (2nd edn), Albany, NY, Harrow & Heston.

Clear, T. (1998) 'Community justice and public safety'. Paper delivered to the Conference of the American Society of Criminology, Washington, DC, 11–14 November.

Cohen, S. (1985) *Visions of Social Control*, Cambridge, Polity Press.

Coleman, R. and Sim, J. (1998) 'From the dockyards to the Disney Store: surveillance, risk and security in Liverpool City Centre', *International Review of Law Computers and Technology*, 12 (1), pp.27–45.

Cook, D. and Hudson, B. (eds) (1993) *Racism and Criminology*, London, Sage.

Cornish, D.B. and Clarke, R.V.G. (eds) (1986) *The Reasoning Criminal: Rational Choice Perspectives on Offending*, New York, Springer-Verlag.

Crawford, A. (1997) *The Local Governance of Crime: Appeals to Community and Partnership*, Oxford, Clarendon Press.

Croall, H. (1992) *White Collar Crime*, Buckingham, Open University Press.

Crowther, C. (1999) *Policing the Underclass*, London, Macmillan.

Davies, M., Croall, H. and Tyrer, J. (1995) *Criminal Justice: An Introduction to Criminal Justice in England and Wales*, London, Longman.

Davis, M. (1993) *Beyond Blade Runner: Urban Control – The Ecology of Fear*, New York, The Free Press.

Donzelot, J. (1979) *The Policing of Families*, London, Hutchinson.

Donzelot, J. (1991) 'The mobilization of society', in Burchell et al. (1991).

Downes, D. and Morgan, R. (1997) 'Dumping the "hostages to fortune"? The politics of law and order in post-war Britain', in Maguire, M., Morgan, R. and Reiner, R. (eds) *The Oxford Handbook of Criminology* (2nd edn), Oxford, Oxford University Press.

Esping-Andersen, G. (1990) *The Three Worlds of Welfare Capitalism*, Cambridge, Polity Press.

European Commission (1996) *Immigrant Delinquency, Social Construction of Deviant Behaviour and Criminality of Immigrants in Europe*, Brussels, European Community.

European Forum for Urban Security (1994) *Security and Democracy*, Paris, European Forum for Urban Security.

Feeley, M. and Simon, J. (1994) 'Actuarial justice: the emerging new criminal law', in Nelken, D. (ed.) *The Futures of Criminology*, London, Sage.

Ferrell, J. (1996) *Crimes of Style: Urban Graffitti and the Politics of Criminality*, Boston, MA, North Eastern University Press.

Foucault, M. (1977) *Discipline and Punish*, Harmondsworth, Penguin.

Foucault, M. (1991) 'Governmentality', in Burchell et al. (1991).

Garland, D. (1985) *Punishment and Welfare: A History of Penal Strategies*, Aldershot, Gower.

Garland, D. (1996) 'The limits of the sovereign state: strategies of crime control in contemporary society', *British Journal of Criminology*, 36 (4), pp.445–71.

Gordon, C. (1991) 'Governmental rationality: an introduction', in Burchell et al. (1991).

Graham, J. and Bennett, T. (1995) *Crime Prevention Strategies in Europe and North America*, Helsinki, European Institute for Crime Prevention Control.

Grimshaw, R. and Jefferson, T. (1987) *Interpreting Policework*, London, Allen & Unwin.

Hay, C. (1996) *Re-Stating Social and Political Change*, Buckingham, Open University Press.

Hill, M. (1996) *Social Policy: A Comparative Perspective*, Hemel Hempstead, Harvester Wheatsheaf.

Hope, T. (1995) 'Community crime prevention', in Tonry, M. and Farrington, D. (eds) *Building a Safer Society: Strategic Approaches to Crime Prevention*, Chicago, Chicago University Press.

Hughes, G. (1998) *Understanding Crime Prevention: Social Control, Risk and Late Modernity*, Buckingham, Open University Press.

Jefferson, T. (1990) *The Case against Paramilitary Policing*, Milton Keynes, Open University Press.

Johnston, L. (1992) *The Rebirth of Private Policing*, London, Routledge.

Johnston, L. (1996) 'What is vigilantism?', *British Journal of Criminology*, 36 (2), pp.220–36.

Kelling, G. and Coles, C. (1996) *Fixing Broken Windows*, New York, The Free Press.

Lacey, N. and Zedner, L. (1995) 'Discourse of community in criminal justice', *Journal of Law and Society*, 22 (3), pp.301–25.

Levitas, R. (1996) 'The concept of exclusion and the new Durkheimian hegemony', *Critical Social Policy*, 46, pp.5–20.

McLaughlin, E. and Muncie, J. (1994) 'Managing the criminal justice system', in Clarke, J., Cochrane, A. and McLaughlin, E. (eds) *Managing Social Policy*, London, Sage.

Mawby, R.I. (1990) *Comparative Policing Issues: The British and American Experience in International Perspective*, London, Unwin Hyman.

Muncie, J., Coventry, G. and Walters, R. (1995) 'The politics of youth crime prevention: developments in Australia and England and Wales', in Noakes, L., Levi, M. and Maguire, M. (eds) *Contemporary Issues in Criminology*, Cardiff, University of Wales Press.

O'Malley, P. (1992) 'Risk, power and crime prevention', *Economy and Society*, 21 (3), pp.252–75.

O'Malley, P. and Palmer, D. (1996) 'Post-Keynesian policing,' *Economy and Society*, 25 (2), pp.137–55.

Osborne, D. and Gaebler, T. (1996) *Reinventing Government*, New York, Plume.

Reiner, R. (1992) *The Politics of the Police*, Hemel Hempstead, Harvester Wheatsheaf.

Rose, N. (1996) 'The death of the social? Refiguring the territory of government', *Economy and Society*, 25 (2), pp.327–89.

Rose, N. and Miller, P. (1992) 'Political power beyond the state: problematics of government', *British Journal of Sociology*, 43, pp.173–205.

Ruggiero, V., South, N. and Taylor, I. (eds) (1998) *The New European Criminology: Crime and Social Order in Europe*, London, Routledge.

Scraton, P. (ed.) (1987) *Law, Order and the Authoritarian State*, Milton Keynes, Open University Press.

Shearing, C. (1996) 'Public and private policing', in Saulsbury, W., Mott, J. and Newburn, T. (eds) *Themes in Contemporary Policing*, London, Policy Studies Institute.

Simon J. (1996) 'Criminology and the recidivist', in Shichor, D. and Sechrest, D.K. (eds) *Three Strikes and You're Out: Vengeance as Public Policy*, Beverly Hills, CA, Sage.

Simon, J. (1998) 'Managing the monstrous: sex offenders and the new penology', *Psychology, Public Policy and Law*, 4 (1), pp.1–16.

Stenson, K. (1991) 'Making sense of crime control', in Stenson, K. and Cowell, D. (eds) *The Politics of Crime Control*, London, Sage.

Stenson, K. (1993) 'Community policing as a governmental technology', *Economy and Society*, 22, pp.373–89.

Stenson, K. (1996) 'Communal security as government – the British experience', in

Hammerschick, W., Karazman-Morawetz, I. and Stangl, W. (eds) (1996) *Jahrbuch für Rechts und Kriminalsoziologie*, Baden-Baden, Nomos.

Stenson, K. (1998a) 'Displacing social policy through crime control', in Hänninen, S. (ed.) *Displacement of Social Policies*, SoPhi, University of Jyväskylä, pp.117–44.

Stenson, K. (1998b) 'Beyond histories of the present', *Economy and Society*, 29 (4), pp.333–52.

Stenson, K. (1999) 'Crime control, governmentality and sovereignty', in Smandych, R. (ed.) *Governable Places: Readings in Governmentality and Crime Control*, Aldershot, Dartmouth.

Stenson, K. (2000) 'Some Day Our Prince Will Come: zero tolerance policing in Britain', in Hope, T. and Sparks, R. (eds) *Crime, Risk and Insecurity*, Routledge, London.

Stenson, K. and Factor, F. (1994) 'Youth work, risk and crime prevention', *Youth and Policy*, 45, pp.1–15.

Stenson, K. and Factor, F. (1995) 'Governing youth: new directions for the youth service', in Baldock, J. and May, M. (eds) *Social Policy Review 7*, Canterbury, Social Policy Association.

Stenson, K. and Watt, P. (1999) 'Governmentality and the "death of the social"? A discourse analysis of local government texts in South-East England', *Urban Studies*, 36 (1), pp.189–201.

Taylor, I. (1998) 'Crime, market liberalism and the European idea' in Ruggiero et al. (1998).

Valverde, M. (1996) 'Despotism and ethical liberal governance', *Economy and Society*, 25 (3), pp.357–72.

Wilson, W.J. (1987) *The Truly Disadvantaged: The Inner City, the Underclass and Public Policy*, Chicago, Chicago University Press.

Zedner, L. (1995) 'In pursuit of the vernacular: comparing law and order discourse in Britain and Germany', *Social and Legal Studies*, 4, pp.517–34.

Zimring, F.E. and Hawkins, G. (1997) *Crime Is Not the Problem: Lethal Violence in America*, New York, Oxford University Press.

16

Rethinking Violence, Rethinking Social Policy?

Elizabeth Stanko

1 Introduction

The purpose of this chapter is to demonstrate why a challenge to our presumptions about a phenomenon – violence – is crucial to rethinking social policy. I argue here that violence occupies a central position in social life (see also Stanko, 1990). Despite its consequential positioning, its perpetrators and its victims are often cast as marginal to – or different from – those who live 'violence-free' lives. What might account for the way in which violence has been 'decentred' from our everyday lives? What would be the impact of centring violence within our social lives for our understanding of social policy? After all, are we wrong to assume that violence and its aftermath are adequately managed by the criminal justice system, criminal justice policy and, for example, child protection policy? Without engaging in this discussion about the links between criminal justice policy and social policy, we are unable to grasp fully why violence is too often mistakenly conceptualized as an individual problem within criminal justice policy. In my view this treatment of violence as an individual problem runs right through the work of the criminal justice system, social and welfare institutions, social policy-makers, and indeed is how it is understood by the public. As I shall argue, violence, its circumstances and ultimately the potential to minimize its impact tell us more about the nature of *social relations* than about the individual behaviour of individual victims or offenders. Casting the problem of violence as one embedded thoroughly in social relations displays the need for a sophisticated social policy that embraces violence as a social, not individual, problem. This has profound implications for rethinking social *and* criminal justice policy.

2   What do we mean when we use the term 'violence'?

Let me pause here briefly to define what I mean by violence. For my purposes, I shall define violence as any behaviour by an individual that intentionally threatens, attempts to inflict, or does cause, physical, sexual or psychological harm to others or to her/himself. This is a very wide definition of 'violence'. How authorities and individuals label an act varies, depending on the context within which it occurs (Cretney and Davis, 1995). This process of labelling affects whether the behaviour comes to the attention of someone authorized to intervene and to assist the victim or the offender (Glass, 1995; Hoyle, 1998; Kelly, 1988). Depending on the circumstances of intervention, together with the meanings individuals give to it, violence may be considered acceptable, unacceptable, lawful or unlawful (Tomsen, 1997). It is the capacity of persons and institutions to determine which acts are defined as 'violence' that indicates the *social* character of violence.

A brief word about forms of violence. The use of violence and intimidation includes a whole range of interactions and actions, as well as implicit and explicit verbal abuse that both threatens and hurts. Such a continuum of harm not only contains elements of physical, sexual and psychological damage, but these are often targeted to the wider social contexts of individuals' lives. Such damage, many contend, is evidence that individual behaviour, supported by institutional and cultural legitimacy, feeds social exclusion. For example, sexual abuse and threat, by all research findings, impact upon women's lives far more than men's (Kelly, 1988; Stanko, 1995). The high levels of sexual abuse, harassment and threat, feminists argue, underpin gendered discrimination (Stanko, 1985). Yet the major form of violence is that of male-on-male violence (see Polk, 1994; Stanko, 1994). The way in which this form of violence is labelled – as football hooliganism, lads drinking, drug-dealing conflicts, or gang warfare – obscures its links to various forms of masculinities and its intersections with men's relations with and to each other (Connell, 1995; Tomsen, 1997). Such debate about how social differences are maintained through social structures can be found in the scholarly discussions of violence and 'race' (Virdee, 1997; Bowling, 1999), age (Graham and Bowling, 1995), poverty and social assistance (Tolman, 1999), employment discrimination (Bumiller, 1987), homelessness (Stanko et al., 1998a) and so forth.

These challenges to characterizing violence as a phenomenon flowing solely from the hands of individual offenders combine in intricate ways to give new or expanded meanings to violence and its use (see also Polk, 1994). Forms of threat may include name-calling, stalking, vandalism and other forms of intrusive behaviour that make people feel uncomfortable *and* unsafe, that is, under intimidation of violence (Sibbitt, 1997; Gardner, 1995). Moreover, much of the work challenging violence – stemming from the experience of advocacy groups such as Women's Aid, Stonewall, trade unions and local authorities – makes connections between serious forms of violence and verbal abuse. A great deal of effort, for example, is put into elevating the seriousness of bullying and sexual harassment as a blight on the working lives of many people (see Stanko et al., 1998b). Moreover, these campaigns are often waged with and through institutions, such as schools, housing and welfare agencies, and the health service, as a way of engaging with differential treatment of various social groups. Working in this way also has the potential to make explicit that violence is central to the functioning and practice of institutional life. Prominent today, for instance, is a multiplicity of working parties in many settings that address the impact of violence on employers, staff, the public and 'clients' (from schoolchildren to inmates to children in care). Forms of abuse, and the challenges to institutions that have supported or ignored such abuse, have important repercussions on our thinking about how violence works as a form of shorthand for speaking about social disadvantage and relations of power in contemporary society (Stanko et al., 1998b). Similarly, violence as a phenomenon has been made more visible through challenges to institutional practices that define and shape responses to it in a wide variety of settings. For example, the debate about the high levels of violence met by health service staff is as much about physical harm as it is about conditions of work. So, too, bullying at school is addressed as an impediment to learning as much as it is as damage to the health and development of children. However, what continues to hamper our understanding is the dominance of a framework that has long outlived its usefulness, but not its popularity. Violent offenders are still imagined (Young, 1996) as people 'out of control', psychologically disturbed, distant and different from the rest of us law-abiding folk. It is to this imagery that I now turn.

3   Frameworks for understanding violence

It is the intersection between violence and its relationship to the criminal justice system that is key to understanding this intractable imagery of violent offenders. Criminal statutes include murder, rape, assault and robbery within the category of violent crime against the person. On a general level, violent acts are attributed to behaviour of individuals, some of whom may be acting together with others. Linking violent acts to motivation of individuals has a long history. The disciplines of biology and psychology contribute to most of the popular explanations of why an individual would commit an act of violence. Our statistical categories reflect these explanations. The Homicide Index for England and Wales in the UK lists the following categories of motivation: family stress; rage or quarrel; jealousy or revenge; sexual (pathological); in furtherance of theft; faction fighting or feud (gangs or rival groups); ritual killing; pre-menstrual tension; football hooliganism; other (for example, to get rid of wife to marry another woman); motiveless (insufficient information available indicating no apparent motive, or suspect insane, has a history of mental illness, mentally depressed).

There is an assumption that the above motivations for murder somehow 'explain' why it occurs and what its meanings are to those who are victims, offenders or willing participants (as in faction fighting or family feud), or to the wider society. The above explanations try to classify individual pathology or a state of mind as driving the motivation for killing (Cameron and Fraser, 1987). Groups' violence might be cast as a display of group identities, group solidarity or as defence of territory. Here individual pathology becomes steeped in social relations among various kinds of people. 'Rebellion' or group conflicts commonly appear as self-explanatory. Some commentators speak of groups as territorial packs, who act in violence to protect themselves, their family or neighbourhood, or as justifying the use of violence through displays of hatred for other types or groups of people (as in racist or homophobic violence). Some who commit violence are categorized as those who use violence for entertainment or sport. Finally, some types of violence are categorized as natural outcomes of the unregulated, illegal economies of the drug or sex trade. All of these portray the assailant as faceless, nameless, a predator on innocent victims. These offenders are typically referred to as 'evil' or 'wanton beasts' (see, for instance, Soothill and Walby, 1990; Young, 1996). Moreover, whole categories of people may be vilified as potentially psychotically damaged, 'uncontrollable', organically isolated from the rest of law-abiding society. Characterizations of football hooligans come to mind here. These images of violent crime, its perpetrators and its victims intersect with the fact-finding process of law (see, for instance, Kalunta-Crompton, 1999).

The law and its application in situations of violent offence provides the democratic vehicle for the protection of its citizens and mechanisms of redress, should criminal violence happen. In many respects, then, the impact of violence is mediated through a process of individuation – whereby the individual victim – and the individual assailant – becomes severed in many respects from their social contexts. In other words, when violence erupts, somehow only individuals remain affected. The social context, and the social consequence as I demonstrate below, is too often lost in the discourse of blaming one or other party. This discourse of blame also has implications for the way in which we think about victims. In many respects, victims are cast into two categories: those who do not willingly participate in the violence – 'the innocent' – and those who 'deserve' whatever harm befalls them because they either willingly provoked or participated in violence. Such distinctions are continuously made in and outside law. It is important to understand the significance of this separation of 'innocent' and 'deserving' victims. Indeed, the system of criminal injuries compensation is founded upon this very distinction. The Criminal Injuries Compensation Scheme (CICS) provides payment 'at the taxpayers' expense to *blameless* victims of crimes of violence' (Compensation for Victims of Violent Crime, 1999, p.3; emphasis added; see also Miers, 1978). The CICS goes on to describe violent acts as ranging from 'minor assault to unimaginable savagery' (ibid., p.6). The use of this kind of discourse – and especially that which impugns blame to the 'out-of-control' maniac – shows clearly how the law recognizes and sanctions distinctions among forms and meanings of violence.

In many respects, however, the fusing of biological and psychological imagery with 'bad violence' is the most intractable conceptualization in thinking about violence. There is no scope in this chapter to address this distinction in detail. However, one result of this active imagery about 'bad' violence and – for want of another term – 'acceptable' violence, is that those who use and who receive such violence also make such distinctions. Individuals' own resources, cultural histories and knowledge, together with their social, institutional and personal reserves, assist in the resistance to and affect the impact of threats and violence. This is true for both offender and victim (who may be one and the same person). These personal resources are crucially underpinned by social relations. While it is important not to cast the victim of violence as passive, my argument is that victims meet violence within a complex web of personal, situational and social situations. How they manage such violence will be conditioned by the dynamic of the social relations in which they are embedded. Campaign groups – whose activities typically confront the social policies of institutions – advocate on behalf of particular victims of violence as a way to make these social relations and the inequalities of power that structure them explicit (see, for instance, Dobash and Dobash, 1992).

Most people draw on resources other than law to mediate their experiences of violence. This avoidance of law in the protection of citizens or for redress following violence demonstrates the cultural and social power of the distinction between 'bad' violence and 'acceptable' violence. Crime surveys, for example, demonstrate that the majority of incidents that can be classified as legal violence do not come to the attention of the police (Mirrlees-Black et al., 1999). For a variety of reasons – the most commonly recorded is that the incidents were too 'trivial' to involve the police – people exclude their experiences of violence from public scrutiny. In many respects, then, an individual's use of violence is met with another individual's management of it (Stanko, 1990). Moreover, research shows that when an incident comes to the attention of the criminal justice system, the state's interest in punishing violent offenders is affected by people's assessments of the violence they experience (Cretney and Davis, 1995; Hoyle, 1998). Despite strong public commitment to the protection of *all* victims, studies indicate that the individual victim and his or her social characteristics – especially the individual victim's social standing (Cooney, 1994; Stanko, 1981) – strongly influence the police and the prosecution in their decision on whether to prosecute violent offences. In political rhetoric, perhaps, victims of violence are a homogeneous category – all 'innocent' and in need of protection. In reality, many differences and circumstances divide victims and contribute to whether and how the state through its criminal justice apparatus intervenes in violence. In many cases the burden of responsibility to initiate intervention and then to be steadfastly committed to seeing this intervention through is displaced onto the individual. The consequence of this displacement is that many victims of violence rely on the social and emotional support of family and friends or on social institutions outside the criminal justice system.

The central point of my argument thus far is that the distinction between 'bad' violence and 'acceptable' violence acts both to disconnect violence from the social relations in which it is embedded and to mediate criminal justice and other institutional responses to it. While people and social institutions judge incidents of violence through this crude binary opposition, their assessment categories may not necessarily overlap. Many of the challenges to institutions from campaign groups, trade unions, the Health and Safety Executive and the like make the claim that violence is not taken seriously by these institutions as a routine feature of working and everyday life. Despite these challenges, the imagery about danger of violence continues to centre on the 'homicidal maniac' who rarely causes havoc – on the street, in the workplace or at home. Certainly, there are some very dangerous people among the general population and I am not denying the very real harm such people can inflict. However, the data about violence tell a different, more complex story (Stanko et al., 1998b). Familiar, familial and 'ordinary' social encounters (such as between client and server, for instance) provide the settings within which violence occurs. In the UK the *Confidential Enquiry into Homicide and Suicide by those with Mental Illness* found in its preliminary report (Appleby et al., 1997) that those labelled 'mentally ill' were less likely to kill complete strangers. Where those labelled mentally ill did commit homicide, 82 per cent killed members of their own family. Yet the image of the uncontrollable stranger still looms over our knowledge about violence.

This construction points to the way in which thinking about violence has fused with concerns about personal safety, and the growing emphasis on community safety by the police, local authorities and private industry.. In the following section, I will explore the emerging discourses about community and personal safety that have come to dominate our conversations about violence.

4 Anticipating violence: stranger danger as the paradigm of fear

Fear of crime has come to be used as the benchmark of people's concern about crime, especially violence. A standard inclusion among questions on crime surveys – 'How safe do you feel walking in your neighbourhood after dark?' – aims to capture people's assessment of their safety from contact crime (robbery, assault and sexual assault, primarily). While there is a volume of debate in the criminological literature about this question, including much scepticism about the evidence drawn from people's self-assessment of risk, this approach to measuring people's fear of crime remains the most central to criminological debate. There are, however, many paradoxes arising from the research on fear of crime. Those who report most fear also report a wider range of insecurities about other aspects of their lives: job security, ageing, vulnerability to other forms of harassment and abuse, all of which contribute to climates of insecurity (see Hough, 1995). These are also linked to understandings about violence.

Clearly there are many factors that feed people's concerns about safety. One important contribution to fear is people's social resources and experiences of what is often termed 'low-level' violence. Sexual pestering, racist comments, abuse because of one's sexuality, for instance, may not be incidents 'worthy' of criminalization. However, such comments and daily abuse greatly contribute to a climate within which criminal violence can fester (Gardner, 1995; Madriz, 1998).

What is interesting about the 'fear of crime' debates is that the roots of insecurity have been taken outside crime and placed squarely within the commentaries about our social relationships with each other. Many campaign groups have spotlighted particular groups' fear of crime as indicative not only of their relationship to criminal violence, but of their social exclusion, inequality and disadvantage in the wider society (see for instance, Jenness and Broad, 1997; Stanko and Curry, 1997). Thus, violence has become one of the main topics in the political campaigning on behalf of certain groups, such as advocacy for the better treatment of and provision of services to children, battered women, or those harmed by racist or homophobic violence.

Are people's perceived concerns about safety and security appropriately portrayed in explanations of motivations for committing violence? To address this question, we must look at two things:

- How does violence 'work' as a network of threat or a behavioural framework in everyday life?
- What are the consequences of the experiences of and concerns about physical, sexual and psychological violence (whether real or perceived)?

Those who say they *fear crime least* – young men – are by all accounts those *at most risk* of violent crime. Young men are most at risk from offenders who share similar social characteristics – age, 'race', education, economics, and locale. The data show that young offenders and their victims come from similar backgrounds. Moreover, while young women do commit violence, whatever the form of violent encounter (for want of a better term), young men dominate official statistics on violence. And they are most likely to target other men. In making sense of how people assess their risk of violent crime, I suggest, we privilege men's experiences of violence, but do so with a funny twist of logic in which we bring the danger of strangers to the fore, and also change the definition of the vulnerable. As a result, the danger of violent crime becomes a problem for women and the elderly – categories of people to whom most advice about personal safety is directed (see Stanko, 1996). Stranger violence – and the safety of public space – takes its place as the cornerstone in the discourse about community safety. Yet it is in relation to men's violence against men in the street that police are most proactive. For women, the home continues to be the place of most danger, a social fact brought to light by feminist activism over the last twenty-five years, resulting in increased policing of domestic violence. For men, pubs, clubs and the streets provide the locations for their encounters with violence. Myths about generic violence – that the 'stranger' poses similar dangers to all people – feed fear unnecessarily. We must be able to explore how violence affects the lives of different groups and individuals, and particularly where these experiences of individuals reveal features about the everyday lives of different kinds of people. Intervention into violence must be as sensitive as possible to the dynamics and conditions within which people live. These are the conditions that underpin social relations.

Making public space safe – and that often means controlling the visual display of men's fights – demonstrates police competence to control and to secure safe streets. Proactive policing is often aimed at curtailing the violence committed by special groups – animal rights activists, football hooligans, drug gangs, and even 'organized' paedophiles. Certainly such groups do constitute danger to certain people. However, with the exception of paedophiles, few people spontaneously mention the danger posed by these other groups, unless they have been directly affected by them. Mink farmers, for instance, might place the violence of animal rights activists at the top of their list of concerns. Similarly, those who attend football matches might rate hooliganism at soccer matches as a major social problem.

What is important here is to consider how all of these different problems of violence come to define *what violence is* in state discourses about community safety. The following example illustrates this process. In October 1998, a research report was published, announcing that it was now 'official': there are more muggings in England than in the US (Langan and Farrington, 1998). Nicholas Rufford, Home Affairs Editor of the *Sunday Times*, wrote that this study shattered traditional beliefs that England is a 'safe' country. While the rates of homicide and rape are still higher in the United States, the report stated, assault, robbery, burglary and motor vehicle theft are higher in England and Wales than in the US. The release of the official statistics and the *1998 British Crime Survey* for England and Wales in that same week showed violent crime in decline. The *British Crime Survey* (Mirrlees-Black et al., 1999) reported an overall drop in crime of 17 per cent, although 'mugging', the major concern of the Langan and Farrington analysis, clocked an increase of 1 per cent. The 1997 criminal statistics in England and Wales showed violence against the person to have risen by 5 per cent, sexual offences by 6 per cent, but the number of robberies to have fallen by 13 per cent.

Controversy about these figures led the news for a few days. Few analysts chose to ask questions about the nature of the 'violence' they were reporting. For instance, 41 per cent of US robberies, but only 5 per cent in England, involved the use of a firearm. Seven per cent of English murders, as opposed to 68 per cent of US murders, were committed using a firearm. Perhaps being robbed at gunpoint feels less intimidating than being robbed at knifepoint. Perhaps living in a society that has fewer firearms also has a qualitative impact on people's feelings of personal safety. We do not know the answers to these questions from these data. Violence is defined through this media-led debate according to generic, legal categories, and as such is undifferentiated in its forms, meanings and consequences for people. This same *Sunday Times* featured another story that focused on teenaged thugs, rampaging out of control. It portrayed young villains who strike unsuspecting victims at random. Such imagery of violence – especially teenaged violence – is embedded in these data analyses and debates and thus becomes entrenched in much social policy.

What kinds of silences are perpetuated by a reliance on official data about violence? We are left, I suggest, with little useful information about the meaning and motivation of violence to different individuals and different groups; about the impact of violence on those structurally more vulnerable; or about the possible interface between collective support and intolerance of particular forms of violence. Nor do we have a systematic understanding of the patterns of violence as they are reflected in people's varying experiences, or about how particular social policies perpetuate their own violence or produce the conditions of possibility for other forms of violence. It is therefore difficult to devise strategies for challenging forms of violence based on empirical evidence and practical, grounded approaches that arise from a detailed understanding of the above. In contrast, 'stranger danger' continues to loom as the most pressing problem of violence.

How, then, do we think about mapping strategies for challenging violence on to better knowledge about it? I suggest that we could usefully begin to treat violence as having different features. The safety and security of individuals and groups may indeed call for different strategies and social policies.

5   Violence in the context of inequality or disadvantage

Debates about violence are often confused because discussions of the meaning of violence are conflated with assumptions that the seriousness of violence dictates its impact on people's lives. By this I mean that some commentators may begin to label so-called low-level violence as annoying, but not fear-provoking, nor as constituting a blight on people's lives. According to this kind of thinking, sex pests on the street or racists shouting abuse do not pose a serious threat to people's quality of life. But our evidence suggests otherwise. Indeed, harassment over time is now defined as a harm in criminal law (Protection from Harassment Act 1997). Many people name harassment, bullying and other forms of abuse as part of a continuum of violence (see Kelly, 1988). Lesbian, gay and bisexual experiences of homophobic violence in the past five years demonstrate that many report abuse (Mason and Palmer, 1996). So, too, the experience of racist abuse demonstrates that the climate of subordination and inequality is maintained through a continual stream of comments and actions, constantly reminding those in particular groups that they are living within a hostile and intimidating social environment (Sibbitt, 1997). There is further evidence that experiences of violent victimization vary by ethnic group (Fitzgerald and Hale, 1996). These patterns show that individuals bear the costs of social inequality and disadvantage – but individuals bear them differently. Moreover, these patterns have more impact on some lives than on others. The data on the prevalence of domestic violence suggest that nine out of ten women are not beaten in any one given year (Stanko et al., 1998a). Yet a larger proportion of women have the memories of past physical and sexual abuse from partners or boyfriends. Consistently, one in four to one in three women report some experience of domestic violence in their lifetime. The fact that Women's Aid – in England, Northern Ireland, Scotland and Wales – cannot cope with requests for emergency accommodation attests to the significant numbers of women fleeing violence day in and day out in the UK. Conservative estimates show that a woman calls Women's Aid somewhere in the UK every two minutes, and this statistic is generated only by the calls which get through. Domestic violence and abuse of women has been named as a signifier of women's status in society.

Another example. Individuals are subjected to violence as employees. Throughout the UK, there is growing disquiet by workers about the levels of intimidation, threat and violence they experience at work either from managers or colleagues or as a result of unsafe working practices. Information collected by the Health and Safety Executive from a variety of workplaces in the public sector illustrates how staff have to manage violence as a part of their working lives: those who provide services to the public – nursing staff, ambulance drivers and driving instructors, for instance – report varying levels of threat and assault (Stanko et al., 1998b). Many work-based injuries take place where violence commonly occurs between men, such as pubs and clubs.

The Reporting of Injuries, Diseases and Dangerous Occurrences Regulations (RIDDOR) 1995 came into force on 1 April 1996. This legislation includes a requirement to report any incidents resulting in death, major injury, or incapacity for normal work for three days or more. However, reporting of incidents is reduced because the majority of work-based violence does not result in injury requiring three or more days off work; moreover people are concerned about reporting being viewed as a waste of time and money, or fear the loss of licences or of being identified as unprofessional. According to the first RIDDOR report, nurses and nursing assistants reported more injuries than all other professions, including the police.

Physical assaults are part, but not the only part, of the continuum of intimidation. People cope with bullying or verbal harassment from fellow employees, managers and clients. Recasting some kinds of violence as targeted intentionally helps focus strategies to challenge its presence in various locations. Violence in the context of work should not be defined solely in terms of 'dangerous strangers' but in terms of unacceptable conditions of work.

One final point about the data on violence. An analysis of the data on the trends of violence shows that robbery – the most common form of violence that is treated as randomly distributed – has begun to decline in its aggregate (see Stanko et al., 1998b). I would expect that the crime audits prompted by the recent legislation in England and Wales will begin to capture the local features of this form of violence. However, I would like to conclude by offering another insight into the way in which we might continue to think of this form of violence as the most likely to threaten our social fabric. When examining the proportion of people convicted of violent offences, there is another pattern that emerges. Those convicted of robbery receive more sentences of immediate custody than those convicted of sexual offences, and far more than those convicted of various forms of violence against the person (Stanko et al., 1998b). It is not possible to determine whether this is actually based on an assessment of the seriousness of the offence, or whether the contexts within which violence occurs mediates how we view its seriousness. There are, for instance, constant worries by advocates for battered women that very serious crimes of domestic violence are not treated appropriately by the courts. It may be that our fear of strangers is extended to the way in which offenders are sentenced by the courts.

6   Social policy and its impact on violence

There are a number of initiatives under way to challenge violence. Many of these are spearheaded by interest groups – unions on behalf of many workers, women's groups on behalf of women battered and sexually abused, children's advocates on behalf of abused and neglected children, homophile groups on behalf of the 'non-straight', black and ethnic minority campaign groups on behalf of some minorities, self-help groups for the disabled, and supporters of those who have experienced forms of mental illness. Many common analyses of violence question the primacy of a criminological definition and a legal solution that will minimize violence. Such analyses recognize a wide definition of violence that includes threat and intimidation alongside physical and sexual violence. It includes discourses about people's quality of life and their rights to citizenship, good physical and mental health, and decent working conditions within the debates about the criminal harm of physical violence. Moreover, the discourses adopted by such campaigns extend the responsibility to challenge violence way beyond the remit of the courts and the police.

These discourses must now also be placed at the centre of our understanding of the way in which violence works in contemporary life. We must query the persistence of the discourses of biology and psychology as the commonsense explanations of why people are violent. Until we are willing to accept that the wider society produces, maintains and supports the conditions within which violence festers, our social policy to confront violence – which relies almost solely on the length of sentences meted out to convicted violent offenders – is surely hollow. We must admit that social inequalities are a formidable foundation for violence in our midst. Thus, to the extent that social policy is concerned with ameliorating social inequalities, such an admission necessarily links social policy to our thinking about violence.

References

Appleby, L., Shaw, J. and Amos, T. (1997) *The Progress Report of the National Confidential Enquiry into Suicide and Homicide by People with Mental Illness*, London, Department of Health.

Bowling, B. (1999) *Violent Racism: Victimization, Policing and Social Context*, Oxford, Clarendon.

Bumiller, K. (1987) *The Civil Rights Society*, Baltimore, MD, Johns Hopkins University Press.

Cameron, D. and Fraser, L. (1987) *Lust to Kill*, Cambridge, Polity Press.

Compensation for Victims of Violent Crime (1999) *A Consultation Paper*, Home Office, CCN077828, London, The Stationery Office Group.

Connell, R. (1995) *Masculinities*, Cambridge, Polity Press.

Cooney, M. (1994) 'Evidence as partnership', *Law and Society Review*, 28, pp.833–58.

Cretney, A. and Davis, G. (1995) *Punishing Violence*, London, Routledge.

Dobash, R.E. and Dobash, R.P. (1992) *Women, Violence and Social Change*, London, Routledge.

Fitzgerald, M. and Hale, C. (1996) *Ethnic Minorities: Victimization and Racial Harassment*, Research Study No.154, London, Home Office.

Gardner, C. Brooks (1995) *Passing By: Gender and Public Harassment*, Berkeley, CA, University of California Press.

Glass, D.D. (1995) *All My Fault*, London, Virago.

Graham, J. and Bowling, B. (1995) *Young People and Crime*, Research Study No.145, London, Home Office.

Hough, M. (1995) *Anxiety about Crime*, Research Study No.147, London, Home Office.

Hoyle, C. (1998) *Negotiating Domestic Violence: Police, Criminal Justice and Victims*, Oxford, Clarendon.

Jenness, V. and Broad, K. (1997) *Hate Crimes: New Social Movements and the Politics of Violence*, New York, Aldine de Gruyter.

Kalunta-Crompton, A. (1999) *Race and Drug Trials*, Aldershot, Ashgate.

Kelly, L. (1988) *Surviving Sexual Violence*, Cambridge, Polity Press.

Langan, M. and Farrington, D.P. (1998) *Crime and Justice in the United States and in England and Wales, 1981–96*, NCJ 169284, Washington, DC, US Department of Justice.

Madriz, E. (1998) *Nothing Bad Happens to Good Girls*, Berkeley, CA, University of California Press.

Mason, A. and Palmer, A. (1996) *Queer-bashing*, London, Stonewall.

Miers, D.R. (1978) *Responses to Victimisation: A Comparative Study of Compensation for Criminal Violence in Great Britain and Ontario*, Abingdon, Professional Books.

Mirrlees-Black, C., Budd, T., Partridge, S. and Mayhew, P. (1999) *The 1998 British Crime Survey: England and Wales*, London, Research, Development and Statistics Directorate.

Polk, K. (1994) *When Men Kill*, Cambridge, Cambridge University Press.

Sibbitt, R. (1997) *The Perpetrators of Racial Harassment and Racial Violence*, London, Home Office.

Soothill, K. and Walby, S. (1990) *Sex Crime in the News*, London, Routledge.

Stanko, E.A. (1981) 'These are the cases that try themselves', *Law and Society Review*, 16, pp.225–40.

Stanko, E.A. (1985) *Intimate Intrusions*, London, Routledge.

Stanko, E. (1990) *Everyday Violence*, London, Pandora.

Stanko, E.A. (1994) 'Challenging the problem of men's individual violence', in Newburn, T. and Stanko, E.A. (eds) *Just Boys Doing Business*, London, Routledge.

Stanko, E. (1995) 'Women, crime and fear', *The Annals*, 539, pp.46–58.

Stanko, E.A. (1996) 'Warnings to women', *Violence Against Women*, 2 (1), pp.5–24.

Stanko, E.A. and Curry, P. (1997) 'Homophobic violence and the self at risk', *Social and Legal Studies*, 6 (4), pp.513–32.

Stanko, E.A., Crisp, D., Hale, C. and Lucraft, H. (1998a) *Counting the Costs*, Swindon, Crime Concern.

Stanko, E.A., Marian, L., Crisp, D., Manning, R., Smith, J. and Cowan, S. (1998b) *Taking Stock*, Uxbridge, Middlesex, Brunel University.

Tolman, R. (1999) 'Guest editor's introduction', *Violence Against Women*, 5 (4), pp.355–69.

Tomsen, S. (1997) 'A top night: protest, masculinity and the culture of drinking violence', *British Journal of Criminology*, 37 (1), pp.90–102.

Virdee, S. (1997) 'Racial harassment', in Mohood, T., Berthoud, R., Lakey, J., Nazroo, J., Smith, P. and Virdee, S. (eds) *Ethnic Minorities in Britain*, London, Policy Studies Institute.

Young, A. (1996) *Imagining Crime*, London, Sage.

17

Discursive Histories, the Pursuit of Multiculturalism and Social Policy

Gail Lewis

Contents

1	**Introduction**	259
2	**A note on terminology**	261
3	**Discourses of racial exclusion**	265
3.1	1960s–1970s	266
3.2	1970s–1980s	267
3.3	1980s–1997	267
3.4	1997 – 'New' Labour	268
4	**Some evidence from education**	269
5	**Conclusion**	272
References		273

---

1 Introduction

It has long been accepted that social policy as welfare policy and practice has a key role to play in achieving social integration. It does this by ameliorating the excessive inequalities produced by the dynamic of capitalist production (Marshall, 1950; Titmuss, 1958). By articulating the relationship between state and 'people' as part of a set of citizenship rights, state-regulated, produced and delivered welfare has acted as a powerful suturing mechanism and thereby been central to the construction of society. Prior to the 1970s, the ameliorating effects of social policy were largely conceived in terms of inequalities associated with class relations understood as the unequal distribution of, and access to, material goods and services. Indeed this focus on issues of distribution is reflected to some extent in the Beveridge attack on the 'five giants' of ignorance, squalor, idleness, disease and want. However, whilst writers such as Beveridge and Marshall recognized that capitalist social relations inevitably led to distributive inequalities, it was not their view either that capitalism ought to be displaced by some other system nor that inequalities were inherently bad. Thus, it was only the excessive inequalities that needed to be ameliorated and it was this that social policy was to address.

The emergence of new political challenges accompanying radical Marxist and 'new social movement' critiques of the social relations of welfare, resulted in a deepened and widened field of contestation over the inclusions and exclusions which the post-Second World War welfare regime articulated. These critiques identified the welfare state itself as producing inequalities not only in relation to class differentiations, but also those associated with gender, 'race', sexuality, age and disability. Williams (1989) has shown how the post-war welfare state instantiated in the Beveridge reforms yoked together notions of 'work', 'family' and 'race'/nation in a way that constructed a particular image of the British people. Ideas about gender, 'race' and nation have, then, been at the very heart of British welfare regimes for a long time (see also Lewis, 1998a). This chapter takes one aspect of this ensemble and looks at the relation between social policy and the discursive production of the category 'race'. More specifically, the chapter argues that three aspects of this relationship are germane to a rethinking of social policy. First, that social policy draws upon and reflects hegemonic understandings of the category 'race'. Second, that social policy as discourse is constitutive of the category 'race' and as such is implicated in the construction of racialized differentiations, subject positions and subordinations. Third, that the racial inscriptions produced by and embedded in social policy as discourse affect the type and quality of welfare service (and benefit) which groups racialized as minorities receive.

These dimensions of the relation between the discursive production of the category 'race' and social policy are explored through education as a specific site of social policy. Education – i.e. the period of compulsory schooling – has been chosen for a number of reasons. Education is not always seen as an arena of social policy since the latter is often narrowly defined as pertaining to social security, social work, and perhaps health and public housing. In many ways this is a rather peculiar delimiting of the field of social policy, particularly when one remembers that, at least in the British context, government intervention into the family and education developed coterminously upon the site of 'the social', and one of Beveridge's 'five giants' was 'ignorance'. Education can also be seen as a central part of social policy once we remember that the latter is identified as contributing to two elements central to the formation of society. The first, as already mentioned, is the question of the amelioration of excessive inequalities and the promotion of equality of opportunity. In this context schooling has enabled, and continues to be identified in official debate as enabling, children to achieve to the best of their ability, without regard to material or familial circumstance. Schooling has also been identified as a central mechanism for achieving and expressing the relationship between state and citizen. Children, therefore, receive schooling as part of the rights of their parents' citizenship status, and as a means of learning the attributes of citizenship (Sadler, 1916; HMSO, 1990). Schooling in this sense is seen as central to the process of citizenship and social cohesion. Similarly, in terms of the logic of capital and social control, schooling has been cited as a core mechanism in ensuring a general level of skill, literacy and numeracy among the labouring population (Bowles and Gintis, 1976).

These factors point to the centrality of education in both the management and cohesion of diverse social constituencies and in the production of social subjects. In this sense education has long been identified as central to analyses of the processes by which particular groups of pupils become positioned as racialized minorities (CIAC, 1964; Mullard, 1982; Rattansi, 1992; Lewis, 1998b). Education, then, can provide fertile ground for the examination of how social policy constructs relations of inclusion, exclusion and subordination both within welfare and in society more generally.

2   A note on terminology

Before going on to discuss the ways in which social policy is implicated in the construction of the category 'race', racialized differentiations and subordinations, some conceptual clarifications are required. In particular I want to consider the terms 'ethnic minority' and 'nation-state'.

Let me begin with the term 'ethnic minority'. I use it to signal a social location – and not primarily a numerical position. This point needs to be made explicitly for a number of reasons. First, although it should go without saying that the 'other' of 'ethnic minority' is 'ethnic majority', this latter term hardly ever appears in official or popular debate, including in the academic social policy literature. Thus, the relational and social character of these two positions is lost and instead there is a suggestion that to be positioned within either category reflects a natural demarcation. In contrast to terminological formulations which foreground the constructed and relational character of ethnic designations, the term 'ethnic' is increasingly used to reference Britain's racialized populations of colour. Given this, it is necessary to state that both 'minority' *and* '*majority*' are constituted through the processes of boundary formation around notions of something called 'ethnicity' – the precise content of which is historically and socially contingent.

Just as it is necessary to point to the constructed character of ethnic divisions around a binary 'minority'/'majority', so too is it important to be reminded of the diversity of those groups who are positioned as 'ethnic minorities'. Recent research data (Modood et al., 1997) shows increasing diversity among Britain's racialized populations of colour. Whilst members of these groups still have a common experience of racial exclusion, there is also evidence of an increasing complexity of experiences and internal diversification. This suggests that any tendency to homogenizing categorization may lead to an elision of differences among and within racialized populations of colour; and to the denial of the possibility and effects of agency on the part of members of these populations. Thus, 'ethnic diversity' needs to be understood as a complex term referencing at least the following elements: a range of social groups, including those constructed as the (invisible) 'majority', formed around and through numerous cultural and social characteristics; a range of social/economic/political patterns formed around the intersections among 'racial' or 'ethnic' inclusions, exclusions, dominances and subordinations with other axes of social differentiation, such as class, gender, sexuality; a series of social locations or positions within the overall social formation; and individual and collective responses to these exclusions and locations.

From this perspective, 'ethnicity' becomes understood as a *relational process* – in which categories of community and identity are in constant formation at the intersection of actual or imagined cultural (understood as ways of life) heritages and the political/economic/cultural (understood as representations) relations through and upon which racisms emerge and operate. It is around this intersection that boundaries demarcating 'ethnic groups' (within and between 'minority' and 'majority') are formed.

A second point of clarification concerns the idea of the nation(-state). It has become common among social policy academics to use the concept of 'settlement' as a device through which to capture the set of unstable and temporary relationships which are constitutive of, and constituted by, a welfare regime at any particular time (Clarke and Newman, 1997; Hughes and Lewis, 1998). The usual 'settlements' are thought of as economic-political, social and organizational. We can also add an intellectual 'settlement' represented by Fabian social democracy in Beveridge, and, though perhaps more debatable, a New Right mix of neo-liberalism and social authoritarianism in the 'reforms' inaugurated by the Thatcher and Major governments.

To these I would add 'the nation(-state)' as a kind of geo-political/administrative 'settlement'. This term carries two elements: nation as a sovereign state with legal and political autonomy and the right to assign citizenship; and nation as an 'imagined community' (Anderson, 1983) with forms of cultural belonging, inclusion and exclusion.

Chapters 11 and 13 raise issues about the units of space corresponding to a particular form of welfare regime and the impact of globalization on the sustainability of the relatively bounded nation-state. In considering the relation between racialized differentiations and social policy this chapter addresses some of the same terrain, but centres its gaze internally – within the nation-state. In particular I explore some of the ways in which social policy under the government of 'New' Labour is constructing 'the nation' and national belonging.

Nation-states have commonly been taken as the 'natural' political unit within which social policy does and ought to operate. The assumed *naturalness* of the nation-state as the unit bestowing and delivering entitlement to state, private and voluntary sector provision extends to a presumption about the naturalness of the nation as a constituency of belonging, attachment and boundary. In contrast to this I want to suggest that the nation(-state) is also a kind of settlement formed at the intersection of a particularized ethnic or national identity and the universalizing claims of social democracy and citizenship. The nation(-state), then, represents a temporary stability achieved by sublimating the closures effected by ethnic identifications to a 'patriotic' or 'higher' kind of identification (Zizek, 1997) represented by a commitment to something called the 'national interest', usually understood as capital's economic interest (as in, for example, 'Buy British'). In this formulation, the undertow of particularistic (and 'lower') ethnic identifications becomes subordinated to or reconstituted as identification with and commitment to a 'universal', social democratic 'national' economy. Thus ethnic belongings and attachments become obscured and displaced into something called 'national' belonging and attachments – a thing conceived as without and above ethnicity. The implication of this is that 'the national' comes to stand for 'the majority' and all those defined as 'ethnic' automatically become defined as 'other' and 'minority'. In this way the pursuit of multiculturalism becomes understood as the pursuit of tolerance for a range of social groups seen as outside the norm of the national.

In arguing that the nation-state be seen as another kind of settlement I am drawing directly on work by Zizek (1997), the cultural theorist who draws on Lacanian psychoanalysis to develop his analyses. His concern is with issues beyond the scope of this chapter, but his discussion of what he calls 'the Nation Thing' (Zizek, 1995, p.162) raises a number of points which are useful in considering the connections between social policy and the construction of racialized differentiations and subordinations. In particular Zizek's conceptualization is useful because it alerts us to its social and historically contingent character. Post-colonial analysts would also alert us to the tension produced by the porous character of the boundaries of the nation, and the simultaneous attempt to fix these boundaries as solid and natural (Hall, 1996; Rattansi, 1997; Lewis, 1998c). Post-colonial theory therefore provides us with another way of conceptualizing ethnicity and nation as constituted relationally.

There are, then, three key elements characterizing the nation-state – and 'the nation' it putatively contains – which I want to draw on in developing my argument:

- It is social, temporary and unstable – representing a contradictory articulation of the demands of particular ethnic identifications and the universal claims of social democracy, citizenship and capital's 'globalizing' market.
- It is mutually constituted along shifting and contingent boundaries formed in the encounter with a series of significant and abject 'others' – i.e. those nation-states of the overdeveloped 'north' and underdeveloped 'south'.
- Its temporary and contingent character points to the need to constantly remake 'nation' through a plurality of processes which 'fix' the boundaries of belonging and sovereignty. Included among these processes are representations of heritage, the organization of collective memory, processes of national identification and the rights and *responsibilities* of citizenship. However, precisely in the attempt to fix its boundaries (self) by the exclusion of its 'others', the conditions and sites of anxieties over national identity are produced and barriers are erected to a multiculturalism which would lead to an equality of recognition and valorization of *all* social groups, including those constructed as 'minorities'.

The elicitation of these strands enables us to conceptualize shifts in the formulation, presentation and implementation of social policy in a way that analytically centres 'the nation' and the processes of its formation. For my purposes this has three key factors:

- the central role of social policy in attempts to 'fix' the nation around fictions of stability and homogeneity, even while it may also be concerned to meet the particularistic needs of groups positioned as minority;
- the simultaneous and necessary construction of the nation's 'others';
- the degree to which particular policies enhance or inhibit the pursuit of a fully inclusive multiculturalism.

Having identified the approach I adopt to both 'ethnicity' and the 'nation(-state)' I now want to look at the ways in which the government's strategy for social inclusion constructs ethnic diversity and reinscribes particular groups in subordinate and racialized positions.

In this context I suggest that contemporary policy documents define the central issue facing central and local government as how to promote and reconcile ethnic diversity and *simultaneously* resurrect (and become the keeper of) an older version of the British nation – which is seen as ethnically homogenous, benign and 'tolerant'. How, in other words, to align the pursuit of (a narrowly conceived) 'multiculturalism' with a recourse to 'tradition' and an unchanged Britain.

3   Discourses of racial exclusion

In order to explore the ways in which 'New' Labour social policy constructs racial or ethnic subordinations, we need to look at the discursive histories through which 'the nation' and its 'others' have been constructed.

The predominant official approach to the social relations of 'race' and ethnicity has taken four main, often overlapping, directions:

- constructing issues of 'race' as solely about relations between 'black' and 'white' people;
- suggesting that in the British context this is a post-1945 phenomenon;
- arguing that the way to avoid a persistent 'race relations problem' is to link strong/fair immigration legislation with the promotion of an ethos of 'good race relations'/multiculturalism. Indeed it has been common sense for at least thirty years that the latter is dependent on the former;
- constructing the issues as a 'problem' originating externally but one that is now an internal 'problem' located in specific areas, such as 'the inner city', where 'ethnic minorities' tend to be concentrated.

This approach sets up a series of exclusions and amnesias which centre on (at least):

- 'forgetting' the long history of politics and policies aimed at the Irish population present in Britain – if not the UK; politics and policies often articulated through a discourse of 'race' (Hickman, 1998);
- 'forgetting' the long history of politics and policies aimed at the presence of Jewish people in Britain – including the 1905 Aliens Act (and its developments in 1914/1919). This Act can be thought of as the precursor to the wave of immigration and nationality legislation instituted from 1962 onwards that was aimed at

controlling migration and settlement of people from the New Commonwealth and Pakistan (NCWP) who were, or had been, British citizens (Cesarani, 1996);

- 'forgetting' that British governments have long had experience of dealing with 'black/white' race relations – from Elizabeth I's declaration that there were too many 'blackamores' in the kingdom and they should be despatched (Walvin, 1973); to the Sierra Leone project 1786–1791, (Braidwood, 1994); to legislation of 1915 and 1919 aimed at controlling the movement and registration of 'Coloured Seamen' resident in England's port cities, (Tabili, 1994); and the vast administrative and political structures and practices in the erstwhile colonies.

These persistent and active 'forgettings' have made it possible to construct the issue of 'race' as an 'externally' generated issue – 'external' in the double sense of neither originating within the territory of the UK, nor as endemic to the internal (domestic or imperial) politics and trajectory of the UK.

Somewhat paradoxically, given the amnesia at play, these approaches to 'race' have provided the discursive context for a series of laws and policies implemented between the 1960s and 1990s aimed, wholly or partially, at addressing the real and assumed welfare needs of those defined as 'immigrants' and/or 'ethnic minorities'. Some examples, ranging from the 1960s to the 1990s, are: the three reports by the Commonwealth Immigrants Advisory Council (on housing, education and employment) published in the 1960s; Inner City Policy; Section 11 monies; the race relations legislation of the 1960s and 1970s; positive action policies (such as professional training of social workers); and same-race adoption and fostering policies of the 1980s and 1990s.

These illustrate some of the areas identified by central and local government as matters of concern. Remember, too, that this concern was written through a discourse which problematized the presence of African, Asian and Caribbean peoples in Britain. While a discourse of problematization has been a connecting thread across these four decades, it is possible to periodize the approaches adopted by central and local government. The following indicate some very broad contours.

3.1   1960s–1970s

This period can be characterized as focusing on assimilation of racialized groups of colour into existing social, political and cultural formations. This was to be achieved with as little disruption to the 'host' community as possible, and among the policies designed to ensure this were dispersal strategies in schools; dispersal *or* concentration in housing, depending on the individual local authority; Section 11 monies for educational (mainly) and other public welfare agencies; and Inner City Partnership or Programme funds for specifically designated local authorities. The hegemonic discursive thread was such that the presence of racialized populations of colour was seen as (at least potentially) disruptive of a stable and homogenous national entity.

3.2   1970s–1980s

At this time we see the emergence of a cultural pluralist approach. This includes a degree of recognition of the potential contributions (rather than disruptions) that racialized populations of colour can make to life in Britain. A key exemplar is the Swann Report *Education for All* (DES, 1985), but there are earlier examples from the late 1970s, such as the Soul Kids and Black Families for Black Children campaigns within some social services departments.

These were very much locally based initiatives and in many ways went against the trend to construct black families and communities as in some way 'pathological' but nevertheless as 'ethnic'. This is also a time of heightened self-organization with an explicit focus on politics within Britain/UK. This decade was marked by the creation of the category 'mugging'; a huge increase in police/'black youth' antagonism, especially through the use of the 'sus' laws; and a spate of riotous protest by white, black and Asian youth across the country.

3.3   1980s–1997

This was a much more contradictory 'moment' with trends pulling in opposite directions. In many ways it is a 'moment' marking intense ideological struggle over what meanings to attribute to the (now acknowledged) permanent presence of racialized populations of colour in the UK. Thus, these years are marked by contradictory trends. On the one hand, there are New Right attacks on positive action; the 'Tebbitt Test'; attacks upon the idea and values of multicultural education; and a nostalgic 'Little Englandism'. On the other, there are policy developments such as the clause in the Children Act 1989 cautioning local authorities and courts to have due regard to a child's 'race', religion and culture in custody, care or placement orders; the wider influence of the critiques and demands of self-organized groups – such as same-race adoption policies linked to the influence of the Association of Black Social Workers and Allied Professionals

(ABSWAP); and a more general acceptance of the positive contribution that black and Asian British people make to social, economic, cultural and political life.

3.4 1997 – 'New' Labour

Here we seem to be witnessing a shift into a different moment but the delineation of any definitive characteristics is more difficult. In part this is because, at the time of writing, it is only two years since Labour's election victory. However, the difficulties stem from more than the period of time that has elapsed since the election and relate to the ambiguities in the government's own attempts to rethink social policy. As Janet Newman (2000) has pointed out, the government's approach to the public sector in general, and welfare in particular, suggests a double movement both toward and away from the reforms instituted by successive Conservative governments in the 1980s and 1990s. Thus, whilst there is some continuity between 'New' Labour modernization and the new public management of the last Conservative era, there is also a distancing organized around an expanded notion of 'managing for public purpose' (Newman, 2000). This expanded notion is linked to the pursuit of a reconfiguration of the relation between state, 'the people' and welfare. It is also con- nected to the attempt to craft a new identity for the party around a rupture with the approaches and concerns associated with 'old' Labour and social democratic/socialist politics of the last thirty years.

One aspect of this rupture has particular relevance for the con- cerns of this chapter. This is the attempt to proceed *as if* all inequali- ties deriving from the constitution of differences around axes of 'race'/ethnicity, gender, class, sexuality and disability are no longer sources of serious antagonism. A second feature is to dissolve or condense all social inequalities (understood as material and dis- cursive) into the notion of *social exclusion* understood as exclusion from waged work. At the same time it is clear that the government is attempting to institute a new social settlement with the hetero- normative family at its core even while there is recognition of the social changes in gender and household formations which have occurred over the past two or three decades.

These trends of dissolving social inequalities into a single notion of social exclusion; the reinscription of the heteronormative family as the core unit of a stable, law-abiding and responsible citizenry, together with the discursive histories of 'race', coalesce to form the parameters of the government's approach to the question of 'race' in education. I want to illustrate this by looking at the Social Exclusion Unit's White Paper *Truancy and School Exclusion* (SEU, 1998). In particular I contrast some data derived from a number of studies on 'race' and racism in schools with the approach to these issues contained in this document.

4 Some evidence from education

For at least twenty years research on teacher attitudes to and expectations and perceptions of black and Asian schoolchildren (whether born overseas or in the UK) has shown the presence and effects of racial stereotypes (Giles, 1977; Adams, 1978; Rex and Tomlinson, 1979; DES, 1985; Wright, 1985; Mac an Ghaill, 1988; Gillborn, 1990; Ogilvy et al., 1990; Sewell, 1997). Much of this research has been ethnographic in character, focusing on the dynamics of interaction between teachers and pupils from 'ethnic minority' groups. The qualitative character of these studies provides a fruitful complement to more quantitative data provided by, for example, the British Social Attitudes surveys, and allows for a more detailed tracking of the workings and effects of racial stereotypes.

Two quotes taken from studies carried out thirteen years apart establish the terrain:

> . . . heads admitted that many members of staff tended to develop expectations and attitudes towards their [West Indian and working-class pupils'] role and future in English society different from the expectations they would have from indigenous middle-class children . . . Thus . . . the real and perhaps only significance of the terms, 'working-class', 'middle-class' and 'West Indian', as used by teachers to describe children, is the way these terms affect teachers' attitudes, expectations and behaviour. (Giles, 1977, p.6)

> I wish to stress that the imputation of a deliberate challenge to authority . . . was not a crude stereotype held by obviously prejudiced teachers. Rather, it was a way of thinking which was rooted in the ethnocentric assumptions of teachers and their responses to the day-to-day demands made upon them within the school. (Gillborn, 1990, p.37)

This refrain of the co-existence of a lack of any conscious attempt to treat black and Asian school pupils differentially, alongside precisely such differentiating expectations and treatment of these pupils is echoed throughout the research on education.

These effects can be summarized as follows:

- Racial distinctions are applied to pupils of both African-Caribbean and Asian descent but in differential ways, leading to divergent expectations of each group (Ofsted, 1996).
- Such racial distinctions are often based on racial stereotypes of Caribbean and Asian family structures and relationships as, equally but differently, pathological or dysfunctional.

- Pupils of Asian descent are characterized as academically able and diligent, if also quiet and docile; and African-Caribbean-descent pupils are characterized as academically poor and lazy (Mac an Ghaill, 1988; Gillborn, 1990).
- Boys of African-Caribbean descent are assumed to be disorderly and thus to present teachers with behavioural problems (Mac an Ghaill, 1988; Sewell, 1997).
- There is a high level of conflict between white teachers and African-Caribbean descent pupils.
- Teachers and schools themselves often play an active, though unintended, part in the creation of this conflict (Ogilvy et al., 1990; Rex and Tomlinson, 1979; Mac an Ghaill, 1988; Gillborn, 1990).
- There is consistent over-representation in school exclusions of black pupils (i.e. Caribbean, African, or black other) of both sexes (Ofsted, 1996).
- Levels of academic success may be achieved by pupils despite – rather than because of – teacher/school support (Fuller, 1984; Sewell, 1997).

These studies indicate that racial attitudes and stereotypes have a profound effect on the experiences of 'ethnic minority' pupils in schools and that there has been a remarkable stability in the operation of such stereotypes over the past two decades. Moreover, they show that the organizational culture of the school often acts to 'induct' teachers who are new to the school into a set of expectations regarding ability and behaviour. Thus, Mac an Ghaill found that racial stereotypes of Asian pupils as of 'technically high ability' and African-Caribbean children as 'having low ability' were very quickly transmitted to new teachers in the staffroom. In addition any problems that new teachers might be experiencing were often 'explained' as resulting from the racial composition of the school, as opposed to, say, the inexperience of the teacher (Mac an Ghaill, 1988, p.64).

The organizational culture of schools in which racial stereotypes prevail leads, then, to a system of expectations which may become self-fulfilling prophecies. As one prominent educational researcher has noted, drawing on his own and others' research observations, interviews with pupils and an analysis of school punishment records, all suggest that black pupils, of both sexes, are disproportionately criticized and disciplined by white teachers (Ofsted, 1996, p.55). Moreover, this pattern of expectation is not limited to teachers who might be classified as holding to a crudely racist or conservative ideology. Mac an Ghaill (1988) reported finding that in a class containing five pupils of African-Caribbean descent, out of a total of 34 (27 Asian descent, and two white, of unspecified ethnicity), the teacher had identified the five twice as many times as being disruptive. What is significant is that this teacher, of liberal persuasion, had been critical of the dominant social imagery of African-Caribbean-descent pupils operating in the school. This evidence clearly illustrates the power of racial stereotypes to structure the perceptions and behaviours of professionals working in the public sector, a power which is reflected in the patterns of exclusions from schools. This is evident from the Social Exclusion Unit's report (1998) which shows that:

- African-Caribbean-descent pupils are six times more likely to be excluded from school either for a fixed term or permanently;
- they account for 8 per cent of all those permanently excluded, despite comprising only 1 per cent of the total school population (pupils from all 'ethnic minority' groups account for 16 per cent of the school population).

The report also recognizes the indications found in the research evidence, specifically citing the Ofsted (1996, p.11) research showing teacher expectations and the deployment of racial stereotypes. The SEU report identifies the characteristics of the African-Caribbean population of excluded pupils. These are:

- being over-represented in single-parent (lone-mother) house-holds;
- having a higher than average ability yet often being defined as underachieving;
- usually having *not* been displaying disruptive behaviour from early in their school career;
- displaying less evidence of deep-seated mental trauma or ill health.

That the SEU report on *Truancy and School Exclusion* uses data such as this shows awareness and even recognition of the body of research evidence pointing to a racial dynamic *within* the school and classroom. One might then expect that in the recommendations for policy and practice the report would signal a course of action aimed at addressing this dynamic where it is lived or played out – i.e. among teachers and pupils – and not elsewhere, in communities, families or local education authority offices.

It is, however, in the move to policy recommendations that the historical legacies of discourses of 'race' and discourses of family enter to sharply configure the strategy for action and that the evidence of the intersection of racializing practices and the educational trajectories of African-Caribbean pupils disappears. For example, the report begins by citing a number of projects which have succeeded in preventing or decreasing the number of exclusions. These centre on: work with parents and wider community and the development of mentoring schemes. More specifically, in the measures identified to address the issue of exclusion, the racial dynamic in the classroom gets rewritten as a question of behaviour management and data collection. So there are proposals:

- to collect statistics by ethnic group;
- for special Ofsted inspections of schools which have dispropor-tionate rates of exclusion of high-risk groups;
- for the government to ensure that equal opportunities issues, as well as behaviour management, are adequately incorporated in the requirements for initial teacher training, and in-service training;
- that 'a DfEE Task Group consider how to forge a new partnership at national and local levels to tackle the wider problem of raising achievement of ethnic minority pupils. It will also look at what can be done to promote community mentoring in ethnic minority communities' (SEU, 1998, p.25).

This circumvents all the available evidence which pointed to the central role of the teacher/pupil relationship within the school and instead recentres black family formations, black communities and black 'cultures' as the cause of black pupils' over-representation in school exclusions. More widely, because the focus of these recom-mendations is on groups defined in terms of ethnicity, it constructs these pupils, their families and communities as outside the bound-aries of 'the nation' which, I have argued, is defined as an entity without and above ethnic identifications. By identifying the nodal points for intervention as the pupils' families and communities, the report is suggesting that the problem – and solution – to exclusions and underachievement lies in these locations. Pupils therefore arrive at school with 'wrong attitudes' or 'disruptive behaviours' which teachers then have to learn to manage. Moreover, recommendations with this emphasis ignore the fact that the educational experience of children of African-Caribbean descent has been at the centre of much black activism for at least three decades, as the network of supple-mentary schools illustrates. Whilst there is clearly a role to be played by these constituencies, the research evidence suggests that it is a dynamic *within* the classroom/school that is central to the problem. The 'problem', in other words, lies in an institution deemed to be at the heart of the nation and central to its reform.

5 Conclusion

Reading from these discursive histories into the Social Exclusion Unit's White Paper, we can see that the project of multicultural inclusion is constrained from a number of directions. First, it is because the proposals for action in the White Paper reinscribe 'ethnic minority' family formations as in some sense 'the problem' causing some racialized pupils to be disproportionately represented in school exclusions. This in its turn is premised on an active 'forgetting' or denial of the evidence (cited in the document) of the prevalence of a racial dynamic within the classroom and teachers' expectations and fears of 'ethnic minority' children, especially African-Caribbean boys. The inscription of certain family formations as pathological also intersects with 'New' Labour's attempts to establish the hetero-normative family as hegemonic (see HMSO, 1998). This has important consequences for the project of multiculturalism since it disallows the possibility of a field of diverse ethnic identifications, including those bounding the social group defined as the majority. It also precludes recognition and equal valorization of multiple forms of family as a site of production of stable citizens and therefore continues to cast those family forms defined as 'ethnic minority' as not fully included within 'the nation'.

These racialized discourses, set against the pursuit of a hetero-normative family as the universal, construct the limits of 'New' Labour's multicultural project. My argument suggests that the 'New' Labour ideological chain reinscribes 'the nation' as culturally homogeneous and exclusive and thus seriously constrains the pursuit of multiculturalism.

References

Adams, G. (1978) 'Racial membership and physical attractiveness effects in pre-school teachers' expectations', *Child Study Journal*, 8 (1), pp.29–41.

Anderson, B. (1983) *Imagined Communities*, London, Verso.

Bowles, S. and Gintis, H. (1976) *Schooling in Capitalist America*, London, Routledge & Kegan Paul.

Braidwood, S.J. (1994) *Black Poor and White Philanthropist: London's Blacks and the Foundation of the Sierra Leone Settlement 1786–1791*, Liverpool, Liverpool University Press.

Cesarani, D. (1996) 'The changing character of citizenship and nationality in Britain', in Cesarani, D. and Fulbrook, M. (eds) *Citizenship, Nationality and Migration in Europe*, London, Routledge.

CIAC (Commonwealth Immigrants Advisory Council) (1964) *Second Report*, London, HMSO.

Clarke, J. and Newman, J. (1997) *The Managerial State: Power, Politics and Ideology in the Remaking of Social Welfare*, London, Sage.

DES (Department of Education and Science) (1985) *Education For All*, The Report of the Committee of Inquiry into the Education of Children from Ethnic Minority Groups, chaired by Lord Swann (The Swann Report), Cmnd. 9453, London, HMSO.

Fuller, M. (1984) 'Black girls in a London comprehensive school', in Hammersley, M. and Woods, P. (eds) *Life in School: The Sociology of Pupil Culture*, Milton Keynes, Open University Press.

Giles, R. (1977) *The West Indian Experience in British Schools: Multi-Racial Education and Social Disadvantage in London*, London, Heinemann.

Gillborn, D. (1990) *'Race', Ethnicity and Education: Teaching and Learning in Multi-ethnic Schools*, London, Unwin Hyman.

Hall, S. (1996) 'When was "the post-colonial"? Thinking at the limit', in Chambers, I. and Curtis, L. (eds) *The Post-Colonial Question*, London, Routledge.

Hickman, M.J. (1998) 'Education for "minorities": Irish Catholics in Britain', in Lewis (1998a).

HMSO (1990) *Encouraging Citizenship*, Report of the Commission on Citizenship, London, HMSO.

HMSO (1998) *Supporting Families*, London, HMSO.

Hughes, G. and Lewis, G. (eds) (1998) *Unsettling Welfare: The Reconstruction of Social Policy*, London, Routledge/The Open University.

Lewis, G. (ed.) (1998a) *Forming Nation, Framing Welfare*, London, Routledge/The Open University.

Lewis, G. (1998b) 'Welfare and the social construction of "race"', in Saraga, E. (ed.) *Embodying the Social: Constructions of Difference*, London, Routledge/The Open University.

Lewis, G. (1998c) 'Same place, different culture? Thinking welfare through the post colonial'. Plenary address to the Social Policy Association Conference, Lincoln.

Mac an Ghaill, M. (1988) *Young, Gifted and Black: Student Teacher Relations in the Schooling of Black Youth*, Milton Keynes, Open University Press.

Marshall, T.H. (1950) *Citizenship and Social Class and Other Essays*, Cambridge, Cambridge University Press.

Modood, T., Berthoud, R., Lakey, J., Nazno, J., Smith, P., Virdee, S. and Beishon, S. (1997) *Ethnic Minorities in Britain*, London, Policy Studies Institute.

Mullard, C. (1982) 'Multiracial education in Britain: from assimilation to cultural pluralism', in Tierney, J. (ed.) *Race, Migration and Schooling*, New York, Holt.

Newman, J. (2000) 'Modernizing public services', in Clarke, J., Gewirtz, S. and McLaughlin, E. (eds) *New Managerialism, New Welfare*, London, Sage/The Open University.

Ofsted (1996) *Recent Research on the Achievements of Ethnic Minority Pupils*, prepared by Gillborn, D. and Gipps, C., London, Ofsted, HMSO.

Ogilvy, C.M., Boath, E.H., Cheyne, W.M., Jahoda, G. and Schaffer, H.R. (1990) 'Staff attitudes and perceptions in multicultural nursery schools', *Early Child Development and Care*, 64, pp.1–13.

Rattansi, A. (1992) 'Changing the subject? Racism, culture and education', in Donald, J. and Rattansi, A. (eds) *'Race', Culture and Difference*, London, Sage/The Open University.

Rattansi, A. (1997) 'Postcolonialism and its discontents', *Economy and Society*, 26 (4), November, pp.480–500.

Rex, J. and Tomlinson, S. (1979) *Colonial Immigrants in a British City: A Class Analysis*, London, Routledge & Kegan Paul.

Sadler, M.E. (1916) 'An English education for England', *Contemporary Review*, September.

SEU (Social Exclusion Unit) (1998) *Truancy and School Exclusion*, Report by the Social Exclusion Unit, Cmnd 3957, London, HMSO.

Sewell, T. (1997) *Black Masculinity and Schooling: How Black Boys Survive Modern Schooling*, Stoke-on-Trent, Trentham Books.

Tabili, L. (1994) *We Ask for British Justice: Workers and Racial Differentiation in Late Imperial Britain*, Ithaca, NY, Cornell University Press.

Titmuss, R. (1958) *Essays on the Welfare State*, London, Allen & Unwin.

Walvin, J. (1973) *Black and White: Negro and English Society 1555–1945*, London, Allen Lane.

Williams, F. (1989) *Social Policy: A Critical Introduction*, Cambridge, Polity Press.

Wright, C. (1985) 'School processes: an ethnographic study', in Eggleston, S.J., Dunn,

D.K. and Anjali, M. (eds) *The Educational and Vocational Experience of 15–18-year-old Young People of Ethnic Minority Groups*, Warwick, Warwick University Press.

Zizek, S. (1995) *Looking Awry: An Introduction to Jacques Lacan through Popular Culture*, Cambridge, MA, and London, October Books.

Zizek, S. (1997) 'Multiculturalism, or the cultural logic of multinational capitalism', *New Left Review*, 225, September/October, pp.28–51.

18

The Demise of Professional Self-regulation: a Moment to Mourn?

Celia Davies

1 Introduction

In March 1998 the influential Channel 4 television series *Dispatches* broadcast a programme exploring the way in which the General Medical Council (GMC) deals with misconduct of doctors. In their review of over 200 decisions made by this profession-dominated regulatory body, the television researchers found that the majority of doctors against whom complaints were upheld were allowed to continue working. Where they were not, doctors were restored to the register after only a short period. Complainants appeared on screen to express their distress and dismay at the decisions. 'Survey finds convicted doctors treated leniently' ran the headline the next day in the *Guardian* (12 March 1998).

Dissatisfaction with the way in which disciplinary action was being taken by the GMC had been surfacing periodically for more than a decade. Legislation in 1992 had required the GMC to put in place procedures to deal with 'poor performance' in addition to 'serious professional misconduct'. There were doubts, however, as to how effective it would be and continuing dissatisfaction on matters such as how complaints were handled, the appropriateness of the criteria for decision and sanctions, and the overall accountability of the process. And criticism was clearly gathering pace (Allsop and Mulcahy, 1996). The way in which nursing regulates its members had also been in the headlines. For three years in a row, there had been public as well as professional outrage at a decision taken by the statutory body, the UK Central Council for Nursing Midwifery and Health Visitors (UKCC), to restore the right to practise of a nurse convicted of serious crime (Davies and Beach, 2000).

The year 1998, however, was to prove a particularly bad year for the medical profession. A case concerning the deaths of babies undergoing cardiac surgery at Bristol Royal Infirmary hit the headlines in May and caused a huge outcry. A negligence settlement and a full-scale public inquiry called by the Minister kept the matter in the public eye. A gynaecologist in Kent, struck off the register for harming patients, provoked more shocked public comment. Elsewhere a GP was arrested for allegedly killing a number of elderly patients. In the late autumn, *The Times* ran a leading article arguing that doctors should be subject to independent inspection (17 November 1998). The government, already involved in far-reaching changes to the NHS, underlined the importance of measures to monitor clinical performance and added a clause to the 1999 NHS Bill that would give it the capability to take wide-ranging powers to make changes in the machinery of regulation of the health professions.

How are we to interpret these events? Are they to be seen as a healthy questioning of professional prerogative, part of the decline of deference – a working through of the new social movements' demands for change (as discussed, in for example Chapters 1, 3 and 22 this volume)? Do they therefore mark the decisive break with the post-war era in which the professions, and most notably medicine, were 'indispensable partners in the great national task of reconstruction and, within limits, they were to be trusted and encouraged to apply their expertise for the public good' (Clarke and Newman, 1997, p.7)? Or are such events to be regarded as a continuation under Labour of a project to curb expenditure via control of the professions begun under the managerialism and markets era of the Conservatives? Above all, in a world of fallen heroes, where expertise is no longer taken for granted, and where scientific knowledge is increasingly recognized as provisional and fallible, what is the place of the professions in the policy community and what might it be?

This chapter seeks to bring the presuppositions of *professional self-regulation* (PSR) into stronger focus in the rethinking of social policy. It will draw attention to the nineteenth-century origins of today's institutions. It will trace how the contemporary debate about PSR has taken shape under Tory governments since 1980 and will question the self-evident character of Labour's present 'modernization' project for professions. It will call for a much more sustained examination of the position that professions hold – and might hold in the future – as neither saviours nor scapegoats in a new world of welfare.

2   The nature and origins of PSR

PSR is a set of institutionalized practices whereby an occupational group maintains a register of those it deems qualified to practise in a particular field and itself decides on criteria for admission to and exclusion from that register. The status of the register is confirmed in legislation. Those removed from the register are unable to call themselves registered and in most cases are effectively prevented from practising their profession. Those falsely representing themselves as registered can be taken through a legal process and fined. There are variations here in that the relevant legislation may protect the *function* as in the case of midwifery, the *common title* as in the case of medical practitioner (but not the title of doctor) or the title *registered* (as in registered nurse, state-registered chiropodist and so on).

Regulatory bodies comprise a mix of elected and appointed members, the majority of whom are drawn from the profession in question. They are funded by practitioners who pay registration and, increasingly, periodic re-registration, fees. Currently there are *eight* bodies engaged in the practice of professional self-regulation in the health field in the UK. Each profession has a separate regulatory body, some of which have long been established as in the case of doctors, dentists, opticians and pharmacists; others – for osteopaths and chiropractors – have been created more recently. Nurses and midwives, having started separately, now share a unified regulatory structure and a single body; the Council for Professions Supplementary to Medicine offers a regulatory umbrella for a number of others (including, for example, occupational therapists, physiotherapists and radiographers).

All regulatory bodies set overall standards that the would-be practitioner must reach and in various ways oversee programmes of pre-registration education. All also have ways of reviewing individual cases of misconduct and, where it is deemed appropriate, of removing practitioners from the register. There is considerable variation in the ways in which these bodies act in relation to procedures to maintain standards of practice. The publication of codes of conduct and practice has become common in recent years and the imposition of requirements for evidence of practitioners' actions to update knowledge and skills has become more widespread. The rather stronger notion that practitioners should be required to demonstrate continuing competence to such a body not only presents challenges of implementation but is, not surprisingly, deeply controversial among practitioners themselves.

In terms of legislation, PSR is a patchwork of provision, hard to grasp by those not intimately involved with it. Precise powers, organization of functions and membership arrangements vary between bodies and are widely misunderstood by practitioners, press and public. The crucial assumption of PSR, however, and the one firmly adhered to by regulatory bodies, is that PSR simultaneously provides guardianship of the standards of the profession and protection for the public. This claim to independence, to being 'above the fray' in making decisions in the interests of the community as a whole, is what, in theory at any rate, distinguishes a regulatory body from the professional associations and trade unions with which it is often confused.

PSR needs to be situated in its historical context. When the forerunner of today's GMC was set up in 1858, attention centred on distinguishing between those practitioners who had followed an approved course of preparation and those who had not. The public clearly had an interest in identifying those who could be trusted. The profession equally clearly had an interest in keeping out competitors, hence assuring standards but simultaneously raising its status and rewards. A non-interventionist state was happy to grant such powers to the profession.

PSR was part of a wider project of forging a place for the professions in a changing social order. Professional men (*sic*) increasingly came to see themselves as set apart from capital and labour. They worked independently, commanded a fee for service and developed an elaborate etiquette of location and referral which avoided direct competition among their number. They set store by the knowledge they had acquired; they were self-reliant and disciplined. All this gave them a confident sense of themselves as distant from and morally superior to many of their clients. Professionalism in this sense draws on and affirms a particular nineteenth-century notion of bourgeois masculinity (Davies, 1996).

These ideas gave PSR in medicine a distinct favour. Recruiting the right kind of person to medicine, and schooling the recruit in the correct values, would result in properly professional behaviour. It would only be the exceptional few who would need to be disciplined by their peers and actually removed from the register. Medical education, the business of some of the most respected in the profession, would need little in the way of a steer from the GMC. Judgements about who should join the register and who should be excluded were thus not onerous; business could be conducted on an informal basis by a small elite.

These notions were still distinctly serviceable a century later. A Royal Commission set up to investigate the question of PSR in medicine served to confirm just how much of this model was still intact and to give it considerable further endorsement. PSR, the report explained, was best seen as a contract whereby the profession guarantees to the public that it will provide satisfactory treatment (Merrison Report, 1975, para.4). The work of maintaining the register was regarded as important, not least for the self-respect of members of the profession. To ensure that pre-registration education maintained its relevance, a place needed to be found on the GMC for key staff from the medical schools to take a direct part in formative discussions. There was acceptance that doctors might need some encouragement to keep up to date, but detailed descriptions of duties were felt to be inappropriate and any form of continuous scrutiny was distasteful. It was conceded that there was a place for lay input. Given the complexity of the knowledge base, however, the Commission could not see that any except a very small lay input could be relevant (Davies, 1999).

Inevitably PSR in medicine has changed and developed over time. PSR in other areas of health work was never able to work with quite the same assumptions or enjoy the same degrees of autonomy (see Davies and Beach, 2000). Yet its relevance in vastly changed social circumstances and in altered conditions of employment has to be questioned. Margaret Stacey's term as a lay member of the GMC spanned a period before and after the Royal Commission. She vividly described her sense of being drawn into an elite group, debating weighty matters and fulfilling an important and serious public duty to act in the public interest. She accepted the actions of the members of the GMC as well-meaning. But, writing in the early 1990s, she judged the institution as outmoded and in need of radical reform (Stacey, 1992).

As we shall see, a New Right government determined to take on the professions, chose to put its energies elsewhere. Only towards the end of its lengthy term did a model for change emerge. It was left to New Labour to decide what to do with it.

3   Attending and dis-attending to PSR

The Conservative Party came to power in 1979 with an agenda of cutting public spending, bringing the discipline of business principles into the provision of the full array of health, education, welfare and criminal justice services, and increasing efficiency. The trust which had extended to professionals in all these fields was now in question. Active management, contracting out and competition were to be the watchwords of change. New mechanisms of audit and performance review were put in place. For the first time professionals began to face demands to demonstrate quality and effectiveness. There were different potential sites for this confrontation with the professions. Pressure could have been put on registering bodies to make changes to the nature of pre-registration education, to develop new requirements for continuing registration and perhaps to make non-compliance with audit, for example, a disciplinary offence. In practice, the institutions of PSR, where they existed, were largely left alone and indeed allowed in some instances to expand their reach. There have been different judgements about the degree of success or failure of the project of controlling health professionals in the 1980s and 1990s.

Commentators have variously suggested that new managerialist mechanisms have brought success, stalemate, incorporation, or professional recapture (Pollitt, 1990; Harrison and Pollitt, 1994; Ferlie et al., 1996; Dent, forthcoming). Whatever the assessment, however, the focus of government intervention undoubtedly lay with local managerial control, not with re-examining and reshaping the institutional frameworks of PSR. The issue of self-regulatory institutions moved towards the political agenda in health more than once in the years of Conservative control in the 1980s and 1990s, although far right consumer ideas made little headway (see Stacey, 1992, Ch. 13). It was left aside by a government intent on creating a purchaser/provider split and provider competition as the means of ensuring better value for money in services.

Nursing provides a particularly stark case. A protracted battle for change had reached a crisis in 1979, the very year that the Conservatives came to power. New legislation meant an enlarged statutory structure for the nursing and midwifery professions and powers were given to a regulatory body – the majority of whom were drawn from the profession – to 'improve' practice. It was an opportunity the UKCC took with alacrity, developing a code of practice to underline and foster understanding of personal professional accountability and embarking on a fundamental review of the form of pre-registration education. A hard-fought battle on educational reform ensued, with government seeking a path between hostile employers and the wishes of the regulatory body. Yet government not only agreed to postpone its first quinquennial review under the 1979 Act until the UKCC had completed its work, it also set terms of reference which explicitly ruled out any questioning of the principle of self-regulation and ultimately agreed to changes which included strengthening the accountability of the central body to the profession (Peat, Marwick and McLintock, 1989). Nor were opportunities to challenge PSR in medicine taken. Nothing was done, for example, to build on the Monopolies Commission report on restrictive practices in 1988, nor, in an age of consumer rhetoric, to address the consumer-based challenge to GMC practices that came from the organization Health Rights (see Stacey, 1992). The NHS and Community Care Act of 1990 remained silent on the structures for self-regulation of the health professions.

There was no doubt, however, that the statutory bodies were a thorn in the side of a New Right government at this time. Take the matter of training. The establishment of national and Scottish vocational qualifications in 1986 signalled an ambitious, all-encompassing vision of clearly defined levels of qualifications from the most humble to the most advanced. Links and ladders would allow individuals to progress in their chosen spheres. Most importantly, employers would take the lead in defining competencies and outcomes, and learning would be strongly work-based. The professions were not untouched – clearer specification of learning objectives and outcomes started to emerge in curriculum planning. In the main, however, they were distinctly hostile, seeing a wilful disregard of their crucial role in underpinning theoretical knowledge, and a desire to reduce professional expertise to a series of discrete skills and provide substitute cheap labour. Working with the regulatory bodies in health on these matters proved frustratingly slow. In social work, by contrast, where there was no statutory regulatory machinery, notwithstanding vociferous critics, a shorter, competency-based programme of initial education was put in place (Weinstein, 1998). Following the NHS and Community Care Act 1990, regional educational consortia were established in the health field, holding the purse-strings for professional education in areas other than medicine, negotiating with education providers as to types of programme the service needed and numbers who would be funded to complete them. Placing such measures alongside managerialist moves towards tighter performance control – amending consultants' contracts and putting them in the hands of trusts, promoting audit, quality assurance and risk management, for example – it would seem that the Conservative government was not confronting PSR head-on; instead, it was *bypassing* it.

4   Owning and disowning a debate

By the mid-1990s, several new groups were anxious to be included in the regulatory machinery of the Council for Professions Supplementary to Medicine (CPSM). The Council itself was also concerned that its legislation was far out of date, that procedures for disciplining members lagged behind those for medicine and nursing and that there was no easy way of taking forward the growing pressures to ensure that practitioners updated themselves and engaged in continuing professional development. A review of the legislation concerning the professions supplementary to medicine was commissioned by the NHS Executive. JM Consulting started work in July 1995, publishing their report eight months later. For the first time in almost twenty years there was an opportunity to address the concept of PSR directly

– albeit not directly in relation to the most powerful of the health professions, medicine (JM Consulting, 1996).

Finding no clear way forward in the myriad of comments emerging from their consultation, JM aimed to 'reassess the purpose and principles which should guide this type of professional regulation for the coming period' (JM Consulting, 1996, para.11). They recognized that regulation was costly and had drawbacks, and that there were other ways of ensuring standards – through consumer law, complaints machinery and inspection, for example. Only when there were invasive procedures or where unsupervised judgements impacted on health and welfare was there a case for PSR. Protection of the public was the paramount purpose of such regulation and questions of safety should be uppermost. The key problems with current practice were threefold. The register was not acting as a sufficiently powerful tool (although the NHS had agreed to employ only registered practitioners, neither GP fund-holders nor the private sector was compelled to do so). The statutory agencies had lost focus and were drifting into work more properly done elsewhere. The central body, the CPSM, was dominated by its uni-professional boards.

The recommendations which flowed from this included a stronger protection of title, the handing over of the setting of 'aspirational standards' as well as the production of codes to professional associations. Also recommended was a pulling back from detailed accreditation of educational programmes now that these were in the higher education sector. Employers needed to make explicit use of the register, but they also needed the freedom to make changes to working relationships and working practices: it was concluded that regulatory bodies had been wrongly inflexible about this, and that isssues about helper grades were better handled by employers. Also strongly recommended was the creation of an umbrella regulatory body: individual professions had been 'reinventing the wheel' and making idiosyncratic decisions, so it would be more efficient were an overarching Council of Health Professions to take a more strategic view. The Council should include consumer, employer, other professions and lay elements, reducing the power of the individual regulated professions and of the medical profession, which historically had had so strong a role.

Although JM had endorsed the concept of regulation, and continued to refer to PSR throughout, 'state of the art' regulation, as they called it, repositioned PSR dramatically. They were recommending limiting the scope of regulation and changing the participants in it. In effect, they were taking the 'self' out of self-regulation – making a shift from statutorily supported PSR to the statutory regulation of professions. Professions were no longer to be accorded the place they had had in regulating their own affairs. The report was released and endorsed by government in July 1996 with a commitment to work on the detailed drafting of a Bill and to consult interested parties further on this. Nothing emerged, however, before a change of government on 1 May the following year.

Three months on, Labour appointed the same firm of consultants to carry out the second quinquennial review of nursing legislation then due. In January 1998 the interim report revealed thinking on similar lines (JM Consulting, 1998). It looked as if the consultants would again judge that a statutory body had strayed from its paramount purpose of public protection. Once again, there was a vision of a smaller strategic body with a balance of relevant interests beyond the profession, taking an overall view. When the report finally emerged this was confirmed. There was the possibility of protecting the common title of nurse and a strong statement that, for public protection, the register had to mean something. The consultants recommended that registration and renewal of registration be accompanied by a number of things including a statement of good character, a satisfactory result of police checks, evidence of continuing professional development and written acceptance of the code of conduct. The Central Council was to be small and have one-third lay membership. It should commission work rather than carrying it out itself. Its independence from central government was seen as important. This seemed to affirm the correctness of the way in which, as a result of information emerging at disciplinary hearings, it had seen fit to remonstrate with the health authorities and with the government about policies that were unworkable or under-resourced (Davies and Beach, 2000). The nursing report was more detailed and included much about setting and monitoring standards in relation to practice education and conduct (JM Consulting, undated). The emerging clarity of vision of the first report was perhaps more blurred here, yet the challenge to self-regulation was still apparent.

Would the government take the opportunity to bring the two reports together – to reposition PSR and perhaps even create a single council for all the health professions? JM's second report was available to government in the summer of 1998. Doctors had distanced themselves from these reports on regulatory reform, but in the midst of the bad press year for medicine described at the outset of this chapter, government could perhaps have taken a radical view. However, this was also the moment when the detail of Labour's new framework for ensuring quality of clinical services was being unveiled (Department of Health, 1998a). With national service frameworks, a new National Institute for Clinical Excellence, the Commission for Health Improvement and clinical governance at local provider level, the report landed on a crowded regulatory table. Finding legislative time would be problematic – and a number of the recommendations bumped up against debates about and plans for devolution. JM's report on PSR was not released until the following February. It emerged with an announcement that powers would be taken in the forthcoming Health Bill to make adjustments to the statutory regulation of professions. No great debate was envisaged. The professions would be consulted but change could come through the mechanism of an Order in Council and hence would not need to be debated on the floor of the House of Commons.

Thus both Conservative and Labour governments have relegated PSR to the sidelines of reform. As in the previous period, new layers of control were again being added to old (cf. Allsop and Mulcahy, 1996); PSR seemed set to be changed without being directly challenged. A rationale for reform that would reposition professions, designing institutions that would begin to bring them down from above the fray into the fray, went unheeded.

5   An alternative in the air?

A new model of regulation had also begun to take shape in the early 1990s in the field of social services. Professional practice had always been contested and social workers had never agreed upon or achieved PSR in the form it had developed in health. With a different history, there was more of a clean regulatory slate to write upon. Fostered by the Joseph Rowntree Foundation and growing under the umbrella of the National Institute for Social Work (NISW), a wide-ranging review was undertaken (Parker, 1990). Ideas then developed in the hands of a specially constituted action group. This group engaged in a deliberate process of consensus-building among what they saw as the key stakeholders – employers, unions, professional and educational bodies – to develop the concept of a General Social Services Council (GSSC). These plans were rejected by a Conservative government late in its term of office, but were further refined and presented to New Labour (Brand, 1998).

At the heart of this model of regulation is a vision of a body that will act as 'watchdog, advocate and source of information and advice', exerting 'continual and concerted pressure' for the improvement of standards in the care field (Parker, 1990, p.119). Classic PSR's idea of a register is turned on its head. Instead of policing admission through restrictive education and training criteria, the GSSC (subject to agreed vetting procedures) is to include all those in the care workforce, progressively working to promote adherence to its standards, upgrade training, and exclude from practice those shown to be unsuitable. The model envisages standards of conduct – broad and relatively long-lasting statements of values set out in a code, and standards of practice – statements specific to settings, user groups, and levels. Both the standards of conduct and those of practice would

286 RETHINKING SOCIAL POLICY

be regularly updated and would be influenced by both research and public opinion. The GSSC will work to create consistency between its own practice standards, developed in consultation with stakeholders, and the more employer-led occupational standards and those set through the inspection process and by government. It will seek their incorporation into standards of training and qualification and enforce them by the use of powers to exclude from the register.

It is vital for this model that the GSSC is both an independent agency, and comprises all the relevant interests – users, employers, practitioners, educationalists – working together to create and enforce viable standards. The Council 'should operate in ways which users find empowering and not stigmatizing, restrictive, oppressive or otherwise disempowering' (NISW, 1997, p.4) and should model good practice in promoting equal opportunity in all aspects of its work. The model entails a particularly important role for the GSSC in public education. Recognizing that practitioners often tackle 'complex ethical dilemmas where public opinion is uncertain or divided', it identifies a specific task for the new regulatory body to acknowledge this and foster greater public confidence and understanding. It refers to the growing body of research evidence and practice in areas such as mental health, care of older people, child care and adolescent development, which could be of day-to-day benefit to the wider public. Both information-giving and challenge are envisaged:

> Public attitudes have a significant impact on the treatment and wellbeing of service users, and on the morale of those who practise in the social services. Much of the development of good practice requires the public's active consent and support. There may be a need to address public attitudes which contribute to discrimination and social exclusion, to the disadvantage of service users. (NISW, 1997, p.14)

From the earliest days, professional regulation has been presented as protecting the public. Here, however, there is a significant reversal. Where classic PSR starts with the importance of members of the profession guarding the standards of the profession and thereby protecting the public, this model starts with protection of the public, which, if done effectively will enhance the reputation of those working in the field. Furthermore, the GSSC model involves a concept of *a grown-up public* – not necessarily in possession of up-to-date knowledge and research in the field, but open to and interested in it. The task of the GSSC then becomes both to reflect public opinion in practice standards and also to help shape and change it. The centrality of development through dialogue with stakeholders, together with inclusiveness and a commitment to work towards consistency with other standards-making and enforcing agencies, all mark this model out both from classic PSR and from the emerging models of reformed PSR in the health field discussed above. No one should underestimate the learning that would need to take place on the part of all stakeholders – not least the professions – in making a reality of this form of regulation. But these developments represent the clearest statement to date of what a transformed vision of professional regulation might be and how it might work in practice.

The Labour government's response is contained in the White Paper *Modernising Social Services* (Department of Health, 1998b). There is a clear commitment to the establishment of a council (now a General Social *Care* Council not a General Social *Services* Council). In part this acknowledges the recommendations. There is acceptance that existing regulatory models are not appropriate, and there is endorsement of a lay majority and lay chair. Government, however, has not accepted a one-step, inclusive body and proposes only to register different categories of staff once qualifications and training become established for a substantial proportion of staff. It makes much of arrangements for training, prioritizes a new training strategy and offers funds for it. New arrangements for inspection overshadow the GSCC and are not linked to it in a clear way. There is no time-table; the Council will be set up as the legislative timetable allows. Concerns about cost figure large. In all, the coherence and novelty, the excitement of the vision of new-style regulation, are not reflected in the White Paper. Furthermore, the unity around that vision in some areas is faltering. With the strong education and qualification remit of the government's model, some of those involved in the present regime of oversight of social work qualifications are begin-ning to question whether the lay emphasis is viable (see *Community Care*, 25 February 1999, 4 March 1999). White Papers in Scotland (Scottish Office, 1999) and Wales (Welsh Office, 1999), and a consul-tation paper in Northern Ireland (DHSS NI, 1998) hint, however, that with devolution things could be different.

6   Conclusion

The decisions and actions of doctors, nurses, therapists and social workers can often be life-changing ones for people who are vulnerable and ill-placed to question and challenge. The day-to-day work of others in the care team can equally have life-enhancing or life-diminishing consequences for service users. How, then, are we to secure high-quality, relevant services, delivered with competence, courtesy and concern? Nineteenth-century professional self-regulation gave an answer which is now deeply outmoded. It conceived of professionals as part of an elite group, on a higher moral plane than the rest of us, who, by dint of this could almost always be relied upon to act in our interests. It regarded those professionals as independent practitioners, working solo, not in teams, and untrammelled by today's dependence on others for equipment, technical and clerical support and all the other resources that make modern care delivery possible. Knowledge was not developing at a frenetic pace; an initial education served the practitioner longer and better than it does today.

Late twentieth-century governments, intent on root and branch reform of public sector services, proved reluctant to confront PSR. Labour's reforms in health and social care retain regulation at the centre rather than seeing a role for intermediary bodies of the kind that reconstituted professional regulation might entail. By a process of accretion, we now regulate persons, programmes and places. Little surprise, then, if consumers feel confused and professionals feel embattled.

And yet present in the multiple and conflicting proposals for reform is the imagining of a new policy space, in which there is a greater potential to recognize interdependence and foster new articulations of need (cf. Chapter 22 this volume). Its further development requires the constitution not only of new welfare subjects but also of new welfare professionals – able to articulate a place which is a key place, but not pride of place in the debate. We have cause to mourn not the demise of PSR but the limbo life to which it has been condemned – and the lost opportunity for rethinking regulatory policy that this represents.

References

Allsop, J. and Mulcahy, L. (1996) *Regulating Medical Work: Formal and Informal Controls*, Buckingham, Open University Press.

Brand, D. (1998) 'Regulation and the prospects for professions', *Managing Community Care*, 6, December (supplementary issue), pp.43–6.

Clarke, J. and Newman, J. (1997) *The Managerial State: Power, Politics and Ideology in the Remaking of Social Welfare*, London, Sage.

Davies, C. (1996) 'The sociology of professions and the profession of gender', *Sociology*, 30 (4), pp.661–78.

Davies, C. (1999) 'Rethinking regulation in the health professions in the UK: institutions, ideals and identities', in Hellberg, I., Saks, M. and Benoit, C. (eds) *Professional Identities in Transition*, Gothenburg, University of Gothenburg/Swedish Humanities and Social Sciences Research Council.

Davies, C. and Beach, A. (2000) *Professional Self-Regulation: A History of the UKCC, 1969–1998*, London, Routledge.

Dent, M. (forthcoming) 'Hospitals and new ways of organising medical work in Europe', in Thompson, P. and Warhurst, C. (eds) *Workplaces of the Future*, Basingstoke, Macmillan.

Department of Health (1998a) *A First Class Service: Quality in the New NHS*, London, Department of Health.

Department of Health (1998b) *Modernising Social Services: Promoting Independence, Improving Protection, Raising Standards*, Cm 4169, London, Department of Health.

Department of Health and Social Services, Northern Ireland (1998) *Fit for the Future: A New Approach*, Belfast, DHSS.

Ferlie, E., Ashburner, L., Fitzgerald, L. and Pettigrew, A. (1996) *The New Public Management in Action*, Oxford, Oxford University Press.

Harrison, S. and Pollitt, C. (1994) *Controlling Health Professionals*, Buckingham, Open University Press.

JM Consulting Ltd (1996) *The Regulation of the Health Professions: A Review of the Professions Supplementary to Medicine Act (1960) with Recommendations for New Legislation*, Bristol, JM Consulting Ltd.

JM Consulting Ltd (1998) *The Regulation of Nurses, Midwives and Health Visitors: Invitation to Comment on Issues Raised by a Review of the Nurses, Midwives and Health Visitors Act 1997*, Bristol, JM Consulting Ltd.

JM Consulting Ltd (undated) *Report on a Review of the Nurses, Midwives and Health Visitors Act 1997*, Bristol, JM Consulting Ltd.

Merrison Report (1975) *Report of the Committee of Inquiry into the Regulation of the Medical Profession* (Chairman Dr A.W. Merrison FRS), Cmnd 6018, London, HMSO.

National Institute for Social Work GSSC Implementation Group (1997) *General Social Services Council: Principles and Concepts*, London, NISW.

Parker, R. (1990) *Safeguarding Standards*, London, NISW/J. Rowntree Memorial Trust.

Peat, Marwick and McLintock (1989) *Review of the United Kingdom Central Council and the Four National Boards for Nursing, Midwifery and Health Visiting*, commissioned by Department of Health, Scottish Home and Health Department, Welsh Office, Department of Health and Social Services, Northern Ireland.

Pollitt, C. (1990) *Managerialism and the Public Services: The Anglo-American Experience*, Oxford, Blackwell.

Scottish Office (1999) *Aiming for Excellence: Modernising Social Work Services in Scotland*, Cm 4288, Edinburgh, The Stationery Office.

Stacey, M. (1992) *Regulating British Medicine: The General Medical Council*, Chichester, Wiley.

Weinstein, J. (1998) 'The use of national occupational standards in professional education', *Journal of Interprofessional Care*, 12 (2), pp.169–79.

Welsh Office (1999) *Social Services, Building for the Future: A White Paper for Wales*, Cm 4051, Cardiff, The Stationery Office.

19

Exchange and the Metaphor of Exchange: Economic Cultures in Social Care

Maureen Mackintosh

1 Introduction: economics, discourse and social care

This chapter is intended to contribute to the development of a social constructionist economics of social policy. The core of the chapter is a discussion of some research on 'economic cultures' in social care contracting in the mid-1990s.[1] The discussion concentrates as much on methodology as on results, and aims to show that integrating the analysis of culture and discourse into a particular kind of institutional economics can add to our understanding of care contracting processes. At the same time, the chapter suggests that this methodology

opens a way of applying a social constructionist approach to economic
analysis for social policy, and examines some limitations of existing
economics of 'quasi-markets'.

By 'economics' in this context, I mean the study of the ownership,
transfer and use of money and material resources. This includes the
study of how markets work, how production of goods and services is
organized, and how capital is accumulated and invested in production. It is not, of course, only economists who are interested in
these matters, but this is nevertheless the particular terrain of economics. In this chapter, the element of 'economics' is the concern to
understand market dynamics: that is, the way in which markets and
contracting relationships develop a logic of their own which shapes
economic outcomes in terms of who receives what type of services at
what cost.

2 Contracting and exchange in social care

The research project I am discussing set out to bring the analysis
of culture and discourse into the economics of so-called 'quasi-
markets'.[2] That concept, which originates in the economic analysis of
trading relations within private firms, was imported into the analysis
of public sector reform in 1980s and 1990s Britain (Le Grand and
Bartlett, 1993). It refers to the introduction of trading processes – that
is, the exchange of specified activities or outputs for cash – into
working relationships which were not previously understood as
relationships of exchange in this sense. Examples include contracts
for service within public sector bodies between fund-holding 'purchasers' and service 'providers'; the contracting-out of service provision to commercial firms or non-profit organizations; competitive
tendering to provide public services; and repeat contracting by public
authorities for services to individuals from approved lists of external
suppliers.

There are a variety of reasons why such exchange processes might
be characterized as 'quasi'-market rather than simply market
exchange. The contractual relations they create are in many cases
not legally binding: for example, the contracts between central
services, such as Finance, and service departments, such as Social
Services, within local authorities, and the NHS contracts between
health authorities and trusts. Competition is often very limited in
practice, as is the freedom of public authorities to set the contractual
terms of exchange with outside bodies (Walsh, 1995).

However, despite the widespread doubts about whether these
reforms created 'markets', the reforms brought with them a forced
transfer of the *language* of markets and business into the public
sector. However audible or visible the quotation marks, practitioners

have come to employ the language of 'internal markets', 'contracts', 'business units', 'prices', and 'surplus' or 'deficit', as well as 'competitors' and 'customers'. This imposed vocabulary of markets and business ran alongside – but was not the same as – the managerialist vocabulary of quality, responsiveness and customer service (Clarke and Newman, 1997). The two vocabularies overlap particularly in the language of unit costs, cost control, marketing and output measures. Practitioners play around with these vocabularies, distancing themselves from them and using them strategically and as a tool of power; but over time the market language does seem to be becoming naturalized, used more easily and descriptively.

Sociologists have studied some of this transferred vocabulary, notably the use of 'quality' and 'customer', and the managerialist language of empowerment and control (du Gay, 1994; Clarke and Newman, 1997). Economists, however, have on the whole analysed the reformed structures 'as if' they displayed processes of market exchange, while cautioning that competition and information flows were very limited (for example Propper and Bartlett, 1997 for the NHS, Wistow et al., 1996 on social care). Some sociologists studying contracting have also used the contracts and trading language as descriptive: for example, treating the designation of people as 'purchasers' or 'providers' as facts about their roles, despite noting much collaborative activity in practice (Flynn et al., 1997).

The project I describe here began from a rejection of this traditional starting-point of quasi-market and contracting research that accepted the market language as descriptive, in favour of paying specific attention to how the shift to the market language, particularly the more technical economic language of costs, prices, competition and contract, was interacting with behavioural changes in the use of resources within the public sector.

3   Economics without the metaphor of exchange

This theoretical move represents a substantial shift away from the perspective of most economic analysis. Mainstream economics is strongly – though not completely – dominated by what I will call the 'metaphor of exchange'. That is, it tends to analyse all economic relationships *as if* they were processes of exchanging something for something (usually particular qualities and quantities of goods or labour services for money), whether or not the participants in those relationships construe them in this way. Economists have been continually extending this approach to new areas. Relationships between workers and managers within public and non-state sectors, between regulators and regulated, between members of co-operatives, between husbands and wives, adults and their parents, are all now commonly analysed in the economic literature as something-for-something contractual exchange.

The 'quasi-market' literature falls into this tradition, accepting the designation of relationships between institutions and people in the reformed public sector as 'contracts'. This economic concept of 'contract' encompasses implicit understandings and incomplete agreements as well as explicit signed documents, and the quasi-market literature emphasizes the reliance within the public sector on such 'soft' or 'relational' contracting allowing adaptation to changing circumstance.

A methodological difficulty with this framework is that it obscures the process of transition *to* markets. A *general* economic framework that construes economic relationships within the public sector (as elsewhere) as contractual exchange will rewrite a particular *shift* to explicitly labelled exchange (or contractual) relationships as merely a change in the form of exchange. Such a rewriting obscures the issue of why the relabelling of relationships *as* exchange might change outcomes. In order to ask in what sense 'quasi'-market relationships are – or are not – becoming more 'market-like', we need to avoid imposing upon the evidence an analytical framework with an embedded market discourse.

That was what the study I am discussing set out to do, in an exploratory kind of way. It aimed to examine directly how 'market-like' local government services were becoming, through an exploration of economic discourse and its role in institutional change in a set of case studies in two authorities. The theoretical framework drew on 'old' institutional economics, as it is being reworked by some economists interested in evolutionary economic change (Hodgson, 1993). This sort of economic theory is not based in methodological individualism, but admits non-individualist aspects of economic systems, such as cultural norms, as explanatory variables. The definition of 'institution' in this kind of economics includes norms *as* institutions, and focuses on how such norms are established and changed.

The analysis of discourse in the project drew on anthropological work on institutions and organizations, and on discursive analysis by political and organization theorists. I use the concept of 'discourse' as a mutually consistent set of meanings, shared by (some) participants in a particular context. Dryzek (1996, p.109) suggests that a 'politically interesting' discourse will include an ontology, ascription of agency and motive, and some taken-for-granted relationships.

This political theorist's concept of a 'discourse' is recognizably similar to the anthropologist Mary Douglas' concept of a 'thought world' (Douglas, 1987). Douglas sees institutions as encompassing both a thought world or 'cognitive community' of people working with shared meanings, and also the power relations and behaviour understood and sustained through those meanings. She particularly emphasizes the importance of the taken-for-granted or 'naturalized' nature of institutionalized relationships: social conventions become institutions once they take on an apparently 'natural' status and so long as they appear to have a grounding in reason (that is, they are not too arbitrary or transparent). Institutions 'settle' once people find ideas reinforced by experience, and then come to have moral force: they 'make' big ethical decisions for us.

4 'Economic culture' in social care

The project applied this approach to institutional behaviour and change to case studies of the supposed shift to more market-like relationships. The cases relevant to social care included contracting for domiciliary, respite and day care, and residential care; internal trading between central services and main service departments; and the creation of 'business units' within service departments including Social Services.[3] We interviewed officers, from directors to staff providing services, and also managers of partner and contracting organizations. We read documents and attended meetings. We did not talk to service users.

The interviews sought to elicit explanatory narratives of *economic behaviour*: that is, behaviour that uses and allocates material resources. For example, we asked for stories about how prices were set for services, and for whom and on what basis; how tenders were costed and priced; how 'unit costs' were calculated (or guessed at); how competitors (if any) were identified and responded to; how it was decided what services were to be provided (or 'commissioned') and for whom; how decisions were made about what wages to set and whom to employ; how 'business units' were designated and how people in them went about trying to raise revenue or make profits; what services were closed down; and why access to services was granted or refused.

Like all case-study narratives, these include contradictory statements about what happened and why; competing interpretations of motivation and differing explanations; and also cross-checkable statements such as the prices charged to particular people or units, the closure of particular services, or the deficit run by particular units given the accounting conventions.

These narratives were then used as data for the analysis of *economic discourse*. The analysis looked within and across the case studies for shared and competing meanings of key economic terms, and then for sets of consistent meanings of a range of terms, with the aim of seeing whether different and competing discourses (or 'thought worlds') could be identified. The analysis draws upon the use of metaphor, analogy, recurrent narratives and repeated tropes as evidence of sense-making by interviewees. In this framework, concepts of trading and exchange, discussed in this chapter, are just some among many economic concepts that interviewees use as both description and metaphor.

Finally, I use *economic culture* to refer to the mutual interactions of economic behaviour and economic discourse. An economic culture is thus a set of mutually reinforcing economic ideas – or meanings – and forms of behaviour. Neither 'economic behaviour' nor 'economic culture' is currently a standard term in economic analysis even in its institutional variant, and this concept of an institutionalized economic culture is the key link between the methodology of the research and its objectives. I use it here to analyse some aspects of the institutionalization – in Mary Douglas' sense – of the new structures in social care. In other words, I am exploring their economic dynamics: how are expectations of behaviour emerging and becoming stabilized and legitimized, and what does that tell us about the economic implications of the new orders(s)? Are different identifiable types of so-called 'quasi-markets', with different economic implications, emerging from these contested reforms?

5   'Shopping' for social care

Having abandoned the imposition of the metaphor of exchange as a way of analysing a range of varied economic relationships, we set out instead to analyse the way in which interviewees thought about exchange. We looked for recurrent metaphors and similes characterizing some activities – but not others – as trading or exchange. Here are a few of the results from the case studies of social care contracting.

'Contracting' carries a very strong implication of exchange, so case studies of something designated formally as 'contracting' tell us how participants deal discursively with this labelling of working relationships as exchange. A recurrent trope in discussing contracting processes was to characterize some types of contracting behaviour as 'shopping'; this occurred in two contexts.

The first was in contracting for domiciliary care (Mackintosh, 1997a). Some interviewees used 'shopping' images to describe the choice by a social worker, from an approved list, of a supplier of a specified number of hours of care for a client (called 'spot' contracting by some managers). This shopping image was used with a variety of evaluative intents. Two interviewees used it positively. One was a local authority contracts officer, with a commercial training; the other a manager of a commercial care supplier. Both were describing a company feeling in control of its purchases from suppliers; this is the supplier:

if you are a company, and you want to buy something off another company, you look around for a company with a good track record, ring them up and say, what is your price for one of those? . . . That basis is wonderful.

Negative uses of shopping analogies were more common in domiciliary care. A number drew on the lack of control a retail shopper has of what is available. This, for example, is a local authority contracts manager:

So it's not just going into Woolworths and saying, I want twelve Christmas crackers, this will do, but actually saying, what kind of Christmas crackers do I want?

An owner of a small private residential and domiciliary care firm expressed similar sentiments: 'You are not selling bars of soap, are you?'

All of these interviewees used 'shopping' to mean arm's-length buying of pre-specified items; two found that an appropriate framework for organizing the supply of domiciliary care; others did not. One objector wanted more scope to specify what she wanted; the other wanted more relationship with the person paying for the care: 'I like to think of myself as part of the team' (with the social workers).

The second context of 'shopping' imagery was the case study of internal trading within a local authority, in (acrimonious) debates between central services, such as Finance, and departments such as Social Services (Mackintosh, 1997b). Managers in Social Services (as in Housing and Education) sought to use internal 'trading' (the corporate documents always put the concept in inverted commas) to reduce their expenditure on services from Personnel and Finance. They wanted an 'internal invoice' to allow them to see what they were paying for and to pay only for what they thought they needed.

In both authorities, corporate and Finance department officers fought back using shopping metaphors:

Finance manager: . . . some departments are more prone to playing shops than others.
Q: What do you mean by that? What's 'playing shops'?
Finance manager: Well, it means they charge you as soon as they pick up the phone . . . because they think it's commercial and business-like.

In this exchange, a Finance manager is disparaging a retail trading image of commercial behaviour within the public sector, seeking to undermine the confidence of the invoicing demand from the main service departments.

These examples illustrate three major discursive strategies in the interviews towards the construction of working relationships as trading relations within and across the boundaries of the council. The first strategy was to embrace this, accepting the 'shopping' framework. The second was to accept that an exchange, or contractual, relationship existed, but to try to redefine it: here 'shopping' images describe the rejected approach. The third strategy was to reject the whole exchange metaphor head on. Finance officers were particularly willing to do this, refusing to label the internal working processes between departments as invoicing, contracting or trading:

> Q: Would you ditch the trading language if you could?
> *Finance officer*: If it implies that SLA [service level agreements] equals contracts for service at a price, then yes.

6 'Free' trade

Trading and exchange are powerful images. Trading is often seen as a solvent of personal and social relationships, and as a source of power and change. This is part of its attraction: it carries associations with freedom from constraint. Two groups of social care interviewees drew links between exchange and freedom.

The first were lower-level Social Services managers running facilities redesignated as business units. These managers had an acute sense of loss of control: they saw themselves as facing cheaper external competitors within a price-competitive commissioning process:

> Q: What do you have a sense is going to happen?
> *Social services manager*: That, um, well I suppose the inevitable, that we will eventually close down.
> Q: Why is that?
> *Social services manager*: Because I think we are going to be too costly.

Many managers responded to this sense of powerlessness by seeking more 'business freedoms': to change employees' terms and conditions, lower wages, supply services for payment outside the council, and control their own budgets. The demand for internal invoices, just described, formed part of this strategy.

The second group associating trading with freedom were the private (commercial) sector domiciliary care suppliers (Mackintosh, forthcoming). One large company's marketing manager firmly located his firm's activity as individual exchange with clients:

> all the care in the community contracting is really an extension of private patients at home, because that is in effect what they are. It just so happens they aren't paying their own bills.

He, like the smaller firms' proprietors interviewed, wanted to be able to pick and choose clients, and to be able to say, of those he thought too difficult, 'No, I can't manage that one.' This was why he preferred the authority to take a fairly arm's-length, 'shopping' approach to care contracting.

The association between exchange and freedom was thus offered by interviewees who also understood social care contracting (whether they liked it or not) as buying standard items – domiciliary care hours, or respite and nursing-home bed days, or day care days – for cash. The same people expected to see social care provision increasingly organized by commercial firms selling standardized services; and they tended to expect in-house provision to survive only in areas that private providers avoided. They accepted (like it or not) that competition was largely on price (Mackintosh, 1997a), and would tend to drive out higher-cost provision. I will label this set of associated meanings around social care contracting as a 'trading' discourse.

7   'Providers' and 'purchasers'

Interviewees using many elements of this trading discourse did not, of course, generally see these meanings as unproblematic. Local authority officers shared with private sector contractors the view that the 'trading' or the 'market' in care operated between themselves: the person requiring care (whom *no one* called a 'customer') was not on one 'side' or the other of the market. (The quotation above, asserting that the user was 'in effect' a private patient, was part of an argument about how trading with the council should be organized, not a discussion of how clients should be treated.) But if the trading is between organizations, how *does* the client fit into this 'trading' discourse?

The moment you ask that question, the neat distinction between 'purchaser' or 'commissioner' and 'provider' in this discourse starts to disintegrate. One difficulty is the assessment process: the access gate for the client. No one interviewed thought that the assessment process was – or even could be – independent of the providers. Social workers, for example, relied on in-house providers to advise on home care needs:

> Q: You're partly treating your own provider as a purchaser, that is, the supervisors are wearing two hats?
> *Social worker*: Well, that's right.

Neither authority had the resources to reassess frequently. Local authority staff – social workers, contracts officers, commissioners, provider managers – all knew that the quality of social care depended on the providers' relationship to the clients, and that monitoring was necessarily very inadequate.[4]

Interviewees who used the trading discourse to discuss social care contracting thus knew that their categories did not map on to the government-defined 'purchaser–provider split'. The government framework at the time was not, in a straightforward sense, implementable: it could not be made sense of in terms of the market language in which it was couched. Knowing this, people employed the partial sense-making strategy of the trading discourse for a variety of specific purposes. Commercial suppliers used the distancing between supplier and 'shopper' to help to justify rejecting expensive clients. Contracts officers saw the tendering framework as a protection against accusations of impropriety, and a way – even if flawed – to look for value for money. For social workers buying domiciliary care 'hours', it expressed the practice of stretching their budgets by choosing the cheapest.

All parties knew that the visible downward pressure on prices, and the likely downward pressure on quality, from the trading behaviour thus described was a problem for clients. Social workers reacted as shoppers do: paying attention to suppliers' reputation, using informal information, checking suppliers' behaviour when they could, trying to build up stable working relationships with private firms that would discourage the worst kinds of instrumental behaviour by contractors. A contracts officer who started out expressing confidence in the tendering system said, when pressed, that in fact she would prefer to deal with just a few firms, since that would make 'working with them' on quality easier. The commercial firms complained about being undercut by cheaper rivals, but they did not want closer working relations with the authorities. In-house 'provider' managers were the most fatalistic: they knew they were playing a mixed purchaser/ provider role and they did not expect their jobs to survive.

8   Contracting without trading?

Within the same set of social care contracting interviews – and dealing with the same domiciliary care contracting problem – there is a second and distinct economic discourse. This is the second strategy alluded to in section 4 and I will call it the 'partnership' discourse: accepting that a contracting relationship of some kind exists but redefining or minimizing the extent of 'exchange' or 'trading' within it.

The interviewees who took this approach included some who also used the trading discourse. Here is one thoughtful social care contracts manager worrying about defining her role in a 'market' framework:

> We are actually acting as the intermediary, which is the market demand if you like, and it isn't, it shouldn't be, as straightforward as, you know, going to the supermarket . . . because we are supposed to be developmental and moving with the times, and I don't think the market is such that it is going to develop new ideas itself . . . it is not going to work in that straightforward commercial market way. I think we have to do some developmental work and involve providers in thinking it out.

In this reflection the 'market' shifts from including the council – the 'demand' side, or the market 'intermediary' – to referring to providers outside the council who are not going to develop what the council wants to buy. 'Straightforward' seems to mean not requiring the council's involvement in designing provision. 'Developmental work' means collaboration between the council and outside providers, which in turn means moving away from the 'market'.

The involvement of providers – in innovation, in specification, in continuing dialogue, and in taking explicit joint responsibility for clients – is the theme that holds together the alternative discursive approach to social care contracting. In these two authorities, all the relevant initiatives were with non-profit organizations as partners.[5]

In discussing 'partnership' approaches, interviewees sought to redefine the exchanges involved in care contracting to move away from buying individual items of service. The authority was still seen as exchanging a given sum of money for a given amount of service, but both the meaning of the funds, and the form in which they were given, changed. A 'block' contract, guaranteeing a given sum of money, allowed the cash to function like an investment, to support a specified level of service capacity. The contract could even function as an asset, allowing the provider or joint venture to raise a bank loan (Mackintosh, forthcoming). Here is a local authority officer describing a housing-with-care scheme:

> It's a partnership between us and the housing association. The housing association owns the land and we had the cheque book for paying for the domiciliary care. What we are doing is getting a contract for two years for someone to come in and provide domiciliary care to these people . . . and the amount of service people get obviously varies.

In trying to develop partnership-style working relationships, people really struggled with the notion of 'contract'. The 'contract culture' meant an arm's-length tendering process that could block collaborative innovation, because the dialogue such collaboration required was disallowed: 'that's about collusion and inside information and, um, reaching certain competitive requirements'. On the other hand: 'Partnership arrangements *are* contracts, where we actually share our skill resource to help stimulate and develop initiatives within the community sector.'

9   Collaboration and control

The discourse of 'partnership' thus moved away from the vocabulary of buying and selling to a language of sharing and joint action. This discursive move explicitly accepted a provider role in determining on a day-to-day basis the service provided to a group of clients: this is what the speaker just quoted meant by 'the amount of service people get obviously varies'. The 'obviously' seeks to create an air of normality around the fact that the local authority is allowing the housing association to determine the varying allocation of care among its residents and to monitor both its quantity and quality. The housing association would only question the initiating exchange of (block) local authority cash for care services if they felt the total had become insufficient for their residents.

This working relationship had advantages for the housing associations, in that it provided them with substantial control over the projects. The voluntary sector managers interviewed were strikingly willing to take on this role, with its associated financial and political risks (Mackintosh, forthcoming). An economist determined to apply the theoretical 'metaphor of exchange' to this project could see it as the council exchanging financial and management control for risk and cost reduction. But the interviewees did not see it that way. They saw themselves as having reduced the contractual – in the sense of specified exchange – element of the relationship and having replaced it with collaborative finance, innovation and problem-solving. The housing associations *also* saw these initiatives as strategic alliances with councils to build up their own competitive position, and as a way of gaining increasing influence on policy.

10   Two economic cultures in social care contracting

The 'partnership' discourse on social care contracting thus focused the 'exchange' activity on the financial deal that got a project started: closer perhaps to an investment contract than to a retail sale. The rest of the working relationship was discussed in a longer-term framework that made explicit the importance of the provider–client relationship and the provider influence on quality. Social Services managers interviewed expected to pay more for domiciliary care in this framework than in the 'trading' framework of paying by the hour. Price competition was explicitly played down, with local authority interviewees pointing to the benefits of long-term stability, and coping with increasing dependency, as reasons for the higher price per hour assumed in setting the payment under the block contract (Mackintosh, 1997a, pp.90–1).

It is worth emphasizing one major way in which this 'partnership' framework of thought is *not* different from the trading discourse. If rethought from within the economists' metaphor of exchange, both are frameworks of 'soft' contracting: that is, both rely on incomplete specification of what is exchanged and both involve trust of the supplier. The nature of the implicit understandings and the implied incentives for the two parties are, however, quite different. The role of the clients is also different. In the trading discourse, as noted above, the client is virtually absent. The partnership discourse, however, allocates to the provider an explicit role in responding to client needs.

If these two discourses are accepted as distinct sets of meanings of social care contracting, how do we understand their relationship to economic behaviour? The 'partnership' discourse is not limited to discussions of explicit joint ventures with outside organizations; it is also present in a good many of the critical discussions of 'spot' contracting. However, we can think of these two discourses as stabilizing in interaction with two different types of experience, and two different types of contracting partner, in social care.

One set of working relationships and experiences was with the commercial providers. Here there was a mutually reinforcing process of learning and of establishing working assumptions. From a very low start, the number of domiciliary care contracts with the private sector had risen very fast in both authorities. The private sector managers and owners were also drawing on experience as they went along. The developing pattern was, verifiably, of prices being driven down by competition, and a stabilizing pattern of purchase of 'care hours' at pre-agreed prices.

Participants used different discursive strategies to explain this pattern of behaviour: the commercial firms justified it as proper business behaviour, since it suited their preference for control of their client mix and for limiting risk; the contracts officers justified it as even-handed treatment of providers, and the social workers as stretching limited budgets. No one thought the pattern problem-free, and many of the problems revolved around the exclusion of the client from active participation in either 'purchase' or 'provision'. But the story 'worked' in terms of consolidating a risk-averse, price-focused economic culture of contracting.

A similar shared set of working relationships and experiences was operating across the boundaries of the authority around 'partnership' contracting. Again, both parties to the contract were learning. The housing associations had gone into the housing-with-care field very rapidly and competitively. The authorities, too, were trying to work out what the benefits and problems might be. Both sides saw themselves as taking risks, notably in developing long-term working relationships on the basis of one-year council budget allocations. The authorities were, one Social Services director noted, 'mortgaging' their future budget. The housing associations were taking political risks in developing, in effect, a policy role.

The learning process had focused in several partnerships on dealings with clients. Who should set prices? Who dealt with complaints? Who took the responsibility for allocating limited resources? Who dealt, in one case, with a payment strike by residents? The problems had been addressed, in one scheme, by drawing the residents into decision-making, the local authority having to relinquish explicitly some of its policy control and the association having to abandon its earlier strategy of treating domiciliary charges as the authority's problem.

Again, different discursive strategies were used to justify this behaviour. The associations' managers focused on the benefits, in terms of greater financial control and more policy leverage, that flowed from accepting more risk. The local authority contracts officers justified the move away from 'proper' tendering by expressing understanding of the associations' constraints, and by noting that care contracts could never be properly monitored, so partnerships might help to sustain quality. The Social Services managers shared with the associations' managers the argument that total benefits to clients were raised by partnerships: the budget constraint could be loosened.

So two distinct economic cultures were being developed across the boundaries of the local authorities, between the authorities and their 'contractors'. Neither side started out with a distinct culture that it imposed on the other; the assumptions and experiences of the two sides created an evolving culture through a process of mutual learning, argument and increasingly shared ideas. Each participant's behaviour and assumptions influenced the other's. The cultures had distinct material consequences for clients, in terms of the money spent per client and the working framework within which the social care staff were operating.

11 A social constructionist economics of social policy?

I now want to return to the starting-point of this chapter and consider what this kind of analysis can add to a social constructionist analysis of social policy. First, the chapter has shown, I hope, that the exploration of multiple meanings given to economic terms such as 'contracting' can contribute to an understanding of the economic dynamics of social care reform. Two distinct logics of economic discourse and behaviour have been shown to have developed within the problematic formal structures of social care contracting in two local authorities. The particular twist to the story here is the way in which these logics have involved profit-seeking firms and large not-for-profit organizations.

The research is thus an application of a constructionist approach to understanding the direction of economic change in service provision, showing how distinct economic cultures become institutionalized in increasingly taken-for-granted meanings and behaviour. In the economic literature, the research is unusual in its attention to discourse, and in its abandonment of the academic metaphor of exchange. It treats economic language in context, as a symbolic system that people engage with, rework, and seek to legitimize.

Conversely, in the social constructionist context this research is – I think – unusual in its close focus on economic processes. I want therefore to end by suggesting that social constructionist theory of social policy needs to take a more discriminating stance on economic analysis. I am not sure that it has yet got to grips with economic categories and processes, except in terms of locating economic concepts within broader strategies of power. Otherwise, the social constructionist work draws, like the social administration tradition, on the results of mainstream welfare economics of the empirical sort, examining what is spent within the welfare state systems, who receives what, how one might define the redistributiveness of different systems on the basis of different assumptions about the value of benefits people receive (for example, Barr, 1993; Falkingham and Hills, 1995; Goodman et al., 1997).

This latter economic research does not – unlike the quasi-market research – depend heavily on the academic metaphor of exchange. For that reason, it can be drawn upon by a variety of traditions of social theory. In its concern with issues such as defining poverty and inequality, it forms part of the predominant or mainstream social construction of the social policy field. Its implicit policy framework is, however, a voluntarist one. The research is designed to suggest how, given particular policy objectives and values, public money could be better spent. This leaves open to further investigation the social construction of the economic assumptions and processes that shape social policy. I suggest that the kind of investigation of institutional economic cultures of which this chapter is a small example could add to our understanding of those processes.

Notes

1 This project, entitled 'Economic Culture and Local Governance', formed part of the ESRC's Local Governance programme; the financial support of the ESRC and also

of The Open University is gratefully acknowledged. The author is most grateful to Madeleine Wahlberg, the Research Fellow on the project, and to the two local authorities that hosted it. Thanks also to Gail Lewis and other participants at the Open University workshops on Rethinking Social Policy, for comments on an earlier draft. The views expressed here are the sole responsibility of the author.

2 The study included a range of local government services (Mackintosh, 1999); only social care is discussed here.

3 Other case studies, not concerned with social care, included re-tendering of an in-house catering contract; and a 'leisure card' initiative intended to cross-subsidize from profitable leisure services to those requiring support.

4 Mackintosh (1997a, pp.91–6) elaborates this argument. Lewis and Glennerster (1996, p.107) also note the impossibility of closely monitoring domiciliary provision.

5 I am not suggesting that this is necessarily the case: partnerships with commercial providers are a possible approach. However, a survey of social care contracts (Walsh et al., 1997) found that block contracts – an indicator of 'partnership' approaches – tended to be with the voluntary sector.

References

Barr, N. (1993) *The Economics of the Welfare State* (2nd edn), Weidenfeld & Nicolson.

Clarke, J. and Newman, J. (1997) *The Managerial State: Power, Politics and Ideology in the Remaking of Social Welfare*, London, Sage.

Douglas, M. (1987) *How Institutions Think*, London, Routledge & Kegan Paul.

Dryzek, J.S. (1996) 'The informal logic of institutional design', in Goodin, R.E. (ed.) *The Theory of Institutional Design*, Cambridge, Cambridge University Press.

du Gay, P. (1994) 'Making up managers: bureacracy, enterprise and the liberal art of separation', *British Journal of Sociology*, 45 (4), pp.655–74.

Falkingham, J. and Hills, J. (1995) *The Dynamic of Welfare: The Welfare State and the Life Cycle*, London, Prentice-Hall and Harvester Wheatsheaf.

Flynn, R. and Williams, G. (eds) (1997) *Contracting for Health: Quasi-Markets and the National Health Service*, Oxford, Oxford University Press.

Flynn, R., Williams, G. and Pickard, S. (1997) 'Quasi-markets and quasi-trust: the social construction of contracts for community health services', in Flynn and Williams (1997).

Goodman, A., Johnson, P. and Webb, S. (1997) *Inequality in the UK*, Oxford, Oxford University Press.

Hodgson, G. (1993) *Economics and Evolution*, Cambridge, Polity Press.

Le Grand, J. and Bartlett, W. (eds) (1993) *Quasi-Markets and Social Policy*, London, Macmillan.

Lewis, J. and Glennerster, H. (1996) *Implementing the New Community Care*, Buckingham, Open University Press.

Mackintosh, M. (1997a) 'Economic culture and quasi-markets in local government: the case of contracting for social care', *Local Government Studies*, 23 (2), pp.80–102.

Mackintosh, M. (1997b) 'Trading work: discourses of internal exchange in the economic culture of local government', *Public Policy and Administration*, 12 (2), pp.17–30.

Mackintosh, M. (1999) 'Two economic discourses in the new management of local governance: "public trading" and "public business"', in Stoker, G. (ed.) *The New Management of British Local Governance*, Basingstoke, Macmillan.

Mackintosh, M. (forthcoming) 'Flexible contracting? Economic cultures and implicit contracts in social care', *Journal of Social Policy*.

Propper, C. and Bartlett, W. (1997) 'The impact of competition on the behaviour of National Health Service trusts', in Flynn and Williams (1997).

Walsh, K. (1995) *Public Services and Market Mechanisms: Competition, Contracting and the New Public Management*, Basingstoke, Macmillan.

Walsh, K., Deakin, N., Smith, P., Spurgeon, P. and others (1997) *Contracting for Change: Contracts in Health, Social Care and Other Local Government Services*, Oxford, Oxford University Press.

Wistow, G., Knapp, M., Hardy, B., Forder, J., Kendall, J. and Manning, J. (eds) (1996) *Social Care Markets: Progress and Prospects*, Buckingham, Open University Press.

20

Social Justice, New Labour and School Reform

Sharon Gewirtz

1 Introduction

In her seminal work, *Justice and the Politics of Difference*, the American social theorist, Iris Marion Young (1990), draws upon the claims of what she calls new group-based social movements to rethink political philosophy. The particular movements which inform Young's work are those which grew up in the 1960s and 1970s to combat various forms of institutional injustice in North American society: feminism; black, American Indian, Puerto Rican and gay and lesbian liberation movements; and movements of disabled, old and poor people. However, the relevance of Young's work is not limited to the USA. In this chapter I want to use her work to demonstrate how philosophical thinking derived from the new social movements can help us make sense of a specific set of policies, in a specific place, at a specific historical juncture – namely, New Labour's restructuring of English schooling at the end of the twentieth century.

2 Young on justice

Young uses the concept of group difference and the claim of new social movements that contemporary US society contains deep institutional injustices as lenses through which to analyse political theory. I want to draw particularly on Young's conceptualization of oppression as being produced by:

> systematic institutional processes which prevent some people from learning and using satisfying and expansive skills in socially recognized settings, or . . . which inhibit people's ability to play and communicate with others or to express their feelings and perspective on social life in contexts where others can listen. (Young, 1990, p.38)

Young conceptualizes oppression as a family of five processes: exploitation, marginalization, powerlessness, cultural imperialism and violence. In explicating these processes she offers a systematic analysis of the meaning of oppression as used by the diverse groups involved in the new social movements.

The strength of Young's analysis lies in the way in which it incorporates what is good in liberal, Marxist and post-modernist conceptions of justice, whilst overcoming their limitations. Whilst she criticizes liberal conceptions of justice for being restricted to the distributive paradigm, Young nevertheless acknowledges that in thinking about justice we need to attend to patterns of distribution of material goods. Young also usefully draws on post-modern conceptions of justice, such as interdependence and the importance of recognizing, attending to and not repressing the voices and perspectives of oppressed groups. But whilst post-modern conceptions of justice can usefully inform micro-face-to-face interactions, they fail to adequately address macro-structures of oppression. This is where Young's recourse to Marxist and feminist theory is helpful. She draws upon and extends these theories to show how social institutions and structures of various kinds can mediate relations between individuals to produce injustices of exploitation, powerlessness, marginalization, cultural imperialism and violence. This makes Young's conceptualization of oppression a useful tool for analysing the impact of policies such as the use of markets in the provision of public services.

Nancy Fraser (1997) has expressed concerns about the tensions in Young's work between justice as redistribution and justice as recognition and respect of difference. However, whilst such criticisms are valid in certain respects, they do not appear to undermine the validity or attractiveness of Young's framework as a whole which provides us with a wide-ranging set of questions that can be used to inform evaluations of social policies from a social justice perspective.

More specifically (Gewirtz, 1998), in the context of education, they lead us to ask: how, to what extent and why do education policies support, interrupt or subvert:

- exploitative relationships (capitalist, patriarchal, racist, hetero-sexist, disabilist etc.) within and beyond educational institutions?
- processes of marginalization and inclusion within and beyond systems of education?
- the promotion of relationships based on recognition, respect, care and mutuality; or produce powerlessness (for education workers and users)?
- practices of cultural imperialism within and beyond systems of education?
- violent practices within and beyond systems of education?

In what follows, I use Young's framework, and the available research evidence, to consider the extent to which New Labour's restructuring of English schooling is likely to perpetuate or disrupt the injustices in and around schooling which were produced by the New Right education reforms of the 1980s and 1990s.

3 New Labour and the reconstruction of schooling

Successive Conservative administrations in the 1980s and 1990s effected a restructuring of the relationship between the state, economy and educational institutions, contributing to the establishment of a new educational settlement to supersede the previous welfarist settle-ment (Gewirtz, 1997; Fergusson, 1998). Most crucially, the policies effected a shift from a situation in which schools and teachers had a 'licensed autonomy' from the state and the economy to one of 'regu-lated autonomy' (Dale, 1989) in which the state controls from a distance the work of schools and teachers through the mechanisms of a highly regulated market and new managerial modes of control and by creating systems of accountability, inspection and performance monitoring which 'steer' actions and decisions towards targets and set goals. Whilst these mechanisms effectively produced a tightening of control of teachers' work by the central state, they were somewhat paradoxically anchored in discourses of devolution and decentraliza-tion.

The election of the New Labour government in May 1997 and subsequent legislation have provoked considerable debate about whether New Labour policies represent a continuation of or a depar-ture from the previous Conservative reforms. In some respects New Labour education policies appear to support and accentuate the approach of their Conservative predecessors. In particular, New Labour's policy architects advocate the use of markets in education, they are committed to the managerialization of schooling, they promote pedagogic traditionalism and they want to inculcate individual responsibility. However, at the same time there is a new rhetoric of experimentation, revitalizing civic association, education for citizenship, and reprofessionalizing teachers (Gewirtz, 1999). New Labour's leadership has tried to make a virtue out of the apparently paradoxical nature of their policy mix by presenting it as a deliberate strategy of pragmatic eclecticism based upon the principles of a 'third way' between the 'stifling statism' of the Old Left and the rampant market ideology of the New Right.

4   Implications for social justice

So what are the implications of educational New Labourism – the so-called third way – for social justice in education? First, it is important to acknowledge the impossibility of separating out the effects of New Labour policies from those of preceding governments. These effects will necessarily interact with each other as well as with other, non-policy-derived, social and cultural practices and processes to shape what goes on in and around schools; the effects of policies are undoubtedly systemic and accretive rather than politically discrete. In analysing the social justice implications of current policy trends, it is therefore only possible to tease out the likely implications of New Labour policies *in terms of their interaction* with the effects of the policies of previous governments. It is also, at the time of writing, too early to make any definitive statements about what these implications may be, although it is possible to speculate, partly on the basis of what we know about the results of the New Right reconstruction of education in the 1980s and 1990s.

If, for the moment, we conceive of justice in its purely distributional sense, it would appear from the available evidence that the Conservative policies exacerbated injustice through the promotion of inequalities of access to schooling and polarization in the social composition of student intakes. Not only does it appear that children from working-class and particular racialized groups were increasingly concentrated in under-resourced schools, it seems that within schools similar resource redistribution occurred through such processes as the devalorization of special needs provision, setting and the emphasis on providing for 'able' or 'gifted' children (Gewirtz et al., 1995).

Whilst the Conservative policies seem to have effected a redistribution of resources from the least to the most advantaged, New Labour policies suggest a commitment to a degree of *progressive* redistribution: more specifically, the phasing out of the Assisted Places Scheme and the use of those funds to lower infant class sizes, and the targeting of extra resources on schools in localities designated as Education Action Zones (EAZs). However, there are a number of reasons – aside from the relatively limited quantity of funds being redistributed (Plewis, 1998) – why we may have to be sceptical about how extensively redistributive New Labour's education policies will be.

First, New Labour remains committed to the ideas of choice and competition, and, given this support for markets in education, it is difficult to see how the targeting of resources on specific schools through the EAZ policy will be able to interrupt the processes of segregation and polarization which markets seem to produce. Some EAZ schools may 'improve' as a consequence of their additional resources or as a consequence of gaining specialist school status. But there is a possibility that any improvements will be at the expense of neighbouring schools which may lose teachers attracted by the better pay in zone schools and students attracted by the better resources.

Second, looking beyond EAZs to the education system as a whole, the managerial practice of target-setting which New Labour is encouraging is, if we are to extrapolate from past evidence, likely to lead teachers to focus on those students just below the required level, rather than the lowest-achieving students (Gewirtz et al., 1995; Plewis, 1998). And traditional pedagogical practices such as setting by 'ability' and whole class teaching, which are a central feature of the literacy and numeracy hours promoted in primary schools by the Department for Education and Employment (DfEE) under New Labour, also have the potential to further a *regressive* redistribution of resources. I am referring here to a redistribution *away* from students deemed to be 'less able' and, in the case of setting, students from working-class families and particular racialized groups towards those 'able', middle-class, mainly white students who benefit most from setted regimes and whole class teaching. Furthermore, the lowering of class sizes in primary schools to thirty students or fewer may have the perverse effect of redistributing resources in favour of schools in relatively advantaged areas.

New Labour is committed to the involvement of the private sector in the running of schools, which may well exacerbate the regressive distribution of resources which market forces produce. For the likelihood is that private companies, motivated by profit and the desire to demonstrate success, will be reluctant to spend resources on those students deemed to be least motivated and underattaining. In arguing for the value of private sector involvement in the provision of schooling, the government has pointed to the academic success of city technology colleges (CTCs) which are run by governing bodies upon which commercial sponsors have built-in majorities. Rarely is it mentioned, however, that whilst the CTCs may have to take children from across the whole measured ability range, they are able to select students (and their parents) by interview and, at least covertly, on the basis of class and 'race'.

In what ways, then, is the restructuring contributing to the exacerbation of oppression of particular social groups? I now want to use Young's criteria to explore the extent and ways in which teachers and students may be oppressed by New Labour policies.

4.1 Exploitation

Young broadens the concept of exploitation beyond the narrow Marxian sense of pertaining exclusively to the relation between capital and labour (Hunt, 1977; Lawn and Ozga, 1988; Giddens, 1981; Bowles and Gintis, 1976). She defines exploitation as a form of oppression which 'occurs through a steady process of the transfer of the results of the labor of one social group to benefit another' (Young, 1990, p.49). She is careful to distinguish exploitation from the broader category of domination. For Young, domination 'consists in persons having to perform actions whose rules and goals they have not participated in determining, under institutionalized conditions they have not had a part in deciding'. Domination only becomes exploitation when the actions someone has to perform, under conditions they have not participated in deciding, *systematically benefit another without reciprocation* (Young, 1990, p.218). Hence, for Young, 'The injustice of capitalist society consists in the fact that some people exercise their capacities under the control, according to the purposes, and for the benefit of other people.' Loss of control also deprives people of 'important elements of self respect' (ibid., p.49).

Young's conceptualization of exploitation, when applied to the context of schooling, can help us map out the complex web of exploitative relations that exist in and around schools. First, it can help us see how teachers are both exploiters of others and an exploited group themselves. For example, on Young's definition, teachers as professionals are exploiters of non-professionals, in that the 'material' work of non-professionals – like cleaning classrooms, cooking dinners, typing letters – frees teachers for the 'higher' work of 'thinking, designing and calculating . . . making decisions, writing reports, planning, and co-ordinating and supervising' (Young, 1990, pp.218–19). However, since the 1970s a number of commentators, in the UK, North America and elsewhere, have observed that in many ways teachers' work is becoming deskilled, with the diminution of the thinking, designing and calculating parts of the job, as teachers are increasingly expected to execute decisions made elsewhere (Ozga, 1988; Smyth and Shacklock, 1998). Yet even in such circumstances the relationship between teachers and non-professionals in schools is, on Young's definition, exploitative 'because the professionals usually get paid more, get more recognition, and have greater power and authority, even though the work of some non-professionals directly enables their work' (1990, p.219).

On the other hand, teachers themselves can be viewed as exploited in a number of senses. For example, teachers are exploited by those who manage them, in that teachers' increasingly technicist work frees school managers for yet 'higher' work; and the higher pay, power and authority that managers accrue is directly enabled by the work of teachers. Exploitation in schools, as in most other workplaces, is gendered and racialized to the extent that women and some racialized groups tend to predominate in jobs with the lowest pay and status – for example, as classroom assistants and mealtime supervisors – whilst the highest-paying high-status jobs are disproportionately held by white men. It can also be argued that teachers *and managers* in schools are exploited (if less directly) by private employers, in that the benefits of the energy teachers and head teachers expend in 'producing' educated workers enables employers to extract value from those workers, the benefits of which are not transferred back to workers in schools. Furthermore, teachers and managers in schools are exploited by those professional and managerial workers in the private and public sectors who are more highly paid and have more status and authority than those who work in schools. This relationship can be classified as exploitative because the higher pay, status and authority of such professional/managerial groups depend on the existence of the educated labour 'produced' by workers in schools.

The extent and ways in which the web of exploitative relationships in and around schools has been, or is being, *transformed* as a consequence of both Conservative and New Labour policies is a complex issue. Certainly, it is difficult to see how the Conservative policies did anything to interrupt processes of exploitation within schools, and one can argue that the exploitation of teachers was intensified as a consequence of Conservative policies in education and that it will continue under New Labour. It would seem reasonable to conclude that teachers lost out materially under the Conservatives. A number of surveys suggested that they were working longer hours in the 1990s than they were in the 1970s (ILO, 1991; NAS/UWT, 1990, 1991; Lowe, 1991; Campbell and St J. Neill, 1994). At the same time, there has been a long-term decline in teachers' salaries since the fiscal crisis of the mid-1970s in relation to the average increase in earnings of non-manual workers. New Labour's policy on teachers' pay may lead to improvements for those in managerial positions, those passing the new 'performance threshold' and those successful in gaining Advanced Skills Teacher's (AST) status, but seems unlikely to result in significant pay increases for the 'ordinary' classroom teacher. In addition, the 1997 School Standards and Framework Act allows schools in EAZs to disapply the Teachers' Pay and Conditions Order, which may improve pay for teachers in EAZ schools (possibly in return for evening and weekend work), whilst making those in neighbouring schools relatively worse off. New Labour's Green Paper, *Teachers: Meeting the Challenge of Change* (DfEE, 1998), suggests that the number of teaching assistant posts will be increased by at least 20,000 by the year 2002, but no mention is made of increased remuneration for these workers; it is yet to be seen how successful the campaigns for improving the pay and status of classroom assistants and nursery nurses in schools will be.

There is also evidence to suggest that opportunities for participative forms of decision-making and autonomous teacher activity are more tightly circumscribed now that teachers' work is increasingly governed by a technical, rather than substantive, rationality.[1] The introduction into primary schools by New Labour of the literacy and numeracy hours, which prescribe the content of teaching in these areas, is further intensifying this 'technicization' of teaching. Similarly, the high degree of surveillance of teachers, generated by Conservative policies, is likely to be increased under New Labour. New Labour has not only retained the Ofsted regime of inspections, national testing and examination league tables, but is introducing a whole range of new mechanisms to facilitate more central regulation of schooling. For example, there are plans for new appraisal arrangements involving annual assessment of teachers' performance against agreed objectives which will be used to influence teachers' pay; to gain Advanced Skills Teacher's status, teachers will have to meet national standards specified by central government; and New Labour's 'School Performance Award Scheme' will distribute pay awards to teachers and other workers in schools which demonstrate improvement according to central government criteria (DfEE, 1998).

As teachers are increasingly deprived both in material terms and in terms of control, and as their productivity is maximized and central scrutiny of their work heightened, the likelihood is that they will experience intensified exploitation by all of those (employers and professional/managerial workers in both the private and public sectors) whose material and status well-being is dependent on the extraction of value from educated labour.

The picture is complicated by the fact that teachers do not constitute a homogeneous social group but represent a group cross-cut by gender, ethnicity, class background, dis/ability, age and so on. Work needs to be done in mapping the changing degrees, experiences and modes of exploitation of different fractions within the teaching workforce and within school workforces more generally.

And what of students? On Young's definition of exploitation as the transfer of energies from one group to another, students have always been an exploited group. For the way in which students exercise their capacities in the vast majority of schools has never been determined solely by a conception of children's own needs and interests. Rather children's energies are used to augment the interests of others to the extent that what students do in schools is shaped by a perception of what is in the interests of the schools, parents, employers and the state. Arguably, these more instrumental purposes of schooling are becoming more dominant in the reconstruction of education. Various studies have highlighted the more overt commodification of students and the increased adoption of narrow, instrumentalist and didactic pedagogic practices that the restructuring has contributed to producing (e.g. Woods et al., 1997; Smyth and Shacklock, 1998). More specifically, it seems that schools and teachers are being encouraged to value students according to what these children can offer the school – financially and in terms of exam performance. In this way, students have become *objects* of the education system, to be attracted, excluded, displayed and processed, according to their commercial and semiotic worth,[2] rather than subjects with needs, desires and potentials. They are judged and processed on the basis of their capacity to contribute to a school's market success. These judgements not only inform the selective, exclusionary and semiotic practices of schools, they also inform the treatment of students within schools (Gewirtz et al., 1995).

Again it is difficult to see how New Labour's policies will interrupt these processes, given the government's commitments to the market as a mode of co-ordination for schooling; the increased involvement of private companies in the provision of education; and the vocationalization of the curriculum for children living in those 'disadvantaged' areas designated as action zones.

However, like teachers, students are a heterogeneous group. There is, therefore, considerable work to be done in mapping the multiple forms of exploitation that restructuring policies produce or interrupt, and there is a need to focus on the differentiated ways in which exploitation is, or is not, experienced by students of different classes, genders, ethnicities and 'abilities'.

4.2   Marginalization

Young defines marginalization as a form of oppression in which people are excluded from participating in those arenas of social co-operation where most of society's productive and valued activities take place.

The practices produced by the restructuring of schooling marginalize particular categories of children firstly by devaluing them. It seems that children with special needs and working-class children, particularly African-Caribbean and white working-class boys, are all not valued within a 'post-welfarist' policy environment (Gewirtz, 1997) because they are judged troublesome and unlikely to make a significant positive contribution to a school's examination perform-ance or attractiveness in the marketplace (see Chapters 6 and 17 this volume). As a consequence of not being valued, these students tend not to be selected for and are more likely to be excluded from those schools which are the most generously resourced and considered to be the most socially desirable. This in turn means that these groups of students are devalued further. *Inside* schools, the same groups of students are also being marginalized by the practice of setting which is becoming increasingly popular and which New Labour has explicitly endorsed. If we are to extrapolate from existing research on the effects of the grouping of students by 'ability' (e.g. Hargreaves, 1967; Lacey, 1970; Troyna 1978; Ball 1981; Troyna and Siraj-Blatchford, 1993), then it is reasonable to conclude that the combination of these processes of selection, exclusion *and* setting is likely to significantly intensify, amongst marginalized students, the experiences of boredom and perceptions of uselessness identified by Young as key consequences of marginalization.

New Labour strategies of individual 'responsibilization', like family literacy or inter-generational learning schemes, may have the potential to facilitate perceptions of inclusivity amongst members of previously excluded social groups, and hence combat the injustice of marginalization. However, these strategies also have the potential to make people feel they are being constructed as a problem, hence exacerbating their perceptions of marginality. So, much will depend on the way in which such strategies are enacted on the ground.

As far as teachers are concerned, those who are still in work are not marginalized in the sense of being excluded from 'useful participation in social life' (Young, 1990, p.53), although many teachers may *feel* marginalized as a consequence of their experiences of exploitation. Moreover, learning and language support teachers, who are especially involved in dealing with those students who are most marginalized by policies of marketization and setting and the devaluing of special needs, may well be experiencing a form of *reflected marginalization*. Such teachers are certainly particularly vulnerable to the new 'flexible' staffing practices and redundancy (Gewirtz et al., 1995).

4.3 Powerlessness

Just as teachers may feel marginalized by their experiences of exploitation, so many may, justifiably, also feel that they lack power, which Young defines as the ability of people to participate in decisions which affect the conditions of their lives. Whilst some researchers have detected a heightened sense of professionalism amongst *primary* teachers (for example Campbell and Neill, 1994), enhanced professionalism was not a prominent feature of the perceptions of teachers in my own study of secondary schools (Gewirtz, 1997) or of teachers in the primary schools studied by Peter Woods and colleagues (1997). Nor were the 'new' professionalism and collaborative teaching cultures that Hargreaves (1994) describes evident. The experiences of teachers I interviewed came closer to those who participated in Robertson and Soucek's (1991) study of teachers in Western Australia:

> In essence, the changes have meant teachers can participate in making decisions over a limited range of technical issues, not the big ticket items such as: What is it that we want children to know? How do we provide opportunities for students to genuinely participate in the learning process? What does it mean to educate a critical citizenry? (Robertson, 1996, pp.43–4; see also Smyth and Shacklock, 1998)

However, whilst they may have suffered a loss of power in relation to school managers and the state, teachers are not power*less*, nor are they being rendered powerless: they continue to exercise power on a daily basis over students, and some teachers continue to exercise power over other teachers. Most students are more appropriately defined as powerless within schools, since they regularly have power exercised over them, but rarely have the opportunity to exercise power over others (although some do exercise power over other students by various forms of bullying and harassment). Whilst it is difficult to construct a case for arguing that the powerlessness of students has been intensified, there is certainly less evidence now of the social agency of students in the form of rebellion or riot than in the 1970s and 1980s.

4.4   Cultural imperialism

> To experience cultural imperialism means to experience how the dominant meanings of society render the particular perspective of one's own group invisible at the same time as they stereotype one's group and mark it out as the Other.
>
> Cultural imperialism involves the universalization of a dominant group's experience and culture, and its establishment as the norm. (Young, 1990, pp.58–9)

The instrumentalism, narrowness of focus and pedagogic traditionalism of schooling under New Labour, bolstered by the discourses of school effectiveness and improvement, may be viewed as functioning as mechanisms of cultural imperialism in two senses.

First, these mechanisms appear to be marginalizing dissenting voices and squeezing the spaces within which emancipatory practices, which promote what Young calls self-development, can evolve. In transforming the values and rationality of education provision, educational New Labourism seems to be building on the policies of previous Conservative governments (Hatcher et al., 1996) to produce a discursive reconstruction of schooling within which schools are primarily seen as being concerned with the production of measurable short-term learning outcomes. This is reflected in the rise to prominence of the purveyors of the language and practices of school effectiveness and improvement, with their claims to have developed objective instruments for the identification of failings in schools and the facilitation of improvement. As John White (1997, p.52) has pointed out, the emphasis on short-term measurable outcomes, like 'good test scores, GCSE results, low truancy rates or whatever other desiderata the [school effectiveness research] may insist on', means that non-measurable, 'longer-term goals to do with well-roundedness, democratic citizenship, independence of spirit' and so on are neglected (although 'citizenship education' is currently being promoted by New Labour). Despite these serious weaknesses, the discourses of school effectiveness and improvement appear to have become hegemonic. It would also seem that those who question the 'objective educational truths' being 'discovered' by school effectiveness and improvement researchers and who challenge the ideological, pedagogical, social and epistemological assumptions underpinning them are being effectively sidelined in policy terms.

Second, the mechanisms of pedagogic traditionalism and narrowness of focus associated with the restructuring of schooling themselves represent new possibilities for the promotion of culturally imperialist practices in schools, including an ethnocentric curriculum and ethnocentric pedagogies. Cultural imperialism has a long history in English schools. This was highlighted by the 'new' sociologists of education in the 1970s who argued that the way schools were organized and their curricula and pedagogies reflected the experiences, values, interests and ways of learning of dominant (i.e. middle-class) social groups (Young, 1971). This form of critique was extended by feminist and anti-racist educators in the 1970s and 1980s, and gave rise to the advocacy and adoption in some schools of feminist and anti-racist policies and practices (Coard, 1971; ALTARF, 1979; Deem, 1980; Arnot and Weiner, 1987).

I do not wish to imply that prior to restructuring *most* schools or teachers were especially attentive to issues of social justice. Nor do I want to give the impression that in the current era there are not still teachers struggling within their own classrooms to develop practices which are rooted in a recognition of and respect for difference. There are still teachers who, *in spite of* the pressures towards ethnocentrism generated by contemporary policies, are able to develop curricula designed to engage a diversity of students with the kinds of critical political, moral and social issues associated with a politics of recognition (Fraser, 1997) which are not covered in the national curriculum. What I am suggesting is that prior to the restructuring there were more spaces for teachers who wanted to develop organizational practices, curricula and pedagogies which were underpinned by a recognition and respect of diverse identities and by a desire to combat culturally imperialist practices in schools.

It is yet to be seen whether in the aftermath of the Stephen Lawrence inquiry report such spaces will be opened up once again. The government's action plan, published within a month of the report, accepted Sir William MacPherson's (1999) recommendations that the national curriculum be revised to emphasize a valuing of cultural diversity and the prevention of racism; that local education authorities (LEAs) and school governors should have a duty to develop various monitoring and recording strategies in schools to prevent and deal with racism; and that these strategies should become a focus of Ofsted inspections. Moreover, the government's review of the national curriculum explicitly endorsed the need for education to 'enable pupils to challenge discrimination and stereotyping', to 'develop their knowledge and understanding of different beliefs and cultures' and to 'help them form and maintain worthwhile and satisfying relationships based on respect for themselves and for others' (QCA/DfEE, 1999) (see also Ghouri, 1999). Clearly, the implementation of the proposals for personal, social and health education and for 'citizenship education' which are outlined in the curriculum review will need to be studied. But at this point I am sceptical about the viability of successfully incorporating meaningful anti-racist practices, whether through 'citizenship education' or other strategies, into the managerial and traditional pedagogic environments being promoted by New Labour (see also Chapter 17 this volume). For, as I have discussed above, it is these very environments which are likely to generate the kinds of exclusionary practices that anti-racist education needs to combat.

4.5   Violence

> The oppression of violence consists not only in direct victimization, but in the daily knowledge shared by all members of oppressed groups that they are liable to violation, solely on account of their group identity. Just living under such a threat of attack on oneself or family or friends deprives the oppressed of freedom and dignity, and needlessly expends their energy . . . To the degree that institutions and social practices encourage, tolerate, or enable the perpetration of violence against members of specific groups, those institutions and practices are unjust and should be reformed. (Young, 1990, pp.62–3)

Violence, in the form of physical attacks as well as harassment, of a racist, sexist, heterosexist and disabilist nature continues to occur in schools, as it did prior to restructuring. It certainly could not be argued that in general contemporary schools are encouraging the perpetration of violence against members of specific groups. One could mount a case, however, that through the mechanisms of cultural imperialism discussed above New Labour policies may prevent schools from doing as much as they should to challenge the kinds of attitude which underpin group-directed violence (see also Chapter 16 this volume). On the other hand, though, it is important to note that the focus on school 'cultures', which is one of the features of the school improvement research that is currently so fashionable, has had the effect of highlighting the issue of bullying in schools.

5 Conclusion

A rhetoric of social justice is far more prominent in the discourses of New Labourism than it ever was in Conservative discourses. Nevertheless it is difficult to see how New Labour, who remain committed to marketization and managerialization as policy strategies, and who espouse pedagogic traditionalism, will be able to disrupt the injustices produced by Conservative policies. This is despite their claimed commitment to a more humanistic education policy based upon a redistribution of opportunities, revitalizing local democracy, citizenship education, reprofessionalizing teaching and experimenting to improve schooling for 'disadvantaged' children. In general, it would seem from the available evidence and on the basis of the analysis presented in this chapter, that the education policies introduced by New Labour are more likely to exacerbate rather than disrupt these injustices.

However, these outcomes are not guaranteed. It may be that the tensions within what might be termed the neo-liberal authoritarian humanism (Andrews, 1999) of educational New Labourism – between those neo-liberal and authoritarian elements which in part represent intensifications of New Right policies and the newer, apparently more humanistic strands – may be played out differently.

Notes

This is a revised version of 'Post-welfarist schooling: a social justice audit', *Education and Social Justice*, 1 (1), pp.52–64 (1998).

1 The emphasis of technical rationality is upon the development of techniques, procedures and organizational practices which are intended to facilitate the setting and reviewing of objectives, good financial controls and information, cost improvement,

responsiveness and consumer loyalty. The emphasis of substantive rationality is upon the intrinsic qualities of the product or process – here education, teaching and learning.

2 Particular categories of students (for example middle-class white and Indian girls) are seen as valuable not only because of their potential contribution to a school's league table position, but because their presence in the school is seen to symbolize high achievement and therefore can be used as a marketing tool.

References

ALTARF (All London Teachers Against Racism and Fascism) (1979) *Racism in Schools*, London, ALTARF.

Andrews, G. (1999) 'New Left and New Labour: modernisation or a New Modernity?', *Soundings*, 13, pp. 14–24.

Arnot, M. and Weiner, G. (eds) (1987) *Gender and the Politics of Schooling*, London, Hutchinson.

Ball, S.J. (1981) *Beachside Comprehensive: A Case Study of Secondary Schooling*, Cambridge, Cambridge University Press.

Bowles, S. and Gintis, H. (1976) *Schooling in Capitalist America*, London, Routledge & Kegan Paul.

Campbell, R.J. and St J. Neill, S.R. (1994) *Curriculum Reform at Key Stage 1: Teacher Commitment and Policy Failure*, Harlow, Longman.

Coard, B. (1971) *How the West Indian Child is Made Educationally Sub-Normal in the British School System*, London, New Beacon Books.

Dale, R. (1989) *The State and Education Policy*, Buckingham, Open University Press.

Deem, R. (1980) *Schooling for Women's Work*, London, Routledge.

DfEE (Department for Education and Employment) (1998) *Teachers: Meeting the Challenge of Change*, London, DfEE.

Fergusson, R. (1998) 'Choice, selection and the social construction of difference: restructuring schooling', in Hughes, G. and Lewis, G. (eds) *Unsettling Welfare: The Reconstruction of Social Policy*, London, Routledge/The Open University.

Fraser, N. (1997) *Justice Interruptus: Critical Reflections on the 'Postsocialist' Condition*, New York and London, Routledge.

Gewirtz, S. (1997) 'Post-welfarism and the reconstruction of teachers' work in the UK', *Journal of Education Policy*, 12 (4), pp.217–31.

Gewirtz, S. (1998) 'Conceptualizing social justice in education: mapping the territory', *Journal of Education Policy*, 13 (4), pp.469–84.

Gewirtz, S. (1999) 'Education Action Zones: emblems of the Third Way', in *Social Policy Review 11*, London, Social Policy Association.

Gewirtz, S., Ball, S.J. and Bowe, R. (1995) *Markets, Choice and Equity in Education*, Buckingham, Open University Press.

Ghouri, N. (1999) 'Racism log ordered for nation's schools', *Times Educational Supplement*, 26 March, p.4.

Giddens, A. (1981) *A Contemporary Critique of Historical Materialism*, Berkeley, CA, University of California Press.

Hargreaves, A. (1994) *Changing Teachers, Changing Times: Teachers' Work and Culture in the Post-modern Age*, London, Cassell.

Hargreaves, D. (1967) *Social Relations in a Secondary School*, London, Routledge & Kegan Paul.

Hatcher, R., Troyna, B. and Gewirtz, D. (1996) *Racial Equality and the Local Management of Schools*, Stoke-on-Trent, Trentham Books.

Hunt, A. (1977) 'Theory and politics in the identification of the working class', in Hunt, A. (ed.) *Class and Class Structure*, London, Lawrence & Wishart.

ILO (International Labour Organization) (1991) *Teachers: Challenges of the 1990s*, Second Joint Meeting on Conditions of Work of Teachers, Geneva, ILO.

Lacey, C. (1970) *Hightown Grammar: The School as a Social System*, Manchester, Manchester University Press.

Lawn, M. and Ozga, J. (1988) 'The educational worker? A reassessment of teachers', in Ozga (1988).

Lowe, B. (1991) *Activity Sampling*, Hull, Humberside County Council.

MacPherson, W. (1999) *The Stephen Lawrence Inquiry*, CM 4262–1, London, The Stationery Office.

NAS/UWT (1990) *Teacher Workload Survey*, Birmingham, NAS/UWT.

NAS/UWT (1991) *Teacher Workload Survey*, Birmingham, NAS/UWT.

Ozga, J. (ed.) (1988) *Schoolwork: Approaches to the Labour Process of Teaching*, Milton Keynes, Open University Press.

Plewis, I. (1998) 'Inequalities, targets and Education Action Zones', *New Economy*, 5 (2), pp.104–8.

QCA (Qualifications and Curriculum Authority)/DfEE (1999) *The Review of the National Curriculum in England*, London, QCA.

Robertson, S. (1996) 'Teachers' work, restructuring and post-Fordism: constructing the new "professionalism"', in Goodson, I. and Hargreaves, A. (eds) *Teachers' Professional Lives*, London, Falmer Press.

Robertson, S. and Soucek, V. (1991) 'Changing social realities in Australian schools: a study of teachers' perceptions and experiences of current reforms'. Paper presented at the Comparative and International Education Society conference, Pittsburgh, PA.

Smyth, J. and Shacklock, G. (1998) *Re-making Teaching: Ideology, Policy and Practice*, London, Routledge.

Troyna, B. (1978) 'Race and streaming: a case study', *Educational Review*, 30 (1), pp.59–65.

Troyna, B. and Siraj-Blatchford, I. (1993) 'Providing support or denying access? The experiences of students designated as "ESL" and "SN" in a multi-ethnic secondary school', *Educational Review*, 45 (1), pp.3–11.

White, J. (1997) 'Philosophical perspectives on school effectiveness and improvement', in Barber, M. and White, J. (eds) *Perspectives on School Effectiveness and School Improvement*, London, Institute of Education, University of London.

Woods, P., Jeffrey, B., Troman, G. and Boyle, M. (1997) *Restructuring Schools, Reconstructing Teachers: Responding to Changes in the Primary School*, Buckingham, Open University Press.

Young, I.M. (1990) *Justice and the Politics of Difference*, Princeton, NJ, Princeton University Press.

Young, M.F.D. (1971) *Knowledge and Control: New Directions for the Sociology of Education*, London, Collier-Macmillan.

21

Redefining Work and Welfare in Europe: New Perspectives on Work, Welfare and Time

Jane Pillinger

1 Introduction

The nature of paid work and of welfare systems is changing dramatically across Europe and new ways of conceiving work and welfare are evolving. New thinking about time and experiments in working time that link policy objectives of, for instance, equal opportunities or job creation, are leading to some fundamental changes in the making and shaping of both future labour markets and welfare entitlements across Europe. This response to European Union (EU) discourses regarding new forms of flexibility at work and work organization as a result of global competitiveness, reconciles the flexibility that firms need with the security that workers require (European Commission, 1997a).

Cultural, social and economic changes taking place across Europe are inextricably linked to these developments in the EU. This new focus on time policies allows for working time to be related to individual needs over the life cycle in recognition of the tensions between work and family responsibilities. Discourses linking changing work organization and working time to reducing unemployment also introduce new perspectives on the future of social protection, the promotion of equal opportunities and on caring responsibilities (European Commission, 1995, 1997b, 1998a). This chapter shows that there is a direct linkage between new working practices in the public services and the restructuring of welfare across Europe. In turn, time becomes a conceptual tool for understanding new values in time systems and a new culture that has the *quality* of time as a prerequisite of changing social and economic relations.

2   What are the key dynamics of change?

So what are the main shifts taking place in our thinking about time and how do they relate to debates about work and welfare across Europe? As the twenty-four-hour global technological and information society has brought with it new conceptions of time, new thinking about work and welfare is inextricably linked to these changing time frames, and in turn to new patterns of work, leisure, family and personal relationships. There are four main dynamics of this change, which I shall now consider in turn.

2.1   The restructuring of welfare across Europe

In all European countries profound changes are taking place in the modernization and restructuring of welfare services and in new relationships between welfare (particularly the role of social protection) and work. Across Europe the restructuring of public services has to varying degrees responded to market mechanisms and new forms of competition. As a result, a common feature of most European welfare states is a mixed economy of welfare with a shifting emphasis away from the state towards private, voluntary and informal networks of provision (Johnson, 1998). In some countries, particularly the UK, this has led to the introduction of full-scale privatization or contracting out of services, whilst in a large number of European countries this has resulted in the introduction of competition and markets into the organization of state services. For example, Stockholm City Council in

Sweden now requires all of its social and welfare services to be tendered on the open market and this is resulting in a large increase in private and semi-public care provision. In the Netherlands the bulk of social care is now provided by private care organizations. In other countries, for example Ireland and Portugal, the state is now directly funding the voluntary care sector as care needs grow. Another dimension of this increasing diversification in provision is the movement towards allowing users of services to determine who provides their care, whether this be private or public organizations or relatives, neighbours or friends. This has been made possible through the introduction of carers' allowances in a number of countries and particularly through the introduction of Personal Budgets in the Netherlands since 1996 and Dependency Insurance in Luxembourg since 1998 (Pijl, 1997; Weekers and Pijl, 1998).

For historical, political and cultural reasons, welfare systems have evolved in different ways across Europe. The analysis of welfare regimes has been important to an understanding of this diversity of welfare systems, the linkage between welfare and work (Esping-Andersen, 1990, 1996), and particularly in highlighting the absence of a gender analysis and recognition of unpaid care in welfare systems (Lewis, 1992, and Chapter 2 this volume). However, these analyses do not show how demands from users and civil society play a role in structuring welfare, especially in a climate of consumer and user orientations to services (Williams, 1997).

On the one hand, a large majority of Western European countries developed welfare systems based on a relationship between fulfilling social needs and merit/work performance, funded from employer and employee contributions to social or national insurance schemes and some direct taxation. On the other hand, the Scandinavian model developed from a principle of the individual as part of a social collective, whereby universal services and the entry of women into the labour market became the mechanism for fulfilling social needs, financed through direct taxation. Although the Scandinavian model is based on production and financing by the public sector and institutionalized welfare, the trend has been towards more private sector solutions (for example, through insurance premiums and private contribution schemes) in social security systems and the introduction of market-orientated services and contracted-out care and welfare services.

An associated development is the emergence of a new relationship between welfare (particularly the role of social protection) and work, representing a shift towards a discourse that stresses work incentives and a policy that is focused on employability. In part this is a response to concerns that disincentives to work and high unemployment are closely associated with generous welfare systems in the OECD countries (Haverman, 1996). Moreover, the growing costs of welfare across Europe (EU member-states spend 28 per cent of their GDP on social protection) reveal the inability of the labour market to provide adequate protection (Heikkilä, 1999; Esping-Andersen, 1996). This has led to new strategies that link welfare to work across Europe, whether these be workfare orientated, based on active labour market policies, on notions of worksharing (whereby existing work is shared between employed or unemployed people), or based on programmes for a basic income (Heikkilä, 1999).

A policy shift towards a Schumpeterian workfare model (see Chapter 11 this volume) is evident from this shifting policy discourse, linking competitiveness and economic policy, flexible labour markets and reduced public expenditure, with welfare restructuring. In many cases there is an associated trend across Europe towards decentralized services and devolved budgets, and an emphasis on the need to rationalize services and to seek cost-effective solutions to welfare provision, including the promotion of informal care solutions.

2.2　The articulation of user demands

Changing political cultures across Europe are directly linked to a new emphasis on the relationship of the consumer to welfare and a not unrelated growth of user movements and social movements that are articulating new welfare demands and entitlements. As a result, an important dynamic of the future development of both work and welfare is a result of the new demands for improved service provision from users which may have different time frames and time demands associated with them.

As new social movements have developed in recent decades, new concepts of active citizenship and participatory 'direct' democracy are advocated by the EU in order to overcome the shortcomings inherent in the distance of the EU from ordinary people and the 'democratic deficit' whereby the European Parliament has few of the powers that national parliaments hold. The emphasis on citizenship and participation is increasingly needed in order to ensure that the people of Europe stay on board for critical European developments (particularly Economic and Monetary Union). This has led to a rise of non-governmental organizations and users asserting welfare claims in the emerging civil dialogue at the EU level, along with user panels, committees and forums in a number of European countries. This has had the effect of sharpening the focus on citizenship and participation in national and European discourses, resulting from changing social relations and new alliances at the national and European levels (Williams, 1997; Hoskyns, 1996).

Likewise, the EU Social Dialogue brings the social partners (employers and trade unions) into a dialogue to frame and agree new legislation. The recent agreements for directives which have led to the introduction of new legislation across Europe on parental leave (1995), part-time work (1997) and fixed-term contracts (1999) have established new rights to unpaid leave from the labour market after the birth of a child, the right for part-time workers not to be discriminated against, and new rights for temporary workers. These aim to remove some of the worst excesses of flexibility in the labour market and to promote equal opportunities, and are a response to the need to provide minimum protection in an increasingly insecure labour market. These developments in both the civil and social dialogue have led to new notions of participation and new policy networks in a mixed economy of welfare.

Associated with the move to a mixed economy of welfare is the development of new notions of partnerships in welfare, particularly around care, and new pressures to improve the quality and co-ordination of services. The experience of direct payments to users of care services in the Netherlands and the UK and the growth of payments to informal carers in a number of countries, rather than the direct provision of state services, challenge traditional patterns of welfare delivery (Evers et al., 1994). Some of the most interesting partnerships, now emerging in Sweden and Germany, have been alliances between users and providers of welfare (between user organizations, non-governmental organizations, voluntary organizations, trade unions and employers) which have had user empowerment strategies built into the provision of services at their core.

2.3   Changing household and family relationships

New family and household formations, shifting personal and family relationships and new value systems are part of this process linked to changing patterns of work and time over the life course. For example, ageing populations raise new challenges about how care services can be funded, with shifts towards more informal support systems evident in all European countries.

Gender is central to an analysis of time, particularly because women's time falls outside of the commodified time systems that operate in the paid workplace. Women often have to give time as carers; their work, whether it be paid or unpaid, is frequently time-consuming and time-precious (Adam, 1990; Forman and Sowton, 1989; Bettio et al., 1998). Policies that aim to reconcile family and work life by mainstreaming equality in public institutions are central to discourses on working time, in the recognition that work needs to be organized within different time frames for women (European Commission, 1998a; Rubery et al., 1995). In this respect some experiments in making working time more flexible have had the consequence of legitimizing women's exit from the labour market, and so have further undermined women's position in the labour market. For example, working time experiments in Finnish municipalities and health services to introduce a six-hour day, part-time pensions, part-time benefits and work rotation, the bulk of which have been taken up by women, have had this negative consequence. As a result, in a growing number of countries, and particularly in the Netherlands, the collective reduction and reorganization of working time has become strategically important to achieving equality and the sharing of work and family life.

2.4 Restructuring work: changing work and working time

Dramatic changes in work are evident across Europe as the 'Tayloristic' model of production, with work organized in a particular time frame (full-time, five-day-week and male model of continuous employment), and within a particular locality (the workplace) are breaking down so that work has become more precarious and work and home are no longer rigidly separated. Post-Fordism has led to an increase in flexible work, with production organized to time-match the demand for products. The result is an increasing incidence of insecure flexible work, particularly of women's part-time work in the expanding service sector of the economy, a sector that has also seen the extension of services and production into the evening and weekends (OECD, 1998).

Nevertheless, in some cases there are ways in which employees' (especially women's) choices about working time have increased in this new climate of flexibility, whereby flexible working times, as distinct from flexible work, allow for more expressions of diverse time preferences. What is clear, however, is that working time preferences are often constrained by inadequate state support services, for instance for child or elder care, which affects women's participation in either full- or part-time work to different degrees in different European countries.

Changes in work organization and working time, alongside new forms of flexibility at work (largely carried out by women) in the welfare services, have been developing in response to the crisis in welfare funding and the need for cost-savings, along with growing demands to improve the quality of services and to extend provision. Where these developments have linked local service improvements to user needs, the result has been some highly innovatory experiments in local areas, in municipalities and, in the case of Italy, across whole cities. In Italy, city experiments have led to the rescheduling of services to enable social, education, transport and welfare services to be more woman-friendly and user-orientated. These initiatives which place new values on time are some of the most exciting responses to the restructuring of work and welfare since the post-war welfare settlement across Europe. For example, they have led to new policies to redistribute work between women and men and between employed and unemployed people. These will be discussed further in section 5 below.

3 Time as an analytical tool

So how can we make sense of these changes? Social, economic and cultural structures and processes are essentially temporal. Utilizing time as an analytical tool can lead to new understandings about how the social relations of time relate to the social relations of work, care and welfare. As a result, time is critical to women's and men's working time preferences, to strategies to redistribute working time to allow for family-friendly working practices, to equal opportunities, and to informal care. It can also result in new ideas about the redistribution of work (and therefore of time) between the employed people (who experience time deficits and time pressures) and unemployed people (who often have a surfeit of time). If there is a fixed amount of work in the economy, changing working time alongside policies that link work with welfare, based on notions of solidarity, can be highly innovative. Time is an important aspect of social reality, of personal, social and economic life, and therefore of social policy.

In this sense the politics of time is critical. At one level, time is a resource and a commodity. It is a central component of modern industrial societies and indeed is an essential element of Marxist theories of the exploitation and regulation of labour time under capitalism. Economists such as Gary Becker (1965) recognized the scarce resource nature of time and applied it to consumers' use of personal time and domestic activity, while feminist critiques of the social relations of time have stressed that time is highly gendered. Whatever the analysis, time has become a precious resource and making the best use of time is as integral to work organization as it is to family and caring responsibilities; at its most salient Gorz (1982) suggests that of 'all the levers available to change the social order and the quality of life [time] is the most powerful'. Developing innovative responses to the restructuring of both work and welfare across Europe necessarily invokes new thinking about time.

These issues raise some important questions about the delivery and organization of work in the context of new forms of flexibility, of an increasingly mixed economy of welfare and of new welfare strategies across Europe. As a result, time is both commodified and also highly politicized. This new thinking on time, and indeed of changing global and technological relationships, suggests that the organization of time is not fixed.

4 European Union pressures and the future of work and welfare

A number of important developments are taking place at the European level, which are changing the nature of both work and welfare. Whilst EU social policy is largely focused on work-related issues, there is a growing emphasis on the relationship between work and welfare and on recognizing the need for policies that promote social inclusion and social cohesion. With unemployment at 10.8 per cent (18 million officially unemployed) a key priority for the EU has been job creation. These concerns have led the European Commission to recommend solutions to unemployment based on new forms of flexibility, work organization, work-sharing and part-time work, combined with active labour market policies that stress employability and that get people off welfare and into work (see the European Commission's employment guidelines, 1997b, 1998c). In this respect the UK's 'Welfare into Work' policy was highlighted as signalling the right approach to welfare reform (European Commission, 1998b).

The European Commission argues that flexibility at work and new forms of work organization are critical to future employment growth on the basis that 'the prevalence of the standard working week, a standard contract or a standard career within a lifetime job is gradually declining' (European Commission, 1997a, p.19). The growth of part-time work is an expression of this, with 17 per cent of all employees working part-time in 1996 and over 31.5 per cent of all women in employment working part-time. Indeed, women's entry into the labour market in 1996 was largely accounted for by the growth of part-time jobs (Eurostat, 1998).

The European Commission argues that net job creation in the EU will take place in the services, and particularly in the communal services (for instance health care, social care and education) where job growth has remained relatively high against the backdrop of restricted budgets and pressures to reduce levels of taxation, but relatively low in comparison with the USA (European Commission 1998d). This has led to recommendations for more innovative forms of co-operation between the public and private sector, initiatives for local employment development, and the introduction of voucher schemes for care services. This aspect of the EU social policy, outlined in the 1998–2000 Social Action Programme (European Commission, 1998e) also prioritizes action aimed at reducing unemployment, with a focus on drawing on the 'labour reserve of the young unemployed, women and the long term unemployed' in order to reduce the skills gap to enable

Europe to compete in the global economy. Changing working patterns, work organization and improving the skills base of Europe are regarded as the key to greater adaptability alongside the 'need for flexibility for enterprises and security for employees so as to harness the potential of new forms of work organization.' (European Commission, 1998d, p.6).

This discourse has at its core the relationship of economic prosperity and welfare dependency. For the European Commission this is increasingly framed in an approach based on a competitiveness model that incorporates flexible working, employment-friendly social protection systems, with certain minimum protection, for instance for part-time workers or for leave for parental purposes (Bosco and Chassard, 1999; European Commission, 1997a). According to Heikkilä (1999) three interrelated issues are relevant to the linking of welfare and work across Europe: work incentives and social protection; social activation measures which encourage labour market integration; and guaranteed minimum income linked to reintegration measures. At the core of these strategies are policies to integrate unemployed people into the labour market, or, to put it another way, entry into the labour market is the route by which integration into society manifests itself. This discourse assumes that moving out of 'welfare dependency' and into work is universally possible and desirable and neglects women's unpaid caring roles or their choice to pursue a caring role over and above a role in the paid labour market.

5   Rethinking work and time

These issues are closely connected to some of the new thinking on working time and the social organization of time, for instance by introducing family-friendly working time policies, redistributing work between men and women, or job creation through changing working time arrangements. Since the 1980s the trend towards reduced and reorganized working time across Europe has been marked by a blurring of the boundaries between working time and non-working time resulting from economic, social and cultural changes, examples of which are discussed below. Alongside changing family and household formations and women's increased participation in the labour market are new social demands for more free time and a greater desire for employees to have control over their working time (Boulin, 1997; Pillinger, 1998).

Despite many of the negative experiences of flexible work across Europe, enlightened thinking on the future of work, and a growing awareness of the importance of time to these debates, means that a new space has opened up for work to be more closely connected to the lives of women and families and for new arrangements, moving away from rigid patterns of employment and towards more positive forms of flexibility (TUC, 1998; Pillinger, 1998). In many respects it has been the trade unions, particularly in the public sector in the Netherlands, Germany and the Nordic countries, with high levels of female membership, that have been proactive in developing new working time strategies and in the process of modernization have linked important welfare objectives to equal opportunities, time sovereignty, quality of working life and job creation.

A key objective of working time policy is its potential to redistribute work in favour of women's time frames. In Sweden, Denmark and Norway this has led to strategies to maintain the full-time work norm, backed up by state-supported child and elder care, in order to resist trends towards involuntary part-time working. In contrast the Dutch approach, based on a part-time work-led strategy for employment growth, has emphasized the redistribution of work between full-time male employees and part-time female employees, with a particular emphasis on reducing working time in order to support the reconciliation of family and work life (Pillinger, 1998; O'Reilly and Fagan, 1998; Bettio et al., 1998).

The restructuring and reduction of working time are especially important in the public services in order to reduce unemployment, to regulate the nature and incidence of flexible work (part-time and temporary work), modernize and improve the quality of services, improve working conditions, and reduce stress and ill health associated with excessive working hours. Finally, changing working time can enhance possibilities for leisure time, education and parental leave, equal opportunities and the sharing of family and work life. It is worth noting that developments in working time have been taking place at a time of, and in some cases in direct response to, budgetary restrictions in the public sector in all EU countries.

An analysis of time as a resource is now inseparable from collective bargaining activity across Europe. The issue of working time has grown as the link between pay and productivity has been severed in the private sector and where public budgets have been severely restricted in the public sector, leaving limited room to manoeuvre in bargaining for increased pay, and more scope for bargaining for time. This raises some pressing issues about the relationship between pay and time and whether one can be traded off against the other. For example, thinking about time as a 'unit of account' has led to the emergence of innovative ways of accounting for time, for example through time banks. For this reason a work-rich/time-poor analysis can help to redistribute working time in favour of women or the unemployed, through job rotation programmes in Denmark, Finland and Belgium, or strategies to redistribute working time between men and women in the Netherlands or in Sweden as a mechanism to reconcile family time and responsibilities with working time. This has led to an emphasis on how the current organization of working time disadvantages women, carers and parents who frequently have problems juggling working time with family or care time. Let us now turn to look at some examples of experiments in work and time.

5.1   Reorganizing the city or the municipality

Pressures to reorganize and improve the quality of services have led to some innovatory thinking about time. 'Time in the city' projects in over 200 Italian cities are interesting examples of innovatory approaches to service delivery, interconnecting family, work and leisure time with city time schedules. Central to this has been the reorganization and reduction of working hours through local collective bargaining forums of employers, unions and government – the *Concertazione* – which have adopted broad economic, political and social agendas in this respect.

One of the earliest and most successful '*i tempi della città*' projects, in Modena, has developed new practices on working time alongside a network of services from kindergartens to the care of the elderly within this structure. The initiative came from the woman Mayor, Alfonsina Rinaldi, who first raised the problem of working time and its relationship to urban living patterns in response to demands from women in the community, in the then Italian Communist Party Women's Charter. It was also a response to an Italian grassroots legislative initiative, 'Women Change Times', which related women's family and working time experiences to urban policies. The project has monitored working hours and the opening times of municipal and central government departments, shops, businesses and public and private bodies, with a particular emphasis on care services, resulting in the reformulation of working hours to meet citizen needs. This was made possible by legislation in 1990 which gave the local authorities the power to co-ordinate, and where necessary to extend, the working hours of businesses and public services and the opening hours of public offices to meet the needs of the users alongside action to develop an integrated transport strategy. The project was devised from a perspective and in a spirit of public service, especially to enable women to balance their family and work schedules, rather than growing out of a business culture and has been highly successful (in sharp contrast to the UK where longer opening times for shops and businesses have led to disruption of family and social life). Moreover, trade unions believed that workers were providing a better-quality service to citizens and that they were receiving recognition for this, either through bonuses, training or feeling valued. The value of public services was enhanced and the quality of services provided was substantially improved.

The recognition of the importance of city-time initiatives has led to a growing number of time projects across Europe, particularly in experiments in Germany, the UK and France. On a less ambitious scale municipal experiments in Sweden and Germany have led to improved services to local citizens within new work-time frameworks. Partnerships between the trade unions, employers and users have reduced working time as a trade-off for the introduction of flexible work (especially by extending care services into the evening and weekends), while also introducing more choices in working time, extending equal opportunities, and responding to user needs. In many cases these experiments have led to improved services, without additional cost, and in Germany they have helped to reduce growing public deficits. In one municipality, Main-Kinzig, the experiment helped to improve the quality of services to the user while also reducing the public deficit and preventing services from being contracted out or privatized for cost-cutting purposes.

Many working time experiments have been localized and this suggests important new expressions of the importance of the locality in welfare–work–time discourses. This is a reflection of the trends towards decentralized services and new welfare mixes in many countries. The Italian city-time experiments are rooted in the decentralization of services, the articulation of user demands and imaginative responses to the improved delivery of services and the very operation of cities. Likewise, experiments on the redistribution and reorganization of time, the use of time banking and of lifetime working hours suggest a trend towards more individualized solutions and choices in working time.

5.2   Time as a resource

Time is an important resource in the labour market that can be banked or credited for extended leave. Time banks and time accounts systems have been piloted in Italy, France, Germany and Norway and allow for overtime, additional hours worked, periods of high work demand and other bonuses, profit-sharing schemes and incentive payments to be translated into 'banked' time in most cases for up to one year. There are some new proposals to create time banks over a lifetime. These schemes have normally been conceived as a means to reduce the extent and costs of overtime, but increasingly they are viewed as a way of allowing for time to be taken for family responsibilities or leave. In Italy and Spain time banks have been organized through local citizens' networks. In one experiment in the municipality of Barcelona in Spain a time bank has been developed for this purpose, particularly to compensate for the inadequate redistribution of caring and domestic roles between women and men.

5.3   Creating jobs by changing working time: worksharing and job rotation

A growing emphasis has been placed on changing working time in order to create new jobs, as structural unemployment remains high. The possibilities for this have arisen as trade unions have sought trade-offs for flexible working time in the public services, particularly as services have been modernized and extended into the evenings and weekends, whilst also pursuing solidarity strategies with unemployed people. For example, the introduction of legislation in France (Loi Aubrey) in 1998 for a thirty-five-hour working week and a national agreement in the Netherlands for a thirty-six-hour working week have led to job replacement guarantees for reduced working time. In France, social security and tax incentives to employers are linked to increasing job opportunities from reduced working hours with an overall objective to create new jobs for young, unemployed people.

In Finnish municipalities, the introduction of more flexible services and production times has led to the standard eight-hour working day being split into two six-hour jobs. The 6 + 6 working time model has improved and extended care and welfare services, whilst the splitting of one job into two, has created new jobs, particularly for young unemployed people. It is interesting to note that employees working the six-hour shift have not lost pay because of their reduced daily working hours; nor has their productivity reduced. The experiment has been highly successful in showing that it is possible to create new jobs, to extend and improve the quality of services, and allow for a balance between paid work and care responsibilities, through a dual strategy of reducing working hours and creating new jobs. The Finnish government recognizes that the savings on social security payments to unemployed people more than compensate for the financial and social costs of creating new jobs in the public sector.

This spirit of 'job rotation' has been an important feature of the pioneering Danish leave schemes, a model now adopted in a number of countries; these allow for up to one year's leave (subsidized through the social security system) from the labour market for training, care or for sabbatical purposes. The leave schemes remain a key instrument of redistribution of time between employed and unemployed people, through the principles of job rotation and worksharing, and a different way of conceiving working time reductions. Every leaver has to be replaced by an unemployed job-seeker, who in turn gains valuable work experience.

6   Conclusion

Time has social, cultural and political meanings that have a direct bearing on new work–welfare discourses in the EU and the restructuring of work and welfare across Europe. It directs attention to changing values associated with the division of time between work, family and leisure, between women's and men's time, and, as a result, the reorganization of social and economic life at the individual, family or even city/town level. The process of change is complex. Fixed patterns of work around time and place are breaking down, new working patterns and flexibility at work are emerging, and the restructuring of the post-war welfare settlement, bound up with market principles, decentralized services and the articulation of user demands and consumer orientations, suggest that a new settlement based on a work–welfare strategy is in the making. The social relations of work, care and welfare are inextricably linked by time.

In this respect time is part of a new discourse of redistribution and in turn a new form of materialism that raises important questions of how time is distributed and valued. The flexible use of working time has been a critical agent of change in this work–welfare discourse. For instance, new job creation measures have resulted from working time trade-offs and innovative job rotation and work-sharing projects, while the redistribution and reorganization of working time has the possibility to enhance equal opportunities and improve the balance between family and home life. Finally, the work–welfare discourse allows new thinking about the relationship of work to welfare and welfare to work over the life course.

References

Adam, B. (1990) *Time and Social Theory*, Cambridge, Polity Press.

Becker, G. (1965) 'A theory in the allocation of time', *Economic Journal*, 75 (299), pp.473–517.

Bettio, F., Del Bono, E. and Smith, M. (1998) *Working Time Patterns in the European Union: Policies and Innovations*, Report of European Network of Experts on Gender and Employment, Equal Opportunities Unit, DGV, Brussels European Commission, revised edition, May.

Bosco, A. and Chassard, Y. (1999) 'A shift in the paradigm: surveying the European Union discourse on welfare and work', in European Foundation for the Improvement of Living and Working Conditions.

Boulin, J.-Y. (1997) 'From working time to city time: the case for a single approach to time policies', *Transfer*, 3 (4), pp.723–36.

Esping-Andersen, G. (1990) *The Three Worlds of Welfare Capitalism*, Cambridge, Polity Press.

Esping-Andersen, G. (1996) *Welfare States in Transition*, London, Sage.

ETUC/LRD (European Trade Union Confederation/Labour Research Department) (1994) *Time for Working: Time for Living*, London, Labour Research Department.

European Commission (1995) *Social Protection in Europe*, COM(95)457, Brussels.

European Commission (1997a) *Partnership for a New Organization of Work*, COM(97)479 final, Brussels.

European Commission (1997b) *Modernizing and Improving Social Protection in the European Union*, COM(97)102 of 12 March 1997, Brussels.

European Commission (1998a) *Reconciliation between Work and Family Life in Europe*, Luxembourg, Office of Official Publications of the European Communities.

European Commission (1998b) *From Guidelines to Action: The New Action Plans for Employment*, May, Brussels, Commission Communication.

European Commission (1998c) *European Commission Adopts 1999 Employment Guidelines*, October, Brussels, Commission Communication.

European Commission (1998d) *Employment Rates Report 1998: Employment Performance in the Member States*, COM(98)572, October.

European Commission (1998e) *Social Action Programme 1998–2000*, COM(98)295 final, Luxembourg, Office of Official Publications of the European Communities.

European Foundation for the Improvement of Living and Working Conditions (1999) *Linking Welfare and Work*, Luxembourg, Office of Official Publications of the European Communities.

Eurostat (1998) *Labour Force Survey 1997*, Luxembourg, Office of Official Publications of the European Communities.

Evers, A., Pijl, M. and Ungerson, C. (eds) (1994) *Payments for Care: A Comparative Overview*, Aldershot, Avebury.

Forman, J. and Sowton, C. (eds) (1989) *Taking Our Time: Feminist Perspectives on Temporality*, Oxford, Pergamon.

Gorz, A. (1982) *Farewell to the Working Class*, London, Pluto.

Haverman, R. (1996) *Employment and Social Protection: Are They Compatible?*, DEEL-SA/ELSA/SP(96)4.

Heikkilä, M. (1999) 'A brief introduction to the topic', in European Foundation for the Improvement of Living and Working Conditions (1999).

Hoskyns, C. (1996) *Integrating Gender: Women, Law and Politics in the European Union*, London, Verso.

Johnson, N. (1998) *Mixed Economies of Welfare: A Comparative Perspective*, Hemel Hempstead, Prentice-Hall Europe.

Lewis, J. (1992) 'Gender and the development of welfare regimes', *Journal of European Social Policy*, 2 (3), pp.159–73.

OECD (Organization for Economic Development) (1998) *Employment Outlook*, Paris, Organization for Economic Development.

O'Reilly, J. and Fagan, C. (1998) *Part-Time Prospects: An International Comparison of Part-Time Work in Europe, North America and the Pacific Rim*, London, Routledge.

Pijl, M. (1997) 'Quality of care: on whose terms?', in Evers, A., Haverinen, R., Leichsenring, K. and Wistow, G. (eds) *Developing Quality in Personal Social Services: Concepts, Cases and Comments*. Aldershot, Ashgate.

Pillinger, J. (1998) *Working Time in Europe: A European Social Dialogue in the Public Services*, Brussels, European Federation of Public Service Unions.

Pillinger, J. and Campling, J. (1992) *Feminising the Market: Women's Pay and Employment in the European Community*, Basingstoke, Macmillan.

Rubery, J., Smith, M. and Fagan, C. (1995) *Changing Patterns of Work and Working-Time in the European Union and the Impact of Gender Divisions*, V/6203/96-EN, Brussels, European Commission.

TUC (1998) *The Time of Our Lives*, London, Trades Union Congress.

Weekers, S. and Pijl, M. (1998) *Home Care and Home Care Allowances in the European Union*, Utrecht, NIZW (International Centre of the Netherlands Institute of Care and Welfare).

Williams, F. (1997) 'Contestations of gender, "race"/ethnicity and citizenship in EU social policy'. Paper presented to the European Sociological Association Conference, Essex, August.

22

Principles of Recognition and Respect in Welfare

Fiona Williams

1 Introduction

This chapter examines the ways in which the welfare claims from grassroots campaigns, organizations and movements have contributed to a rethinking of social policy. It starts from the view that these forms of political activity, whilst never homogeneous, have, nevertheless, contributed as profound a political critique of the post-war welfare state as those from the New Right and New Labour. In so doing they have highlighted a critical political question of whether it is possible to combine a commitment to *universalism* in policies whilst respecting a *diversity*, or particularism, of identities, practices and beliefs. The chapter offers a tentative conceptual answer to this question by drawing on the history of welfare struggles and campaigns since the 1970s to provide a common framework of principles of recognition and respect for a reordering of the social relations of welfare.

2   A new politics of welfare

Since the 1970s forms of welfare activism emerged from both the 'new' social movements (around gender, 'race'/ethnicity, sexuality and disability) and those campaigning organizations and self-help groups which developed to stake claims for welfare as *claimants* or *users* of particular services – for example, carers, users of psychiatric services, and users of maternity services – or as *providers* of alternative services, such as refuges or support systems for people with AIDS (Williams, 1989; Taylor, 1993; Oliver, 1996; Beresford and Turner, 1997; NCVO, 1997; Hoggett, 1997). Their claims exposed the limitations of a 'false' universalism, a limited egalitarianism and an exclusive rather than inclusive citizenship inherent in the post-war welfare state (Williams, 1989; Clarke and Newman, 1997; Lister, 1997; Hughes and Lewis, 1998). In doing this they also highlighted new social risks – for example domestic violence, racial violence, forms of discrimination, child sexual abuse, lack of autonomy, rights circumscribed according to sexual preference, health risks from pollution. The identification of these risks emerged from claims against cultural and social injustices caused by the unequal relations of power in society. These relations were refracted in welfare through the hierarchical relations between providers and users, through the constitution of moral categories of desert and medical categories of physical, mental and sexual invalidity, and through forms of restricted access to resources by marginalized social groups. In common with the New Right and New Labour discourses these new politics of welfare have constructed the notion of an *active welfare subject*. However, the emphasis of those making new claims has not been on the self-interested consumer active in the market of welfare, nor on the enlightened consumer-citizen actively exercising their responsibilities in paid work for self, family and community, but upon the reconstitution of the welfare subject as an active citizen articulating their needs in the democratic organization of welfare services.

While this new politics of welfare has been diverse as well as particularist, in the sense of staking out specific needs, it is nevertheless marked by a more general claim that extends beyond the *redistribution of goods*. This centres upon claims for the realization of personhood and well-being, for cultural respect, autonomy and dignity.

3   The politics of recognition

The term 'the politics of recognition' has been used by some political theorists to capture the nature of struggles by subaltern, marginalized and excluded groups to assert their equal moral worth (Honneth, 1996; Taylor, 1994; Fraser, 1995). These struggles signify the attempt to reject the systematic disrespect or misrecognition of a group's 'culture or way of life, the dignity of their status as persons, and the inviolability of their physical integrity' (Anderson, 1996, p.x). Such a description could also be applied to new struggles in welfare.

According to Charles Taylor, 'Due recognition is not just a courtesy we owe people. It is a vital human need' (1994, p.26). In a historical analysis of the significance of recognition struggles he describes how, from the eighteenth century, the collapse of social hierarchies with fixed statuses derived from the 'natural' order and their replacement with a democratic ideal led, on the one hand, to universalist politics which emphasized the equal dignity of all, and, on the other, to the development of a modern notion of identity. Furthermore, the greater the questioning of the preordained, the more numerous the struggles for the recognition of previously excluded identities/groups (for example, women, minorities). However, the universalizing logic of the first process pulls against the particularizing logic of the second, producing a tension between universalism and particularism. The attempt to resolve this tension requires, according to Taylor, a continual reassessment of our horizons of taken-for-grantedness or 'common sense'.

Honneth (1996) emphasizes the *moral* grammar of social conflicts and proposes that the preconditions for self-realization are rooted in the struggle to establish mutual recognition (rather than in the struggle for existence). Crucially, however, mutual recognition is relational, or dialogic; personal identity depends upon social relationships to develop and sustain it. Honneth identifies three modes which make this possible: close relationships of love and friendship which grant self-confidence; legally institutionalized relations for the development of rights, granting self-respect; and networks or communities of shared values which provide an individual with a sense of worth and self-esteem. In terms of the political, his theory takes us beyond rights as the basis for self-realization and into the moral landscape of social conflicts over worth, and also beyond the idea that 'interests' alone fuel collective action. These need to be related, he argues, to 'the everyday web of moral feelings' (Honneth, 1996, p.161).

Nancy Fraser's contribution to the debate (1995) insists on the importance of acknowledging issues of redistribution. She therefore talks about the politics of *redistribution and recognition*, saying that strategies for greater egalitarianism cannot have one without the other. The corrective is an important one. It applies to welfare struggles in Britain where claims for recognition have almost inevitably involved some element of redistribution.

The remainder of this chapter attempts to draw out some key 'principles of recognition and respect' which have emerged from the struggles and claims over welfare by new social and welfare movements. These are necessarily speculative at this point. They lay no claim to be universal and should be seen as reflective of claims emerging within a specific time and place. They attempt to extend the moral vocabulary of the social relations of welfare and thus focus upon issues of recognition and respect, but this does not mean that they are separate from the issues of how to pay for welfare. They have to be seen as part of, not an alternative to, a commitment to meeting people's needs for a basic income, employment, health care, housing and education. As such they address the social, cultural and political elements of current moves to a new welfare settlement. Glenn Drover and Patrick Kerans argue that the claims-making of new welfare movements involves three 'stakes': identity, resources and relationships (1993, p.5). I would suggest that the seven principles of recognition outlined below cluster around respect for identity, the quality of relationships and the challenging of boundaries, as well as distribution of and access to resources (which I do not spell out here). In addition, although they have been generated by groups with *particular* interests, nevertheless there are ways in which their claims raise issues of *general* interest; they flag up new norms governing behaviour and social relations, as well as common aspirations and concerns.

4   Principles of recognition and respect

4.1   Interdependence

In the 1970s the Campaign for the Legal and Financial Independence of Women was established to challenge women's dependent status in relation to social security rights, taxation, tenancies, mortgages, bank accounts and so on (McIntosh, 1981). In the 1980s the Independent Living Movement developed from local campaigns by disabled people (Morris, 1993). Central to both these campaigns was a challenge to the way in which welfare institutions, policies and professionals construct particular social groups as dependent and unable to exercise autonomy in certain areas of their lives. The construction of women as financially dependent on their husbands not only limited their access to some benefits, it also captured their assumed subordinacy to their husbands in relation to other areas – in decision-making, in relation to sexual relationships or spending power. For disabled people, their dependency was constructed as a grateful passive dependence upon those relatives or professionals who 'looked after' them. As for older people, their institutionalization often represented the stripping of autonomy and privacy and an exclusion from social life. In contrast, the Independent Living Movement seeks independence for disabled people in their daily lives, in achieving mobility, in parenting, in pursuing paid work, in living in places and with others of their own choice (Priestley, 1999).

These examples illustrate the way dependency has become the focus for grassroots resistance (see Chapter 3 this volume). However, at the formal political level discourses of dependency are infused with moral disapprobation, especially when associated with 'welfare dependency' – an imagined culture that is said to have developed into a deviant underclass (Murray, 1990). In this scenario dependency is seen as a condition resulting from the receipt of benefits and is counterposed to empowerment and independence gained by paid work in the market. This narrowing of the notion of independence as market-based, and of the notion of dependency as behavioural rather than enforced or resisted, has served to obscure the struggles against dependency of those whose routes to labour market freedom, or economic independence, are more risky and tortuous – women with children, disabled people, the chronically ill, older people. Moreover, welfare benefits and services have provided for women, disabled and older people the means to *escape* from the undesirable dependency upon oppressive relationships. Furthermore, that those who are claiming welfare are seen as dependent, no matter how fully engaged or responsible for others they may be, hides an understanding of their agency, especially when those who are market dependent are seen as independent. Contemporary discourse in Britain also labels lone mothers who prefer to stay at home to look after their children as welfare dependants whereas their married counterparts are seen as exercising choice. This dichotomy between the extra-market dependant and the fully integrated paid worker fails to recognize that this worker's independence is achieved through hidden systems of support by those who care for that worker's children, clean his/ her house, buy and cook his/her food, and so on (see Chapter 1 this volume). Personal autonomy is only achieved through collective effort.

Rather than promoting the dependence/independence dichotomy, we could propose *interdependence* as the principle which brings into play all those emotional, material, physical networks of unequal reciprocity, and creates the basis for autonomy. It also emphasizes a *collective* commitment to individual welfare and an individual commitment to collective welfare. It acknowledges that we are all necessarily dependent on others, but that there is a need to challenge the institutions, structures and social relations which render some groups unnecessarily dependent. This connects to the second principle: that of care.

4.2 Care

One important way in which welfare states construct a boundary between public rights and responsibilities and private duties is the extent to which they recognize, remunerate or socialize the work involved in caring for and/or supporting children, older frail or sick people, people who are disabled and require support. On the whole, this work has been assumed to be the unpaid responsibility of women in the home. In the 1960s and 1970s women's demands focused upon improving childcare support facilities for women to enable them to work and this was followed by an attempt to get women's caring of older and/or sick and/or disabled family members recognized. All of this was a radical departure from the post-war welfare settlement in which informal care was an invisible and taken-for-granted area of welfare (Land and Rose, 1985).

Local carers' groups and carers' organizations and later a National Carers' Organization campaigned for the right of women to benefits for caring responsibilities, especially married women who had been denied (until 1986 when it was challenged by the European Court) a care allowance on the basis that care was part of a married woman's natural duty. More research revealed the extent to which caring responsibilities involve financial, emotional and physical costs to women (Finch and Groves, 1983). As more claims were made women had to confront the difficult issue of whether by demanding a wage for carers they would simply reinforce the idea that caring is women's work. Other strategies have included demanding, or creating, the conditions for men to share caring responsibilities, or following what has been called the 'residential route' (Finch, 1984). However, this strategy, with its resonances of institutionalized care, has been profoundly problematic for people requiring support. Care may assume duty and responsibility, it may involve love and commitment, but, as disabled people have pointed out (see Chapter 3 this volume), the emphasis upon care and the notion of care as unvalued and oppressive labour obscures the fact that caring is also a *relationship* which may involve unequal relations of power between the carer and the cared-for person.

The principle of care requires us to heed not only the needs and interests of the carer but also the needs and interests of the cared-for person. People who require support have demanded the choice as to who cares for them, where and how. For many disabled people, the very concept of 'care' cannot be disentangled from a notion of dependence; it sits uneasily with a view of empowerment which leads to respect, choice and control (Morris, 1993). Thus, one of the strategies to enable disabled people to pursue independent lives has been the demand for direct payments – that is, for disabled people to receive cash payments in order to employ carers of their own choice and to determine the type of support and assistance they require.

'Care', then, requires recognition but also careful negotiation of the different interests caught up in its discourse and practice. Care suggests duty, responsibility, obligation, power, control, oppression, conflict, altruism, love, solidarity and reciprocity. We all at some time care and are cared for. The focus upon care that different groups and campaigns have brought provides us with a grounded set of ethics with which to balance the twentieth-century preoccupation with the ethic of paid work at the centre of our values, duties and rights. The ethics of care assume relationships which are bound by mutual interdependence. Its practice involves the values of attentiveness, responsiveness, competence and responsibility, negotiation and mutual recognition (Tronto, 1993; Sevenhuijsen, 1998). This means that it is through caring and being cared for that we take account of the needs of others, not in an abstract way but in terms of their specific contexts, and this provides a grounding for the civic virtues of responsibility, tolerance and an awareness of 'otherness', of diversity and competing claims. The values of care can, then, inform concepts of citizenship: they involve concepts to do with responsibilities and relationships and they can engender practices of moral deliberation and dialogue grounded in everyday activities. It is the boundaries of these concepts of care to which we turn next: intimacy.

4.3 Intimacy

The care relationship is often but not always an intimate one; the intimate relationship is usually, but not always, a relationship of care. The intimate sphere covers relationships based upon mutual exchange of love based upon family ties (parenting, marriage, kinship), friendship, sexual relationships, as well as paid care relationships. It has been argued that there have been a number of key shifts in the ways we understand intimate relationships (Beck and Beck-Gernsheim, 1995): they are less about duty and more about mutually agreed commitment; they are less about achieving status and more about negotiating an identity; they are less about authority and obedience and more about consent; they are less about tradition and more about trust; they are less about honour and more about respect. However, to identify these shifts in emphasis is not the same as saying that this is what characterizes intimate relationships (Jamieson, 1998). However the aspiration that relationships can and should be more democratic reflects a response to the women's movement questioning of unequal gender relations. The pursuit of claims for women's autonomy in terms of rights to earn a wage, to expect help with household duties, to claim fair shares on divorce, to leave relationships where power was abused, have all influenced the democratization of relationships both between men and women and between mothers and fathers and children. Women's debunking of patriarchal authority has also partly contributed to a greater understanding of children as active subjects (see Chapter 6 this volume).

It is not simply the detraditionalization and democratization of gender and parent–child relations which have influenced these shifts. The attempt to shift the focus of concern about relationships to their mutuality rather than their conventionality reflects the campaigns by gay and lesbian movements to gain recognition, rights and respect. The freedom to chose one's sexual partner, to have that relationship respected and to have access to the rights enjoyed by heterosexual couples (joint tenancies, pensions, custody, parenting and so on) have been part of these movements' claims (Carabine, 1996).

Whilst on the one hand there has been pressure for the state to recognize diversity of form in intimate relationships, there has also been pressure for the state to intervene to protect the vulnerable who are victims of violence and abuse in intimate relationships (see Chapter 16 this volume). Campaigns against child sexual abuse, domestic violence and sexual abuse of disabled children, adults and older people in institutional and residential care characterize an approach to intimacy which places much higher value upon personal autonomy and empowerment within personal relationships. It is an approach that also recognizes the potential for the abuse of power in unequal relationships. Connected to these issues is the fourth principle: that of bodily integrity.

4.4 Bodily integrity

The history of welfare interventions is, in part, the history of the identification and classification of healthy/productive and unhealthy/unproductive bodies and fit and unfit minds (Foucault, 1965, 1973). The power of the professions of medicine, social work and education to observe and assess the body and the mind required the physical surrendering by patients of their bodies as well as the surrendering of their own knowledge about their bodies. However, from the 1960s a wide range of campaigns began to resist this.

Campaigns by women for reproductive rights – over contraception, abortion, infertility treatment, medical treatment in childbirth, campaigns against ECT treatment, campaigns by older people in residential homes for the right to look after their own medications; campaigns against racial violence and abuse on housing estates, and in communities by the police; campaigns against rape, sexual violence and abuse; campaigns against corporal punishment in schools and homes; campaigns against the practice of 'virginity tests' by immigration officials on young women migrants and visitors from Asia and Africa; campaigns to grant the right of asylum to rape victims; campaigns against sex trafficking and sex tourism and child prostitution; campaigns to 'normalize' disabled and different bodies – all of these centre upon the right of the individual to protect their body against external or internal risk and abuse. The body is a site of control, resistance and pleasure; it is inscribed with the social relations of power in which it exists. The title of the famous health-care manual *Our Bodies, Ourselves* (Phillips and Rakusen, 1978) reflects the way in which our bodies mark the physical boundaries of our sense of self, our own dignity and self-respect (see Chapters 8 and 9 this volume). In these terms, respect for the integrity of the body is fundamental to the maintenance of the autonomy of the welfare citizen. With the demystification of professional knowledge and techniques, this is also the prerequisite of any policy which encourages people to maintain their own bodies as healthy.

4.5   Identity

It was suggested earlier that due recognition of identity, as both a sense of self and a sense of belonging, offered a vital way for understanding individual struggles for self-realization and collective struggles by subaltern groups against disrespect. David Taylor has outlined the significance of these two aspects of identity – which he calls ontological (sense of self) and categorical (sense of belonging) – for the social relations of welfare (Taylor, 1998). He argues that by exploring how 'individuals build up a sense of coherence through their multiple identifications' we can 'understand the way in which individuals form attachments to social movements and enter into political agency – in this case around struggles for welfare' (ibid., p.341). At the same time, 'categories of identity act back upon their incumbents, often ascribing ontological characteristics to their members' and in this way 'identity categories become inscribed in welfare discourse, positioning their subjects with ascribed characteristics' (ibid., pp.341–2). It is possible to see these processes at work in the recent history of welfare, each demonstrating the significance of the demand for proper respect for identity in the practice of welfare.

In relation to ethnicity, the migrants who came to Britain after the Second World War were mainly Commonwealth citizens who, formally at least, had access to the social rights of the welfare system.

However, restrictive criteria of eligibility, such as length of residence, prevented access to public housing, and lack of information, language barriers and lack of respect for different cultural practices led to a denial of their rights. The assumption was that those of different ethnic backgrounds would or could be forced to assimilate through strategic development and implementation of social policies. In practice, the material conditions of these groups' existence, such as mothers engaged in paid employment or living in restricted residential areas, were fed back as negative culturally ascribed characteristics. The subsequent struggles around health care, education, community and social care were both about claiming cultural respect and about the redistribution of rights and goods to which their current or previous citizenship entitled them. Ultimately they were challenging Britain to come to terms with itself as a culturally and racially diverse society.

However, there are problems with notions of diverse cultural and ethnic identities. First, the concept of diversity can obscure the fact that ethnic groups (including those seen as the 'silent' majority) may be hierarchically positioned and not simply living in harmony together. Campaigns by African-Caribbean mental health groups to challenge the incarceration of disproportionate numbers of their young men in prisons and mental hospitals were a challenge to racist stereotyping of the cultures of the Caribbean rather than simply a demand for cultural diversity. The very fact that the word 'ethnic' commonly refers to minority ethnic groups suggests that those of white, English, Christian ethnicity can take their ethnicity so much for granted that they do not have to reflect upon or define their own identity (see Chapter 17). Second, tolerance of cultural diversity may ignore differences *within* those ethnic groups – of class, gender, sexuality or age. Third, cultural/ethnic categories may be imposed upon groups in static or essentialist ways which ignore the fact that time and place reconfigure and hybridize cultural/ethnic identities of both 'minority' and 'majority' groups. Indeed, this kind of essentialism can give rise to a justification for separatism – they have their schools, we have ours – but without shifting the relations of domination and subordination between different ethnic groups.

The categories constituted through welfare policies and practices have also become the focus for resistance. For example, disabled people have grasped hold of the administrative/medical category of 'disabled' and turned it into a political identity of enactment and empowerment.

It is common, in contemporary politics, to invoke a network of solidarity and duty which moves effortlessly from the individual to family, community and nation. Without reference to identities these may be insufficient as the bases of inclusion, solidarity and support. The multiple identities which create forms of belonging, solidarity, resistance and support for groups (some of whom may be excluded from family or community or nation) may cut across, indeed, may reconstitute the very meanings of family, community and nation.

4.6   Transnational welfare

One of the biggest challenges to twenty-first-century welfare societies is the boundary of the nation-state. The assumption of the twentieth century has been that our access to civil and social rights is bounded by national/territorial/geographical boundaries (see Chapters 11, 13 and 17 this volume). What we have seen over the last ten years is the redrawing of national boundaries, the creation of supra-national boundaries such as the EU and the increase in people, especially women, crossing those boundaries as migrants, refugees and asylum-seekers. In many European countries migrants have limited access to social, civil and political rights yet they are part of a political economy which depends upon their labour. Furthermore, in those welfare systems which perpetuate the use of nationality as one of the criteria of eligibility to social rights, denial of social rights to those racialized 'others' who are not nationals is commonplace, as is the scapegoating of those groups as 'scroungers'. The racialization of welfare politics has become more pronounced in many Western and Eastern European countries in recent years (Faist, 1995). One of the areas where this has manifested itself in Britain is in the withdrawal of rights to cash benefits and social housing to asylum-seekers.

However, the transnationalism in markets, corporations, agencies and political institutions has been matched by transnationalism in social movements, especially in their capacity to forge international links at grassroots levels. This is also reflected in the growth of global conferences (such as the women's conference in Beijing in 1994); in the growing significance of non-governmental organizations (NGOs) as political actors and mediators; and in the internationalization of anti-poverty strategies of organizations such as Oxfam, which now focus on strategic alliances between poor communities in the North and the South (Bronstein, 1998). One example at the EU level is an organization of 'Black and Migrant Women' which has been campaigning within the European Women's Lobby (EWL) since 1992 for, amongst other things, independent legal status for black and migrant women, distinct from their partners and fathers; emergency provisions for women who are subject to domestic and other violence; and a recognition of the specific legislative discriminations and abuses experienced by women applying for asylum (EWL, 1995, pp.255–7; Williams, 1997). How far the EU reinforces nationalisms by conflating citizenship with white, Christian Europeanness or moves towards a multi-ethnic, multi-faith, post-national citizenship (Delanty, 1995) will affect the possibilities for meeting the welfare needs of those most affected by changing boundaries and globalization.

4.7   Voice

This final principle runs through each of the other principles discussed. Underpinning the challenge to users as dependent subjects, the interrogation of the care relationship, the assertion of diverse and democratic forms of intimacy, the recognition and respect of bodily integrity, the diversity of identities and the questioning of nationality as a basis to rights, is an assertion that the experience of the users of welfare services and their own definition of their needs are central to the organization and delivery of welfare services. At the same time, the proliferation of self-help groups is testimony to the claim that people themselves can develop and share their own forms of knowledge and care. What this challenges is the power of expert knowledge to monopolize the definition of what is wrong with us and what we need to right it. It demands a democratizing of the relationship between users and providers both collectively and individually. It demands a sharing of expert and lay knowledges.

This suggests a different interpretation of the *active* welfare subject. The New Right envisaged a new power for welfare users as consumers in the welfare market exercising their choice. This left largely untouched the relations between providers and users of welfare. However, the new managerialism ushered in by the New Right brought with it a commitment to consult with user groups or, say, with parents and communities in relation to education, which, in areas where those groups are strong, provided a space for collective voices to be heard. New Labour has reinforced this managerialist approach to the assessment of a diversity of individualized needs, while also, in places, acknowledging the importance of users having access to a variety of expert knowledge (see *Our Healthier Nation*, HMSO, 1998). However, the approach by both Conservative and Labour governments, where citizens/consumers become active and empowered is less in the articulation of these needs than in the exercising of duties and responsibilities to themselves, family, community, taxpayer and state. The social movements have focused more directly upon the democratization of provider–user relations as the site for the pursuit of active citizenship. In this situation needs are both individual, but also, in so far as they are discursively constructed through forms of social differentiation that are shared, they are *collective* needs. It is on this basis that users may collectively reinterpret their needs and influence the relations of power between individual providers and users.

This latter version of active citizenship depends upon a radical and pluralist notion of democracy which can both account for and address the competing claims of different groups. Some have called this 'the politics of a differentiated universalism' in which universalism is the commitment to an equal moral value and inclusion of all, and its differentiation reflects people's own definitions of their diversity, but challenges the structured differentiation which renders some groups unequal and/or excluded (see Young, 1990; Mouffe, 1992; Lister, 1997). The political strategies for pursuing this depend upon developing solidarities based upon the respect of difference: not the solidarity of the lowest common denominator, nor the solidarity that presumes all will forgo their particularities in aiming for a common goal; rather it is the pursuit of unity in dialogues of difference.

5 Conclusion

In the earlier discussion of recognition politics, the point was made that the pursuit of the mutual recognition of worth has also involved claims for the redistribution of goods. If groups simply pursue the politics of recognition without addressing socioeconomic inequalities, then they will simply win social justice for some in their group, but not for others. On the other hand, the singular pursuit of issues of economic inequality can make invisible cultural injustices which render some groups more vulnerable to economic exploitation (Fraser, 1995). This chapter has outlined seven principles of recognition and respect – recognition for interdependence and care, respect for intimacy, bodily integrity and identity, recognition of transnational boundaries and of voice. In so far as these generate claims involving the redistribution of goods, then these, too, go beyond conventional thinking to include the redistribution not simply of wealth but of work and time (see Chapter 21 this volume) and of care and space. The intersection of the principles of recognition and respect with these dimensions of redistribution can begin to provide a shared vocabulary with which to write our individual and collective welfare scripts.

Note

This is an abbreviated and amended version of 'Good-enough principles for welfare' published in the *Journal of Social Policy* (2000, vol. 28 (4), pp.667–87). The issues in the chapter are also elaborated in *New Principles for Welfare*, Cambridge, Polity Press (forthcoming).

References

Anderson, J. (1996) 'Translator's introduction', in Honneth (1996).

Beck, U. and Beck-Gernsheim, E. (1995) *The Normal Chaos of Love*, Cambridge, Polity Press.

Beresford, P. and Turner, M. (1997) *It's Our Welfare: Report of the Citizens' Commission on the Future of the Welfare State*, London, National Institute for Social Work.

Bronstein, A. (1998) 'Social policy: different place; same problem'. Plenary paper presented at the Social Policy Association annual conference, University of Lincoln, 15 July.

Carabine, J. (1996) 'A straight playing-field or queering the pitch: centring sexuality in social policy', *Feminist Review*, 54, pp.31–64.

Clarke, J. and Newman, J. (1997) *The Managerial State: Power, Politics and Ideology in the Remaking of Social Welfare*, London, Sage.

Delanty, G. (1995) *Inventing Europe*, Basingstoke, Macmillan.

Drover, G. and Kerans, P. (eds) (1993) *New Approaches to Welfare Theory*, Aldershot, Edward Elgar.

EWL (European Women's Lobby) (1995) *Confronting the Fortress: Black and Migrant Women in the European Union*, Brussels, European Parliament, Directorate General for Research.

Faist, T. (1995) 'Ethnicization and racialization of welfare state politics in Germany and the USA', *Ethnic and Racial Studies*, 18 (2), pp.219–50.

Finch, J. (1984) 'Community care: developing non-sexist alternatives', *Critical Social Policy*, 9, pp.6–18.

Finch, J. and Groves, D. (eds) (1983) *A Labour of Love: Women, Work and Caring*, London, Routledge & Kegan Paul.

Foucault, M. (1965) *Madness and Civilization*, New York, Pantheon Books.

Foucault, M. (1973) *The Birth of the Clinic*, London, Tavistock.

Fraser, N. (1995) 'From redistribution to recognition? Dilemmas of justice in a "post-socialist" age', *New Left Review*, 212, pp.68–92.

HMSO (1998) *Our Healthier Nation*, London, The Stationery Office.

Hoggett, P. (ed.) (1997) *Contested Communities: Experiences, Struggles, Policies*, Bristol, The Policy Press.

Honneth, A. (1996) *The Struggle for Recognition*, Cambridge, Polity Press.

Hughes, G. and Lewis, G. (eds) (1998) *Unsettling Welfare: The Reconstruction of Social Policy*, London, Routledge/The Open University.

Jamieson, L. (1998) *Intimacy: Personal Relationships in Modern Societies*, Cambridge, Polity Press.

Land, H. and Rose, H. (1985) 'Compulsory altruism for some or an altruistic society for all?', in Bean, P., Ferris, J. and Whynes, D. (eds) *In Defence of Welfare*, London, Tavistock.

Lister, R. (1997) *Citizenship: Feminist Perspectives*, Basingstoke, Macmillan.

McIntosh, M.(1981) 'Feminism and social policy', *Critical Social Policy*, 1, pp.32–42.

Morris, J. (1993) *Independent Lives? Community Care and Disabled People*, Basingstoke, Macmillan.

Mouffe, C. (ed.) (1992) *Dimensions of Radical Democracy*, London, Verso.

Murray, C. (1990) *The Emerging British Underclass*, London, IEA Health and Welfare Unit.

NCVO (National Council of Voluntary Organizations) (1997) *Basic Needs, Basic Rights, Report from the Conference in Birmingham*, 3 March, London, National Council of Voluntary Organizations.

Oliver, M.(1996) *Understanding Disability: From Theory to Practice*, Basingstoke, Macmillan.

Phillips, A. and Rakusen, J. (eds) (1978) *Our Bodies, Ourselves: A Health Manual by and for Women*, Harmondsworth, Penguin.

Priestley, M. (1999) *Disability Politics and Community Care*, London, Jessica Kingsley.

Sevenhuijsen, S. (1998) *Citizenship and the Ethics of Care: Feminist Considerations on Justice, Morality and Politics*, London, Routledge.

Taylor, C. (1994) *Multiculturalism*, Princeton, NJ, Princeton University Press

Taylor, D. (1998) 'Social identity and social policy: engagements with postmodern theory', *Journal of Social Policy*, 27 (3), pp.329–50.

Taylor, G. (1993) 'Challenges from the margins', in Clarke, J. (ed.) *A Crisis in Care? Challenges to Social Work*, London, Sage/The Open University.

Tronto, J. (1993) *Moral Boundaries: A Political Argument for an Ethic of Care*, London, Routledge.

Williams, F. (1989) *Social Policy: A Critical Introduction, Issues of Race, Gender and Class*, Cambridge, Polity Press.

Williams, F. (1997) 'Contestations of gender, "race"/ethnicity and citizenship in EU social policy'. Paper presented to the European Sociological Association conference, University of Essex, 26–30 August.

Young, I.M. (1990) *Justice and the Politics of Difference*, Princeton, NJ, Princeton University Press.

Index

Printed in the United Kingdom
by Lightning Source UK Ltd.
107022UKS00001B/112-129